1L OF A RIDE:

A Well-Traveled Professor's Roadmap to Success in the First Year of Law School

Third Edition

Andrew J. McClurg

Herbert Herff Chair of Excellence in Law
Cecil C. Humphreys School of Law
The University of Memphis

WEST
ACADEMIC
PUBLISHING

ISBN: 978-1-63460-789-6

To my students—past, present, and future.

ACKNOWLEDGMENTS

It's appropriate that a book written for and about law students was shaped every step of the way with the help of law students. Students who provided direct assistance are thanked below, but I'm indebted to all of my students collectively. Even after thirty years as a law professor, I learn something new from law students nearly every day.

One of the many fortunate aspects of being a law professor is working with talented research assistants, all of whom epitomize what it means to be a great law student. Research assistants at the University of Memphis Cecil C. Humphreys School of Law who contributed to this book include Kaitlyn Abernathy, Joshua Baker, Shea Barker, Chelsea L. Brown, Quynh-Anh Dang, James Duckworth, Lindsey Gill, Russell Hayes, Sally Joyner, Julia M. Kavanagh, Jane Marie Lewis, Natalie Fox Malone, Taylor Oyaas, Megan McKenzie Reed, Elizabeth Rogers, Meredith Blake Stewart, James Stone, Mary L. Wagner, and Todd V. Williams.

Special thanks to the students who shared their case briefs, class notes, and course outlines so that readers can learn from authentic samples of these crucial law school documents. All of those students were either research assistants or are listed below.

Since beginning work on the first edition in 2006, I've solicited comments from hundreds of law students, mostly through surveys, but also informally via email, Facebook, and conversations in and out of the classroom. Most of them are current or former students at the University of Memphis, but they also include former students of mine at the University of Arkansas at Little Rock School of Law, Florida International University College of Law, and Golden Gate University School of Law, as well as students from other schools.

Over the years, the following students and former students have provided comments or other assistance: William D.

Albright, Lauren M. Armstrong, Monica Barba, Shea Barker, David Barman, Jennifer M. Baum, Christopher N. Bell, Willem H. Bermel, Jonathan E. Bettis, Matthew K. Bishop, Anna Vergos Blair, Daane J. Blocksma, Peter G. Bolac, Bianca F. Brasher, Christopher G. Britt, Chelsea L. Brown, Kimberly G. Brown, Wilson S. Bryan, Katie Burch, France Caldwell, Amanda G. Carpenter, Joseph D. Cassidy, John C. Catmur, Jessica H. Chandler, Courtney Clothier, Christopher B. Connolly, Aaron B. Crafton, Caroline W. Crawford, Edwin Cruz, Kyle R. Cummins, Anne B. Davis, Tamara Davis, Adam R. deNobriga, Andrew S. DeShazo, Carolan M. Deutch, Rachel D. Dyer, Carl T. Eppler, John M. Escue, Jamie Ewing, Libba Fyke, Charles F. Fleet, Sharon A. Fortner, LaTaya Franklin, Caroline E. Gabriel, Matthew P. Gabriel, Tyler C. Ginn, Whitney Goode, Michele B. Gwinn, Jennifer D. Haile, Blake W. Hazlerig, Kevin P. Henson, Katherine L. Herriman, Jayniece R. Higgins, Richard T. Hoehn, Mackenzie R. Hogan, Amy E. Holland, Megan R. House, Laurence B. Howard, Taylor Hughes, Sheryl T. Hurst, Christian R. Johnson, Michele L. Johnson Spears, Sally Joyner, Yael Julian, Christine Jurado, Terri Keinlen, Erica R. Kelley, Marissa A. King, William Kruse, Erin Kubisiak, Cloteal LaBroi, Denise Lambert, Laura J. Lee, Ashley M. Levins, Erno D. Lindner, Jonathan A. Lindsey, Abigail M. Mabry, Chandra Madison, Tanesha L. Matthews, Kevin M. McCormack, Brandon F. McNary, M. Elizabeth McNinch, J. Bradley Mercer, Jonathon M. Meredith, Matthew E. Miller, Kate L. Moore, Robert G. Morgan, Charles M. Molder, J. Aaron Mullis, Katie Myers, Benjamin R. Newman, Donald P. Nicholson, Zachary S. Ogale, Daniel L. Owens, Holly Palmer, Alexander Y. Pao, Lacy Papadeas, Brian A. Parker, Laura Partlow, Laurie Peterson, Bryce H. Phillips, Galen P. Pickard, William M. Plosser, Joshua C. Powell, Susan Price, Adam C. Ragan, Allison S. Raines, Debra Reece, Emma J. Redden, Horace A. Reid, Monica R. Rejaei, William A. Roach, Carson L. Rogers, Schaefer K. Rowe, Ashley Jordan Russell, Caroline E. Sapp, Erica J. Scott, Benjamin T. Seamon, Seth M. Segraves, Reginald E. Shelton, Steven D. Shirley, Lakeisha D. Sisco-Beck, Jeffrey S. Smith, John D. Smith, Mary Katherine Smith, Sara Elizabeth Smith, Shayne Smith, Dylan M. Spaduzzi, Ryan J. Spickard, Allison J. Starnes-

Anglea, Bridgett L. Stigger, Kendall F. Stivers, Brittany L. Strung, Matthew A. Thomas, Neely Campbell Thomas, Sarah M. Turner, Christopher J. Tutor, Pablo A. Varela, Gregory H. Wallace, Bridget M. Warner, Cameron M. Watson, Rachel D. Whitaker, Chad M. Wilgenbusch, Joanna L. Williams, Smith Nall Wilson, Dina Windle, Justin Wojciechowski, Jason J. Yasinksy, and Erin C. Young. Thank you to all! I apologize if I left anyone out.

The comments from law students and their significant others in Chapter 23, addressing the impact of law school on outside relationships, are borrowed from my book, *The "Companion Text" to Law School: Understanding and Surviving Life with a Law Student* (2012). They were obtained from surveys administered to more than 200 students and their partners at the University of Memphis, California Western School of Law, and the Seattle University College of Law. All of those contributors are named in the acknowledgements to *The "Companion Text" to Law School* so I won't relist them here, but I want to say thanks again.

I also received help from many law professors. Particular thanks to the five legal writing professors who generously contributed so much of their time and expertise to Chapter 18: Kimberly K. Boone, Christine Nero Coughlin, Sandy C. Patrick, Joan Malmud Rocklin, and David Walter. Mary Pat Treuthart read and commented on a draft, offering her usual insightful, blunt, and often hilarious wisdom. Other professors who shared their expertise include: Thomas E. Baker, Coleen M. Barger, Sara R. Benson, Leslie Burton, Markita D. Cooper, John M.A. DiPippa, June F. Entman, Barbara Glesner Fines, Judith D. Fischer, Elizabeth P. Foley, Jose Gabilondo, Larry Howell, Barbara Kritchevsky, Nancy Levit, Ernest F. Lidge, III, Jana R. McCreary, Kathleen A. Miller, Steven J. Mulroy, Martha M. Peters, Janet L. Richards, Ruth Anne Robbins, Ediberto Román, David S. Romantz, Daniel Schaffzin, Katherine Traylor Schaffzin, Eugene Shapiro, Sheila J. Simon, Kevin H. Smith, Stephen Smith, Andrej Thomas Starkis, Meredith A.G. Stange, Brenda L. Tofte, Grace C. Tonner, Barbara J. Tyler, Nicholas L. White, and Jodi Wilson.

Thanks to Chad Christensen, a project manager for the Law School Survey of Student Engagement, for providing unpublished data from the 2016 survey. At the University of Memphis, research librarian Jan Stone tracked down hard-to-find sources and faculty assistant Linda Hayes was there to assist at every step. Finally, I'm grateful to all the great folks at West Academic Publishing for their assistance and support. It's an honor to be part of such a distinguished publishing family.

A few passages were borrowed from my books: *The "Companion Text" to Law School: Understanding and Surviving Life with a Law Student* (2012) and *The Law School Trip: The Insider's Guide to Law School* (2001).

PROLOGUE

_____

For three decades as a law professor, at several schools across the country, I've watched first-year law students—"1Ls"—make the same mistakes: in their approach to studying, behavior in and out of the classroom, exam preparation, exam performance, and overall mindset toward law school. Sometimes these mistakes result from following bad advice, but more often they occur simply because students don't know what to expect or what is expected of them when they arrive at law school.

The consequences of these missteps vary. Some students flunk out, of course, but more often the mistakes prevent students from maximizing their potential, meeting their own high expectations, and living happy, well-balanced lives. Even many students who end up excelling in law school struggle dispiritedly to cope with the stress and anxiety that come from having to compete in the high-stakes 1L race without prior training and on a route lacking clear markers.

My partial remedy—and the goal of this book beginning with the 2008 first edition and continuing in this 2017 third edition—is to provide new students with a candid, beginning-to-end roadmap to the first year of law school, including the navigational and other tools to complete the sojourn scholastically accomplished and emotionally intact.

If you've done any looking around, you know that a bunch of other "how to succeed in law school" books exist. What makes this book distinctive?

- **Written by a law professor with a wide range of experience teaching different kinds of students at different law schools.**

As you approach law school, lots of people—lawyer acquaintances, other law students, and authors of books like this one—will be giving you advice about how to succeed. Your first question to any of us should be: "Who are you to be giving me advice?"

I've taught thousands of students at six law schools, from the West Coast (San Francisco) to the East Coast (Miami), and points in between (Boulder, Little Rock, Memphis, and Winston-Salem). These include law schools in each tier of the *U.S. News & World Report* law school rankings. I have experience teaching every kind of law student: affluent students, low-income students, private-school students, public-school students, young students just out of college, older students with families and established careers, single parents, brilliant, average, and struggling students, kids whose parents were law school deans and those who were the first in their family to attend college, urbanites, ruralites, full-time day students, part-time night students, diverse students, and students with disabilities. I've taught students who went on to become great judges and students who went on to become great bartenders.

My teaching credentials include six teaching awards, excellent student evaluations at six law schools, articles and book chapters about law teaching, and teaching presentations for organizations such as the Institute for Law School Teaching and the Association of American Law Schools. My publishing record includes several books and dozens of scholarly articles that have been cited in more than 600 books, articles, and court opinions. As a legal commentator, I've been quoted by National Public Radio, the *New York Times*, *Washington Post*, *Time*, *Politifact*, *U.S. News & World Report*, and dozens of other media sources.

Additionally, I once was a successful law student. In 1980, I graduated third in my class at the University of Florida College of Law, where I was a member of the law review and Order of the Coif, an honor conferred on the top 10 percent of graduates at select law schools. While my memories of the first year of law school are distant, some of them remain quite clear, which says a lot about the impact of the 1L adventure. I still remember my first day of law school orientation, first class, first Socratic interrogation, and first exam.

That my own law school memories still have relevance tells you something important to know about U.S. legal education: it's deeply rooted in tradition. While changes are occurring, for the most part, particularly in the first year, "[t]ypical classroom instruction at most law schools today would be familiar to any lawyer who attended law school during the past hundred thirty years."[1]

I don't claim to have the only right answers about succeeding in law school. Be wary of anyone who does. Any advice-giver making such a claim knows little about the wide variations in the learning styles of law students and teaching styles of professors. As with the law itself, many of the relevant questions about how to succeed have more than one answer depending on the particular student and professor. Indeed, the very definition of "success" is subject to different answers. I base my advice on what will be most helpful to the largest group of students.

- **Provides a comprehensive beginning-to-end roadmap of what to expect in the first year.**

A large part of what makes the first year of law school so stressful and frightening is not knowing what to expect. For several years, I polled my entering Torts students with this question:

As you begin your 1L quest, what is your dominant feeling?

- Confidence
- Excitement
- Lack of confidence
- Pride
- Stress
- Fear or anxiety
- Uncertainty

"Uncertainty" was the most common answer. "Stress" and "Fear or anxiety"—much of which is generated by uncertainty—also received many votes. To reduce your uncertainty and enlarge your comfort zone, this book explains what to expect as a 1L and

---

[1]   Roy Stuckey et al., Best Practices for Legal Education 98 (2007) [hereinafter Best Practices for Legal Education].

how to respond when it happens. Essentially, it answers the questions, "What is the first year of law school really like and how do I make the most of it?"

The first year is the most important year in the three-year U.S. law school curriculum (four years for part-time students). The first year is where students acquire the basic knowledge and tools of legal analysis that carry them through the rest of law school and beyond. Think of it as the foundation on which all subsequent building blocks for becoming and being a lawyer are laid. It is also the year that tends to define students, both academically and in terms of their overall attitude and approach to law school.

While most of my advice applies to the entire first year, we'll concentrate on the all-critical first semester. The first semester is where students learn to read cases, write case briefs, take class notes, compose course outlines, deal with the Socratic teaching method, and develop either good or poor classroom, study, and exam strategies. Those first fourteen weeks forge the critical-reasoning skills that law professors like to call "thinking like a lawyer."

- **Offers *candid* advice and information.**

I try to be candid in depicting the good, bad, and ugly of law school. To keep myself honest in that regard, I approached the book from this standpoint: If my daughter decided to go to law school, what advice would I give her? I wouldn't necessarily tell her everything law schools or law professors would want her to hear. I'd be bluntly honest.

For example, I'd be less than candid if I didn't tell you that the past decade has witnessed several worrisome trends in legal education. Due to a tepid legal job market that commenced with the Great Recession of 2008 and continues today, law school enrollment has shrunk significantly because of a much smaller applicant pool. With too many law schools competing for too few applicants, admissions standards have declined at most schools (which could be viewed as bad news for legal education, but good news if you're a beneficiary of the lower entrance barriers). Likely related, bar passage rates have fallen in a majority of states over the past several years, dramatically in many cases. Consult Chapters 2 and 3 for more information about each of these items.

But trends were made to be reversed and as of this writing in 2017, there are some signs things may be leveling off. In the meantime, there's still plenty of good news. Law schools remain remarkable learning places populated by talented professors and energetic, hard-working, and passionate students.

- **Addresses each aspect of academic success, including the top five habits of successful law students, effective class participation, case-briefing, note-taking, outlining, exam preparation, and essay and multiple-choice exam strategies.**

You may already be aware that grades, particularly early grades, are important to opportunities both within and outside of law school, more important than in other graduate programs and employment sectors. Any suggestion to the contrary would be a misrepresentation. The finding of a 1980s national study of higher education remains true today: in no other educational discipline do early grades have as much impact as they do in law school.[2]

This isn't to say that people without high grades can't or don't succeed in the legal profession. Quite the contrary is true. Many of the most successful and impactful lawyers in America were average students. I laughed when a colleague told me her law school has a nice basketball court for students bearing a plaque reading "Donated by a *C* Student."

But it's a fact that high GPAs and class rankings open doors not available to students who lack them, both in law school and in the real-world job market. Within law school, students with good grades have better opportunities to obtain scholarships, positions as research assistants to professors, and law review

---

[2]   The survey by the Association for the Study of Higher Education studied stress in undergraduate, graduate, law, and medical students, concluding with regard to law school: "[I]n no other university setting do grades have the importance at such an early point in one's education." NEAL A. WHITMAN ET AL., ASS'N FOR THE STUDY OF HIGHER EDUC., STUDENT STRESS: EFFECTS AND SOLUTIONS, ASHE-ERIC HIGHER EDUCATION RESEARCH REPORT NO. 2 53 (1984).

membership. Outside of law school, many law firms and judges won't interview people who are not in the top quartile of their class. At the end of an academic year, I asked my students to name one thing they wish they had known when they started law school. One student responded: "I wish I had known how important law firms find class rank to be."

Although substantial grade inflation, discussed in Chapter 14, has occurred in law schools over the past decade, it remains true that high grades in law school are harder to come by than in most other graduate programs. Because grades play such a crucial role, a large portion of the book is devoted to helping you "make the grade." I can't promise that if you follow my advice, you will ace your courses or finish at the top of your class. Mathematics dictates that in every law school class since the dawn of time only 10 percent of students finish in the top 10 percent. Ninety percent don't. But I firmly believe—and many readers over the years have attested to it—that following the advice in this book will substantially improve your chances of succeeding at a higher level than you otherwise would.

If you're looking for shortcuts to success in law school, this may not be the book for you. While it does offer important tips for being efficient—a critical time-saving attribute of successful law students—I'm sorry to report that students who make a habit of cutting corners simply do not succeed at the highest levels in law school. Most students "succeed" in law school in terms of not being academically dismissed, including many students who cut corners. But if your definition of success is something higher, cutting corners isn't a viable option for most students.

But don't take my word for it. In response to a year-ending question to list one piece of advice students would give to someone starting law school, one student wrote:

> I read some books before I started law school: [*Title omitted*] and [*Title omitted*]. Both were helpful, but it seems that most of the pre-law, self-help books are geared toward helping students find the easy way out. For example, one of the books I read had a whole chapter on book-briefing and gathering outlines from others. Well, the people who book-

brief and don't do their own outlines usually don't do well. I would emphasize in your book that there is no easy way through law school.

And this came from a kid I jumped all over on the second day of class for arriving late. Law students, God love 'em.

- **Focuses on practical advice that can be followed by any student from day one.**

One of the problems with a lot of advice students receive about how to succeed in law school is that it can't be readily followed. I learned this in seeking feedback from other law professors. Reduced to its essence, much of their advice amounted to "learn to read better," "learn to write better," and "learn to think better." Easier said than done. This book focuses on practical advice that can be followed by any student from the first day of law school.

- **Addresses "emotional success" in addition to academic success.**

People are starting to lose it a bit, egos flying, etc. One girl started crying the other day because she threw a french fry at this kid, just playing around, and he flew off the handle because it hit his laptop.

—First semester update from a 1L

Here's an early warning: law school takes an emotional and physical toll on a substantial percentage of students, even those who enjoy it and perform well. Studies of law student psychological distress, as you will see in Chapter 19, do not paint a pretty picture.

Most advice in law school prep books, including this one, is geared toward maximizing academic success by traditional barometers: grades and class rank. But as important as grades are, they are by no means the only measuring sticks of law school achievement. Exploration, empowerment, happiness and well-being, learning for its own sake, building relationships, becoming a professional . . . there are many components of law school success.

At many stops along the road to academic success, this book offers advice for reducing stress and leading a healthy, balanced law school life. Several chapters are specifically devoted to these issues. Don't let this book or law school make you lose sight of the most important goals of life, which do not include writing the top exam in Contracts.

- *Shows* **with anecdotes and examples.**

Showing is more effective than telling, so many anecdotes and examples are used to make and illuminate points, including samples of authentic Socratic dialogue, student case briefs, student course outline excerpts, student class notes, and exam questions and answers.

Nearly all of the examples come from the subject of Torts. Simplistically, Torts is the study of monetary liability for personal injuries, both physical and psychological. Torts is a good subject to use as a vehicle for exploring law school's first year because it is a required first-year course at all schools and many of the basic principles and fact patterns of tort law are comprehensible without extensive background or explanation. It is also a subject with which incoming students have at least some familiarity due to the widespread coverage of tort lawsuits and the tort system by the media.

A cautionary note: I picked and constructed simple examples that can be processed by pre-law, admitted, and new students. Don't be misled into thinking law is as straightforward or easy as some of the examples might make it appear.

- **Includes a student voice with comments from real 1Ls.**

To stay in touch with the modern 1L experience from a student perspective, I continually seek input from law students. Their interesting, insightful, and sometimes poignant comments add confirmation, as well as balance to (and relief from) the drone of teacher talk that will be bearing down on you for the next many pages.

While the limited student populations surveyed do not empirically represent the entire universe of law students, in terms of student reactions to the trials and tribulations of the 1L experience, my guess is that they come very close. This is attributable to the remarkable uniformity in the basic structures and institutions of the first year of law school throughout U.S. legal education. In teaching at schools in different parts of the country, I've always been struck by the core likeness of law students. At schools great and small, all 1Ls struggle to learn the same material under the same teaching methodologies and evaluation formats.

In quoting student comments, I made style, punctuation, and grammar adjustments, but did not change their meaning.

- **Backs up advice with empirical research.**

Scores of studies have been conducted about law students, legal education, and teaching and learning in general, yet this research is often overlooked in giving advice to law students. To boost confidence (yours and mine) in my recommendations, I researched and discuss many of these studies. Did you know that students who sit in the front of classrooms get higher grades than those who sit in back? That women voluntarily participate in law school class discussions at lower rates than men? That the conventional wisdom to not change initial answers to multiple-choice questions is backwards? Some of the research on these and other points might surprise you.

- **Includes input from other law professors.**

To broaden my view I solicited input from other law professors all along the way. In particular, in Chapter 18, five experienced legal writing professors from different law schools answer important questions about legal research and writing courses, part of the required first-year curriculum at all law schools. As you will soon learn all too well, no 1L courses generate more attention, angst, and complaining from students.

- **Written in a reader-friendly voice.**

Who wants to read several hundred pages of boring law professor advice? I wouldn't, so I try to keep you engaged with a lively voice and touch of humor. My credentials for attempting to occasionally amuse you include four years as the monthly humor columnist for the *American Bar Association Journal*, editor of Lawhaha.com, and author/editor of two books in the seemingly oxymoronic genre of "legal humor."

Note on the New *1L of a Ride Video Course*

In 2016, West Academic Publishing released the *1L of a Ride Video Course*, a twelve-part video series that can be used separately or as a supplement to the book. You might already be holding a copy of the book with the video access code printed on the inside cover.

The videos feature award-winning Professors Christine Coughlin (Wake Forest University School of Law), Meredith Duncan (University of Houston Law Center), Nancy Levit (University of Missouri-Kansas City School of Law), and, of course, yours truly. Along with an introductory video, the videos cover these topics:

- Planning Ahead and Biggest Fears
- Structure and Role of U.S. Courts
- Socratic and Case Methods
- Overview of the First-Year Curriculum
- First-Year Sample Course: Torts
- How to Read and Brief a Case
- The C.R.E.D.O.—Top Five Habits of Successful Law Students
- Essential Study Techniques
- Legal Research Basics
- Legal Writing Basics
- Managing Stress and Maintaining Well-Being
- Professionalism

Although experts disagree about the reliability of classifying people as "aural" or "visual" learners, there's no question that many students benefit from seeing and hearing in addition to reading. Studies show that educational videos can reinforce reading, enhance student comprehension, and help accommodate diverse learning styles.

Research also suggests that students learn better when a one-on-one connection is established with teachers. In the book, I try to achieve that by using a personal, first-person voice. One Amazon reviewer wrote: "Professor McClurg has this extremely personal way of speaking in the book, making you feel like he's standing right in front of you and guiding you, so you know you are not alone." Aw, so nice. In the video course, though, we really are standing right in front of you and guiding you. And you're not alone, unless, of course, you want to be, in which case you can just hit pause.

If you have access to the video course, an obvious question is, "What should I do first? Read the book or watch the videos?" It depends on your most immediate goals and how you learn best. Some people may want to watch the videos first to get a big-picture overview. Maybe it's early in your law school application process and you're not quite ready to get into the nitty gritty details. If you're closer to starting law school, it might be better to tackle the book first and use the videos for reinforcement. Either approach is fine. Just don't make the mistake of only watching the videos and thinking you have it all covered. A lot gets left out in ten-minute videos. The videos are aimed at basic, first principles.

Keep Your Roadmap Handy

Like all roadmaps, you'll want to keep this one handy throughout your 1L trip. If you were taking a real one-year road trip, you wouldn't just glance at the map before you backed out of the driveway and toss it aside. You'd review it each time you entered new territory or faced a new fork in the road.

If you haven't started law school yet, read the entire book to get the big picture, then return to consult particular chapters as they become more directly relevant in your 1L journey. Much of the advice is very specific. If you haven't started law school yet, you won't be able to remember or process it all.

For example, as scintillating as the subject is, reading the chapter (Chapter 13) on how to compose a course outline before law school starts isn't going to imprint all the details you'll need to know when it comes time to start preparing your own outlines. The same holds true for several other chapters, including those on case-briefing (Chapter 11), note-taking (Chapter 12), exam preparation (Chapter 15), essay and multiple-choice exam strategies (Chapters 16 and 17), legal research and writing (Chapter 18), maintaining well-being (Chapter 20), dealing with the second semester (Chapter 21), and co- and extracurricular activities (Chapter 24).

Buy some highlighters and mark the heck out of key passages as you read. That's what you'll be doing with your other law school books, so it will be good practice. Consult the index for answers to specific questions.

I hope you enjoy reading and learning from this book as much as I enjoyed writing it. Most important, I hope you'll actually follow the advice. Occasionally I receive student comments along the lines of "I learned that lesson the hard way." Learn it the easy way. It's all in here!

TABLE OF CONTENTS

1L OF A RIDE:

A Well-Traveled Professor's Roadmap to Success in the First Year of Law School

Third Edition

CHAPTER 1

DESTINATION LAW SCHOOL

Get ready to embark on a wild ride unlike anything you've ever experienced, packed with thrills, chills, and probably a few spills. Being a 1L will challenge you like you've never been challenged. Law school and a law degree offer the potential for great rewards, but at a cost. The first year of law school will be one of hardest years of your life. Law school will profoundly alter the way you think, and view and interact with the world around you. Your 1L experience will change who you are, whether you want it to or not.

But you may already be tired of hearing or reading these kinds of dire proclamations and predictions. Perhaps you've encountered them in other prep books. Maybe they even sound like clichés by now. "Yeah, yeah, law school will be hard. I'll be changed. Whatever. Everyone says the same thing. I can handle it."

The best analogy I have for explaining how law school will both take you by surprise and forever alter you involves becoming a parent. When I was an expectant dad many years ago, friends and family told me the same kinds of things about becoming a parent. "It will change your life forever." "It will be the hardest thing you've ever done." "Say good-bye to your old life."

I thought they were exaggerating. It wasn't like I was uninformed. I'd read the essential baby and parenting books and even attended parenting classes. I cruised blissfully through the entire event thinking, "I'm prepared. I'm prepared. I'm prepared." Then five seconds into my first encounter with infant projectile vomiting, it was, "Augh! I'm not prepared! I'm not prepared! I'm not prepared!"

Like being a parent, one can truly understand and appreciate the first year of law school only by experiencing it, so let's start by looking at some reactions from those who did. On the last page of my first-semester Torts exam, I sometimes insert this bonus question: "Write the name of a song or a song lyric that best describes your feelings about the first semester of law school." (It doesn't count for any points, so don't get your hopes up that law school exams are that easy.) Below are some of the responses. Lyrics are in quotation marks.

While we can't attach deep psychological meaning to these answers, dashed off hastily and perhaps in jest, the students' spontaneous associations are nevertheless revealing. Their first-semester playlist reflects the rollercoaster ride of emotions inherent in being a 1L, including:

Stress, anxiety:

- Help!—The Beatles
- Chalkdust Torture—Phish
- Under Pressure—Queen/David Bowie
- I Wanna Be Sedated—The Ramones
- Panic—The Smiths

Disorientation, madness:

- Highway to Hell—AC/DC
- "They won't let me out, they won't let me out (I'm locked up)."—Akon
- Basketcase—Green Day
- Welcome Home (Sanitarium)—Metallica
- Crazy Train—Ozzy Osborne

Exhaustion, frustration, hostility:

- A Hard Day's Night—The Beatles
- Welcome to the Jungle—Guns N' Roses
- "I'm gonna knock you out. Mama said knock you out."—LL Cool J
- Rat Race—Bob Marley
- We're Not Gonna Take It—Twisted Sister

Melancholy, depression:

- A Hard Rain's A-Gonna Fall—Bob Dylan

- Long Road to Ruin—Foo Fighters
- Paint It Black—The Rolling Stones
- "Reflections of the way life used to be."—The Supremes
- Another One Bites the Dust—Queen

Self-doubt:

- "I fought the law and the law won."—Bobby Fuller Four
- "What the hell am I doing here? I don't belong here, I don't belong here."—Radiohead
- Should I Stay or Should I Go?—The Clash
- Should Have Been a Cowboy (instead of a lawyer)—Toby Keith
- Livin' on a Prayer—Bon Jovi

But don't let these answers bring you down. They were solicited at the end of a long, tough semester, seconds after the students completed a grueling three-hour exam. And even then—even in the very worst of times—many students expressed excitement, hope, optimism, and pride, as in:

- I Feel Good—James Brown
- I Will Survive—Gloria Gaynor
- "Here I am, rock you like a hurricane."—The Scorpions
- Nothing's Gonna Stop Us Now—Jefferson Starship
- We Are the Champions—Queen

Every time I use the song question, one or more students quote the Grateful Dead, describing the first semester as a "long, strange trip." And indeed it is. So what are we waiting for? If you haven't already started, law school is probably looming on the not-too-distant horizon. It may be just months away, perhaps only weeks. You're probably wondering what you should be doing and feeling. Let's find out.

CHAPTER 2

PRE-TRIP PLANNING: WHAT TO DO BEFORE YOU ARRIVE

Incoming students naturally feel like they should be doing something to get ready for law school before they get there. They should be, but not necessarily the things they think they should be doing. Below are two pre-arrival "To Do" lists, one for intangibles and one for tangibles. Law students and law student advice usually focus on the tangibles, but the intangibles are just as important and some of them are harder to accomplish.

Pre-Arrival "To Do" List: The Intangibles

Be excited!

Be excited about going to law school. It's a big deal and you should treat it that way. Approach it with enthusiasm, not dread (distinguishing dread from a healthy apprehension), and certainly not apathy—nothing would be worse than that. My experience observing law students has taught me that President Harry Truman got it right when he said he had studied the lives of great people and "found that the men and women who got to the top were those who did the jobs they had in hand, with everything they had of *energy and enthusiasm*."

Law school is an entry pass to an exclusive club offering unique challenges, opportunities, and rewards. Your degree will grant you the power to single-handedly change people's lives for the better. That's what ordinary lawyers do every day.

In my original draft of this chapter, to inspire you, I talked about some big, important lawyers and how their big, important cases changed history. It was all true. Experience has shown time and again that lawyers are the only group with the conviction and courage to consistently stand up and fight for justice when it's unpopular to do so. Lawyers created the liberties we cherish and have fought to protect them for more than two hundred years. Thirty-three of the fifty-five framers of the U.S. Constitution were lawyers. Twenty-six of America's forty-four presidents—nearly 60 percent—studied law.[3] Tales about lawyers who altered the path of America could fill this and many other books.

But a conversation in the hallway with a 2L caused me to change course. As I was walking into class, he came up and recounted a dispute he'd been having with his landlord. He said he was able to resolve it because a lawyer offered to help him without charge because he was a broke law student. The student told me: "Professor, I'm going to remember that when I become a lawyer. I'm going to remember what it felt like to have no money and no power and no voice and how that lawyer helped me."

That brought back to me the real heart and soul of what it means to be a lawyer. Big cases change history, but the smallest and simplest cases often have the biggest impact on ordinary people. I decided to cut the history lesson and tell you instead about a very tiny case I handled as a young lawyer. It was a pro bono case, meaning there was no fee involved. The Jacksonville, Florida legal aid organization called and asked if I would help an elderly man being sued by a home improvement contractor for breach of contract. I was tempted to say I was too busy— which was true, such is the life of a young litigation associate, as many of you will learn—but I accepted the case.

My client was a man in his eighties whom I'll call Clarence Jackson. Mr. Jackson had shown up at the legal aid office clutching a packet of papers, explaining to the intake interviewer that he had signed a contract with a home improvement contractor to have some repairs done on his house for $1,000. That was a lot of money back then, especially for a man living on Social Security. He said the contractor didn't complete the work properly, so he refused to pay. The contractor hauled off and sued him, threatening to take his house away.

I drove out to the house on a hot, humid summer morning to meet Mr. Jackson. The house was in a neighborhood on "the other side of town" that I had never visited. Honestly, it wasn't much of a house. It was very small and very old, but

---

[3]   Donald Trump holds the forty-fifth presidency, but is only the forty-fourth president. The discrepancy comes from Grover Cleveland, who was elected as the twenty-second and twenty-fourth president, with Benjamin Harrison wedged in between.

exceptionally well-kept. Mr. Jackson greeted me at the door and I took an instant liking to him. He was a gentle, soft-spoken man. He wore overalls and I felt ridiculous standing on the porch sweating in my lawyer power suit. He invited me in, showed me pictures of his kids and grandchildren, and gave me some iced tea. We sat in the living room looking over the contract and the legal complaint, then he took me on a tour of the premises.

He pointed out the shoddy workmanship by the contractor: bare, wrong-sized fascia boards nailed haphazardly at the roof line, a toilet that poured water out the bottom every time it was flushed, a new window several inches too small for the opening, etc. I remember getting mad. The nerve of that contractor to not only do such slapdash work, but sue Mr. Jackson and scare the heck out of him by threatening to take his home away.

I took some pictures with a Polaroid camera (this was long before the days of digital cameras) and went back to my office to prepare an affidavit for Mr. Jackson to sign and a motion for summary judgment in the lawsuit. Summary judgment is a way for a court to dispose of a case without a trial. We had a hearing on the motion in the judge's chambers. At the end, the judge granted our motion—dismissing the case—but with all the legalese the old man misunderstood. He thought we lost. When the judge adjourned the hearing, Mr. Jackson put his hand on my shoulder and said, "Thank you, Mr. McClurg, I know you did a good job. I guess some things just can't be helped." I said, "Mr. Jackson, it's okay. We won."[4]

He couldn't believe it. Literally. Maybe he went in believing the system would be stacked against him. When the victory finally sunk in, he kept repeating, "Thank you, thank you, thank you." I was embarrassed. I was still in my twenties. Here was a man who had done and seen far more than I ever had. But for just a little bit of my time, I'd changed his life.

A few days after the hearing, the receptionist buzzed me and said, "There's a man out here who *says* he's your client." Mr. Jackson did not fit the profile of the firm's usual well-heeled clientele. I walked out to the receptionist area and there stood

---

[4]   Of course, I don't recall the exact words of the conversation in this or other anecdotes sprinkled throughout the book. I recount their substance to the best of my ability.

Mr. Jackson, still wearing overalls. He said he wanted to pay me and pulled a wad of bills from his pocket. He said it was a hundred dollars. I explained again that his was a pro bono case and that he didn't owe me anything. But he kept insisting he had to do something for me. Finally, he said, "Mr. McClurg, I'll tell you what. You come over to my house on Saturday and I'll cook you supper." I had insisted he call me by my first name, but he never did.

I went. And to this day I've never felt more proud to be a lawyer than that afternoon, sitting in that old man's blazing kitchen—he didn't have air conditioning—eating the dinner he made for me.

America is filled with "Mr. Jacksons"—people who desperately need help with legal problems that may seem small from the outside, but which dominate their lives. Our system entrusts the awesome responsibility to give that help to one group: lawyers. People tend to think of doctors as the only life-saving profession, but make no mistake: lawyers have people's lives in their hands every day.

Start law school feeling proud about becoming part of a noble and honorable profession. Don't let the people around you sour you on studying to be a lawyer. The public has a love-hate relationship with lawyers. On the one hand, they're fascinated with the law and lawyers, as shown by the never-ending stream of books, movies, and television programming about them. On the other hand, people are quick to malign lawyers. Even total strangers may feel comfortable telling you lawyer jokes.

True story: I went on a canoeing trip with a group of law professors. You can imagine what a rollicking adventure that was. The woman at the canoe rental place asked what I did and I said, "Law professor." Without hesitating, she said, "I hate lawyers." Without hesitating, I said, "I hate people who rent canoes." She was shocked and appalled I would say something so rude. Although the irony escaped her, I felt good about standing up for my profession. Plus, I really do hate people who rent canoes.

Lawyers aren't perfect, and there are rotten apples in the bin of every profession, but as a fellow named Harrison Tweed said more than half a century ago: "With all their faults, [lawyers] stack up well against those in every other occupation or profession. They are better to work with or play with or fight with or drink with than most other varieties of mankind." Trust that the haters and joke-tellers will be the first ones calling when they get in trouble.

Let the power of the law to right wrongs invigorate you. Let the grand tradition of lawyers in America make you proud. Law is power. Knowledge of law is *em*powering. So get ready to be unstoppable. Prepare to set the world on fire! Figuratively only, since that would be a tort.

Be excited! If you're enthusiastic about law school, the workload will be more tolerable and you'll enjoy the experience much more.

Get your life in order.

The first year of law school is all-consuming. The workload and volume of material you will be expected to master will be unlike anything you've ever encountered. To maximize your chances for success, you need to enter law school with your full focus on it.

Life distractions should be resolved before you get there. Don't be a procrastinator when it comes to getting your housing or financial aid firmed up. Having to work out kinks in either while starting school will not only take away needed time and energy, it will add extra stress you don't need. Law school will provide plenty of that.

If you're in a turbulent intimate relationship that you know deep down is going to end at some point anyway, the summer before law school might be a good time to kiss it goodbye. Don't drag it out until after law school starts. Law school can take a heavy toll even on good relationships. See Chapter 23. No reason to jeopardize your success by wasting emotional energy on a relationship that's already on life support.

For part-time evening-division students, employment conflicts are the biggest challenge and number one reason for failing to succeed. "Ti-ii-ii-ime is *not* on your side"[5] if you're going to be attending law school at night while working full-time. You will need a detailed time management plan before you get to law school. Chapter 22 addresses the unique challenges faced by "night" students and nontraditional students generally.

Health issues are another source of interference with law school success. Unfortunately, people have less ability to control them than many other potential life distractions. If you face serious health issues as law school approaches, consider the prognosis for the immediate future, recognizing that the stress of law school can aggravate health conditions. If the immediate prognosis is not good or unclear, postpone law school until your health issues can be resolved. Schools often will grant deferments to admitted students for health reasons, meaning you can enroll the next academic year without having to reapply.

Do not plan weddings, extended vacations, or pregnancies during the first year of law school. To the fullest extent possible, clear your calendar of major events from August through May.

Approach law school like a full-time job.

Key to success is approaching law school with a proper mindset. Transposing a classic U.S. military recruiting slogan, law school's not just an adventure—it's a job. If every law student approached law school as they would a full-time job, more would excel at it. Accept that law school is going to be a full-time endeavor marked by long, sometimes tedious hours. Accept that you're going to have to sacrifice a lot of the leisure time you enjoyed in your pre-law student life.

Think about it. Suppose that instead of going to law school, you accepted a career-type job in your field of undergraduate study, a job offering potentially great rewards for good

---

[5]   *See* THE ROLLING STONES, TIME IS ON MY SIDE (Verve 1963). This song became the Stones' first top ten single in the United States. Notice those big and small capital letters? Virtually unknown to the rest of the printed universe, they are vitally important to correct legal citation style per *The Bluebook*. You'll hear more about *The Bluebook* in future pages, but for an early insight into the compulsively detailed world of legal citation style, *The Bluebook* even has specific rules for referencing song titles. *See* THE BLUEBOOK: A UNIFORM SYSTEM OF CITATION R. 18.7.1, at 188 (Columbia Law Review Ass'n et al. eds., 20th ed. 2015) (setting forth rules for citing to audio recordings).

performance, as well as the possibility of getting canned for poor performance. Would you:

- Show up late for work?

- Browse the web during important company meetings?

- Arrive unprepared for a meeting with your boss?

- Stay out late partying on nights when you know you have to get up early and go to work?

- Search for ways to cut corners rather than giving your best effort?

Hopefully, the answer to each question is *no* (if not, that's a whole other conversation we need to have), yet some law students follow these behavioral patterns in law school. If you approach law school as a full-time job, you will have already charted a course toward success.

Forget what you think you know about law.

You've heard the adage that a little knowledge is a dangerous thing. Nowhere is this truer than when starting law school. On the first day of Torts, I tell my students that if they think they know something about the law, *please* try to forget it. Why? Because everything people think they know about the law when they get to law school is wrong, incomplete, taken out of context, or not in the form your professors will want you to know it.

Beginning students without any legal background are sometimes alarmed when it seems that some of their classmates already know a lot about the law. Perhaps these students took a few undergraduate law courses. Some may have worked as paralegals at law firms. Don't worry. The latter may know something about how law is practiced in real life, but no one without a legal education really knows anything about "the law." Most important, no one coming to law school knows anything about law that will help them perform academically in the first year.

Trust that law school will teach you what you need to know, or at least give you the tools to acquire that knowledge. That's why you can go to law school with an undergraduate degree in religion or art history, but can attend medical school only with a background in science. Arrive at law school imagining your brain as a fresh sponge, right out of the package, ready to absorb a whole new world of information and way of thinking.

Expect and embrace uncertainty.

New law students arrive expecting the law to be a neat and tidy catalog of black and white rules they can memorize and, by doing so, become successful students and lawyers. They're perplexed and frustrated to discover that so much of law is awash in shades of gray. "It depends" is the most accurate answer to many legal questions. Students also struggle with the fact that the complex pieces of law do not fit neatly together like a jigsaw puzzle.

Part of this indeterminacy stems from the fact that the U.S. is a "common law" legal system. Most of the rest of the world, including all of Europe and Latin America, follows what is known as the "civil law tradition." Common law is judge-made law, derived from and developed through case precedent. In civil law systems, law is derived primarily from codes—i.e., books of neatly organized statutes promulgated by legislators. In theory, judges have no power to make law in civil law systems. Their job is to follow the rules set forth in the codes. (It doesn't really work that way in practice because all legal language requires interpretation.)

Exasperated by the indefiniteness of the law, U.S. law students sometimes utter comments such as, "Why don't they just write all the rules down in one place? That way, we'd know what the law is!" Without realizing it, they're advocating for a civil law system. Someone actually tried to do that once. In the eighteenth century, Frederick the Great implemented the Prussian Code under Prussia's civil law system. The Prussian Code stands as an attempt to install what so many U.S. law students desperately wish for: a detailed compendium of rules intended to foresee and govern the entire range of human conduct. The Prussian Code contained more than 17,000 provisions, but it was a failure. Seventeen million provisions would not be enough.

When I workshopped a chapter of this book with a group of law professors, I asked them to name the most important traits of successful law students. Immediately, one of my colleagues blurted, "The ability to embrace uncertainty!" Accept before you arrive at law school that much of law is vague and malleable, as it must be to address the ambiguity of language and the infinite permutations in facts that comprise legal disputes.

Here's an example from criminal law to give you a taste. A federal statute, 21 U.S.C. § 924(c)(1), imposes a mandatory minimum enhanced sentence of five years for one who uses or "carries" a firearm during and in relation to the commission of a drug-trafficking crime. Sounds clear enough. Everyone understands the meaning of "carries," right? Surely such a simple word could not lead to a protracted legal dispute.

In *United States v. Foster*,[6] the police arrested the defendant for drug-trafficking when they found methamphetamine in his pickup truck. They also arrested him for "carrying" a firearm during the commission of a drug-trafficking crime after finding a gun in the bed of his truck under a buttoned-down tarp. Was he "carrying" the gun within the meaning of the statute? The trial court ruled that he was, but after nine years of appeals, a federal appellate court held he wasn't and reversed the conviction. Nine years to determine the meaning of *a single word*. Well, at least that issue was finally settled . . . until the U.S. Supreme Court came along a year later and ruled in a different case that transporting guns in vehicles *does* constitute carrying them.[7] Welcome to law school!

Students who fixate on searching for *the* answer to every legal question can drive both themselves and their professors mad. Arrive open to the idea that the answer to many legal questions is a range of possibilities, frequently dependent on the facts of the case, rather than a single rock-solid right answer. Embrace uncertainty.

---

[6]   133 F.3d 704 (9th Cir. 1998).

[7]   Muscarello v. United States, 524 U.S. 125, 126–27 (1998) (holding that one "who knowingly possesses and conveys firearms in a vehicle" is carrying them within the meaning of the enhanced sentencing statute).

Define "success" for yourself.

Figure out what you want out of law school before you get there. "Success" can mean different things to different people. For most incoming students, success means achieving at a high academic level and this book operates on the assumption that "grade success" is a primary goal for most readers. But not all students come to law school with the intent to graduate at the top of their class. Many part-time students with existing careers, for example, attend law school to advance their lives and careers in a practical way. They're interested in getting a law degree, not necessarily a law degree with honors.

Of course, all students have a goal of succeeding at a level high enough to avoid being academically dismissed. Hopefully, your aspirations are higher than that bare minimum, but if not, filter the advice herein in accordance with your own goals.

But success also has meaning beyond academic achievement. Most students care about *more* than just grades. In addition to academic success, they care about things like justice, exploration, enlightenment, general happiness, and becoming a "professional."

Define success for yourself. Literally. Put it in writing. Begin the sentence with "My definition of success in law school is . . ." and complete the sentence. If your idea of success includes several components, make a list. Putting it in writing will force you to think more concretely about what you really want and need out of law school. Revisit the definition as you progress through the first year. If you notice it changing, stop and consider why. As discussed later, law school has a sneaky way of changing one's goals and values.

Pre-Arrival "To Do" List: The Tangibles

Some tangible tasks also should be on your pre-law school "To Do" list, although perhaps not the ones you think. Let's take a look.

Develop a financial plan.

You need a plan for financing your legal education, paying particular attention to ways to keep your student loan debt as low as possible. You're probably familiar with the daunting financial challenges facing new law graduates due to the combination of a challenging job market and high student debt-loads.

A challenging legal job market. The Great Recession of 2008 inflicted a big hit on the legal job market. The recession is over, but the job market still hasn't fully recovered. What gives?

Several explanations have been offered. Clients are demanding lower costs, often placing caps on fees, forcing firms to abandon the traditional billable-hour, sky's-the-limit model. Firms have responded in a number of ways, including reducing associate hiring and resorting to more contract lawyers. Technology plays a role that is only going to increase. Artificial intelligence now allows machines to do jobs in minutes—document review being a notable example—that traditionally took young associates, billing by the hour, days or weeks to perform. In 2016, a prominent law firm announced it was "hiring" a robot to sift through bankruptcy documents.[8] Some work, including legal research and document preparation, is being outsourced, sometimes to other countries. DIY "lawyering" is thought to be cutting into some of the bread and butter work of small practitioners, such as preparing simple wills or leases. Meanwhile, mandatory arbitration clauses in contracts and legislative restrictions on lawsuits may be shrinking the litigation job market, particularly in the once-staple field of personal injury law.

In short, dramatic paradigm shifts are occurring in the structure of the legal job market that make it unlikely it will ever return to the glory days where jobs were readily available to all graduates.

ABA data showed 62.4 percent of 2015 law graduates were employed in jobs requiring a law degree within ten months of graduation,[9] while an additional 13.8 percent held "JD Advantage" jobs; i.e., jobs for which a Juris Doctor degree is not usually a requirement, but is considered an asset.[10] Some of the

---

[8]   Karen Turner, *Meet 'Ross,' the Newly Hired Legal Robot*, WASH. POST, May 16, 2016.

[9]   ABA SECTION OF LEGAL EDUC. & ADMISSIONS TO THE BAR, 2015 LAW GRADUATE EMPLOYMENT DATA (2016).

[10]   *Id.* The ABA offers this definition of JD Advantage jobs:

graduates in both of those categories were in short-time or part-time positions. Most of the other grads were also employed after ten months, but some in jobs unrelated to having a law degree. Just under 10 percent were unemployed and seeking jobs.

Here's what I tell my students about jobs and what I truly believe. Work as hard as you can in law school and trust that the job situation will work itself out. It might not work out exactly like you planned. It might work out better than you planned. Maybe you don't get the job at the big law firm you fantasized about. Instead you accept a job as a prosecutor only to find that was your true calling all along.

It also might not work out like you want *at the very beginning.* Increasingly, I see graduates settling for "Meh" jobs starting out because that's all they can find, but after they get a couple years of experience, they move on to much better jobs. The trend is explainable in part by the fact that, unlike in the old days, legal employers lack the resources or patience to train new lawyers who don't know much about the actual practice of law. This issue is related to the drive toward more "experiential learning" in law schools, discussed in Chapter 5.

Take heart in the fact that the comprehensive *After the JD* study, tracking 5,000 lawyers over time, found that lawyer salaries trend significantly upward as the years pass.[11] Also

---

A position . . . for which the employer sought an individual with a J.D., and perhaps even required a J.D., or for which the J.D. provided a demonstrable advantage in obtaining or performing the job, but which does not itself require bar passage or an active law license or involve practicing law. Examples of positions for which a J.D. is an advantage include a corporate contracts administrator, alternative dispute resolution specialist, government regulatory analyst, FBI agent, and accountant. Also included might be jobs in personnel or human resources, jobs with investment banks, jobs with consulting firms, jobs doing compliance work in business and industry, jobs in law firm professional development, and jobs in law school career services offices, admissions offices, or other law school administrative offices. Doctors or nurses who plan to work in a litigation, insurance, or risk management setting, or as expert witnesses, would fall into this category, as would journalists and teachers (in a higher education setting) of law and law related topics.

Id.

[11]   D. Benjamin Barros, *Review of* After the JD III, *A Law Professor's Take,* Ass'N AM. L. SCH. (last visited Feb. 10, 2017) [hereinafter D. Benjamin Barros, *Review of* After the JD III, *A Law Professor's Take*] (observing that the most recent data, released as part of the "third wave" of the study, show that, except for solo practitioners, "lawyer salaries continue to trend up significantly over their first ten years of practice"). See Chapter 21 for more discussion of the *After the JD* study.

worth noting is the data in Chapter 3 regarding shrinking law enrollment, which will likely pay dividends to future graduates due to a balancing out of supply and demand in the job market.

Heavy loan debt. More worrisome to me than the job market is the student loan debt situation. According to data collected by Law School Transparency, 2015 law graduates borrowed an average of $119,000. The average debt was $96,000 for public schools, $132,000 for non-profit private schools, and $154,000 for for-profit schools.[12] Data collected for the 2015 Law School Survey of Student Engagement, to which 21,849 students responded, showed that roughly 30 percent of participating students anticipate graduating with more than $120,000 in loan debt, up from 16 percent in 2006.[13]

It's almost impossible to avoid law school debt these days, due mostly to rising tuition, including at previously inexpensive public law schools. But I'm convinced that students could shave a significant percentage off their debt by: (1) making wiser choices about where to attend law school; and (2) living more frugally once they get there.

In choosing a law school, don't rely solely on the *U.S. News & World Report* rankings, as too many students do. Look at the big picture. Compare tuition and the cost of living among cities, while also looking at each school's bar pass and employment rates. Attending a private law school in an expensive locale can double or even triple your loan debt compared to a public school in a city with a low cost of living. Depending on the school, it might be worth the extra outlay, but in many cases it isn't.

Be sure to investigate and vet scholarship opportunities. If you're an attractive candidate, you can often negotiate with a school for more scholarship money. Beware, however, of conditional scholarships with strings attached, such a requirement to maintain a high GPA. The ABA now mandates that law schools publicize the number of conditional

---

[12]   *Law School Financing, Federal Investment in Legal Education: Class of 2015*, LAW SCH. TRANSPARENCY (last visited Feb. 10, 2017). This source also allows you to search for the average student debt-load at individual schools.

[13]   LAW SCH. SURVEY OF STUDENT ENGAGEMENT, 2015 ANNUAL SURVEY RESULTS: HOW A DECADE OF DEBT CHANGED THE LAW STUDENT EXPERIENCE 1, 10 (2015).

scholarships awarded and the number that have been yanked during each of the previous three academic years.

Once you arrive at law school, do everything *reasonably* (law's favorite standard of conduct) within your power to keep your spending low. Live communally, with roommates or your parents, to cut housing costs—the largest and most easily controllable consumption expense of all.

Heavy debt will not only weigh down your bank account for many years, but bear on you psychologically. Chapter 20 gives more tips for addressing this major un-doer of student well-being.

You should be aware that the job market and loan debt issues discussed above have led some, including some law professors, to attack law schools for offering a poor return on investment, and in extreme cases, as a "scam." Be informed. Read up on these critiques, but in the end, the most important question to ask yourself is whether you really want to be a lawyer. If you do, don't abandon your goal, but make good choices about the best ways to accomplish it.

Buy some books (but not as many as everyone wants you to buy).

Books, books, and more books. Everywhere you turn. Thick books. Expensive books. Distinctive red, blue, black, brownish-red, and gray books. If the law could have intimate relations, it would be with a book. It wouldn't be pretty, but a lot of things in law aren't. This section breaks down the different types of books associated with starting law school and offers advice on what to buy and when to buy it.

• **Law school recommended reading lists.** Some law schools may inadvertently perpetuate a belief among incoming students that they should be trying to learn about the law before getting to law school by posting lengthy recommended reading lists. Some of the recommended books are deep, dense tomes about jurisprudence and legal history, such as Karl Llewellyn's *The Bramblebush: On Our Law and Its Study* (1951) and Edward H. Levi's *An Introduction to Legal Reasoning* (1949). These are classics that should be read at some point in every lawyer's life. But laboring to comprehend this dense material before law school, especially without any context, may spike your anxiety level and fry your synapses before you ever cross the law school's threshold.

Certainly, much good would come from reading the great books about American jurisprudence and legal history. In a perfect world with unlimited free time, every law student, lawyer, and law professor should read them all. We'd be smarter, better-informed, and more capable readers and thinkers. But, of course, most people don't have that kind of time. The good news is that you don't need to read any of the heady tomes to do well in law school.

If you're determined to do serious legal reading prior to law school, choose books that explain the institutions and functioning of American government, particularly the structures and roles of courts. Avoid all books that purport to teach law per se.

• **"How to Succeed" books.** Many of the recommended reading lists include less lofty books from the "how to succeed in law school" genre. A variety of these books exists. Most of them offer good information and advice. Some of the books written by law professors are excellent. This one, of course, is indispensable. (Successfully fought off urge to insert smiley-face emoticon, for which I know you are grateful.)

I intentionally did not look at other law school prep books while composing this one because I didn't want to be influenced by them, even if only unconsciously. After I finished the manuscript to the first edition, I did scan several of them. What I discovered was affirming. Much of the advice is not only consistent with my advice, but remarkably identical to it. Not all of it though. I came across advice in books written by non-law professors that was at times amusing, without intending to be, and at times downright scary. Sift through all advice in law school prep books, including this one, with a discerning eye. Avoid books that offer shortcuts to success.

• **Inspirational books.** For enjoyable inspiration about your new pursuit, check out one of these page-turners showing the power of lawyers and the law to change lives:

- Jonathan Harr, *A Civil Action* (1996). A tenacious, flamboyant lawyer gives his all in taking on a large corporation accused of dumping cancer-causing solvents into the groundwater in Woburn, Massachusetts. John Travolta and Robert Duvall starred in an inferior 1998 movie version.

- Anthony Lewis, *Gideon's Trumpet* (1964). A small-time criminal named Clarence Earl Gideon changes history by appealing his burglary conviction to the U.S. Supreme Court, resulting in a landmark decision establishing the Sixth Amendment right to counsel for indigent criminal defendants. Henry Fonda played Gideon in a 1979 movie version, but the book is better.

- Harper Lee, *To Kill a Mockingbird* (1960). This Pulitzer-winning tale of Southern lawyer Atticus Finch's defense of a wrongly accused man in a racially charged rape trial is not only the best legal book ever written, but one of the best books, period. In a questionnaire, I ask incoming students, "What made you want to become a lawyer?" A 1L said she read *To Kill a Mockingbird* as a high school freshman and Atticus Finch's courtroom speech set her on her legal career path. The movie version won three Oscars. Gregory Peck's depiction of Atticus Finch earned him the ultimate cinematic accolade. In 2003, the American Film Institute named him the number one movie hero of all time. Imagine that: a lawyer is America's top film hero.

- **Study aids.** You will become very familiar with law school "study aids." A study aid is a book that, unlike your casebooks, clearly explains the law in a particular subject area, either in an outline or treatise-like format. Study aids have traveled an interesting journey through legal education. When I was in law school, our professors threatened us with mayhem if they laid eyes on a study aid in class. Professors referred to them derisively as "commercial" study aids, as if expensive casebooks are distributed by non-profit organizations. While some professors still look down on study aids, many actually recommend them to students.

Law school study aid series generally break down into four basic types: (1) outlines of the law in particular subject areas, sometimes keyed to popular casebooks; (2) treatise-like works that explain the law of a subject area in an expository non-outline format; (3) exam-prep series containing practice essay and/or multiple-choice questions and analyses (many of the outline series also contain practice questions); and (4) "canned brief" series containing case briefs of all of the cases appearing in particular casebooks. One of the most frequently used study aids, CALI (Computer-Assisted Legal Instruction), is free to law students. CALI is a non-profit consortium of law professors, who have prepared sets of online practice questions in most subject areas.

The overall quality of modern law school study aids is high because most are written by law professors who are experts in the field. At last count, there were more than fifty different *series* of law school study aid books. Some series feature dozens of titles. The long-running West Nutshell Series has books in more than 160 subject areas. The sheer length of the list of available study aids should convince you not to rush out and start buying any of them until you acquire more information about what you really need.

That so many study aids exist flags one of the oddest aspects of legal education. Law is the only educational discipline where students feel compelled to routinely buy external books to explain what they're supposed to be learning from their assigned books. I surveyed a 1L class asking how many study aids the students purchased during the first year and the answers ranged from zero to twelve, with an average of four. One student said he snatched up twenty-five study aids from a 3L in exchange for paying the 3L's bar tab at the annual Barrister's Ball (the law school prom), one more reason to socialize with your colleagues. My strategy in law school was to find one good study aid for each course.

Study aids can be helpful not only in elucidating legal doctrine but in casting what you're learning into a coherent framework that makes it easier to see the big picture. Depending on the professor, they can be a lifesaver. Some professors just aren't very good at or concerned about conveying the law they expect you to know for the exam in a clear or organized fashion.

Just don't make the mistake of substituting study aids for reading your casebook assignments and taking good notes in class. Study aids are useful only as a supplement to, not a replacement for, your casebooks.

• **Books required and recommended by professors.** The only books you absolutely must buy are those your professors assign as "required." Your law school will post a list of these books on its website and probably email it to you as well. For most courses, your main required book will be a "casebook." See Chapter 7 for a discussion of casebooks and the case method of teaching.

Some casebooks come with paperbound supplements (sold separately, of course) containing new cases and statutes designed to keep the book up-to-date until the next edition comes out. It's easy to overlook the supplements, so take your time when reviewing the list and make sure you get everything you need.

Buy all required texts and make sure you buy the *correct edition*. Casebooks are updated in new editions every few years. Because the page numbers always will be different, an outdated edition is worthless even if 99 percent of the content stays the same. You won't be able to follow the assignments and you won't be able to follow along in class without the correct edition. When the professor says, "Let's read the court's holding at the top of page 825, four lines down," you don't want to be lost. Required texts simply are not an item to skimp on.

An age-old quandary faced by higher-education students at every level is whether to buy new or used books. Law school texts are expensive. Some new casebooks cost more than $250. 1Ls can expect to fork out $1000 or more for new first-semester books. Used books cost less, but even when I was a destitute law student, I opted for new books, and you should do the same if you can manage it financially.

You want to be able to learn the law and legal analysis without the distraction of someone else's (and maybe several persons depending on how old the book is) thought pattern memorialized by highlighting, underlining, and marginalia. For all you know, that someone could have flunked out of law school. As one student put it, "I advise people coming to law school to not buy used books because some idiot will have highlighted everything you don't want to know in every case." But even if you could lay your hands on the used book of the person who wrote the top exam for the course, you're still better off learning from a clean slate.

Most law book publishers, law school bookstores, and online booksellers such as Amazon allow students to rent books for a semester at a lower cost. While students are technically allowed to write or highlight in rented books, they're discouraged from doing it too much. Amazon's textbook rental terms, for example, admonish renters to "limit your writing and highlighting to a minimal amount[,]" advising that a failure to do so may result in the renter being charged full price.[14] The last thing you want to be worrying about while you're trying to digest a complex judicial opinion is whether you're doing too much writing or highlighting in the book.

Also, many law students like to keep their books rather than resell or return them. Some students think they will be useful to consult in the future when taking other courses or working at a law firm, but in the meantime, casebooks make sharp-looking additions to home bookcases. Once you're a law student, you'll notice when watching TV or movies that office backgrounds often have law books in the bookshelves, even if it's not a lawyer office. I kept my casebooks for years before selling them at a garage sale. Interestingly, people snapped them up, perhaps another indicator of the public's fascination with law.

Law book publishers also offer e-casebooks, although I've never seen a 1L using one, and advise against it for several reasons. First, as discussed later, many law professors prohibit computers in class. Second, it takes more time and multitasking (a proven mental distractor) to highlight and insert marginalia in an e-book or PDF. Third, you're not going to be able to flip back and forth easily among pages, as many law professors do during class. Fourth, while there is no definitive verdict as of yet,

---

14   *Textbook Rentals FAQ*, AMAZON (last visited Feb. 10, 2017).

some studies suggest that reading from a computer screen may impair concentration and comprehension compared to reading from hard copy material.[15] In one study, 92 percent of college students surveyed said they concentrate better when reading print materials.[16]

Don't attempt to read even your required books prior to starting law school, other than your first assignments, of course. Not only will it be a waste of time, it will be counterproductive because you won't have a proper foundation or context to understand what you're reading. Nor will you remember any of it when you start school. I once had a go-getter student who spent the summer before law school reading and briefing the cases in her casebooks. When she boasted this fact to me at the beginning of the semester, I cringed. I respected her for being so motivated, but knew she had made a grave error. I told her to throw away everything she had prepared and start fresh, but she didn't listen. She attempted to rely on her pre-prepared briefs in the first semester. Sadly, because she was dedicated and a very nice person, she did not make it past the first year.

At most, skim through your casebooks to get a feel for how they are structured. Look at the table of contents. Read the preface. Okay, I know you won't be able to resist taking a peek at some of the cases, but don't try to understand them until you get to law school.

In addition to required texts, many professors list one or more *recommended* texts. Some of them might be study aids. With regard to books that are merely recommended, even by the professor, you may want to hold off buying them until you get

---

[15]   *See, e.g.*, David B. Daniel & William Douglas Woody, *E-textbooks at What Cost? Performance and Use of Electronic v. Print Texts*, 62 COMPUTERS & EDUC. 18 (2013) (finding that student motivation rather than format may be the most significant factor in reading comprehension, but also finding that students reading from an electronic format were more likely to multitask); Anne Niccoli, *Paper or Tablet? Reading Recall and Comprehension*, EDUCAUSE REVIEW (Sept. 28, 2015) (summarizing studies showing a strong preference by students for print materials and that e-book readers are more likely to take short-cuts that may undermine comprehension, but also conducting a small independent study of students in a Coast Guard class showing no difference in test results); Erik Wastlund et al., *Effects of VDT and Paper Presentation on Consumption and Production of Information: Psychological and Physiological Factors*, 21 COMPUTERS HUM. BEHAV. 377 (2005) (finding that reading from a computer screen requires dual tasks, which can lead to performance deterioration and increased tiredness and stress).

[16]   Emma Pettit, *Does Reading on Computer Screens Affect Student Learning?*, CHRON. HIGHER EDUC. (June 22, 2016) (interviewing author of study).

more information. Some professors may list several recommended books, none of which you really need. Or they may list several study aids, any one of which would suffice. The exception is if the professor has recommended a *single* study aid for the course. A professor generally would do that only if he or she had personally reviewed and approved of the content as consistent with the way the prof teaches the course. Buy it.

• **Law dictionary.** A crucial part of the first year of law school is learning the language of the law. Especially at the beginning, you'll be inundated with foreign words and phrases. Some professors expect students to look up all unfamiliar legal terms and will express disapproval if they call on you in class and you don't know the meaning of a term.

In the old days, all new law students purchased a copy of *Black's Law Dictionary*, the classic legal dictionary. It's a book with a long, useful shelf-life. The hardcover version makes for a nice gift request from relatives, but the paperbound version will suit most needs and sells for much less.

Because definitions of legal terms are easily found online, many modern students dispense with buying or rarely use their hard copy legal dictionary. Beware, however, that some online legal dictionaries give inaccurate or incomplete definitions. Additionally, *Black's* is available on Westlaw, a computer research service with which you will become very familiar, and other legal dictionaries are available on LexisNexis, Westlaw's competitor.

Discover your "law-learning personality."

Most law students are bright people. Beyond that, it's hard to generalize about them. As is true of any large group of people, an entering law school class contains a wide variety of personality types. Teaching and learning styles that work best for some students don't work as well for others. Similarly, not all law school advice works equally well for all people. If you're interested in figuring out your own learning style, an excellent tool is available to do just that.

Many years ago, a college English professor auditing Torts introduced me to the Myers-Briggs Type Indicator (MBTI), an instrument for measuring personality preferences based on

Swiss psychologist Carl Jung's research into psychological types. The MBTI is designed to help people understand certain core personality preferences that affect the way they gather information, make decisions, organize their lives, and interact with people and the world around them. If the name sounds familiar, it could be that you've already taken the MBTI in a different educational or career context. The MBTI is widely used by universities, corporations, and government agencies. Millions of people take it each year.

The MBTI identifies sixteen psychological types based on eight paired personality preferences:

Extraversion[17] **vs. Introversion** (how we direct and develop our energy—inward or outward—and interact with the world around us)

Sensing vs. Intuition (how we perceive and take in information upon which to make decisions)

Thinking vs. Feeling (how we make decisions)

Judging vs. Perceiving (the ways we organize our lives and operate in the world)

A person's type is a four-letter combination of their preferences as to all four pairings. For example, I'm an ENFJ (Extraverted, Intuitive, Feeling, Judging). Each type has strengths and weaknesses for adapting to different educational, employment, and relationship settings.

Several excellent books have been written about the MBTI and psychological typing, but law students have the benefit of an MBTI book written just for them: *Juris Types: Learning Law through Self-Understanding* (2007).[18] Authors Martha and Don Peters are MBTI gurus who spent decades researching the MBTI and its application to law students. *Juris Types* is filled with practical information about the learning strengths and weaknesses for each of the sixteen MBTI types in tackling the

---

[17]   Not a typo. Extraversion, not extroversion, is the correct spelling in this context.

[18]   MARTHA M. PETERS & DON PETERS, JURIS TYPES: LEARNING LAW THROUGH SELF-UNDERSTANDING (2007).

core challenges of law school: studying, classroom participation, and exam-writing.

Let's use Extraversion and Introversion as an example. The Peters' research shows that Extraverts find it easier to participate in class and enjoy working in study groups, while Introverts may not be able to access and demonstrate their knowledge as easily when called on in class and may prefer solitary over group study. Extraverts tend to write more on exams, but may analyze problems at a superficial level due in part to an absence of external verbal cues. Introverts may engage in deeper internal analysis, but may not write down everything they've mentally processed.[19] For each type, the Peters offer strategies about how to maximize strengths and overcome challenges. If you're curious about how your personality is cut out for the different ways of learning law, take the MBTI (it's available online for a fee) or track down your old results if you've taken it before and check out the Peters' book.

Even if you don't take the MBTI, it's important to be aware that students have different learning styles. As Professor Chris Coughlin recommends in Chapter 18, one way to bolster your self-understanding is to look back on your educational experiences and "determine whether there is a common denominator in the teachers, environments, situations, and subjects in which you responded most positively and successfully." While Coughlin's suggestion is directed at legal writing courses, it applies across the board. Think also about the other side of the coin: to which kinds of teachers, environments, situations, and subjects did you *not* respond positively?

In addition to helping you succeed at a higher level, developing an awareness of your learning preferences can help you overcome confusion and self-doubt arising from differences between the ways you and your classmates are experiencing law school. You'll better understand, for example, why some of your classmates love the way Professor X teaches, while you find her impossible to follow, or why you love contract law and hate constitutional law when your best friend feels exactly the opposite.

---

[19]   *See id.* at 26–30.

Address learning disabilities.

If you have or think you might have a learning disability, you may be entitled to accommodations such as longer time for exams or being permitted to take them in an isolated room. A student who suffers from ADHD (Attention Deficit Hyperactivity Disorder) offers the following information and suggestions on how and when to address the issue:

> For 0Ls who have or might have a learning disability and are still in undergraduate school, I recommend you call the disability services office at your undergraduate institution and inquire about the cost of doing the requisite disability testing there. If testing is expensive or unavailable, then call the law schools to which you've been accepted and inquire about testing there. Testing can cost much less at a school with a graduate psychology department and an active psychological counseling and testing center than at a private psychological testing office.
>
> If you are moving great distances and are on anti-anxiety or ADHD meds, you'll need recent testing so that a psychiatrist in your new location will treat you. Particularly in the case of ADHD meds (colloquially regarded as "steroids for the brain") and law students, psychiatrists are reluctant to prescribe these drugs because of abuses. Because of a presumption that law students are seeking them for performance enhancement, rather than genuine need, *you must get the testing done before you set foot in orientation.* Work with your disability services counselor and develop a plan that works for you. Don't be too proud, and don't worry about what others say about any testing accommodations you might receive.

Key in the above advice is the italicized portion, which bears repeating: *Get the testing done before you set foot in orientation.* I have known many students who either were not aware of or were reticent about acknowledging a learning disability until after they performed poorly on their first set of law school exams.

Buy a notebook computer and become adept at typing on it.

Buying and becoming adept at using a notebook computer may seem like ridiculously obvious advice, but with the proliferation of smart phones and tablets, the advice is actually more relevant today than when it appeared in the first edition of *1L of a Ride* nearly a decade ago. Although I couldn't find any research supporting it, I have a theory that some new students lack the computer *keyboarding* skills they'll need to be successful law students.

If you've ignored developing your regular typing skills or allowed them to wither because of smart phones and tablets, you could be in for a rude awakening when it comes to taking class notes, composing course outlines, typing your law office memoranda in Legal Research and Writing, and taking exams.

I recently graded a set of exams where the level of sloppy typing astonished me. On one exam, I counted and circled more than a dozen misspelled words in a single paragraph. Examples included "plantiff," "defedant," and "in the frist place." Other students eschewed capitalization and punctuation. The content of some of these exams was actually quite good, but the students' grades still suffered.

Folks, you're not writing text messages. Typing with your thumbs on a smart phone or composing email on a tablet keyboard is a different skill than typing long documents—under time pressure—on a traditional computer keyboard. You need to be able to type quickly and accurately.

By the time you're getting ready to enter law school, it's too late to perfect reasoning, reading comprehension, and actual writing skills, but you do have time to hone your word processing and typing skills.

Buy other essential school supplies.

In addition to your books and a decent laptop, here are some other products you should consider investing in before showing up at orientation:

- **Box of highlighters.** You'll need more, but one box will get you started. I still use monochromatic yellow, but many students use a color-coded highlighting system when reading cases, with different colors for the facts, procedural history, case holding, and reasoning.

• **Large backpack or airline carry-on-type bag with wheels.** You're going to be carting around a ton of stuff in law school. Casebooks are thick and heavy. You'll also have your computer and charging cord, study aids, research for your legal research and writing course, and personal items. Most students opt for large backpacks, but many go for luggage on wheels. Today's law school classrooms look like a combination of a Sierra Club base camp and gate area at LaGuardia.

Forget style. Functionality is the key. This comment from a 1L about things she wished she knew at the beginning of law school made me smile:

> I remember the first day I brought this cute laptop bag thinking of how professional I looked. When I got to school I realized that I couldn't fit any of my books in it. And after seeing everyone with their huge backpacks the first day, as soon as I got out of class I went and bought a huge backpack of my own. I think I ended up with one of the biggest backpacks in the class!

• **Day planner.** One of the top habits of successful law students is that they are extremely well-organized. Chapter 10 explains why you need to assiduously keep track of time in your new law school life. While some students rely on electronic calendaring, you might be surprised by how many stick with old-fashioned day planners made of real paper, in part because they're not just using them as event reminders, but to carefully plot out their daily and weekly schedules. If you go the paper route, get a planner with calendar spaces large enough to insert several items per day.

• **Three-ring binders with tabbed dividers.** Three-ring binders are an efficient way to organize and keep track of loose print materials. Not too long ago, nearly all students used them, often one for each course, in which they kept their class notes, case briefs, outlines, course handouts, etc.

Today, most students rely on computers as digital binders, but even those students will end up with a variety of hard copy documents during a semester that need to be kept organized. Here's how one current top student described her binder use:

> I use one three-ring binder per semester, filling it up with any piece of paper that I am given or print or cases I've researched for Legal Methods [the name of our law school's course in legal research and writing]. I keep it separated by class, with papers either in chronological order or in a topical fashion if it logically flows better. I particularly enjoy having it for big documents professors give to us. It provides me with a safe, easily accessed place to keep important materials.

• **Heavy-duty three-hole punch and stapler.** To go with any binder notebook, spring for a heavy duty three-hole punch. You don't want to be jamming holes in the paper with the binder ring like back in elementary school.

Similarly, you'll be turning in multi-page assignments that will require stapling. Do not use the fold-and-tear method you picked up in the fourth grade. Talk about an unprofessional look. In the most recent fall semester I was talking with our faculty assistant as she was collecting the first batch of legal writing assignments. I asked what she thought about the new class. "They're a nice group, but they all need to buy staplers!" she said, as she disassembled paper after paper where students had used the fold-and-tear method to hold the pages together. Invest in a stapler that can drill through at least fifteen pages.

• **USB stick.** If you use cloud storage, good for you, but if you don't you'll need a USB stick to back up all of your computer work (class notes, course outlines, legal writing assignments). One of the most common disasters befalling law students is a crashed or stolen computer resulting in the loss of their precious course work. More about this in Chapter 12.

• **Printer.** Many students don't own computer printers, relying instead on law school printers. But law student printer accounts usually have page limits, the printers are often tied up or out of service, or you might not be near one when you need it. Get your own printer.

Relax and enjoy!

Finally, here's a "To Do" task that's easy to get behind. Surprising as it may sound, one of the best ways to prepare for law school, assuming you have your life in order, is to just kick back and enjoy your summer. Unless you plan on attending another graduate program after law school, the summer before law school may very well be your last chance until retirement to enjoy an extended summer break. Your law school summers will be filled with law clerking jobs, internships and externships, or summer classes. On graduation, you'll only have about fifteen minutes to celebrate before knuckling down to start studying for the bar exam.

Take a vacation. Exercise. Eat well. Get in good physical shape. Enter law school rested and ready to go. One of my 3L research assistants, proofreading this section, wrote to say he had a fond memory of reading *1L of a Ride* the summer before law school while floating on a raft in a swimming pool. That sounds good to me!

CHAPTER 3

FEAR FACTOR: TOP FIVE LAW STUDENT WORRIES

"Come to the edge," he said. They said, "We are afraid."
"Come to the edge," he said. They came. He pushed
them . . . and they flew.

—Guillaume Apollinaire

If you're stressed out about starting law school, take comfort in the fact that you have lots of company. Every 1L you meet, whether they show it or not, will be feeling the same way. Two weeks into the first semester, I asked a group of students to name their "biggest surprise" about law school. One student wrote: "My biggest surprise is that everyone feels the same way that I do. My insecurities are shared among most of my 152 peers. That provides tremendous comfort in that I am not the only one feeling overwhelmed, scared, stressed, and excited all at once."

Not only are your new colleagues as anxious as you are, they're stressing about the same things. Every year I distribute a questionnaire to new students that includes the question, "What is your greatest fear about law school?" Everywhere I've taught, all across the country, the answers have been the same since I started teaching during the Nixon Administration.

No, I'm not really that old. Close, but not quite. The only new entries to emerge in recent years are fears about the job market and loan debt. While those are legitimate concerns, here, we'll stick to actual law school fears. This chapter addresses five common law school fears:

- Failure/failing to meet personal expectations.
- Socratic method/getting called on in class.
- Not understanding the material.
- Detrimental impact on non-law school life, especially relationships.

- Not being able to keep up with the workload.

I'd like to assure you that these fears are baseless, but I can't. Each of the fears has a legitimate grounding in reality. The problem is that students don't properly calibrate them. They exaggerate some fears, while underestimating others. Let's look at them individually.

Failure/Failing to Meet Personal Expectations

Failure is the most common answer to my fear question. Here I have good news. If failure is defined to mean failing to achieve and maintain the GPA necessary to remain a student in good standing, the picture isn't as bleak as many imagine. For 2013–2014, the average first-year attrition rate for academic reasons was only 3.39 percent.[20] That figure is misleading because low-performing students often see the writing on the wall and voluntarily withdraw before they are academically dismissed, but even considering attrition for all reasons, the average drop-out rate was only 6.57 percent.[21]

But low academic attrition rates are misleading for another reason. You need to know that major changes have occurred in law school applications and enrollment that make predicting a student's ultimate success harder than ever before.

In large part because of the weakened job market that began with the Great Recession, the number of law school applicants fell for several consecutive years. From 2006 to 2015, annual law school applications dropped by almost 40 percent.[22] In an effort to preserve the quality of their student body profiles (and *U.S. News* rankings), law schools responded by cutting enrollment, in many cases substantially. Despite an increase in the number of

---

[20]   Jerry Organ, *Part Two: The Impact of Attrition on the Composition of Graduating Classes of Law Students, 2013–2016*, LEGAL WHITEBOARD, Oct. 2, 2015 (compiling and analyzing attrition rate data).

[21]   *Id.*

[22]   *End-of-Year Summary: ABA (Applicants, Applications & Admissions), LSATs, Credential Assembly Service*, LAW SCH. ADMISSION COUNCIL (showing that law school applications dropped from 88,700 in 2006 to 54,500 in 2015).

accredited law schools from 200 to 204, law schools enrolled 28 percent fewer first-year students in 2015 than in 2010.[23]

(On the bright side, the number of incoming students leveled off in 2015 and 2016[24] and the number of LSAT takers increased in 2016. Jeff Thomas, director of Kaplan Test Prep's prelaw programs, said the increase in LSAT takers suggests law schools might be experiencing a "fragile recovery."[25] Let's hope he's right.)

Even with the enrollment cuts, however, most law schools are admitting students today who would have been rejected a few years ago. In 2014, the president of the National Conference of Bar Examiners (NCBE) sent a memo to law school deans, offering as an explanation for declining bar pass rates that takers are "less able" than in the past.[26]

It would be reasonable to expect academic attrition rates to increase given the lower profiles of entering law school classes, and this may be happening at some schools, but there is no evidence yet of widespread increases in attrition rates. One reason, as discussed in Chapter 14, is that most law schools have mandatory grading curves, some of them quite high, and have not, as of yet, adjusted curves downward to account for the declining profiles of incoming students.[27]

But even assuming the risk of academic attrition remains small, the risk of not achieving the ultimate objective of passing the bar exam and obtaining a license to practice law is

---

[23] ABA SECTION OF LEGAL EDUC. & ADMISSIONS TO THE BAR, 2015–2016 ANNUAL REPORT: THE YEAR IN REVIEW 14 (2016) (showing total first-year enrollment of 52,448 for fall 2010 and 37,907 for fall 2015).

[24] ABA data show that first-year enrollment held steady between 37,000 and 38,000 for the 2015 and 2016 fall entering classes. ABA SECTION OF LEGAL EDUC. & ADMISSIONS TO THE BAR, 2015 V. 2016 CHANGE IN 1L ENROLLMENT (2016).

[25] Debra Cassens Weiss, *Number of LSAT Tests Administered Jumps Nearly 8 Percent; Is Optimism or Scheduling the Reason?*, ABA JOURNAL (Jan. 18, 2017) (discussing 8 percent increase in LSAT takers in December 2016 over 2015 and speculating the increase might be attributable to a scheduling change, but also reporting that LSAT takers increased by 2.7 percent from June to December in 2016 compared to the same period in 2015).

[26] Memorandum from Erica Moeser, President, Nat'l Conference of Bar Exam'rs, to Law Sch. Deans (Oct. 23, 2014) (referring specifically to the drop in pass rates between 2013 and 2014).

[27] Organ, *supra* (making this point and observing that mandatory grading curves are "likely to produce a similar percentage of 'at risk' students year over year even though the objective credentials of each entering class have declined").

increasing. Bar passage rates have plummeted in a majority of states over the past few years. Overall average bar pass rates fell to 58 percent in 2016, the lowest percentage in ten years, while the average score on the February 2017 Multistate Bar Examination declined to the lowest point in the history of the exam, first administered in 1972.[28]

Your takeaway from this should be that now, more than ever before, you need to apply yourself fully to maximize your chances of ultimate success.

Meanwhile, more well-founded for most students than the fear of flunking out is the commonly expressed fear of not living up to one's own high personal expectations. One student answered the "greatest fear" question in my questionnaire by saying: "Failure, not as in failing a class or performing poorly. My fear is primarily that I will not successfully meet or exceed my own expectations." Another lamented: "Not being smart enough. I have always been the smart one and the one everything came easy to. What if I don't stand out like I always have? What if it doesn't click with me?" A third student set a specific bar: "Failing (as in anything below a *B–*)—and yes, I know that is an unreasonable standard for my first year of law school!" Yes, that is an unreasonable expectation, depending on your school's first-year grading curve. Don't be shocked to see one or more *C*s on your first grade report.

Law schools are full of high achievers. Instead of competing against students like your undergraduate roommate who sat in his dorm room smoking a bong and listening to Pink Floyd all night, you're competing against motivated, talented people with lifelong track records of academic accomplishment. Okay, some of them may still be smoking a bong and listening to Pink Floyd, but only after they've read and briefed all their cases for the next day.

Law students, like everyone, are susceptible to what is known as "superiority bias"; that is, they often overestimate

---

[28]   Debra Cassens Weiss, *Multistate Bar Exam Scores Drop to Lowest Point Ever; Is There a Link to Low-End LSAT Scores?*, ABA JOURNAL (Apr. 12, 2017). Results by state for 2016 were mixed, with pass rates going up in some states and down in others (e.g., a modest increase from 2015 in New York and a thirty-two year low in California).

their abilities in comparison to those around them.[29] A survey showed that 77 percent of Stanford MBA students rated their quantitative abilities above the median as compared to their peers.[30] If you come to law school expecting As or to finish in the top 10 percent of your class, you're likely to be disappointed. At most law schools, As remain scarce and due to a sticking point called math, since the birth of class rankings, 90 percent of students don't finish in the top 10 percent.

The happy news is that it doesn't take As to be a successful law student. I always tell my students, "In law school, B is the new A." Still, they don't listen.

Once I was in my office working at my computer. I had just posted the Torts grades (by anonymous exam number) outside the door, which was common in the days before online grades. Out of the corner of my eye I could see students coming and going to check grades. Working at my computer, I pretended not to notice, both to give them privacy and avoid having to deal with their disappointment until they had time to process it.

I noticed a young man I'll call Devin standing in the hall studying the grade sheet. He stayed there a long time. I liked Devin. He overcame a lot of odds to get to law school. He participated in class, seemed well-prepared, and struck me as a dedicated student. After a couple of minutes, I finally turned to look at him. His disappointment was palpable. He appeared to be wiping tears. He must have flunked, I thought. I felt terrible. Our ensuing conversation went something like this:

Me: Hey, Devin, how're you doing?

Him: [disconsolately] Not too good, professor.

Me: What's wrong? [As if I didn't know.]

Him: I—I didn't do very well. I'm really disappointed in myself.

---

[29]   See Ezra W. Zuckerman & John T. Jost, *What Makes You Think You're So Popular? Self-Evaluation Maintenance and the Subjective Side of the "Friendship Paradox"*, 64 SOC. PSYCHOL. Q. 207, 207 (2001) (stating that most people making comparisons between themselves and others "judge themselves to be 'better than average' on a variety of traits, skills, and socially desirable dimensions").

[30]   *It's Academic*, THE REPORTER 14, 15 (Apr. 24, 2000).

Me: [hesitantly] What grade did you get? That's if you want to tell me. You don't have to.

Him: I only got a *B+*.

Me: A *B+*? Devin, you got a *B+*? That's *B* as in boy?

Him: [hangdog face] That's right, professor.

Me: Devin, I want to jump across this desk right now both to give you a hug for doing so well and also to strangle you for scaring the bejeezus out of me.

Lower your performance expectations or you'll drive yourself and those around you insane even if you're a good student.

Socratic Method/Getting Called On

Another great fear of law school, which I vividly recall experiencing as a beginning student, is being victimized by the Socratic teaching method, which emphasizes cold-calling on students to recite and analyze cases from the assigned reading in a question and answer format; i.e., being publicly interrogated. As one student articulated it:

> I was terrified of being called on—not of the act itself, but of the all-consuming silence that would follow the calling of my name, as eighty other people waited to see if I would sink or swim. Having a multitude of witnesses to a potential humiliation was a very unpleasant thought. Yet though my hands shook the first time I heard stentorian tones say "Ms. _____," and I felt sick with nervous apprehension with every question the professor posed—one after another after another—when he turned to someone else, I felt as if I had passed some test.

The student's reaction to the Socratic method mirrors that of many students, both her initial fear and subsequent relief and satisfaction when she realized she could, in fact, "pass the test" of this unique rite of passage in American legal education. Chapter 7 explains the Socratic method, so we'll postpone in-depth discussion of it. For now, let me assure you that the horrors of the Socratic method are greatly exaggerated and that being terrorized by professors should be at the very bottom of your worry list.

Not Understanding the Material

A third frequently expressed fear is not understanding the material. While this anxiety could be seen merely as a variation of the failure theme, it falls into a discrete category. The *no comprende* fear is much more immediate. Students worry they will arrive in this new academic world and find that the legal rules they're supposed to be learning are unintelligible ciphers and, worse, that they are the only ones without a decoding manual. The fear is commonly reflected in answers to my "greatest fear" question such as "that I would be the only person to not understand the reading" and "that everyone will 'get it' and I won't."

I'm happy to report this fear is also overblown. Coming into law school, the law naturally seems inaccessible and unfathomable because it's a complete unknown. Some of the first cases students are required to read confirm their worst fears.

Below is an excerpt from a famous Torts case decided in 1616 by the King's Bench in England commonly assigned in the first week of law school. The case, *Weaver v. Ward*,[31] is the earliest known decision expressly recognizing that a defendant might not be liable for damages for a purely accidental injury occurring without fault. But it's doubtful many students ever figure that out from the opinion itself, which reads like this:

> And upon demurrer by the plaintiff, judgment was given for him; for though it were agreed, that if men tilt or turney in the presence of the King, or if two masters of defence playing their prizes kill one another, that this shall be no felony; or if a lunatick kill a man, or the like, because felony must be done animo felonico; yet in trespass, which tends only to give damages according to hurt or loss, it is not so; and therefore if a lunatick hurt a man, he shall be answerable in trespass; and therefore no man shall be excused of a trespass (for this is in the nature of an excuse, and not of a justification, prout

---

[31]   80 Eng. Rep. 284 (K.B. 1616).

ei bene licuit), except it may be judged utterly without his fault.

Er, could you run that by us again? Why couldn't those old English judges speak . . . well, English? Don't worry. Modern opinions aren't nearly as bad. Once you get past the moldy-oldies still included in casebooks because of their historical significance, the reading gets easier because most modern judges write lucidly and in plain English. Take a look, for example, at the judicial opinion in *Robinson v. Lindsay* reprinted in Chapter 11 as part of a case-briefing exercise. Compared to *Weaver v. Ward* it reads like a *My First Reader*.

As with so many other challenges that seem overwhelming when we first encounter them, learning the law becomes less intimidating with each passing day as students begin to figure out basic legal terms and procedures. One of my favorite parts of teaching 1Ls is watching the satisfaction, even joy, as the light bulbs start to go on, as students realize, "Hey, I really can understand this stuff! I really can learn the law!"

Don't get me wrong. A lot of the material is difficult and not all students grasp the law equally well. Some legal topics (the law of "future interests" in Property comes to mind as a quintessential 1L example) do approach utter incomprehensibility, but even those riddles can be unraveled by most students if they put in the necessary effort.

Damage to Non-Law School Life, Especially Relationships

A fourth oft-repeated fear is the toll that law school will take on a student's outside life, especially their relationships with friends, families, and significant others. This fear is well-grounded. Not only does law school put your relationships at risk, stormy relationships can put your law school success at risk. In one study of stress in law school, the number one "crisis" cited by students for falling behind in their studies was a relationship crisis.[32]

---

[32]   Marilyn Heins et al., *Law Students and Medical Students: A Comparison of Perceived Stress*, 33 J. LEGAL EDUC. 511, 520 (1983).

Because the first year of law school is so all-consuming, law students somehow manage to both drive their loved ones crazy with obsessive talk about law school and neglect them at the same time. Quite a feat. Resentment, conflict, even dissolution of the relationship can result. Chapter 23 explores the impact of law school on outside relationships, so we'll wait until then to cover the topic.

Not Being Able to Keep Up with the Workload

This last fear deserves, in real rather than imagined terms, the top ranking on worry lists about law school. In the 1992 presidential race, matching Bill Clinton against President George H.W. Bush, political consultant James Carville came up with Clinton's election-winning campaign strategy. To keep the campaign simple and on message, Carville instructed campaign workers to remember, "It's the economy, stupid." Adapting Carville's slogan to law school, "It's the workload, stupid." Remember this when you find yourself obsessing about less important things like getting on called on in class.

Effectively managing the workload will be one of your primary law school challenges. Asked how law school differs from undergraduate school, one student explained:

> About the only similarity between undergraduate school and law school is that it is school. Other than that, law school is an entirely different caliber—requiring so much more than undergrad that it does not even compare. When law students say we must get ready for class, it doesn't mean the same thing as it did in undergrad. When people ask "When will you be done studying?" there is actually no good answer because we could probably spend every waking hour outside of class studying and still not be done. The only answerable question would be "When are you going to stop studying tonight?"

Many people who do not succeed in law school or who succeed at levels below their potential just weren't prepared to handle the overwhelming workload. They did not arrive at law school with either the mindset or an organized plan to each week: carefully read (and reread) 100–150 pages of dense legal analysis, compose case briefs for twenty or more complicated judicial opinions, and attend 14–16 intense class hours. They weren't primed or prepared to compile lengthy course outlines, research and write (and rewrite) intricate memoranda and briefs in their legal research and writing courses, and still juggle the other parts of their lives, including family and other relationships and, for part-time students, full-time employment.

They fall behind early . . . and never catch up. Nothing, I repeat, nothing will portend lack of success more than falling behind.

* * *

Overall, a healthy trepidation starting law school is not only a good motivator, but appropriate given what you're about to embark on. I'm not talking about counterproductive, paralyzing fear, which inhibits learning, but an informed apprehension that law school is going to challenge you in ways you've never been challenged.

To not have some anxiety about law school doesn't make one brave, but foolish, clueless about what the person is getting into. In every entering class, at least one student responds to my fear question with an answer such as "No fear" or "Nothing scares me." Pay attention to the words of this formerly fearless student:

> As a U.S. Army Major, I was used to long, hard work. The work in law school is very different and in many ways harder. In retrospect, I wish I had more fears and concerns than what I did as I was not overly concerned about anything. Fear is a very powerful motivator, and had I been more fearful I probably would have worked harder and done better.

We'll talk more about the sources of 1L stress, including tips for reducing and managing it. In the meantime, if you find yourself feeling alone in your fears and doubts, take solace from one of my favorite quotations, by motivational educator Stan Dale:

> It all changed when I realized I'm not the only one on the planet who's scared. Everyone else is, too. I started asking people, "Are you scared, too?" "You bet your sweet life I am."

"Aha, so that's the way it is for you, too." We were all in the same boat.

Instead of dwelling on your fears, buckle your life preserver and enjoy the wild river journey with your new mates, soothed by the knowledge that, as Dale said, you're all in the same boat.

CHAPTER 4

WHAT KIND OF STUDENT DO YOU WANT TO BE? TWENTY LAW STUDENT TYPES

Most people arrive at law school with at least some hope that they will become a great law student. Generally, their perception of "great" is quite limited: a high GPA and class rank. Many attributes apart from grades work to define students, both to their peers and to the faculty and staff of the law school. Happily, unlike grade performance, students have substantial control over most of these other defining qualities.

This chapter contains a list of twenty types of law students. There's spillover among the categories, with students usually displaying traits of more than one type. Some of the types evoke positive associations, while some carry clear negative connotations. Several, however, are two-sided coins, with both positives and negatives.

It's worth thinking in advance about the types of law student you want to be and which types you don't want to be.

From the moment you arrive at law school, many people—students, faculty, and staff—will be forming opinions and making judgments about you based on how you conduct yourself. Often, these opinions are inaccurate, based on limited evidence such as classroom performance, social interactions, or rumor. But one's perception is their reality. Thus, in perusing the list below, think not only about the type of student you want to be, but how you want to be perceived by others. Here are twenty law student types:

1. The Frequent Participator. The Socratic method of law teaching involves a lot of question-asking by the professors, including many "What do you think?"-type questions. Most first-year law school class sections include a small number of students who are willing to volunteer answers and comments more frequently than the other students.[33] And to them I say: Thank you! From a professor's perspective, a Frequent Participator beats the heck out of the student who sits silently through the course, never engaging. The most interesting, exciting, and memorable parts of law school classes always involve class discussion.

Unfortunately, people who frequently participate may get labeled by the law school slur, "gunner." It's a shame because the fear of being labeled as a gunner deters many students with good ideas and answers from participating in class.

Ideally, everyone in a law school class would participate at a roughly equal level, but that's just not the reality of group dynamics. Most students never volunteer at all. Someone has to pick up the slack. When in doubt, choose to participate. The benefits of regular class participation, as explained in Chapter 8, are many, and far outweigh the risk of being labeled a gunner.

2. The Regular and Occasional Participators. Between the extremes of the Frequent Participators and the Stealth Student (see below) are all the other students who make some effort to voluntarily participate in class discussions. Since the Regular and Occasional Participators include a substantial percentage of the class, they're not really discrete types. Nevertheless, they're worth identifying because voluntary class participation of any type—as it involves a public display of courage, preparation, and analytical ability—does help define students. Even occasional voluntary participation will earn you most of the benefits that come from class participation.

3. The Stealth Student. Stealth Students manage to blend into the surroundings so well that their very existence remains unknown, at least to the professors. Needless to say, Stealth Students don't voluntarily participate in class. They don't do *anything* in class that would draw attention to themselves. They don't arrive late, rustle paper, or talk to their seat neighbors. In extreme cases, they may hold their breath and fail to blink for the entire class hour.

---

[33]   Frequent Participators are usually men. As discussed in Chapter 7, studies show women voluntarily participate in class discussions at lower rates than men.

In professor-speak, Stealth Student sometimes has a secondary meaning as the student who manages to remain completely anonymous during the semester only to blow everyone out of the water come final exam time. Every class seems to have a curve-busting Stealth Student of this type. Of course, you can't really choose to be a Stealth Student in this sense of the term. You can elect to seek anonymity (see Backburners below), although I recommend against it.

4. The Backburner. In Chapter 6, I recommend sitting in the front of the classroom for a variety of reasons. Here, I merely list Backburners as a type of law student and explain how they may be perceived by professors.

First-year classes are usually divided into two or more sections. Although smaller than they used to be at most schools due to shrinking law school enrollment, class sections still usually comprise upwards of fifty students. As such, they are held in large classrooms where, depending on the design of the room, students who sit in the back can become essentially invisible, which indeed is the goal for many. Back row students tend to be less engaged in class than their closer-to-the-front colleagues.

Professors may interpret the Backburners' disengagement as part of a bad or bored attitude toward the course and learning the law. This is not always a fair assessment because many excellent students choose to sit in back. I asked one good student why she sat in the back and she said, "I just don't feel comfortable with everyone looking at the back of my head."

Understandable, but class sizes and room configurations may create barriers even for Backburner students who want to be engaged. The Backburners don't generate bad reputations with professors. The bigger problem is that unless they make an effort to participate they don't generate *any* reputation because they remain anonymous, unlike . . .

5. The Front Row Crowd. From an alternative universe, or at least the other side of the room, are students who choose to sit in front. Professors like the Front Row Crowd because they appreciate them sitting there and also because professors *get to know* them. Some of this connecting may be attributable to the personalities of people who choose to sit in front, but part of it is simply a matter of proximity. I usually arrive to class ten minutes early to get set up. With nothing else to do, I chat with the students in the front while I'm hanging out at the podium. We talk about music, sports, their current law school gripes—a variety of matters. I get to know them and they get to know me. See Chapter 9 on the value of getting to know and getting known by your professors.

6. The Know-It-All. You can imagine what law professors think about students who believe they know more about the law and legal education than their professors. Know-It-Alls sincerely believe that within weeks or even days of starting law school, perhaps due to supernatural phenomena, they know the law and understand how to succeed in law school better than people who have devoted their lives to these endeavors. These students can be amusing, but are mostly irritating.

I will never forget the student who, after three days of law school, bopped into my office, plopped down in a chair, and said: "Professor, you do a pretty good job, but I'd like to give you some suggestions on how to improve your teaching." Come exam time, the Know-It-Alls are often exposed as Turns-Out-They-Didn't-Know-Much-At-Alls.

7. The Chronically Late. Every first-year class has a couple of students who, left to their own devices, will regularly arrive late for class. Because their arrival is disruptive in a public way, it won't take you long to spot them. Most professors will not tolerate the Chronically Late, although some do, to the annoyance of the rest of the class. See the section on classroom etiquette in Chapter 6 for more about the importance of being punctual.

8. The Slacker. Regrettably, every law school class includes its share of Slackers, students who do not read their assignments, brief their cases, attend class regularly, etc. In the 2016 Law School Survey of Student Engagement, 6 percent of participating first-year students admitted they either often or very often failed to read assignments prior to class.[34] Even worse

---

[34] LAW SCH. SURVEY OF STUDENT ENGAGEMENT, LAW SCHOOL REPORT 2016 (2016) [hereinafter 2016 LAW SCH. SURVEY OF STUDENT ENGAGEMENT].

than the regular Slacker is the Bragging Slacker, students who actually take pride in boasting about how they don't read their assignments or brief the cases, as if there were something appealing about being lazy and irresponsible.

No surprise: professors have a natural lack of regard for this type of student. As one would expect, Slackers flunk out of law school at disproportionate rates.

9.   The Overconfident Without Cause. Most first-year law students are at least somewhat fearful and intimidated by the Jupiter-sized amount of dense, foreign material they're expected to master, but every entering class has a few students who approach law school from a "What, me worry?" perspective. They're marked by their casual attitude toward diligent studying. Overconfident students often are bright, and perhaps sailed through undergraduate school with minimal effort. They seem to be unaware of the fact that the same holds true for most of their classmates.

Overconfident students rarely achieve at a high level in law school because their cavalier attitude diminishes their motivation to do all the tasks necessary to excel (e.g., brief cases, prepare course outlines, work practice exams). No person, regardless of credentials, has just cause to be overly confident about succeeding in law school.

The Overconfident Without Cause are distinguishable from the Know-It-Alls. Unlike the KIAs, the OWC don't assume they know all the answers. Their laidback self-assurance keeps them from even thinking about the questions. One reason they're overconfident is because they haven't thought deeply enough to know what they don't know.

10. The Insecure Contrary to Evidence. At the opposite end of the continuum from the Overconfident Without Cause are the Insecure Contrary to Evidence. These are students who worry themselves sick—sometimes literally so—because they're convinced that everyone around them is smarter than they are. They have a tendency to preface statements about the future with "If I don't flunk out. . . ." Their self-deprecation is sincere. They truly doubt their ability, even when their credentials would suggest such extreme insecurity is unfounded.

Here's a confession: I was a certified member of the Insecure Contrary to Evidence crowd as a first-year law student, to the point where I sought medical treatment in my first semester for stress-induced gastrointestinal issues. I even considered quitting law school. Despite entering law school with a high LSAT score and undergraduate GPA, I was convinced I was a total dolt as I sat in class listening to my brilliant classmates expound. "How did they think of that? Why couldn't I have come up with that? They're so much smarter than me!" I tormented myself with these thoughts.

When the first set of grades came out, I was happy to discover that my insecurities were misplaced. I landed in the top of my class and stayed there throughout law school. My experience is a common one. Many of the Insecure Contrary to Evidence end up as top students. One reason may be that, because of their insecurity, they are motivated to work harder to overcome their perceived shortcomings. Another factor is that they see and worry about the little details and complexities of the law—the same fine points that escape the notice of the Overconfident Without Cause and which are so important to performing well on law school exams.

11. Mr./Ms. Reliable. How professors love these students! It takes a while to figure out who they are because they tend to volunteer infrequently (some of them may overlap with the Insecure Contrary to Evidence). But once they become known to the professor, everyone else will know who they are because professors will call on them disproportionately. These are diligent students who are *always* well-prepared. They're life preservers when the class is wallowing in a mire of cluelessness or unpreparedness. When the going gets tough, the professor will turn instinctively to a Mr./Ms. Reliable. They're the "go to" guys and gals of the class.

No great shock, members of this group usually do well in law school. If you're already a law student and find yourself getting called on disproportionately for no apparent reason, maybe you've been identified by the prof as a Mr./Ms. Reliable. Of course, you might also have been identified as a Slacker whom the professor wants to make an example of, so don't start patting yourself on the back until you've figured it out. Because of their generally quiet demeanor, more Mr./Ms. Reliables exist than are identified by the professors, which is yet another good reason to contribute voluntarily in class. You want the professor to know if you're a Mr./Ms. Reliable.

12. The Nattering Nabob of Negativism. Borrowing a phrase that former Vice-President Spiro Agnew (under Richard Nixon) used in 1970 to describe the media, in all social environments we regularly encounter people who whine and complain about everything. Nothing is ever right for these folks. A disproportionate number of injustices seem to befall them. In law school, they complain about their professors, assignments, classmates, their lunch. You name it, they're unhappy with it.

For some people, complaining is just a bad habit, but some individuals are bitter and unhappy by nature. Law school is going to be stressful enough as it is. Letting it consume you with negative energy is not only unhealthy, but an unattractive quality. If you're unable to develop a positive attitude, at least try to minimize your outward manifestations of negativity. Like our parents taught us, if you can't say something nice, you're better off saying nothing.

A tangible downside of bad-mouthing people is that just about everything one says about a classmate or professor will get passed along to others because of the marble-sized world that is law school. Be positive. Keep a sense of humor, including about yourself. It's healthy to be able to laugh at yourself. Continual complaining about your trials and tribulations and constant bad-mouthing of others is just going to make you and those around you feel worse.

Avoid associating with confirmed Nattering Nabobs of Negativism, lest they drag you into their drag of an existence.

13. Curious George/Georgette. Curious George was a children's book character created in 1941 by H.A. Rey and Margret Rey. A mischievous ape, Curious George's defining characteristic, as his name suggests, was his unquenchable curiosity. Curious George was a lovable character, as are most students who fit into this type. Whereas many students want to know the bare minimum they need to know to succeed in law school, Curious Georges/Georgettes always want to know *more* than they need to know. Their curiosity leads them, for example, to look up the note cases following the principal cases in their casebooks, track down the unabridged versions of the principal cases to learn more facts, or research the actors, places, and history surrounding the cases and case events.

A classic example is the Curious Georgette who, on reading an old case about the consent defense to intentional torts involving a woman who was vaccinated against her wishes on board a ship sailing "from Queenstown to Boston," decided she needed to know more about Queenstown. Because the plaintiff claimed not to have understood the ship's signs explaining that everyone would be vaccinated, the student was curious what language the woman spoke. Her research turned up the factoid that Queenstown was the final port of call for the Titanic on its doomed, maiden voyage. Interesting tidbit, but not the type of information that will be helpful come exams.

Professors appreciate CGs. With so many students uninterested in learning anything beyond "the rules," how could they not? On the other hand, while intellectual curiosity is an admirable quality that should be encouraged, students need to be careful about how they allocate their scarce time.

A subcategory of the Curious Georges/Georgettes includes students obsessed with the great "What if?" These are students who, instead of focusing on the case facts or the hypothetical facts posed by the professor, insist on exploring their own extreme fact scenarios to test the application of legal principles. Within reasonable bounds, this is a valuable mental exercise, as a large part of learning to analyze law does indeed involve applying legal rules to changing fact patterns. Many what-if inquiries are excellent questions that lead to interesting and illuminating discussions, so don't be discouraged from posing them. They become a problem only when a student repeatedly flogs issues with what-ifs taken to absurd lengths. If a Civil Procedure professor discussing personal jurisdiction queries "What if the defendant was served with process in another country?", a What-If Curious George/Georgette will want to know "What if he was served with process on another planet?"

14. The Party Animal. Despite the heavy workload, most law students seem to find plenty of time to socialize. This is healthy, of course. The bonding that occurs among first-year students is one of the great byproducts of the "trial by ordeal" method of legal education. But some students quickly become known as partiers first and law students second, sometimes a distant second. Because most law school socializing involves consuming alcohol, being known as the class Party Animal often carries other negative associations with it. Party Animals are rarely top-performing law students, although they often are quite popular.

15. The Star of Rumor Central. Law schools are cloistered, competitive environments where everyone likes to know and talk about everyone else's business. Rumors, some of them fantastical, swirl with frequency. Sometimes they contain a kernel of truth, but like the old pass-it-along game, the stories get more distorted each time they're retold. Reading this, a research assistant wrote in the margin: "Rumor passing in law school is worse than it was in high school!"

In response to a survey question asking students to identify their biggest surprise about law school, another student wrote:

> Honestly, my biggest surprise has to do with my fellow classmates and all the students in law school. I almost feel like I am back in high school again. There is so much drama between guys and girls as well as just between girls. I thought at this age, people would be over worrying about who likes who, etc., but that does not seem to be the case. I guess that's what happens when you are with the same seventy people every day, all day!

With everyone watching everyone else, you need to be cautious in your behavior, both academically and socially, to avoid ending up as a target of gossipmongers. Frequently, the wholly innocent get caught up in the gossip web. If you regularly hang out and study with a person of the opposite sex (or possibly the same sex), do not be surprised if rumors begin circulating that the two of you are "sleeping together."

Not all law school rumors are unfounded. Often, gossip attaches itself to people who behave in ways that predictably lead to gossip. Be cautious about alcohol, drugs, and sexual activities. Very little remains private in law school. Avoid letting people take untoward pictures of you at social gatherings. Embarrassing pictures can come back to haunt people. Most employers, including most legal employers, scour the internet for information about recruits when making hiring decisions.

16. The Evaluator/Judger. These two closely related types are sometimes the same person, but not always. Both spend a disproportionate amount of time sizing up the competition, the Evaluator by keeping close tabs on everyone's progress and the Judger by overtly rating his classmates as smart or not smart, often based on their classroom comments. Evaluators are obsessed with knowing everyone's grades and comparing them to their own. At one school, in the days when grades were still publicly posted on the "wailing wall" or "wall of shame" (as students called it), we had to change the entire anonymous grade-number system because an Evaluator took the time to collect and chart the grades of every 1L by exam number.

As for the Judger, who may also qualify as a Know-It-All, it is presumptuous in the extreme for any 1L student to believe he is qualified to evaluate the knowledge and analytical abilities of his classmates. It probably goes without saying that overt Evaluators/Judgers are not well-liked by their classmates.

17. The Class Joker. As someone who appreciates humor and the value of it for bolstering the sense of community and energy level in law school classrooms, I love Class Jokers. Most first-year sections will include at least one real character. These are people who like attention and appear to enjoy being the subject of good-natured ribbing from the professor. When the going gets tough or tedious, an appropriate Class Joker can add a much needed spark of energy to a class.

By "appropriate Class Joker," I am excluding students who go overboard in trying to be funny, diverting the focus of the class discussion. Appropriate Class Jokers know their place in the hierarchy. Think of the appropriate Class Joker as the law school equivalent of a sidekick to a late-night talk show host. They can get away with some gentle limelight-seeking, but remain cognizant of their primary role as the "straight man."

18. The Lightning Rod. As with the Class Joker, most law school classes have at least one Lightning Rod, a person willing to express strong and sometimes outrageous opinions about the issues being discussed in class. Often, these views can be associated with either the far left or right of the political spectrum. Sometimes their opinions are politically incorrect. Not all professors share my view, but I like having Lightning Rods as students, even when I disagree with their views, because their opinions prompt other students who normally would not participate to jump into the fray. The surest identifier of a Lightning Rod is a person whose classroom comments ignite a sea of waving hands. Some Lightning Rods offer their opinions with a wink and a nod to the professor, knowing full well the role they're fulfilling.

A truly passionate Lightning Rod may open himself to derision from classmates in much the same way as a true gunner, and, in fact, these categories sometimes overlap. Unfortunately, fear of peer disapproval deters many non-Lightning Rod students from offering honest opinions about charged issues, of which there are many in law.

A classic example from Torts is the famous Iowa "spring-gun case," *Katko v. Briney*,[35] which you are likely to study. Marvin Katko sued Edward and Bertha Briney after he broke into their unoccupied farmhouse intent on stealing property and ended up losing a portion of his leg to a shotgun the Brineys had wired to the bedroom door. The jury awarded Katko substantial compensatory and punitive damages. The Brineys had to auction eighty acres of their farm to pay the judgment. Katko won on the principle that the law values life over property. From teaching the case for many years, I know that a large percentage of students in every class vehemently disagree with the result that a criminal could recover damages from a homeowner whose property he unlawfully invaded, but they're often afraid to express their disagreement until a Lightning Rod opens the door with a comment such as, "The S.O.B. got what he deserved."

19. The Cheater. From a professor's perspective, the only student type worse than the Slacker is the Cheater. People who cheat in law school are likely to cheat in the practice of law, hurting their clients and tarnishing a profession that is already

---

[35]   183 N.W.2d 657 (Iowa 1971).

held in low regard by many. The good news is that the nature of law school exams makes it difficult to cheat effectively. The bad news is this doesn't stop some people from trying. At every law school where I have taught, incidents of alleged cheating have occurred. Sadly, several students at different law schools have reported to me that cheating not only occurs, but is common, although I can't vouch for the accuracy of such indictments.

Of course, whether you decide to be a Cheater isn't going to be influenced by any advice I give you. Nor do you need a book like this to apprise you of the potentially severe consequences of cheating, which can include being suspended from law school or not being permitted to sit for the bar exam. You're the one who has to look in the mirror every day.

But here is some advice that may help honest souls. In some situations involving accusations of academic misconduct, I've come away convinced that the cheating was inadvertent or at least not motivated by a wicked intent. These incidents often involve students who, faced with a dilemma as to what is or isn't proper conduct, resolve the question in their favor without seeking guidance from the professor.

For example, cheating allegations arise disproportionately in first-year legal research and writing courses where gray areas may exist in the rules regarding matters such as collaboration and plagiarism. Instead of simply asking the professor for guidance when a question of right or wrong arises, the student makes a choice on his own—giving himself the benefit of the doubt—which turns out to be the wrong choice. Even if an accused student is ultimately spared sanctions, he suffers the trauma of being investigated and risks a tarnished reputation. In many cases, the student could have avoided any problem simply by seeking clarification from the professor. You cannot go wrong by following that course of action: when in doubt, ask the professor.

Related to overt academic cheating are violations of course policies. A common example is using personal computers to multitask on the internet during class. Most professors have explicit policies against this, which many students violate. I assume students do this because they think the violation is de minimis, but students can't pick and choose which rules are important. Professors not only take violations of course policies personally as a sign of disrespect, it diminishes their faith in the offender's capacity to be an ethical lawyer.

20. The Earnest Hard Worker. Last, but certainly not least, is the Earnest Hard Worker. Don't be misled by the negative types listed above. While the negative types tend to stand out more than the positive types, they are a distinct minority overall. The Earnest Hard Workers, I'm happy to report, represent a majority of law students. Some of them achieve high grades, some don't. But even Earnest Hard Workers who don't come out at the top of their class earn the respect of those around them, both students and professors. I happily write strong recommendation letters on behalf of Earnest Hard Workers even if they received less-than-stellar grades in my courses.

* * *

There you have them. Twenty law student types. Make a list of the types that appeal to you, the types that don't, and the in-between types. Think about the list, then put it away. Revisit your list during the first semester to see whether you're living up (or down) to your aspirations.

CHAPTER 5

THE FIRST-YEAR CURRICULUM: WHAT TO EXPECT

Here's a list of the courses I took as a 1L in 1978:

Civil Procedure

Contracts

Criminal Law

Legal Research and Writing

Property

Torts

Here's a list of the courses you are likely to take as a 1L:

Civil Procedure

Contracts

Criminal Law

Legal Research and Writing

Property

Torts

Hm, can we detect a pattern here? Nowhere has resistance to change in American legal education been more apparent than in the static nature of law school curricula. As discussed below, changes are occurring, but they are unlikely to dramatically impact your first-year experience.

The primary purpose of this chapter is to give you a feel for what I call the "Big Five" doctrinal courses that most full-time[36] 1Ls will be immersed in, if not submerged under: Civil Procedure, Contracts, Criminal Law, Property, and Torts. Because your other first-year required course—Legal Research

---

[36] Part-time students usually take only two of these doctrinal courses per semester, along with Legal Research and Writing.

and Writing—is a skills course and totally different beast, it gets its own chapter (Chapter 18).

There are three basic types of law school courses:

(1) *Doctrinal courses.* These are courses in which the primary goal is to teach a body of substantive rules—or doctrine—in a particular area of law, while also developing students' ability to conduct legal analysis. At most schools, all of your first year courses except Legal Research and Writing will be doctrinal courses.

(2) *Experiential and other skills courses.* As described in the next section, a major push is on for law schools to add more experiential courses. "Experiential learning" is a relatively new term in legal education, used to describe courses designed to impart practical knowledge and skills rather than knowledge of the law itself. Such courses have traditionally been, and often still are, called "skills courses."

Experiential courses come in three varieties: simulation courses, clinics, and field placements (typically called externships).

Simulation courses are courses where students perform assignments under the supervision of a faculty member designed to provide experience "reasonably similar to the experience of a lawyer advising or representing a client or engaging in other lawyering tasks . . . ."[37] They can include courses in negotiation, client counseling, mediation or arbitration, and document drafting.

Clinics involve students working on real cases representing real clients, in a particular area. The subject matter is limited only by a particular law school's clinical choices, which are often dictated by grant availability or other financing issues. As examples, there are clinics in areas such as juvenile justice, elder law, environmental law, tax law, domestic violence, landlord-tenant law, health law . . . the possibilities are pretty much endless.

---

[37] STANDARDS & RULES OF PROCEDURE FOR APPROVAL OF LAW SCH. 304(a) (AM. BAR ASS'N 2016–2017).

Externships involve students earning credit working outside the law school under the supervision of practicing lawyers. They were traditionally limited to working at public agencies and non-profit entities, in part because ABA interpretations of accreditation rules prohibited students from receiving credit for any type of paid externship, such as by working at a private law firm. In 2016, however, the ABA House of Delegates approved a rule change eliminating the prohibition on paid externships, opening the door for law schools to award credit for them.[38] A few schools have already changed their rules to allow paid externships.[39]

(3) *Seminars and other upper-level writing courses.* ABA Accreditation Standard 303(a)(2) requires students to engage in at least one substantial writing experience after their first year. Traditionally, most students satisfied this requirement by taking a seminar. These are small (usually limited to ten or twelve students), subject-matter specific courses in which students typically write a scholarly or other substantial paper and make a presentation. Seminars can be offered in any subject area. For example, I teach seminars in privacy law and gun violence.

As law schools add more skills courses, including advanced writing courses, options may expand for students to satisfy the upper-level writing requirement by means other than a seminar. (As an aside, note that an extra benefit of being a member of the law review—see Chapter 24—is that the writing requirements for law review usually satisfy the law school's upper-level writing requirement.)

The Drive Toward Experiential Learning

Before we delve into the Big Five first-year courses, you should be aware of a major curricular shift occurring in legal education. A withering criticism of law school curricula is that

---

[38] ABA SECTION OF LEGAL EDUC. & ADMISSIONS TO THE BAR, REPORT TO THE HOUSE OF DELEGATES, RESOLUTION 5 (2016) (eliminating Interpretation 305-2, which provided that law schools may not grant credit for participation in an externship for which the student receives compensation).

[39] Katie Thisdell, *Externships for Pay and Credit*, 26 NAT'L JURIST 9 (2017) (reporting that five schools have approved paid externships and that the "vast majority" of schools are studying the issue).

they are too focused on doctrinal courses, failing to prepare students for the actual practice of law. The criticism is longstanding, having been raised in three respected, influential reports—known as the *MacCrate Report*,[40] the *Carnegie Foundation Report*,[41] and *Best Practices for Legal Education* report[42]—over the past twenty-five years. In recent years, legal employers have added to the call by complaining that law schools should be turning out graduates who are more "practice ready."

The traditional law school curriculum is somewhat of an odd arrangement if one stops to ponder it for, say, two seconds. To prepare doctors to practice medicine, medical schools require years of clinical training involving hands-on patient care. Law schools require nothing of the sort.

In the last edition, I cited data from a comprehensive 2012 ABA curriculum study showing that schools were finally moving, albeit slowly, in the direction of adding more skills courses.[43] The movement has gained momentum since then, boosted by a new ABA accreditation standard requiring "one or more experiential course(s) totaling at least six credit hours" as a condition of graduation.[44]

The changes remain modest and are unlikely to convert graduates into being "practice ready,"[45] but after many years of just being talked about, experiential and other skills-based learning have a strong wind at their back. Most skills-based courses are in the upper-level curriculum. The major exception

---

[40]   ABA Section of Legal Educ. & Admissions to the Bar, The Report of the Task Force on Law Schools and the Profession: Narrowing the Gap (1992) (called the "MacCrate Report" after the chair of the task force, Robert MacCrate).

[41]   *See* William M. Sullivan et al., Carnegie Found. for the Advancement of Teaching, Educating Lawyers: Preparation for the Profession of Law (2007) [hereinafter Carnegie Foundation Report].

[42]   Best Practices for Legal Education, *supra*.

[43]   ABA Section of Legal Educ. & Admissions to the Bar, A Survey of Law School Curricula: 2002–2010 (Catherine Carpenter ed., 2012).

[44]   Standards & Rules of Procedure for Approval of Law Sch. 303(a)(3) (Am. Bar Ass'n 2016–2017).

[45]   In addition to a continuing shortage of clinical and other substantial experiential opportunities, a big obstacle to efforts by law schools to turn out "practice-ready" lawyers is that, unlike medical schools, where students pursue clinical experience in fields in which they intend to practice, law school experiential opportunities are not tied, except randomly, to the field of law that the student will ultimately pursue.

will be your required first-year Legal Research and Writing Courses (see Chapter 18).

Other Curricular Innovations

While we won't delve into them in detail, be aware that law schools are experimenting with other curricular innovations, including accelerated degree programs (two years instead of three years), hybrid in-person/online programs, and enhanced technology training. Due to declining bar pass rates, many schools are also investing heavily in bar preparation courses that are integrated into the regular curriculum.

The "Big Five" First-Year Doctrinal Courses

Below is a short summary of the first-year doctrinal courses that most 1Ls will take. Having a rudimentary sense of what each course involves will help you know what to expect and give you a better context for processing the rest of this book. At a minimum, when you see your course list for the first time, it won't feel like reading a menu at a foreign restaurant.

Civil Procedure

All civil lawsuits are controlled by a set of procedural rules, cleverly titled "The Rules of Civil Procedure." The Rules of Civil Procedure tell the lawyers and parties what they must do and may do in the pretrial and trial stages of a lawsuit, as well as how and when to do it. Criminal cases are controlled by a similar set of rules, but courses in criminal procedure are reserved for the upper-level curriculum.

The Federal Rules of Civil Procedure, which are the focus of most 1L courses on the subject, govern lawsuits in the federal courts. Each state has its own set of civil procedure rules to govern civil lawsuits in their respective court systems, but those rules track the federal rules for the most part. The Federal Rules of Civil Procedure contain eighty-six rules, but you will closely study only a small number of them.

You'll spend a lot of time studying cases, many of which predate the adoption of the Federal Rules of Civil Procedure, that developed the key concepts governing questions such as which court has jurisdiction to hear a particular case, whether a court has jurisdiction over the parties to a case, and which court system's rules (federal or state) of substantive law apply to a case.

Unlike your other first-year courses (except Constitutional Law, which is a first-year course at roughly one-half of law schools), many of the cases in Civil Procedure are U.S. Supreme Court cases. You will quickly learn that Supreme Court cases are different from and more difficult to digest than the state court cases that will predominate in your first year. They're usually longer, include more policy analysis, and often contain a maze of concurring and dissenting opinions that must be pieced together to discern the holding of the Court.

A substantial portion of "Civ Pro," as students call it, is devoted to the topic of "personal jurisdiction." A court has the power to hear a lawsuit only if it has jurisdiction over all the parties—i.e., the authority to make binding decisions on them. The basic concept is that each party to a lawsuit must have some connection to the court's geographic jurisdiction for the court to have personal jurisdiction over them.

Sound easy? It's not. Personal jurisdiction is one of the most difficult and heavily tested issues in Civil Procedure. (A good tip to remember across the board is that professors generally like to test on the most difficult material, not the easiest.) Depending on your professor, you might spend several grueling weeks studying the evolution of personal jurisdiction rules via a chronology of famous Supreme Court cases.

Each case modifies the one preceding it, leaving some students wondering why they can't just study the last one, since it contains the most up-to-date treatment of the law. The answer is that a full understanding of complex legal doctrine sometimes can be achieved only by studying its historical evolution. It's probably a fair statement to say that in most Civil Procedure courses, students cannot excel without a thorough understanding of the law of personal jurisdiction.

Every 1L course has at least one classic case that all law students remember studying. For Civil Procedure, that case is *Pennoyer v. Neff*,[46] a complicated artifact about personal

---

[46]   95 U.S. 714 (1877).

jurisdiction with little modern relevance. Quoting Shakespeare's *Macbeth*, one law professor said about *Pennoyer*: "Confusion now hath made its masterpiece."[47] When I was a student, I'm not sure my understanding of *Pennoyer v. Neff* ever progressed beyond wondering why the case wasn't called *Mitchell v. Neff*, since the party who started the whole mess was not Pennoyer, but a colorful lawyer named J.H. Mitchell.

Other topics commonly covered include: "the *Erie* doctrine" (governing whether state or federal substantive law applies in a federal case), motions to dismiss and summary judgment (mechanisms for judges to dispose of cases without a trial), res judicata and collateral estoppel (rules for deciding whether a case or claim that has already been heard once can be re-litigated), and class actions (a type of mass lawsuit that can involve hundreds or even thousands of plaintiffs).

As with all courses, student reactions toward Civil Procedure vary. One student consultant said it was one of her most "boring" courses, while another said it was "fun." Another student, who liked the course and loved the professor, said:

> This is not the most exciting class you will take. It is difficult to get excited about Rule 41, or 65, or any of the rules for that matter. They just aren't very "sexy." And honestly, I never heard any of my classmates come out of a Civil Procedure class and say, "Man, that was awesome. I can't wait to see how that Rule 18 issue is gonna turn out tomorrow!"

On one issue, near unanimity of student opinion exists: Civil Procedure is one of the most difficult first-year courses. This is attributable in part to the fact that the subject matter is unfamiliar ("Not even covered on TV!" wrote one student) and also because the rules are technical and not intuitive. Moreover, civil procedure rules are studied in the context of cases involving other areas of law (e.g., a contract, property, or tort dispute), which you'll be learning about at the same time you're trying to learn Civil Procedure.

---

[47] Wendy Collins Perdue, *Sin, Scandal and Substantive Due Process: Personal Jurisdiction and Pennoyer Reconsidered*, 62 WASH. L. REV. 479, 479 (1987).

Contracts

Contracts focuses on the formation, performance, and breach of oral and written agreements. Much of the course focuses on the three essential ingredients to the formation of a binding contract: offer (a person has to make an offer to enter into a contract), acceptance (the other person has to accept the offer), and consideration (each party must give something of value to the other as part of the bargain). Infinite permutations exist regarding each of these requirements that make them much more complex than they might sound. One student advisor offered this capsule overview of the three requirements:

> This course is all about three words: offer, acceptance, and consideration. From the beginning of the course these three words are drilled into your head constantly. Chances are, if you're not paying attention in class one day and you end up getting called on, answering with one of the three "magic words" will at least get you in the ballpark of the correct answer. (Of course, I'm certainly not advocating drifting off in class.)

> This course began with a simple question, or at least what I thought was a simple question: What constitutes an offer? You will find that there are rarely any simple questions in law school. There's always something lurking under the surface of a seemingly simple question. We read and discussed LOTS of cases initially just trying to determine whether or not an offer was made. For me, this was interesting because as our professor correctly explained, we enter into contracts every day of our lives. From signing a credit card receipt to an apartment lease to accepting your first job offer after law school—we all have experience dealing with contracts even though we may not think about it.

> After addressing whether or not an offer was made, we examined what it means to accept an offer. Now, you might be thinking at this point, "Duh, I know what an offer is and how to accept it. Can they just go ahead and give me my law degree already?" That line of thinking would be a mistake. As you will learn, acceptance can be manifested in many ways, and one can be held to that manifestation even if they

claim accepting the offer was not their intent. Be on the lookout for one of the most famous and interesting acceptance cases, *Lucy v. Zehmer*,[48] which involved a negotiation between two intoxicated parties for a piece of farmland. One of the parties jokingly signed over his farmland on the back of a restaurant check thinking that the negotiation was done in jest. However, as he soon found out, this was considered a valid manifestation of acceptance and he had to sell his farm. (One moral of this case: Don't drink and sell farmland. The two don't mix.)

The third piece of the Contracts puzzle is consideration. In my opinion, consideration was the most difficult of the three major concepts to understand. Whether or not a party gives consideration for an offer is a difficult question, and often court opinions will differ on seemingly similar cases with similar facts. Additionally, I found that most of our exam questions dealt with the issue of whether or not consideration was given to constitute a valid contract. Don't feel too bad if you have no idea what I'm talking about now. Trust me, you will spend an inordinate amount of time discussing consideration during your Contracts class, and you'll likely be just as confused as I was afterwards. (Just kidding . . . I hope.)

In addition to offer, acceptance, and consideration, you'll learn about the scope of contractual obligations, remedies for breaches of contracts, excuses for performance such as impossibility, and something called the parol evidence rule, which relates to what, if any, extraneous evidence outside the contract can be considered in interpreting it. No point trying to explain it here. As a student who finished number one in her class wrote: "I still could not fully explain to you how the parol rule operates."

Like Property below, the facts in Contracts cases can be detailed and complex, making the cases more time-consuming to read and brief than most cases in Torts or Criminal Law.

---

[48]   84 S.E.2d 516 (Va. 1954).

Criminal Law

Criminal Law is the study of criminal offenses and defenses, primarily the former. Because criminal cases are intensely covered by the media and are a favorite subject of law-related books, television series, and movies, students arrive at law school thinking the subject area will be heavily emphasized. But Criminal Law is the only first-year course that takes students outside the realm of civil litigation into the darker world of crime and how the legal system responds to it.

Like Torts, Criminal Law is highly "element"-based. All criminal offenses are composed of elements that must be proved by the prosecution beyond a reasonable doubt. If any element is missing, a completed crime has not occurred. A great deal of class time is devoted to understanding the two most fundamental elements of a crime: actus reus (the criminal act itself) and mens rea (the mental state required to be convicted of a particular crime).

You'll study the elements of core crimes such as homicide, theft, and burglary, as well as the elements of "inchoate crimes" such as attempt, conspiracy, and solicitation. Inchoate crimes, which can be tricky to understand, are offenses for which a defendant can be convicted even where the object crime is never completed. If Amanda hires Bluto to kill Carl, that's a crime even if Carl is unharmed. Defenses to crimes also have elements that must be proved.

Making matters more difficult, because modern criminal law is mostly statutory, you probably will have to study and compare the common law (judge-made law) to statutory law (laws passed by legislatures). Learning to read, interpret, and parse statutes is a different skill from learning to read and interpret cases. Confusing matters even more, it's possible you'll be required to study and compare both the English *and* U.S. common law *and* both the Model Penal Code (a uniform code of criminal law often used as a model for criminal statutes) *and* the criminal statutes actually adopted in your state. This could mean that for one criminal offense, such as homicide, you might be required to learn the distinct elements under English common law, U.S. common law, the Model Penal Code, and your state's criminal statutes. If your Criminal Law course is taught in this fashion, making charts can be an effective strategy for keeping the elements straight.

But it might be taught in a *completely* different fashion. In Chapter 9, I discuss the difference between professors who teach from a primarily practical perspective and those who teach from a primarily theoretical perspective. These divergent approaches can occur in any course, but Criminal Law is a prime candidate for theoretical teaching among 1L courses. Instead of focusing on all the detailed rules and elements, your Criminal Law professor might choose to concentrate (as mine did) on big-picture policy issues, such as the societal policies and theories underlying criminal punishment and sentencing. The difference in these teaching approaches is like night and day for students.

One pitfall to watch out for is that some important doctrines of criminal law parallel similar doctrines under tort law. Criminal Law usually is a one-semester course taught in the second semester, while Torts is usually taught in the first semester or both the first and second semesters. As one student said, the overlap can be "both a blessing and a curse" because, while it's comforting to approach a topic with which you already are familiar, important differences exist in the details between criminal law and tort law. For example, "assault" under criminal law is a different concept from "assault" under tort law. Make it a point to keep the two subject areas separate in your mind.

One upside of Criminal Law is that, as in Torts, many of the cases have interesting, even juicy fact patterns. Where else are you going to find a case like *Regina v. Dudley*?[49] This classic from England is the chilling tale of some castaways who, after being stranded on a lifeboat for twenty days with nothing to eat but two cans of turnips and a turtle, cannibalized a seventeen-year-old cabin boy. Four days later they were rescued by a passing ship. Oops! Back in England, the three survivors faced a variety of criminal charges, including assault with a deadly molar and abdominal possession of a fibula. Also, murder. The crewmen defended on the ground of "justification." The defense of justification says you can commit a crime without penalty so long as it is committed in the interest of avoiding a greater harm.

---

[49]   14 Q.B.D. 273 (Queen's Bench 1884).

The defendants argued it was better that one cabin boy die than all four of them starve to death, which isn't a bad argument. But oops again. The defendants never consulted the cabin boy for his thoughts on the matter before slitting his throat and feasting on him. The court rejected the defense.

A downside is that Criminal Law itself can be less than scintillating. Learning it often requires a lot of memorization of the different elements of different offenses. Students coming out of Criminal Law often experience polar-opposite reactions. Some students go into the course thinking they won't like it and come out wanting to practice criminal law. Others complete the course swearing they will never have anything to do with a criminal case.

Property

In Property, students study the principles of law governing the ownership and transfer of personal property (stuff not attached to land) and real property (land or structures attached to land). Your Property casebook, for example, is an item of personal property. The floor you slam it down on out of frustration with the law of future interests is part of real property. Most of Property—and most of what you will be tested on—will focus on the law of real property.

Your first assignments in Property may cover cases going back to the 1800s. Unlike the law of most other subjects, which has evolved over time, many of the rules governing property rights were frozen in place centuries ago. Thus, historical context is more important to understanding Property than some other 1L courses.

In approaching Property, keep in mind this big-picture point: a person does not "have" real property, but rather has an "interest" in real property. That interest can be purchased, found, gifted, inherited, sold, lost, given away, or devised. The interest can be absolute or conditional. It can be partial or whole. Much of the study of property is simply how the law treats various interests in real property.

Well, "simply" may be a bad word choice. Property is filled with alien concepts such as adverse possession, restrictive covenants, the fee system, marketable title, and, of course, future interests. I recall Property being my hardest first-year course and it was all because of future interests. The law of future interests is a maze-like set of rules regulating the ability of one to control interests in land in the future, such as by way of a will or trust.

One famous future interests rule—the Rule Against Perpetuities—is so ridiculously complicated that the distinguished California Supreme Court once suggested it would be impossible for a lawyer to commit malpractice for misunderstanding the rule.[50] You gotta love that, along with the fact that some of the satellite doctrines under the Rule Against Perpetuities have names that sound like old blues tunes. The "Bad as to One, Bad as to All" and "Unborn Widow" rules could have been classic hits for Muddy Waters. The only thing most lawyers remember about the Rule Against Perpetuities is that, for reasons never fully explained, "twenty-one years" is important to property law.

It's all very confusing, so don't fret too much if your class notes on the Rule Against Perpetuities end up looking like this:

Professor's lecture: No contingent future interest in a transferee is good unless it must vest or fail to vest within twenty-one years of the death of some life in being at the time of the creation of the interest.

Student's notes: No astringent foosball interest?? . . . must vest OR FAIL TO VEST . . . twenty-one years . . . death . . . life in bean . . . creation? interest?

Professor: The rationale for the rule is straightforward. It's designed to limit efforts by grantors to restrict the free alienation of property by burdening it with contingent future interests.

Student: Rationale for rule straightforward—designed to limit grantees ORS . . . something, something, something— SLOW THE **** DOWN!—Alien Nation of Property? . . . BUY STUDY AID!

---

50 *See* Lucas v. Hamm, 364 P.2d 685, 690 (Cal. 1961) ("[F]ew, if any, areas of the law have been fraught with more confusion or concealed more traps for the unwary draftsman. . . . [A]n error of the type relied on by plaintiffs does not show negligence. . . .").

Professor: The simple way to understand the rule is to remember that it all has to do with the vesting or failure to vest of a contingent future interest within the lifetime of a measuring life or twenty-one years after that person's death.

Student: Simple way to understand rule is to remember that it all has to do with ... TWENTY-ONE YEARS, TWENTY-ONE YEARS, TWENTY-ONE YEARS ...

Fortunately, precisely because it is so convoluted, the Rule Against Perpetuities usually isn't a major focus of a Property exam. But the rest of the law pertaining to future interests often is because, as mentioned, professors often opt to test more difficult material over simpler material. While future interest rules are technical and tricky, once you get a handle on them, they're easy to apply.

Unlike the law in many subjects, where hues of gray dominate, the rules in Property are more black and white. As a consequence, more definite "correct answers" exist to property law questions. As one student advisor wrote, "Many property problems operate exactly like math problems." Once you master the rules, it's easier to apply them with confidence than in courses with more abstract rules.

Torts

You may think you have no idea what a tort is. Perhaps you think it's a dessert, but that's a "torte." In fact, Torts is a subject with which entering students have at least some familiarity, whether they realize it or not. Who, for example, hasn't heard about the infamous (albeit grossly distorted) McDonald's coffee spill lawsuit? That was a tort case. So are the lawsuits you hear or read about involving prescription drugs and medical devices, asbestos, tobacco, and defamation and invasion of privacy. Medical malpractice suits are tort cases. So are automobile accident suits. Basically, any time a person is physically or emotionally injured through the conduct of another, whether in a train derailment or through cyber-bullying, the potential for a tort suit arises. Tort law is also part of a controversial national political agenda known as the "tort reform movement" that receives substantial media attention.

A tort is a civil wrong other than a breach of contract (which is also a civil wrong) for which the law allows the plaintiff a right of action for money damages. Like Criminal Law, Torts is highly element-based. All torts consist of a set of elements, each of which must be proved by the plaintiff to make out a successful claim.

Most Torts courses begin with a study of the seven basic intentional torts: assault, battery, false imprisonment, intentional infliction of emotional distress, trespass to land, trespass to chattels, and conversion (the latter two relate to interferences with personal property). This is followed by a study of the basic privileges or defenses to the intentional torts: consent, self-defense, defense of others, defense of property, recovery of property, and necessity (such as eating the cabin boy in *Regina v. Dudley*).

Students enjoy learning about intentional torts because the case facts are interesting and the rules are straightforward and easy to organize. They are a good "learning bike" for new law students in the first few weeks of law school. For the same reasons, a lot of the examples used in this book will involve intentional torts.

The bulk of every Torts course is the topic of negligence. Simplistically, negligence law is the study of liability for money damages when a person or entity fails to exercise reasonable care and that failure causes injury. Negligence principles are mostly intuitive but can be difficult to get a firm grasp on because they are so amorphous.

What, for example, is "reasonable care"? Suppose a car accident occurs because the driver was distracted reading a text message. The driver probably failed to exercise reasonable care, but what about the sender of the text? Is it negligent to send someone a text message? What if the sender knew the recipient was driving and would read the text? Under such facts, a New Jersey court said the text sender could be found negligent and accountable for the accident injuries.[51]

You will grapple with puzzles like this daily in Torts. The words "reasonable" and "unreasonable" will creep into your

---

[51]   Kubert v. Best, 75 A.3d 1214 (N.J. Super. Ct. App. Div. 2013).

everyday vocabulary and contribute to your driving the non-law students around you out of their minds.

Depending on the number of credit hours allotted to Torts, topics of study apart from intentional torts and negligence may include strict liability (of which products liability is the largest component), wrongful death, tort damages, and defamation and privacy.

Tort cases, like those in Criminal Law, can make for interesting reading because of the human element involved when people injure each other, either intentionally or negligently. Sex,[52] drugs,[53] and rock and roll[54]—Torts offers a little of everything.

Torts is where students study one of the most famous and memorable cases in American jurisprudential history: *Palsgraf v. Long Island Railroad Co.*,[55] a wacky, confusing case with opinions from two heavyweight judges about an exploding package of fireworks that supposedly knocked a heavy scale on top of Helen Palsgraf at the Long Island train station in 1924. I always tell my students that *Palsgraf* may be the only law school case that *every* lawyer remembers. Several students have tested this assertion, always reporting back that the lawyers they ask about the case still remember it. Try it out.

Students sometimes think Torts is "easier" than other first-year subjects. It's true that many of the basic principles of tort law are not intellectually difficult, but like all subjects, Torts is full of little twists and nuances that make it more complicated than it first appears. And like all subjects, it has its own unusually difficult topics, with "proximate cause"—one of the elements of negligence—being the signature example.

---

[52] *See, e.g.*, Doe v. Moe, 827 N.E.2d 240 (Mass. App. Ct. 2005) (suit against ex-girlfriend alleging that negligence during intercourse caused plaintiff to suffer a fractured penis).

[53] *See, e.g.*, Hegel v. Langsam, 273 N.E.2d 351 (Ohio Ct. C.P. 1971) (suit by parents of college student against university alleging negligence in not protecting their seventeen-year-old daughter from using drugs).

[54] *See, e.g.*, McCollum v. CBS, Inc., 249 Cal. Rptr. 187 (Cal. Ct. App. 1988) (suit against rock singer Ozzy Osbourne on behalf of teenager who committed suicide after listening to Ozzy's song, *Suicide Solution*).

[55] 162 N.E. 99 (N.Y. 1928).

Even assuming the law of one course is measurably easier than the law of another course, it would be a mistake to treat the course differently in terms of the amount of your studying and preparation. You're not competing against the course. You're competing only against other students in the course. As I always remind my students: "There are just as many low grades in Torts as in other subjects."

* * *

Your level of interest in and enjoyment of any particular course will depend partly on your personality type and learning preferences. Students who are more comfortable with concrete rules may love Property. Students who prefer abstractions and possibilities may prefer Torts and, if offered in the first year, Constitutional Law. Your relative enjoyment of particular courses also will be heavily influenced by the professors teaching them. Good teachers can make any subject come alive, while ineffective teachers can make even the most interesting material dull. Similarly, organized, well-prepared teachers with good communication skills can make even the most complex material accessible and understandable, while disorganized or unprepared teachers can render even simple material obtuse.

CHAPTER 6

THE FIRST DAYS: STARTING OUT RIGHT

The first days of law school are exciting, memorable, and usually quite stressful. Everything is a blur because it's all so new: new people, new physical surroundings, a whole new language, and a mysterious new teaching methodology. It's enough to make anyone nervous. Even professors get nervous on the first days.

The heartening news is that the comfort level in law school classrooms increases quickly. When I walk into Torts on the first day of class, it's so quiet one could hear a Xanax drop. But with each passing day, students get more familiar with each other, their surroundings, and their professors. They're relieved that the Socratic method is not nearly as torturous as rumored, that law professors are by and large nice folks who are good at what they do and care about their students, and that they can actually grasp the legal principles being taught.

As in every other setting, familiarity breeds comfort and relaxes tension. Within a couple of weeks, it sounds like I'm walking into a rowdy pub as I approach the classroom door. Instead of silence, I'm greeted with a cacophony of excited chatter and laughter.

You want to get off on the right foot in these first days. Missteps can result in embarrassment, risk branding you in a negative light, facilitate your falling behind, and, in general, create extra stress that can interfere with learning. The advice in this chapter is designed to help you come out of the blocks smoothly and cleanly as you begin the 1L race.

Getting the Most Out of Orientation

All law schools conduct an orientation for incoming students, usually in the week immediately preceding the commencement of classes. Orientations vary in length and scope, from two to as long as six days. Most orientation programs are two or three days.

Students often find orientation frustrating. Who can blame them? Attending law school requires so much advance groundwork—from taking the LSAT to completing lengthy applications to arranging housing and financial aid to reading books like this one—that by the time law school actually rolls around, students walk through the doors champing at the bit to get going. But it doesn't work that way. First, it's orientation time.

A former student once drew an interesting analogy between law school orientation and having sex for the first time:

> You've waited all your life. You've dreamed about it, planned for it, obsessed over it, visualized it, practiced for it, and now the day finally arrives that you get to actually DO IT. You're totally psyched, when all of a sudden a bunch of people burst into the room and say: "Stop! You cannot have sex right now. Before you can have sex, you must sit down and listen to us tell you for a week what it is *like* to have sex."

Students tend to take two diametrically opposed approaches to orientation: they either disregard it or immerse themselves in it with total devotion. Both approaches can be counterproductive. Blowing off orientation certainly is a poor way to get started on such a big, new adventure in life. As discussed below, some orientation events will be of value to you. Equally important, not acting professionally during orientation reflects poorly on you.

The people responsible for organizing and running orientation are acutely tuned into negative attitudes, disparaging comments they overhear, and who doesn't attend required events. One of them may pass the information on to one or more of your first-year professors, as in: "You have a student in your section—Mr./Ms. Blank—who skipped out on orientation." Or: "You're not going to believe what I overheard this kid in your section say during the reception." Upper-level student orientation mentors and group leaders also sometimes relay information to faculty about the new students they encounter.

Here's a specific example of what I'm talking about. On the first day of orientation, a colleague came into my office, clearly irritated. He said he had just met with the entering class to do a case-briefing exercise. The new students were supposed to have registered for the Legal Research and Writing TWEN course site (see below) and downloaded a case for the exercise. From data available on TWEN, my colleague was able to determine before going into the orientation session that eight of the new students had failed to download the case. What did he do? First and foremost, he formed a bad impression of the eight students. Second, he purposely called on them during the exercise to expose their unpreparedness to the entire entering class. Third, he informed me and perhaps other first-year professors about their lack of preparation. This is not the way you want to begin your new career: with a bad reputation before the first class has been held.

On the other hand, depending on the rigor of the orientation, immersing yourself in orientation as if your life depended on it is not a great idea either. I taught at one law school that had a six-day orientation, which included a lengthy session on the Saturday before school started when the students would have been better off at home preparing for their first week of classes. Just reading the schedule of events, many of which went well into the night, was exhausting. Some of the events required substantial reading to prepare for them.

It was all well-intended and each individual event had value, but it was simply too much packaged together. I watched the students arrive at the start of orientation eager and bright-eyed and leave Saturday afternoon looking like they had just finished first-semester exams. When classes began the following Monday, many of the students already looked worn out.

I suggest a middle-ground attitude and approach to orientation in which your goal is to maximize the benefits while conserving your emotional and physical energy. Simply keeping in mind that orientation doesn't technically "count" for anything should help keep your stress level in check and preserve some psychic energy. Take it seriously, but not gravely.

If the school assigns background reading as part of orientation, by all means read it, but don't wear yourself out fretting over every line you don't understand. Pay particular attention to assignments pertaining to practical study skills, such as case-briefing or outlining. These crucial skills take time and practice to develop, so you want to take advantage of early opportunities to start learning about them. If the school holds a "sample class," be sure to prepare for it. These usually involve one assigned case to read. You don't want to be remembered as "that student" who showed up unprepared for the sample class.

Here are some things to focus on during orientation:

Get your first-week assignments.

Your first week of assignments will probably be posted on the law school's website prior to orientation, but if not, be sure to track them down during orientation. Legal education starts on day one.

Buy your books and pick up other course materials.

If you haven't already bought your books online or otherwise, buy your required books at the law school or university bookstore as early during orientation as possible. Not infrequently, snafus occur in book orders that result in the bookstore running out of books. Stress reduction, not enhancement, is the order of the day. You do not want to be scrambling around trying to locate an alternative source for the first week's course assignments because the bookstore ran out of books. See Chapter 2 for more information about what books to buy.

If for whatever reason you are unable to obtain a book before classes start, borrow a classmate's book and make a photocopy of the assignments for the entire first week. If you don't know any classmates, go to the professor and ask for help. She should be able to provide you with a copy of the assignment or lend you an extra copy of the book.

Some professors may also have handouts for you to pick up before classes start, so be sure to grab those. As usual, early birds get the worm. I always put a sufficient number of handout packets for Torts in a box outside my office, but they somehow always run out. Students either take more than one package or students from the other section mistakenly grab one. This invariably results in some last-minute stragglers standing sheepishly at my door asking if I have extra copies or, worse, starting classes without having read parts of the initial assignment.

Register for your professors' online course sites.

Most professors use online course sites such as TWEN and LexisNexis Web Course sites. TWEN is an acronym for The West Education Network, operated by Westlaw. LexisNexis Web Course sites are built on the Blackboard platform. Westlaw and LexisNexis are the two major competitors in the arena of online legal research. Depending on the individual professor and type of site, online course sites may be used to access course materials (including syllabi, assignments, classroom policies, course calendars, etc.), participate in online discussions, receive and submit online assignments, work through quizzes, link to CALI (Computer-Assisted Legal Instruction) exercises, exchange email with your professors and classmates, and more.

Professors often use the email function of their online course sites to communicate with the class, including sending information about first assignments, class policies, and the like. Thus, register for these sites as soon as passwords are made available to you.

Be sure to check your law school email account once a day *at a minimum*. My colleagues and I have noticed a trend: too many modern law students are overlooking important email messages from their professors. It might have something to do with students relying on smart phones rather than traditional computers or maybe there's just too much email in the world. Whatever the explanation, if a professor sends out an email on Tuesday changing the assignment for Wednesday, you're going to want to know about it.

Get a locker.

Most law schools offer student lockers for a nominal fee. At the beginning of law school, you might not be sure whether you'll need or use a locker. But unless you absolutely can't afford it, you're better off getting one if the opportunity is presented, especially if you're at a school where there are not enough lockers to go around. Even if you end up not using it every day,

having a place to securely stash some of those heavy books will
come in handy.

Listen to advice, but sort it carefully.

Everyone will be giving you advice on how to succeed in law
school, especially upper-level students. Upper-level students
love to give advice to incoming students. Sometimes it's good
advice. When I started law school, an upper-level student told
me to buy the *Gilbert* study aid for Criminal Law. He explained
that while our professor would focus on theory in class, come
exam time he would expect us to know and apply black-letter
law (i.e., the actual legal rules). Sure enough, class discussions
were geared almost exclusively toward theory. My class notes
were a garbled mess.

I followed his advice. I bought and studied the *Gilbert* for
Criminal Law. The moment I started reading the final exam,
which was my first law school exam, I knew that study aid was
the single best purchasing decision I had ever made. The exam
questions were classic issue-spotting/problem-solving essays
requiring mastery of the black-letter rules we never learned in
class. I received my first *A* in law school in Criminal Law.

But upper-level students also give some really bad advice,
much of which involves ways to cut corners, so be wary of what
they tell you. Although it will be socially awkward, if an upper-
level student starts piling on the shortcut advice, ask the person
about his or her GPA or class rank. You could phrase it like this:
"Thanks for all the advice. Did it work for you?"[56]

Law professors also give advice to incoming students. Law
professor advice may be more reliable overall than student
advice, but it might not be as practical or realistic. For example,
I have a hard time picturing my Criminal Law prof explaining:
"I'm not really going to teach you much actual law in this course,
but I will expect you to know it all for the final exam, so I'd advise
you to run, not walk, to the bookstore and get your hands on the
Gilbert study aid for Criminal Law." Law professors may also go

---

[56]   Be aware, however, that students have been known to prevaricate about their
grades. At the end of answering a question about what advice they would give to a close
loved one starting law school, one student added: "Oh! And one more thang! Law
students lie about their grades. They do. If seven people tell you they received an *A* in
Civil Procedure or Property, some of them are lying."

to the opposite extreme from giving shortcut advice, saying you will have to sacrifice every single second of your waking life to survive in law school, which is not accurate. If you follow the C.R.E.D.O. in Chapter 10, you can both succeed in law school and have time to enjoy life.

Both learning and teaching styles are idiosyncratic. You're likely to receive conflicting advice even from professors. Don't be overwhelmed by it all. Process all advice before acting on it.

Socialize.

Most orientations include one or more social events where students can meet and mingle with their classmates and some of the professors. Take advantage of these. Having a close network of supportive law school friends is invaluable to your success and well-being. Because all 1Ls are in the same overcrowded lifeboat, most people jump at the chance to make friends in these early days.

If you spot one of your first-year professors at these events (they'll usually be wearing name tags), go up and introduce yourself. This is hard for a lot of people to do, but as elaborated on in Chapter 9, there is value in getting to know and being known by your professors. The fact that they're attending the event (most profs don't) means that they're probably approachable people. Don't worry. They're not going to ask you deep legal questions, but they may default to the classic introductory question, "What made you decide to come to law school?", which is the law professor socializing equivalent of "What's your sign?" or "What's your major?" So have an answer for that one. Do not, under any circumstances, say, "Because my parents always said I was good at arguing." It may sound clever to you, but: (a) professors have heard it ten thousand times; and (b) it's a silly reason to go to law school.

Also make an effort to introduce yourself to the law school staff, such as librarians, faculty assistants, and employees in the registrar and admissions offices. These people can help you a lot. Treat them with respect, even deference. Some of them get treated shabbily by hierarchical professors and snotty students. They'll appreciate the courtesy and can do a lot to make your law school life easier and better.

Some law schools serve alcoholic beverages at these functions. Be careful about consuming alcohol as a way to calm your nerves. This is not a good time to get intoxicated.

Make a friend.

While socializing, keep your eyes out for potential new friends. Every law student needs a dependable friend who will be there for them when the going gets tough. (*I'll be there for you, when you screw up in class; I'll be there for you, when your answers get trashed . . .* [57])

Fortunately, making friends in law school is easy because of the psychological bonding effects of group terror. In a famous social psychology experiment, researchers put a group of monkeys in the same cage with a group of lions. Monkeys and lions usually don't socialize because the lions eat the monkeys, which causes hard feelings. Early in the experiment, it appeared events would follow this customary pattern as the lions began chasing the monkeys and the monkeys began bonking the lions on the heads with coconuts.

At this point, the researchers inserted a Contracts professor into the cage who began conducting a Socratic dialogue about the doctrine of promissory estoppel. An amazing transformation occurred. The lions and monkeys immediately locked paws and began singing pub songs. Within a few minutes, the lions were giving the monkeys foot massages and the monkeys were encouraging the lions to get in touch with their inner cubs.

Okay, that wasn't a real experiment, but the basic point is sound. I can be shy, but on my first day of law school orientation I was desperate to make a friend. We were packed like matchsticks into an auditorium, sitting in alphabetical order. Speaker after speaker took the podium, but the only thing I remember them emphasizing was the lack of bathroom facilities in the law school. I'm sure they talked about other things, but that's what stood out. The way people went on and on about it, adequate restroom facilities seemed to be the most important issue in legal education.

---

[57]   With apologies to the Rembrandts.

After the speeches, we were divided into groups, still in alphabetical order. A 3L took our group on a tour of the law school. We traipsed in single file down hallways, through classrooms, and finally into the library, where in a narrow aisle between the stacks a large puddle blocked our passage. Everyone, including our 3L tour guide, stood stymied, staring at the puddle, until the guy behind me deadpanned, "I guess they weren't joking about the bathrooms." In the stress of the circumstances, this struck me as hilarious. I turned and introduced myself to James H. "Mac" McCarty, Jr. Mac and I went on to form a study group together and even became roommates. We spent many law school days and nights working and playing together.

Every student will find their own "Mac" in law school. I guarantee that the friendships you develop will be one of the best features of your legal education. Some of them will last a lifetime.

Visit your classrooms.

A great trial lawyer taught me the value of always visiting a courtroom in advance of a trial or big hearing to check out the lay of the land and get a feel for it. Familiarity with a place or situation prompts brain neurons known as "place cells" to fire, making us feel comfortable and at home. Studies show, for example, that if a person is shown a geometric shape for just one-thousandth of a second, far too quickly to register in the conscious mind, the person will like that shape better the next time they see it.

Visiting all your classrooms during orientation week will not only raise your comfort level, it will eliminate the added stress you'll suffer if you have to hunt them down for the first time in the rush between classes during those first days. Knowing where the rooms are also will help you avoid the embarrassing predicament of arriving late to class, something you want to avoid (see below). Moreover, an early visit will allow you to contemplate in advance where you want to sit, since you will be stuck in that seat all semester.

Don't Overcommit to Extra Activities

When you arrive at law school, you'll be besieged by upper-level students, and maybe some professors, to engage in a variety of "extra" or "outside" activities apart from your course work. A partial listing includes student organizations (including student government), community service projects, and social and political causes. It's all great stuff. Activities like these make students well-rounded people, assist others in need, and offer valuable networking opportunities.

The danger for 1Ls is that taking your eye off the ball by diverting time and focus from your studies risks damaging your academic success. First-year law school grades are disproportionately important. They determine who gets to continue in law school, keep scholarships, get research assistant positions, be eligible for law review, and have a dramatic impact on early job opportunities.

In the past, 1Ls were largely insulated from outside activities, but in recent years I've watched, fretting, as 1Ls have ratcheted up their involvement. A few reasons explain the shift. First, students are repeatedly told that networking is helpful to getting a job. It can be, but passing the bar and getting good grades are much bigger keys. Second, as student bodies have shrunk due to the declining pool of law school applicants (see Chapter 3), student organizations and other activity sponsors are in need of more warm bodies. Third, although some studies refute the conventional wisdom that Millennials are more service-minded than their predecessors, modern law students seem genuinely committed to making the world a better place.

I said at the beginning I'd offer you the same advice I would give my own kid if she were going to law school. While it's difficult advice to give because of the significant benefits of outside activities, I emphasize to my 1Ls that "it's okay to say no" when asked to participate in extra activities and I tell you the same thing here. Don't feel compelled to take on extra activities as a 1L. If you insist on doing so, don't overcommit.

The simple truth is that most 1Ls who take on heavy voluntary activities do not perform at a high academic level.

There are exceptions, of course, but you're safer assuming you will not be one of them.

As a check, I reached out to three high-achieving students, all of whom participated in substantial extra activities as upper-level students, seeking their honest feedback about my advice. In short, all of the students cautioned against taking on major extra commitments in the first year.

The class valedictorian wrote back saying:

> I would have to say that I agree with your theory of not getting too involved during your 1L year. My first semester I would attend lunchtime meetings for different organizations to determine where I would like to get involved in the future, but that was pretty much the extent of my involvement in anything. The rest of my time was dedicated to studying and preparing for class every single day.

She went on to explain how she slowly forayed into outside activities beginning halfway through her second year.

Another top student recommended more strongly that 1Ls eschew all outside law school activities:

> I do not think 1Ls should get involved in student organizations. . . . I did not become involved in student organizations and focused on preparing for classes, periodically reviewing notes, and outlining. When I wasn't working on school stuff, I spent my time relaxing with family and friends. I think this was one of the best decisions I made throughout law school. It allowed me to start out OCIs [On-Campus Interviews] with a high rank, which resulted in summer clerkship offers that eventually turned into permanent job offers. This was all from only my first-year grades. Those 1L grades literally defined my career path.

A third top student began her reply by touting the many benefits of her outside activities, but added:

> Having said all that, I don't necessarily disagree with your assertion at all. I was not involved in anything outside of school my first semester, and I only really jumped into stuff

with PALS [Public Action Law Society] after knowing I was on solid footing grades-wise first semester. I don't think I ever realized as a 1L how much my grades mattered (as crazy as it is, my employer for the future only ever saw my 1L grades). . . . Employers don't care nearly as much about your "outside involvement," and the best way to distinguish yourself in my experience is to be as competent as possible and as high in your class as possible.

Go all in the first year. Give academic success your best shot. Stay focused on it. Save major involvement in extra activities for your 2L and 3L years. They'll still be there. See Chapter 24 for more information about co- and extracurricular law school activities.

Start Thinking About Study Group Partners

As you're getting to know your new classmates during the first days and weeks of class, think about whether they might be good matches for a "study group," a popular law school study method. While it might seem too soon, cliques form early in law school and once formed can be hard to break into. Study groups tend to naturally evolve from them.

Study groups usually comprise three to five students who meet regularly throughout the semester to compare class notes, prepare course outlines, and work through practice exams. Working with a group allows individual members to clarify and correct their understanding of the law while also serving the important function of periodic review of the material. Study groups also function as valuable social and emotional support networks.

Whether you will benefit from a study group depends on two principal factors: your individual learning style and the "fit" among the group members. Extraverts, for example, may take to group study better than introverts. I joined a study group early in my first semester of law school because I thought it was the thing to do. I might have been influenced by the fact that study groups were featured so prominently in the movie, *The Paper Chase*, which we were all very much into at the time.

The group was made up of me and my new buddy Mac and a woman named Lynn. Three weeks in Lynn had the good judgment to quit. Her reason was something like: "All you two ever do is debate. We never get anywhere." She was right. Mac and I wasted hours of precious time arguing every point, in part just for the sake of the debate. In retrospect, my only surprise was that it took Lynn three weeks to jump off that train wreck. After that, I rarely participated in group study. I discovered I studied more effectively on my own.

But many students swear by study groups. Asked for the number one piece of advice she would give to a close loved one starting law school, one student said:

> Group study is key! I formed a study group (leading to great friendships) with two other classmates, and we surrounded ourselves with class discussion throughout the day. To our surprise, all of our ranks after the first semester were inside the top ten. The odds of it being purely coincidental seem pretty minimal.

Whether to join a study group is a classic example of a law school decision where you should let *your* personality and learning style—not someone else's advice—guide your decision-making. Join a study group if it feels right to you. Don't if it doesn't.

Before forming or joining a study group, think hard about the people with whom you'll be collaborating. Discuss your objectives and strategies in advance. Make sure they are clearly articulated and everyone in the group is on the same page. When you meet, stay on task. Keep socializing separate from study sessions. Socializing is an add-on benefit of a study group, but business should be business when you gather to study. Plan separate social events for the group.

Take a (Good) Seat

The Socratic method entails professors calling on students frequently. To do that effectively in large classes, they use seating charts. Your professors will pass around a seating chart—sometimes with advance notice but sometimes on the first day—and you'll be stuck in that seat for the entire semester. Some students even grow emotionally attached to their seats:

Sometimes I feel as attached to my seat as to my loved ones. I always get to exams early to sit in my same seat. Even in later semesters, I always try to get that same seat. It has become a comfort zone of normalcy and reliability in the midst of the chaos.

In the chapter on types of law students (Chapter 4), I differentiated the Backburners from the Front Row Crowd in general terms. Let's investigate in more detail why you should resist the natural temptation to sit in the back.

Non-law school educators have conducted a variety of studies on the relationship of seat choice to student personality-type and academic performance. They support one proposition quite clearly: students who choose to sit in the front of the room are generally better students. They have higher GPAs, participate more frequently in class, and receive better grades in the course.[58]

Several studies have linked this better performance to personality differences between students who choose to sit in front and those who choose the back. In other words, the research suggests that students who sit in front by choice do better because better students choose to sit in front. Correlatively, students who sit in the back tend to have more negative attitudes about school and being engaged.[59]

Does sitting in back actually *cause* poorer performance? Study results are mixed.[60] Nevertheless, common sense suggests several reasons why seat choice could improve your law school experience.

You can hear much better in front. Under the Socratic method, much of the talking is done by students. While most law

---

[58] *See* Mary Ellen Benedict & John Hoag, *Seating Location in Large Lectures: Are Seating Preferences or Location Related to Course Performance?*, 35 J. ECON. EDUC. 215 (2004).

[59] *See* Herbert J. Walberg, *Physical and Psychological Distance in the Classroom*, 77 SCH. REV. 64 (1969).

[60] *Compare* Katherine K. Perkins & Carl E. Wieman, *The Surprising Impact of Seat Location on Student Performance*, 43 PHYSICS TCHR. 30 (2005) (finding that students in the back of the room were six times as likely to receive *F*s in the course as students sitting in the front of the room), *with* Steven Kalinowski & Mark L. Taper, *The Effect of Seat Location on Exam Grades and Student Perceptions in an Introductory Biology Class*, 36 J.C. SCI. TEACHING 54 (2007) (finding no difference).

professors speak loudly enough for people in the back to hear them, most law students do not. Moreover, students usually are facing the front when speaking, naturally detracting from the ability of students behind them to hear what they're saying. On several occasions, I've sat in the back of law school classrooms observing other professors' classes, dismayed by my inability to hear student comments even in well-designed classrooms. Many law school classrooms are not well-designed. They're acoustical black holes.

You'll also be able to see better. Many professors use technology, such as PowerPoint slides projected on a screen, as visual aids, but many others still write on the board. Generally, anything a law professor deems worthy of taking the time to write on a board is important. Despite their sometimes larger-than-life personas, many professors write on the board in normal-sized (i.e., small) handwriting.

There are fewer focus-breakers to contend with up front. As discussed below, many students misuse their laptops to browse the web, etc., which is distracting to the students around them. Fewer students in front of you means fewer of these distractions.

Also, people in the very front tend to get cold-called on less often than other students. One reason is that it's hard for students in back to hear them. They may also fall below the professor's sight-line. Finally, even if only unconsciously, professors may want to reward them for their front-row courage.

One of the largest benefits of sitting up front is that your professors are more likely to get to know you and there are definite benefits attached to that (see Chapter 9).

Even assuming seating has no effect on academic performance, sitting in front will change the manner in which you experience law school. You'll be a participant in your class community, rather than merely an observer from a different zip code. Have you ever attended a play or concert and sat in the front? It's like attending a completely different event compared to sitting in the back. It's well established by research that active learning is much more effective than passive learning and being close to the action means that students in front almost can't help but be engaged in the class.

Make a Habit of Backing Up Your Computer Work Daily

From day one, make a habit of backing up all of your computer work daily, including your case briefs, class notes, outlines, and drafts of assignments for your legal research and writing courses. This rule is so basic, yet every year I hear sad stories from students who lost all of their computerized materials when their computers crashed or were stolen. Last year one of my students lost everything when his computer burned up in a car fire!

Options for backing up computer materials include: (1) cloud storage; (2) USB sticks; or (3) emailing documents to yourself.

Three different manuscript readers, all of whom have witnessed the terrible consequences of student computer disasters, urged me to emphasize more strongly the need to frequently back up your work, so let me repeat: **REGULARLY BACK UP ALL YOUR COMPUTER WORK!** Is that enough emphasis?

Classroom Etiquette

Law school classes are conducted more formally than most undergraduate classes, especially in the first year. For example, traditionally, all first-year professors referred to students by their surnames, although today's young profs are much more likely to use first names. The expectations of student conduct and performance are substantially higher than in undergraduate programs. To avoid embarrassing yourself, offending your professors, and hurting your academic performance, follow these guidelines for classroom etiquette:

Be prepared.

As mentioned above, you will receive assignments *in advance* of the first class for each course. Don't get caught being anything less than fully prepared, particularly in the first days. An early unpleasant classroom incident could taint your view of law school, as well as how you are viewed by others.

Many law professors follow an approach of being much sterner at the beginning of a course and then gradually becoming more laidback as the semester progresses. The goal is to set a tone in line with the expectations of a professional school. It's always easier for a professor to move from being strict to less strict, whereas it's nearly impossible for a professor to move effectively in the other direction; that is, from being easygoing or friendly to strict. This approach and mentality means that professors are more likely early on to "make examples" of students who commit classroom infractions.

For most professors, there is no legitimate excuse for being unprepared on the first day of law school. Here are some sample explanations from unprepared students and the likely mental reaction of the professor:

Student explanation: "I didn't know we had assignments for the first day."

Professor's thought process: "Everyone else figured it out. Therefore, you are either lying or mentally defective."

Student explanation: "The bookstore ran out of books."

Professor's thought process: "You should have tracked down a book somewhere else, photocopied the assignment from a classmate's book, or come to me for help."

Student explanation: "I had a family emergency yesterday when I intended to prepare for class."

Professor's thought process: "You shouldn't have waited until yesterday."

What exactly does "being prepared" mean? As to each principal case assigned, you should know: (1) the relevant facts; (2) the procedural history that resulted in the case being heard by an appellate court (e.g., the trial court dismissed the complaint filed by the plaintiff and the plaintiff is appealing, or the trial court gave a legal instruction to the jury that the defendant asserts was incorrect and the defendant is appealing); (3) who won the case; (4) the substantive legal issue in the case; (5) the rule adopted by the court to resolve the substantive issue; and (6) the court's reasoning. We'll talk much more about these components in the case-briefing chapter (Chapter 11).

Be on time.

Don't arrive late to class. Most law professors expect students to be punctual. It's distracting to everyone when students arrive late. Nevertheless, even when this expectation is made clear to students during orientation and in course materials, the beginning of a new school year is often marked by uncomfortable incidents in which one or more students stroll casually into the room after class has begun, only to be publicly called out for it by the professor.

When students arrive late to my class, I give them what my students call, affectionately or not, "the evil eye." I stop everything and maximize discomfort by watching in silence as the student fumbles toward his seat. Why do I do it? Not to be cruel. I don't enjoy embarrassing students. I do it as a deterrent. I do it to let students know they have entered professional school, where learning is taken seriously. I do it because in the real legal world lawyers are expected to be on time.

My first job after law school was as a law clerk to U.S. District Court Judge Charles R. Scott, Middle District of Florida. Judge Scott taught me many valuable lessons about both life and law, including: don't ever show up late. He was a kind man with a great sense of humor and judicial temperament, *except* when lawyers disrespected the court by arriving late to hearings or trials. I can still picture the scene at a trial where one of the lawyers came back late from lunch, with everyone, including the jury, waiting. In his booming voice, Judge Scott said, "So, counselor, I suppose you think your time is more valuable than the court's time and the time of these good jurors, sacrificing their jobs and families to serve their civic duty." I remember looking at the jurors, who were nodding along, as if saying "damn right," and thinking, that lawyer just lost his case. Better to learn these lessons in law school.

Of course, unexpected events arise that can cause even the most diligent students to arrive late. If that happens to you, simply apologize to the professor before (via email if you know you're going to be late) or after the class. Punctuality rules are aimed principally at the Chronically Late (see Chapter 4), those students who, without some kind of deterrent, will regularly barge into classes late.

I'll share two inside secrets with you about punctuality. First, your classmates may not tell you, but they don't appreciate the distraction of late-arriving students either. I hear from these students all the time. They're paying a lot of money to get the best education they can.

Second, many professors will not openly react to students who arrive late even though they care deeply about it. I remember a colleague at one school who stormed into my office seething about a particular student who routinely arrived late. I recall the term "sonofabitch" being liberally sprinkled throughout the conversation. I asked the professor why he didn't simply lay down the law on punctuality. He said he didn't like conflict and that it didn't fit his personality. Carrying a deep-seated grudge against the tardy, however, apparently did.

Having said all that, you will learn that some professors really don't care about students being on time. A few profs even make a habit of arriving late themselves.

Mute electronic devices.

Yes, of course it's a no-brainer, but it still happens, so it's worth mentioning. One of my former colleagues actually gives a "cell phone quiz" if a phone goes off—a real pop quiz that counts as part of the final grade.

Don't misuse your computer.

Unless otherwise specified by your professor, computers may be used in class only for taking notes. Do not use it to browse the web, play games, send messages, or any other purpose. This is a much bigger issue among law professors than you could imagine. Many law professors ban computers in class. Many others (including yours truly) are truly torn. They want to eliminate computer multitasking in class, but don't want to hurt students by taking away an important writing tool students depend on.

I'm a realist. I know from experience this is a piece of advice that many people will ignore. That's why I'm going to engage in what might seem like overkill on the subject in the hope your rational self-interest will persuade you to make the right decision.

Good Reasons Not to Multitask on Your Computer in Class

You can't learn as effectively. The law is complex. In most courses, a majority of what you will need to know for the exam will be derived from classroom elucidation of the reading assignments, not from the reading itself. It will require 100 percent of your mental processing power.

Some students scoff at the Luddites who doubt their prowess at multitasking, who dare to question their ability to learn the Rule Against Perpetuities and check sports scores at the same time. But studies show unequivocally that the human brain cannot engage in simultaneous tasks without the performance of one or both tasks suffering.

Research shows people lose considerable thinking-time each time they switch tasks, are more prone to commit cognitive errors while switching tasks, and that habitual multitasking may permanently change the thinking process in ways that make it difficult for people to focus even when they want to.[61] A 2015 survey-based study of more than 350 college students found that frequent in-class multitaskers received lower grades, even after taking into account their perceived skill at multitasking.[62]

One study found that multitasking does not necessarily decrease the overall ability to learn, but negatively affects the kind of learning used to acquire new concepts and information and to engage in deep analysis—learning abilities that are crucial to law students. Researchers did MRI brain imaging of twenty-somethings engaged in dual-task learning. The brain imaging showed that multitaskers engaged in "habit learning" rather than "declarative learning." Habit learning relies on a portion of the brain used for repetitive skills, whereas declarative learning involves a portion of the brain used for storing and recalling information. The researchers concluded

---

[61]   Anne Enquist, *Multitasking and Legal Writing,* 18 PERSP.: TEACHING LEGAL RES. & WRITING 7, 7–8 (2009) (discussing each of these items).

[62]   Saraswathi Bellur et al., *Make It Our Time: In Class Multitaskers Have Lower Academic Performance,* 53 COMPUTERS HUM. BEHAV. 63 (2015).

that even though people can learn while multitasking, they can't learn the material as well or adapt it to changing conditions.[63]

In short, while some people are adept at doing several tasks simultaneously, they can't do them all well because of the brain's limited processing ability. The result is that if your professor is explaining personal jurisdiction at the same time you're messaging your pal to see what time everyone is meeting for happy hour, something's going to give. Also be aware that students underestimate the amount of time they spend off-task on their computers in class. In one study, a student was found to be opening an average of 173 different windows per lecture.[64]

It's rude and disrespectful to your classmates. One complaint students have about computer bans in classes is that they are paternalistic. Basically, this amounts to an argument that students enjoy an inalienable academic right to shoot themselves in the foot. Assuming arguendo that students possess this liberty interest, it overlooks that students who abuse computer privileges cause harm to the energy and dynamics of the entire class when they mentally "check out."

Closer to home (aka your assigned seat), playing around on your computer is distracting to nearby classmates. As one student complained about messaging, "One message sent during class has the possibility of distracting six people: two persons on each side of the recipient, the recipient, the sender, and perhaps two people behind the recipient. That's a lot of downtime in class for one little message."

Most professors have explicit policies against it. Violating any explicit class policy can constitute academic misconduct. Occasionally, computer misuse even crosses the boundary into the realm of overt cheating. Incidents have occurred where students have messaged answers to professors' questions to their classmates being called on.

Everyone can see what you're doing. Not only are you violating class policy and the professor's trust by misusing your

---

[63]   *See* Karin Foerde et al., *Modulation of Competing Memory Systems by Distraction*, 103 PROC. NAT'L ACAD. SCI. 11778 (2006).

[64]   *See* James M. Kraushaar & David C. Novak, *Examining the Effects of Student Multitasking with Laptops During the Lecture*, 21 J. INFO. SYS. EDUC. 241, 246 (2010).

computer, you're doing it in front of a large group of eyewitnesses. Some students will lose respect for classmates who violate explicit law school or class rules. Some will rat them out to the professor. The professor, in turn, whether or not she ever addresses the issue with you, may never trust you again.

If you're a well-intentioned student who wants to stay on task but fears you simply won't be able to resist the siren call of the internet during class, turn off your wi-fi before class or download a program (many are available) that allows you to block internet access or access to particular sites during specified time periods.

In general, in conducting yourself in class, keep in mind that your professors can see what's going on out there in the classroom. It always cracks me up that some students seem to think they're protected by a Harry Potter-type cloak of invisibility just because they're sitting in a group of people. Professors notice when students yawn, smirk, sigh heavily, roll their eyes, talk to their seat neighbors, or appear to be playing on their computers. Behave professionally in the classroom.

* * *

Following the suggestions in this chapter will help you get off to a solid, trauma-free start in law school. Just as important, following the advice will put you on the right path to becoming a professional, which is what you are training to be. While most of the admonishments are common sense, some law students routinely ignore or violate them, often proclaiming ignorance.

Don't think you're too smart to fall prey to them. Conceit can make you blind to the obvious.

CHAPTER 7

THE SOCRATIC AND CASE METHODS

"Mr. Smith, what's a tort?"

Except for the student's name changing, those are often the first words I utter at my initial Torts class of a new academic year. No introduction, no "Let's get to know each other" chatting, no overview of the class or review of class policies, not even a "Hi, I'm McClurg." I enter the classroom, set my book and notes on the podium, look at the class roster, pick a name, and ask the question. I'm expecting the textbook answer—literally. When a student gives the right answer (it's not a difficult question—the definition is in the second sentence of the initial reading assignment), I start leading the student through a series of hypothetical fact patterns designed to explore what conduct might or might not qualify as a tort under the definition. And, in the words of legendary comedian Jackie Gleason, *awaaaaay we go* with the Socratic method of law school teaching.

Despite continuing criticism, the Socratic method has been, is, and will likely remain law school's "signature pedagogy."[65] The Socratic method involves professors calling on students, typically without prior notice, to recite and analyze cases (i.e., written judicial opinions) and the legal principles raised therein. Most incoming law students are at least somewhat familiar with the Socratic method, usually through having heard exaggerated horror stories about it or from fictionalized accounts in movies such as *The Paper Chase* and *Legally Blonde* or books like Scott Turow's *One L*.

When I was a law student, my main question about the Socratic method was "Why?" Why are the professors doing this to us? Why all the questions? Why no answers? Why don't they just tell us what the law is? Here's why.

---

[65] *See* CARNEGIE FOUNDATION REPORT, *supra*, at 23–24 (characterizing the Socratic method in these terms).

How a Man Named Christopher Columbus Langdell Changed Your Life

The Socratic method is credited to and named after Socrates (470–399 BC), a Greek philosopher who engaged in continuous questioning of his students in a quest to discover moral and ethical truths. Along the way, he exposed fallacies in their reasoning, first, by getting students to commit to certain positions, and then by asking questions designed to expose contradictions or other flaws in those positions. A hallmark of his method was that he only asked questions. He rarely provided answers.

The origins of the Socratic method in law school teaching are traceable back to the 1870s and the inception of what is known as the "case method." To make any sense of the Socratic method, one must understand the case method. The two methods are inextricably intertwined.

In the old days, law was taught in U.S. law schools principally through a lecture method. Students would read explanations of the law in textbooks, professors would expand on that law in lectures, and students would be tested principally on their ability for rote memorization. But in the 1870s along came Christopher Columbus Langdell, the man credited with, or blamed for, irrevocably changing the way U.S. law students learn.

Langdell, a professor and later dean of Harvard Law School, believed that true mastery of the law could not be achieved by simply memorizing it. Rather, students had to develop a facility for *applying* legal principles to the varied fact patterns that lead to legal disputes, what he called "the ever-tangled skein of human affairs."[66] By understanding how law is applied, Langdell believed students would be able to transfer what they learned in one context and apply it in other contexts. To implement his vision, he came up with the idea to replace explanatory textbooks with "casebooks" filled with appellate judicial opinions.

---

[66]   Peggy Cooper Davis & Elizabeth Ehrenfest Steinglass, *A Dialogue About Socratic Teaching*, 23 N.Y.U. REV. L. & SOC. CHANGE 249, 263 (1997) (quoting Langdell).

I still recall coming home from the bookstore before starting law school with my shiny new casebooks. I sat down and opened my Contracts book with excited anticipation. I was about to learn "law" for the first time! But I couldn't find any; well, not any I could make sense of. There was no explanation of contracts law, not even a definition of what constitutes a contract, just hundreds of pages of judicial opinions, many of them old and opaquely written. I started reading the first case, but couldn't make heads or tails of it. I had no idea what the point was. If I had known then about Christopher Langdell, I probably would have cursed him. Casebooks haven't changed much. While most modern casebooks do contain explanatory notes following the cases, the cases themselves remain the primary vehicle for learning law in U.S. law schools.[67]

Under the case method, students are expected to do the heavy lifting. Instead of sitting passively listening to lectures, the case method requires students to think critically and discover the law on their own in response to questions posed by the professors.[68] The Socratic dialogue method of teaching developed as an instrument for implementing the case method. Think of it as the steering mechanism that guides the case method vehicle.

How It Works

The classic portrayal of the Socratic method in law school came from the 1973 movie, *The Paper Chase*, based on John Jay Osborn's book of the same name. Actor John Houseman won an Oscar for his portrayal of the curmudgeonly, imperious Professor Charles Kingsfield, a fictional Contracts professor at Harvard Law School, who torments first-year student James T. Hart, played by Timothy Bottoms. The movie is a classic that all first-year law students should watch.

---

[67] Some law book publishers are introducing new series of law school textbooks that go much lighter on judicial opinions and heavier on explanation and examples. West Academic Publishing's *Learning Series* is one example.

[68] *See generally id.* (exploring the history and present use of the Socratic method); David D. Garner, *The Continuing Vitality of the Case Method in the Twenty-First Century*, 2000 BYU EDUC. & L.J. 307 (2000) (providing history and summary of the case method).

In the movie, Kingsfield is a terror, famously instructing his Contracts students in that great John Houseman voice: "You come in here with skulls full of mush and leave thinking like a lawyer." When poor Hart screws up in class, Kingsfield tells him: "Mr. Hart, here is a dime. Take it, call your mother, and tell her there is serious doubt about you ever becoming a lawyer."

Is this a dated portrayal of legal education? Of course it is. You can't make a phone call for a dime anymore. You can't even find a pay phone. Today, Hart would simply minimize his Netflix screen and send his mom an iMessage. Houseman's performance was exaggerated for dramatic effect, but it did capture the essentials of how the Socratic method operates. The traditional model incorporated these essential components:

- Cold-calling on a student from a seating chart.

- Asking the student to "state the case," which entails narrating the facts and other aspects about the case, such as its procedural history, issue, holding, and reasoning.

- Testing the student's understanding of the case with more questions, which often include hypothetical fact patterns that require the student to interpret and apply the legal principle(s) from the case. This is the component of the Socratic method most closely connected with the oft-stated goal of the method to teach students to "think like a lawyer."

- Failing to offer concrete answers to the questions asked based on the assumption that the students, through the dialogue, should be able to figure out the answers on their own.

Depending on the skill and technique of the professor, for students, the whole thing can come off as resembling a bizarre treasure hunt in which neither the professor nor the casebook provides the answers—at least not directly. In fact, most of the answers are contained in or inferable from the judicial opinions in the casebooks, but they're often hidden between the lines.

Rumors of the Death of the Socratic Method Are Exaggerated

Some have proclaimed the demise of the Socratic method in U.S. law schools. One professor, an advocate of the method, wrote that "[p]opular myth has it that the Socratic method is pervasive in American law schools," adding that "nothing could be further from the truth."[69] But a different writer said "[t]he Socratic Method remains the primary method of law teaching today."[70]

Who's right? Both. The disagreement stems from problems in defining the Socratic method. In its original form as a dialectical "flight of the imagination through a world of allegories, parables and myths,"[71] the method is not only dead, it probably never lived in legal education in the first place because most law professors and students simply do not possess the skill or knowledge to carry it out.

In its modern law school image as a teaching method where the professor "hides the ball" and then humiliates students who can't find it, that too is clearly on the wane. Most professors, especially younger ones, practice what they call a "modified Socratic method," which is much less harsh than the traditional version. More on that in the Facts and Myths section below.

But broadly defined as a style of teaching in which professors call on students, usually without warning, expecting informed, intelligent answers as part of a back and forth exchange (as opposed to simply lecturing), the Socratic style does indeed remain the dominant teaching methodology in U.S. law schools, at least in the first year.

Before proceeding, it should be noted that professors do use other teaching approaches. Most professors do at least some

---

[69] Donald G. Marshall, Socratic Method and the Irreducible Core of Legal Education, Presentation at Law Alumni Distinguished Teacher Inauguration (Jan. 19, 1994), in 90 MINN. L. REV. 1, 2 (2005).

[70] Cynthia G. Hawkins-Leon, The Socratic Method-Problem Method Dichotomy: The Debate Over Teaching Method Continues, 1998 BYU EDUC. & L.J. 1, 5 (1998).

[71] Paul N. Savoy, Toward A New Politics of Legal Education, 79 YALE L.J. 444, 468 (1970).

lecturing. Some do a large amount of it.[72] Some professors use a "problem method" in which students read cases and/or textual explanation and apply them to solve written problems, but the problem method usually entails Socratic-style questioning. Some doctrinal professors[73] assign drafting or other skills-based exercises and some use small-group breakout discussions and projects. But if you ask any former or current law student what first-year law school classes are like, they're likely to focus on the Socratic method.

With So Much Criticism, Why Do Professors Still Use the Socratic and Case Methods?

The Socratic and case methods have faced resistance since their inception. Common criticisms include that the methods are intimidating, humiliating, alienating, bewildering, and inefficient, yet most first-year professors continue to use them. Why? Because we genuinely believe that the combination of the Socratic and case methods is the most effective way to train new law students to develop the critical-thinking skills they will need as lawyers.[74] Like a lot of students, I was terrified of the Socratic method back in law school. As a professor, however, I came to appreciate the usefulness of dialectical questioning as a tool for teaching students to discover knowledge on their own. Also, it's fun scaring the hell out of people.

Seriously, in the right hands the Socratic and case methods can be excellent tools for guiding students to "think like a lawyer," which simply means learning to reason well. As

---

[72]   Current data does not exist, but Professor Stephen Friedland surveyed law professors back in the mid-1990s to determine how they teach. He sent out approximately 2,000 questionnaires, to which he received 574 completed responses. Ninety-seven percent of the respondents said they use the Socratic method at least some of the time in first-year courses, with 30 percent reporting they use it most of the time, and 41 percent reporting they use it often. Comparatively, only 31 percent of the professors surveyed reported that they use a lecture method "some of the time" in first-year courses (a percentage that soared to 94 percent in upper-level courses). *See* Steven I. Friedland, *How We Teach: A Survey of Teaching Techniques in American Law Schools*, 20 SEATTLE U. L. REV. 1 (1996).

[73]   In your Legal Research and Writing course, which is a "skills course," you will be largely spared the Socratic method.

[74]   After visiting sixteen law schools across the country, the authors of the 2007 *Carnegie Foundation Report* on legal education concluded that "nearly all the law faculty" with whom they spoke endorsed the case-dialogue method as the best way to train 1Ls in "the craft of legal reasoning." *See* CARNEGIE FOUNDATION REPORT, *supra*, at 66.

Langdell recognized, you could memorize all the legal rules in the world, but still be a lousy lawyer. Good lawyering is about problem-solving and the Socratic and case methods are intended to force students to learn by doing rather than simply by being told how it is done.

The difference in the way 1Ls think about legal problems at the beginning and end of the first year is dramatic. Even the Socratic-haters would be hard-pressed to deny that they really did arrive at law school with "skulls full of mush," yet exited the Socratic arena as facile thinkers and astute legal problem-solvers. Look at this comment from a 1L two weeks away from finishing his first year:

> Just the other week I was eating lunch with some of my section friends and reading through a case for class. Without thinking, I said something like, "Don't you all think that we are so much better at reading cases now?" They looked at me like I just stated the most obvious thing in the world. I had just never really thought of it like that. When you stop and think about the evolution of your abilities from the beginning of the year to the end, it is really astonishing.

Another student recognized, "When the professor is asking questions and things finally 'click' in my head, I'm much more likely to understand and remember what I learned than if the professor had just told me straight out."

The Socratic method has benefits in addition to fostering legal reasoning skills. It helps train students to think on their feet and articulate their reasoning, vital abilities for any lawyer. It provides a strong incentive for students to be prepared, substantially enhancing the quality of the classroom experience for all involved. While the level of preparation varies among students, 1Ls rarely come to class unprepared, a big difference from most undergraduate classes. One big reason is that they don't want to be publicly embarrassed in front of their peers and professors if called on.

The Socratic method also facilitates a much more interesting exploration of legal issues than pure lecturing, the principal realistic option in large first-year classes. As one student said:

I love how different the classes in law school are as opposed to undergrad. I love the non-lecture format of classes because they are so much more interesting. Though I was scared of the Socratic method, I find it to be a much better way to learn and makes class much more interesting.

Is it a perfect methodology? Far from it. First, the success of the method is heavily dependent on not only the preparation and intellectual level of the students, but the skill of the professor. As one colleague commented in reading this chapter, "Some professors do it well, but I'm not sure that's the norm." Some professors simply ask questions to see who is prepared or ask random questions without using the answers as means to an end. As one student wrote: "It annoys me when professors use a Q & A just to see if we prepared a brief, rather than to engage in a genuine Socratic dialogue designed to expose fallacies and reveal truth."

Also, the large size of law school classes renders most students passive bystanders in the process at any given time. A true Socratic dialogue envisions one-on-one instruction or small group tutorials. But even students who aren't directly participating learn from watching and listening to Socratic dialoguing. The *Carnegie Foundation Report* on legal education observed that one way in which the Socratic method enhances student intellectual development is through *modeling*; that is, the students learn by watching and modeling the cognitive skills of the professor displayed during case-dialoguing.[75]

Other shortcomings of the Socratic method are discussed in the Facts and Myths section below, but when all is said and done, I remain convinced that the Socratic method, while imperfect, beats the viable alternatives for training 1Ls to conduct legal analysis.

---

[75]   The *Carnegie Foundation Report* classified law school case-dialoguing as a type of "cognitive apprenticeship" in which student intellectual development occurs through faculty-student interaction. Observing professor-student Socratic exchanges at sixteen law schools, the report's authors observed professors employing four basic apprenticeship teaching methods identified by cognitive theorists: *modeling*, by demonstrating in class the type of cognitive skills the professor seeks to instill in the students; *coaching*, by providing guidance and feedback; *scaffolding*, by providing support for students who haven't yet mastered critical-thinking skills; and *fading*, by encouraging students to go it alone when they've shown themselves prepared to do so. *See id.* at 60–61.

Sample Socratic Dialogue

With that introduction, let's see what the Socratic method looks like in action. Back in the day, when I taught at the University of Arkansas at Little Rock School of Law, I asked a research assistant to videotape several Torts classes in preparation for a presentation at the Institute for Law School Teaching. The following excerpted transcript from one of those tapes will give you an idea of how the Socratic method works.[76]

The issue under discussion is defamation law (i.e., libel and slander), a topic that, when covered in first-year Torts, is taken up near the end of the course. Specifically, we were exploring the famous 1964 U.S. Supreme Court case of *New York Times v. Sullivan*,[77] where the Court held the First Amendment limits the ability of states to award tort damages for defamation of public officials.

Without being overly specific, the Court imposed a high hurdle known as the "actual malice" test that public officials (later extended to include any public figure) are required to prove to recover damages for defamation. The test requires a public official to prove that the defendant knew the defamatory statement was false or published the statement in reckless disregard of whether it was true or false, which the Court later interpreted to mean that the plaintiff must prove the defendant subjectively (i.e., personally, in his own mind) entertained serious doubts as to the truth of the statement. Ever wonder why you don't hear about more defamation suits being brought by public officials or public figures? *New York Times v. Sullivan* is the reason.

On the video, the back and forth exchange set forth below, which explores the application of the *New York Times* test to a hypothetical, was lively, rapid-fire action. The tone of some of my questions, not apparent from the cold text, was sarcastic. But by this point, the students knew how to play the Socratic game.

---

[76]   Reading this Socratic excerpt, one of my research assistants noted that my Socratic dialoguing at the beginning of Torts was "far less laidback" than at the end of the course, which is when the discussion below took place. As previously mentioned, many professors tend to be tougher, for lack of a better word, at the beginning of a course than at the end.

[77]   376 U.S. 254 (1964).

They didn't take my questioning personally, nor should they have. The discussion involves three students, whom I'll call Mr. Forbes, Ms. Davidson, and Ms. Carvel and label as S1, S2, and S3 in the transcript.

The discussion began with a good deal of lecture and dialoguing about the case itself. We pick it up just after, in good Socratic fashion, I got Mr. Forbes to commit himself to the desirability of the actual malice test as a means for protecting free speech:

Me: Mr. Forbes, let me give you a hypothetical. Suppose we have a candidate running for public office. He's running for governor of the state. He's a man who has led an exemplary life. As far as we know, there are no blemishes on his record of any significance. Shortly before the election, an anonymous source calls the state's largest newspaper and says "I have personal information that this person has sexually abused children." The reporter tries to ask questions, but the caller says, "I'm sorry. It's just too personal. But the people need to know." Then hangs up. The newspaper publishes the allegation that the person running for governor is a child molester. It's false—completely false. Can he win? Can he prove actual malice under *New York Times v. Sullivan*?

S1: Did the newspaper know that it was false?

Me: All they knew is what I've told you. It was a tip from an anonymous source. They didn't check it out. They didn't investigate it.

S1: I don't think the plaintiff can prove actual malice. He can show negligence. They obviously should have investigated. But that's not enough.

Me: Why can't he prove actual malice?

S1: It doesn't satisfy the test.

Me: Should they be able to get away with that? This person's life has been ruined. He lost the governorship. Would you vote for somebody if there were allegations out there that they had abused children?

S1: I don't know. I think probably not.

Me: We can certainly imagine a lot of people thinking that, "Even if it's *possibly* true, I don't think I want that person as governor."

S1: Public officials have to put up with a lot of things that are said about them that I think we know as a society, often times, are questionable whether they're true or not.

Me: Is that a fair price to expect a person seeking government office to pay? Should they have to put up with that? Ms. Davidson? [Raised hand to volunteer.]

S2: I'd just say that's an oversimplified hypothetical because people in the news business just aren't going to take one anonymous tip and publish something like that, something that's so defamatory and inappropriate. So they're going to follow up and—

Me: Let's suppose in this case they didn't follow up.

S2: But they are not going to do that because they know they're going to get sued and lose.

Me: But that's my question, are they going to lose? Mr. Forbes said they're not going to lose.

S2: Under the actual malice test? Well, I guess they wouldn't lose unless what the newspaper did was reckless disregard for the truth.

Me: Based on the facts I gave you, do we have any evidence that they knew it was false?

S2: No.

Me: Do we have any evidence that they in fact, and can we prove, that they entertained—in their heads—serious doubts as to whether it was true or false?

S2: No, I guess not.

Me: So that would mean that under the actual malice test, the newspaper would win.

S2: But I think that those instances are so rare that we need to protect it just as much as we need to protect the times when it's true.

Me: So you're a fan of the actual malice test?

S2: I think, well, I don't know, I'm not sure I really like the actual malice test, but I like protecting free speech at all costs.

Me: Well, then you love the actual malice test because that's basically what it does. It protects speech at almost all costs. Here, the cost is that an innocent person who has led an unblemished life has had his life completely ruined by a false, unsupported allegation and has no remedy.

S2: I think the court said in *New York Times v. Sullivan* that the value of free speech to society is worth more than one person's reputation. We have a greater good that we're concerned with and that's the public's right to free speech. It's a utilitarian view.

Me: That is what they did, but, of course, it's not going to be just one individual. It's going to be some number of individuals. The question is, where do we strike the balance between free speech and the states' interest in protecting the reputational rights of its citizens? Did the court strike the balance in the right place? In this case, you feel comfortable that this person's life has been ruined by a false allegation and he has no remedy whatsoever? He's just "one individual." One very sad individual.

S2: I think he'll have a remedy.

Me: What remedy?

S2: They have spin doctors who work for them. They'll fix it somehow.

Me: Oh yeah, it's easy to get around an allegation of being a child molester. It's no big deal, just spin it a little. "Oh well, I wasn't a child *molester*, I was a . . ."—how are we going to spin that one?

S2: It's a shame, but it's the price we pay to protect free speech. So yeah, it's too bad, but I don't have a high opinion of public officials anyway.

Me: Ms. Carvel? [Raised hand to volunteer.]

S3: I was just going to say because they are public officials, they have an opportunity to speak to the public and defend themselves.

Me: Okay, that's true.

S3: Also, because they are unprotected, I think people will look at those statements and not take them as seriously because they are commonly done.

Me: Ms. Carvel, I've heard some of the most audacious stories about people right here at the law school. Have you heard any? About the students, the faculty. I'm thinking surely people couldn't possibly believe that. But then talking to students, I realize people do believe them—just because someone says it, people believe it. If you print it in the newspaper, don't you think a lot of people are going to believe it, even if it's completely preposterous?

S3: Yeah, but I go back to the person is probably going to be able to defend themselves. I agree there are a lot of negative aspects to it, but they are in a position to defend themselves compared to a person who is not a public figure.

Me: That's a very good point, and what we're going to see at the next class in *Gertz v. Welch* is that the Supreme Court has constructed different, more protective rules for private figure defamation plaintiffs. One of the main rationales they give is that public figures have greater avenues for self-help. Okay, so the guy comes out and says to a room full of cameras, "I am not a child molester," and that's just going to make it all go away?

S3: No, it's not.

Me: No. He's still going to probably lose the election, isn't he?

S3: I don't know. I hear so many different things in politics, and so many of them are false. Maybe in Brazil where I'm from, it's worse. I don't know. We just hear all kinds of things about politicians, and I don't believe them.

Me: You don't?

S3: I don't.

Me: So if you were going to vote for this person for governor, and it came out in the state's largest newspaper that someone has accused him of sexually abusing children, it wouldn't affect your decision? You'd just dismiss that.

S3: I don't know if I'd dismiss it.

Me: You'd still vote for him?

S3: Maybe.

So there you have it, your first authentic Socratic dialogue. It wasn't so bad, was it? If you saw the video, you'd see the students seemed to be enjoying it. After almost an entire year of case-dialoguing, they knew that the tales of terror they heard about the Socratic method prior to coming to law school were a myth. Let's explore that and other myths, as well as some facts, about the present-day Socratic method and its intimate companion, the case method:

Ten Facts and Myths About the
Socratic and Case Methods

1. **The Socratic method strikes fear in the hearts and minds of 1Ls. FACT.** There's nothing quite like being called on without prior notice in front of a large group of peers and expected to speak articulately and intelligently about a question you've never thought about before. It's enough to make anyone anxious. Imagine your name is Smith. You're sitting in class minding your own business. The professor is talking at a hundred miles an hour when all of a sudden:

Mr. Smith! A shoots at B, but misses and hits C, who loses control of her car and crashes into D, driving a school bus full of children—H, I, J, K, L, M, N, O and P—down a winding mountain road. The school bus careens into a gas pump at the same instant lightning hits the pump. In the explosion, E, a piece of glass, hits F, walking his dog, G, nearby. G gets loose and bites Q, a law student, carrying an armload of casebooks up a staircase. The books fall on R, causing head injuries. R is rushed to the ER by EMTs, gets CPR from an RN and an IV from an MD, but it's too late. He's DOA. Who wins? [Three second pause.] Quick, quick, Mr. Smith! We don't have all day.

There's no way around it. Even when wielded in a humane manner, which it almost always is these days, the process is inherently intimidating. One of my favorite law school stories involves the very first person I ever called on as a Torts professor. I asked a student to state the facts of a case. In a very nervous voice, she did so quite suitably. Trying to give her affirmation, I said, "Yes, those are the facts in a nutshell." The student became visibly distraught. I later learned she thought I was accusing her of having not read the case and simply swiping the facts from the West *Nutshell Series* study aid for Torts. Those crazy law students.

One common fear students have about the Socratic method is that they will blank out when called on. Although rare, it does happen. In fact, it happened to me. My Constitutional Law professor was a Socratic traditionalist in the truest sense. I arrived at every class anxious about being called on. One day the professor called on me in that smug, challenging way some professors enjoy. I don't remember the question or even the subject matter. I only remember a cloud of anxiety enveloping my brain to the point where it stopped functioning. I heard the professor repeat "Mr. McClurg?" No response. Time passed, probably just a few seconds, but it seemed longer. Still no response. He finally moved on to another student. I share this story with my first-year students and they seem to find it comforting.

Don't worry. You've got this. After your first encounter with the Socratic method, you'll look around and go, "Hm, I'm not bleeding. No one's laughing at me. I guess McClurg was right." In the meantime, relax. It's just terror.

2. Professors use the Socratic method to intimidate and break down students. MYTH. In writing this book, I came across several articles by law professors talking about the degrading, alienating, and hostile wielding of the Socratic method, and wondered who the heck they were talking about. When I finished the manuscript, I thumbed through a law school prep book that compared the Socratic method to Darwin's theory of natural selection, warning that "only the strong will survive."

Trust me. While surviving the entirety of the first year is difficult, surviving the Socratic method is not. I've taught at several law schools and am acquainted with many law professors. I do not know a single professor who uses the Socratic method to *intentionally* bully or break down students. My experience is consistent with Professor Paul Brest's that "[t]he terrorist version of the Socratic method has almost disappeared."[78] Asked in a survey to name the biggest surprise about law school, a 1L wrote: "What is the big deal about the Socratic method? It is written about like it's some kind of torture. I have yet to see anyone really crucified."

Professors use the Socratic method for the reasons described above—not for the purpose of intimidating students.

3. The Socratic and case methods are inefficient ways to convey information. FACT. One longstanding gripe from law students about the Socratic method is the large amount of class-time consumed in back and forth discussion. "More law could be taught if professors just lectured," they insist.

It's true. More *rules* could be taught by lecture. But that overlooks that the primary goals of the first year are to train students to reason well and solve legal problems. Learning rules is only one part of that.

As a student, it's hard to appreciate these goals because mastering legal reasoning is a gradual process and we live in an instant-gratification society. Compare studying law to working out at the gym to build and tone muscles. Many people give up too quickly because they don't see immediate results. But those who stay with it for a few months will be standing in front of a mirror one day saying, "Wow, check out those six-pack abs!" It's

---

[78]   Paul Brest, *Plus Ca Change*, 91 MICH. L. REV. 1945, 1948 (1993).

the same with law. After a few months, you'll be standing in front of the mirror saying, "Wow, check out those flabby abs, but at least I know how to apply the Model Penal Code to decide whether conduct constitutes a conspiracy!"

4. Under the Socratic method, law professors only ask, not answer, questions. MYTH. This may have been true in the past, but not anymore. Even most Socratic traditionalists lecture at least some of the time. Elizabeth Mertz conducted a study of first-year Contracts classes at eight law schools and found that the percentage of class time devoted to lecture ranged from 21 percent to 95 percent.[79]

In addition to doing at least some explaining via lecture, most professors will attempt to give concrete answers to student questions that have concrete answers (many legal questions don't), although it is common for law professors to turn the question around on the student. "What do *you* think?" is a classic, frustration-inducing law professor response to student questions.

Professors don't do this to embarrass students or because they're too lazy to answer questions. Remember, a goal of the Socratic method is to force students to learn by doing. So, for example, if we were discussing the defense to negligence known as "implied assumption of risk" and a student asked me to clarify a point of law involving the defense, I'd happily do it. But if the student asked, "Would it be implied assumption of risk for a person to accept a ride from a drunk driver?", I'd say "What do you think?" because I would want the student to try to reason through the puzzle by applying the rules we learned.

5. In law, there are no right answers, only good arguments. MYTH. I've heard professors espouse this view. It's catchy, but false. Many legal questions have clearly right or wrong answers. If the professor asks you to state the elements of the tort of battery, you either know them and can state them (right answer) or you don't know them and can't state them (wrong answer). If the professor asks for the court's holding in a case where the court made the holding clear, you'll be giving a right answer if you can state the holding accurately and a wrong

---

[79]   *See* Carnegie Foundation Report, *supra*, at 51–52 (discussing Mertz study).

answer if you can't. In general, many of the questions posed in connection with Socratic case *recitation* are likely to have right and wrong answers.

On the other hand, it's true that in law many questions do not have objectively right or wrong answers. Many legal standards are vague, purposely so because they must be applied to an infinite variety of factual permutations, that "tangled skein of human affairs" of which Langdell spoke.

Questions soliciting your opinion or other subjective assessment of a result, rule, or policy—we can call them "What do you think?" questions—also lack objectively right or wrong answers. Or stated another way, such questions can have more than one right answer. This doesn't mean professors won't challenge your answers. They very well might, even if they agree with you.

Back at the beginning, I advised you to "embrace uncertainty" precisely because the law is so indeterminate. But don't make the mistake of thinking everything in the law is gray.

6.   Professors penalize students who don't know the answer or who are unprepared for class. MYTH as to the first part and, depending on the professor, FACT as to the second part. Most professors show patience for prepared students who don't know the answer to a question and empathy for prepared, but obviously nervous students, who fumble with their answers. Note the caveat *prepared*. While some professors allow students to simply take a "pass" when called on (sometimes limited to a certain number of passes per semester), most first-year professors expect students to be prepared for each class. Professor responses to unprepared students vary widely, but can include: no response, a scowl, placing a mark by the student's name on the seating chart, ranting at the student, asking the student to leave the room, or lowering the student's grade. If the class as a whole is unprepared, some professors will simply walk out.

As with arriving late, you need to know that lack of a visible response to a student being unprepared does not mean the professor doesn't care about it. The professor will most likely note and remember it. At a minimum, being unprepared will lower the esteem in which professors hold a student.

7. The Socratic method entails cold-calling on students without prior notice. FACT, but undergoing change. Part of what makes the Socratic method anxiety-provoking is the element of surprise. Traditionally, law professors, especially first-year professors, cold-called on students randomly.

As to who gets called on, it varies by professor. I usually look at the seating chart before class and jot down the names of four or five students who I haven't heard from much or recently. Some professors use a more scientific method, keeping track of how many times they've called on each student. Others may randomly draw names from a stack of cards, as if they're awarding door prizes instead of interrogation. Subjective factors can increase your chance of getting called on, including things like: the professor knows you're reliable, the professor thinks you're unprepared, you're wearing a bright yellow shirt, you came up to talk to the prof before class and are fresh in her memory, or you arrived late to class.

Many professors use a system where a small number of students are designated in advance to be in the Socratic hot-seat on a particular day, although this method is used more in upper-level courses. The advantage of this method for the professor and class is that, because the students know in advance when they're going to be called on, they are usually well-prepared, raising the level of classroom discussion and reducing time wasted by engaging unprepared students. The advantage for students is that they can relax and concentrate on learning on the days when they are not "on panel," as the system is sometimes called. The downside is that many students take advantage of the system, using it as a license to not prepare on days they know they won't be called on.

Finally, there may be a trend, particularly among younger professors, to eschew cold-calling on students and rely exclusively on volunteers. As a general rule, reliance on volunteers increases by all professors in upper-level courses.

8. Because the chances of getting randomly called on in a large first-year class are small, it's a rational risk to not prepare and roll the dice. MYTH. The first part is true. In a large first-year class, the odds of getting called on in any particular class on any particular day are small—but not lottery-odds small. A lot depends on the professor. Some professors call on only a few students in a single class, sticking with them for a long time. Others call on many students, asking only one or two questions per student.

I can turn the low-odds argument around as a reason why you should *always* be prepared. Precisely because you won't get called on randomly very often in a large class, it's important that you don't screw up your only opportunities to look good when you do. Unless you volunteer, you might not have an opportunity to redeem yourself.

Of course, the biggest risk of not preparing for classes is that you won't learn the material and won't do well in the course.

9. If you give a wrong answer during Socratic questioning, you'll be humiliated in front of the professor and all of your classmates. MYTH. No one likes to be publicly embarrassed. A central component of the angst generated by the Socratic method is the fear of "looking stupid" in front of the professor and one's peers. This is a needless worry, for several reasons. First, most students simply aren't listening that closely to what other students say in class, particularly as the year wears on. Those in the back can't hear a lot of student comments and many students who can hear are more interested in hearing what the professor has to say about the question.

Second, if it's a hard question, most of the rest of the class won't know the right answer either. Thus, many students won't even recognize a wrong answer unless and until the professor points it out, at which point they'll be concentrating not on the wrong answer you gave, but on trying to get the right answer down in their notes.

As for the professor, she's up there trying to orchestrate a large class and doesn't have time, even if she had the inclination, to stop and focus on wrong answers. Additionally, wrong answers don't trouble professors unless the professor believes the student is unprepared. When students approach me after a class apologizing for giving a "dumb" answer, I often don't remember what they're talking about.

Coincidentally, the day I was editing these paragraphs, I came out of Torts and found a student waiting for me at the bottom of the stairs. She said she wanted to apologize for her classroom performance. I remembered calling on her, but didn't notice any shortcomings. I told her so. She proceeded to reel off three perceived failings: "I said 'I don't know' to one question, but I did know. I had it in my notes. I just wasn't thinking right about it. Then I said 'I'm not sure' to another question. Finally, I was going to give the right answer on one question but you corrected me before I had time to finish." Bless her heart, as we say in the South. I thought she did fine. We tend to be our own harshest critics.

Now, it's true that if a student says something that is *way* off-base, some students might snicker or talk about it after class. But you just have to ignore those kinds of people and trust in karma. Their time will come.

Here's a little secret about the Socratic method that may also ease your mind about giving a wrong answer in class. In truth, at least for questions involving hypotheticals, the very last thing the professor wants to hear in many situations is a quick, correct answer because it spoils the Socratic treasure hunt. Often, when professors pose hypothetical fact situations, what they prefer is an answer that's just wrong enough to allow the professor to artfully nudge the student down the Socratic path toward insight, but not so wrong that the only path is directly to another student. So take heart—some wrong answers are actually welcomed by the prof!

10. The Socratic method has a negative impact on women and minority students. Partly FACT as to practical effect. A substantial body of academic literature discusses the barriers women and minority students traditionally have faced in law school. One area where I see continued disparity—and I'm not suggesting it's the only area—is in classroom participation.

Several surveys have showed that women students voluntarily participate less frequently in law school classes than male students. One example is a 2012 study from Yale Law School, which involved monitoring 113 class sessions in twenty-one courses.[80] The study detected some progress in gender parity regarding class participation, but still found that men participated at higher rates than women, especially in large classes. Comparing the data to a 2002 Yale Law School study of the same issue, the report concluded that, ten years later, women were only 1.5 percent more likely to speak up.[81]

Reasons offered by scholars as to why the Socratic method negatively impacts women include increased feelings of alienation and fear, the adversarial and competitive nature of the method, sexist attitudes by some male professors, an interest in protecting the sanctity and integrity of one's beliefs, less willingness to engage in grandstanding, a lower interest in dominating class discussion, and—I love this one because it's so true—better recognition by women than men of the limits of one's knowledge. In short, male students, as a group, are more willing to engage in the adversarial, competitive "sport" of the Socratic method than women.

Studies also show that minority students volunteer in law school classes at lower rates.[82] The obstacles to participating may loom even larger for minority students because of the under-representation of persons of color at many law schools. Experience has shown me that the smaller the number of any group in a class, the less likely it is that individual members of the group are willing to inject themselves into class discussions.

Because class participation carries several advantages (discussed in Chapter 8), not participating in class can have an adverse impact. Professors want to hear from all of their students. More important, your classmates need to hear from

---

[80] YALE LAW WOMEN, YALE LAW SCHOOL FACULTY & STUDENTS SPEAK UP ABOUT GENDER: TEN YEARS LATER 3 (2012).

[81] *Id.* at 23.

[82] *See* Carole J. Buckner, *Realizing Grutter v. Bollinger's "Compelling Educational Benefits of Diversity"—Transforming Aspirational Rhetoric into Experience*, 72 UMKC L. REV. 877, 887–88 (2004) (discussing the value of class participation and studies showing that minority students participate in law school classes at disproportionately lower rates than non-minority students).

you. *Professors call on people who raise their hands, regardless of gender, race, or other identity traits.* Band together with like students and commit to join the fray. There's strength in numbers. Even a small group of students can unify to build a stronger, mutually supportive whole.

* * *

So there you have it, the full story behind law school's unique teaching methodologies. Hopefully, this look under the hood of the Socratic and case methods has assuaged your anxieties about them, while also persuading you that there is indeed method in the madness.

CHAPTER 8

REASONS TO PARTICIPATE IN CLASS AND TEN TIPS FOR DOING IT WELL

A law school class can and should be a vital and exciting learning environment. Many of the issues discussed in law school have enormous implications for society. Indeed, the most controversial issues of our time are rooted in the law: abortion, civil liberties, environmental policy, gun regulation, healthcare, LBGTQ rights, presidential power . . . the list could go on and on.

If every student committed to being a participant in classroom discussion, even if only occasionally, law schools would be much more interesting places. When Socratic dialoguing and discussion are firing on all cylinders, the atmosphere in law school classrooms can be electric. The professor, however, is only one cylinder. No matter how much energy and effort he or she puts forth, stimulating classroom experiences cannot happen without the help of prepared, engaged students.

Unfortunately, too many 1Ls choose not to voluntarily participate in class, often because they're intimidated. Some students no doubt perform a cost-benefit analysis and decide it's easier and safer to just stay on the sidelines. I understand that decision. The problem is that students undervalue the return on participating in class, while, as discussed in the previous chapter, exaggerating the potential risks. This chapter explains the upside of being a class participator and offers ten tips for doing it successfully.

The Benefits of Class Participation

Class participation carries several benefits, both tangible and intangible. First, active student participation in class discussions adds to the energy level and sense of community in the classroom, making for a more lively and memorable experience for everyone. Class hours in courses where students actively participate fly by compared to courses where lecture predominates. Lecturing may be less intimidating than active dialogue and discussion, but it's also approximately five million times more likely to induce drowsiness.

Second, you will better remember the classes in which you participate and feel more satisfaction about your law school experience. I sat through the first half of my 1L year in silence, except when I got called on. Part of me wanted to participate, but I was afraid. The second half I started to open up a bit, raising my hand here and there, and immediately felt better about myself and my law school career. Instead of sitting in class thinking, "I wish I could be one of those brave people who volunteer," I thought, "Hey, now *I am* one of those brave people."

Third, participating will help sharpen your oral communication and group-speaking skills, essential abilities for lawyers of any stripe.

Fourth, your professors want to get to know you, but with so many students, we can't realistically accomplish that unless you speak up from time to time. As discussed in Chapter 9, getting to know and getting known by your professors carries its own benefits. Volunteering in class is one of the most effective ways to become known by your professors.

Fifth, if you volunteer even once in a while, you will get called on less often when you are not volunteering. In fact, there's an inverse relationship between how often students raise their hands to speak and how often they get called on randomly, because professors want to hear from as many students as possible. Wouldn't you rather speak up at a time when you already have something to say than wait until the professor cold-calls on you?

Finally, class participation brings the possibility of the tangible benefit of a grade raise, although this should be at the bottom of your list of reasons to participate. Many professors raise grades for class participation. In a system where class ranks often depend on hundredths of a grade point, even modest grade raises can have an effect.

Law school can be a scary place, but I encourage you to go to classes willing to discuss the material. Your thoughts and opinions are valuable and your contributions to class discussion will help make law school a more enjoyable, meaningful, and memorable experience for everyone.

Ten Tips for Shining in Class

Whether we're talking about voluntary or involuntary participation (i.e., getting cold-called on), *any* student can shine in class by following these tips and reminders, which are aimed both at bolstering your performance and preventing you from making a bad impression:

1. Come to every class prepared. This is the threshold requirement for any successful participation. If you're prepared, you have nothing to fear from the Socratic method. Wrong answers from prepared students do not bother professors. But if you're not prepared, you're a sitting duck.

2. Commit to being a participator. Many students actually do want to participate, but leave their participation to the professor's decision to call on them. In other words, they don't volunteer. But given the large number of students and the small number who get called on randomly in a typical class, that's not a good participation plan.

Commit yourself to being a participant in class discussion. You don't have to participate every day to make a lasting, good impression in class. Just commit to doing it on a semi-regular basis. Here's my challenge to you: make a vow (and keep track of it) that at a minimum you will voluntarily participate at least *one time each week* during your first semester of law school. I'm not even talking about once a week in each class, although that would be great. Just once a week total, ideally mixing up your participation among different courses. The typical semester is fourteen weeks long, which means that following this vow will commit you to speak in class voluntarily only fourteen times during the entire semester. Even this modest level of participation will gain you many of the benefits of class participation.

Three Ways to Participate

Ask a question. Asking questions is an easy way to participate. It's quite possible the professor could turn it around on you and ask, "What do you think?", but more often than not the professor will just answer the question. Even if the professor turns the question back at you, chances are you'll do fine since it's something you've thought about at least a little bit or you wouldn't have asked the question.

Volunteer an answer. If a professor asks a question to which you know the answer, raise your hand! Professors ask some hard questions, but they also ask a lot of easy ones. I was disturbed when a research assistant told me that many students won't volunteer to answer easy questions because they don't want to be seen as someone who tries to answer easy questions.

That's silly. The professor wants someone to answer them or she wouldn't be asking. Moreover, what may seem easy to you probably isn't easy to everyone. You'll get just as much credit for volunteering to answer an easy question as a hard one, with better odds of giving a right answer.

Offer an opinion. The Socratic method often functions in two parts, beginning with one-on-one case-dialoguing and progressing into a generalized, inclusive class discussion of the issue. At this stage, professors often seek answers about what students think the law should be, rather than simply what it is as espoused in the case. Since opinions cannot, by definition, be demonstrably right or wrong, you have little to lose by joining in such discussions. Of course, the professor may want to explore the basis for your opinion since gut feelings don't cut it as legal analysis, so be ready for follow-up questions that might require you to defend your opinion with reasons.

3. Know your professors' class preparation expectations. Law professors are unique individuals. Much of the advice in this book needs to be construed and applied within the context of your particular professors. We will revisit this crucial point. Here, we're talking only about class preparation expectations.

Some professors simply ask a student to state the facts of the case as a springboard for a broader class discussion, while others will stay with a student for a long time and expect him/her to be able to recite the case forward and backwards. Some professors will routinely ask about the procedural history of the case, while others will rarely or never ask about it. Figuring these things out will make it easier for you to prepare for class.

Asked to compare the second semester to the first, a student said that the second semester was easier in part because she and her classmates knew what to expect in terms of class preparation from each professor:

> We know that certain teachers will not call on you if they have called on you in a recent class, at least not usually twice in one week. For example, if I am called on to participate in class on Monday, I am usually safe for the rest of the week in that course. So I might not re-read the assignments right before class as I usually would to make sure I am extra-prepared. On the other side, some teachers really do call on people at random and therefore students know they always have to be ready because the teacher is unpredictable. This is just one example of how to learn and "work" the system.

Getting to know your professors' preparation expectations takes some time, but you can speed up the process simply by making it a point to stop and think about it. Take notice of which components of cases Professor X asks about on a regular basis.

4. Approach the Socratic method as a game or sport. A common criticism of the Socratic method is that it takes on the appearance of a game or sporting event. But so what? Most people enjoy games and sports. That should make it more, rather than less, palatable. Instead of approaching the Socratic method with dread or terror, look at it as a potentially fun type of "brain game." Keep your wits about you. Free your brain from the shackles of fear. And remember, the goal of the game is not to win. The goal is simply to play the game.

Many professors still execute the Socratic method in the style of its creator: they seek to get the answerer to commit to a position, then, through questioning, attempt to expose the contradictions or fallacies in that position. They sometimes do this by leading students down a garden path, then cutting their legs off at the end of the path. Your goal is to make it to the end of the path with your limbs intact. Cues that you're on your way down the path can take the form of statements such as, "Well, let's change the facts just a little," or "Suppose instead of what happened in the actual case, the plaintiff . . ."

The purpose of the game is to sharpen critical-thinking skills. Untrained legal minds think too narrowly about the consequences of adopting particular legal positions. One way to teach students to think beyond the immediate case is, once a student has committed to a position, alter the facts, ask her to apply her position to the new facts, and test whether she agrees with the results. (See the Socratic dialogue excerpt in the preceding chapter for an example.)

If a professor is leading you down the path, you'll be confronted with a recurring choice: (1) stick with your original position, which may now appear absurd in light of the altered facts; (2) modify your position; or (3) distinguish the professor's new factual situation from your position.

If you believe in your position, don't feel compelled to change it simply by the nature of the questioning. As often as not, the professor will agree with you and will simply be playing devil's advocate. On the other hand, as Emerson said, "A foolish consistency is the hobgoblin of little minds." If the new result would be clearly absurd and cannot be distinguished from the original facts and position, there's nothing wrong with conceding your original view may need revising. Frequently, however, the best course is to try to distinguish the new situations posed by the professor from your original position. Again, trust your brain and reasoning instincts.

5.   Give yourself permission to fail. Some students who are well-prepared and perfectly capable of discussing the issues in law school reading assignments freeze up in class because they put too much pressure on themselves to succeed. They have a hard time answering questions about a case even though they know the answers. If a friend came up to them before class to discuss the same case, they'd be able to do it with no problem. Why? Because they wouldn't be thinking, "Omigod, everyone's watching me. I don't want to look stupid."

By giving yourself permission to fail, you'll stop trying so hard and actually perform better. This advice is commonly given to public performers. I first encountered it taking acting lessons. It works. I follow it when teaching. Law students aren't the only ones who feel exposed when talking in front of a large group of people. Law professors get nervous too. Reading a draft of this chapter, one veteran colleague commented, "I still can't eat before class!"

Don't worry about making a mistake. It happens to all of us and is no big deal. Give yourself permission to fail so you can stop trying too hard.

6. Don't be afraid to disagree with professors. A major point of the Socratic method is to stimulate a true dialogue—a back and forth colloquy between the professor and the student. But this can only work if the student is willing to partake in the back and forth. Most professors welcome and appreciate students who challenge them with contrasting legal arguments and policy positions. The problem is that most students are reluctant to dissent from their professors' views, either because they don't believe it's possible they could be right and the professor wrong or don't want to appear disrespectful.

Generally, you want to limit outright disagreement with the professor in class to policy-based or other open-ended issues, rather than the fine points of black-letter law. Most experienced law teachers know their subjects well, so there's a much greater likelihood that you will indeed be "wrong" in contending with the professor on a point of pure law. Moreover, even if you're right— which certainly can happen because professors are sometimes wrong—it's probably not a great idea to call out the professor in class.

A colleague at another school told me of a brazen incident in which a professor made a legal point in class, and a student took it on himself to email the author of the casebook *during* class, questioning the professor's interpretation of the law. The author apparently wrote back saying the student had it right and the professor was wrong. The student then used the email to show up the professor in class. Now, there's a case for banning computers.

If you think the professor is wrong on the law, approach the professor after class and raise your point in the form of a question, as in: "Professor, I wrote down that you said *a, b, c,* but this note in the casebook seems to say the law is *x, y, z.* I'm having a hard time reconciling them." Any professor not suffering a major insecurity complex (there are some of these, by the way) will readily admit their error, thank you for pointing it out, and insist on correcting it to the entire class at the next meeting.

7. Don't take it personally if a professor or other student challenges your position. Students come to law school with varying degrees of skin thickness. Some sensitive students will fall apart if you look at them the wrong way, while others would hardly notice if you zapped them with a Taser. Professors frequently challenge students to explain or defend their positions even when they agree with the position. This is part of the Socratic process. Don't take it personally.

A research assistant told me a tale about a classmate who volunteered to answer a question in class during his first semester. The professor replied in a condescending tone, "Why would you think that?" Later, the student swore that he'd never volunteer in class again. All I can say about that is "Gimme a break!" Lawyers have to be able to defend and explain their positions. If you make an argument to a judge and she says, "Why would you think that?", you can't fall apart and swear to never go to court again.

I once represented a pro bono divorce client. We were in the judge's chambers for what I thought would be a simple five-minute motion hearing. The walls were lined with other lawyers waiting for their cases to come up. To my dismay, the judge decided to transform the mundane hearing into a debacle, berating my client and then refusing to sign an order I prepared because it contained the phrase "among the parties." "As my eighth-grade English teacher taught me, Mr. McClurg," he said sarcastically, "when you're dealing with only two people, you say *between* the parties, not *among* the parties." It was embarrassing.

Folks, it ain't pretty out there practicing law. It makes law school look like summer camp. I'm sympathetic to the sensitivities of students and don't condone professors treating students rudely, but at some point you just have to suck it up and realize that responding to questions, even sarcastic ones, is simply part of being a lawyer.

Other students also may challenge your position in class discussions. I love it when this occurs and results in a good back and forth exchange. Hearty debate is what great law school class experiences are built upon. Unfortunately, it happens much less than it used to. Older students are much more willing to challenge both their professors and classmates, which is one reason teaching in part-time evening programs (i.e., night school) is a lot of fun.

8. **If you're unprepared, have the good sense to keep your mouth shut.** Not infrequently, students ask questions that are directly answered in the reading material, leading to the sound inference that they haven't read the assignment carefully. This is a particular pet peeve of law professors. If you're not prepared, lie low and pray you don't get called on. Don't take it on yourself to announce to the class: "I'm not prepared and I'll prove it."

In a similar vein, don't come to class early to read the assignment five minutes before class starts. Professors get irritated when they arrive early and see students skimming the reading assignment in their unmarked books for what appears to be the first time. You might as well wear a sign saying, "I'm not prepared!" Some professors will purposely call on such students to expose them.

9. **Redeem yourself.** If you get called on and come across as unprepared, whether you are or not, redeem yourself by volunteering at a later point. Most professors are forgiving souls who will respect the effort. If you're prepared and the professor asks you a question to which you don't know the answer, simply say, "I don't know," but, if possible, toss in another relevant comment about the case to show you're prepared.

If you should happen to blank out when called on, approach the professor after class and explain what happened to avoid having the professor think you were unprepared. I once called on a woman who gave no answer at all. I concluded she was unprepared. Fortunately, two of her classmates came up after class and told me she was prepared, but had simply freaked out.

10. If at first you don't get called on, try, try again. Some students get discouraged from participating after they raise their hands once or twice and the professor doesn't call on them. They either think the professor is intentionally ignoring them or they just can't muster the courage for repeat attempts.

Don't take it personally if you raise your hand and the professor doesn't call on you. Managing discussion in a large class isn't as easy as it may look. The professor's mind is racing to stay ahead of the discussion at the same time he's asking or answering questions, many of which come from left field. In an active discussion, ten hands may be raised at the same time.

Also, to keep from falling behind, the point comes in all class discussions, even the most stimulating ones, where the prof has to make the decision to cut things off and move on. Don't give up. No professor I know would intentionally ignore a volunteering student on a repeated basis except in the case of a notorious gunner who always wants to dominate the class discussion.

CHAPTER 9

LAW PROFESSORS

When I was a kid, I loved watching reruns of *Leave it to Beaver*, a sitcom about the misadventures of young Theodore Cleaver ("the Beav"). Beaver had a teacher named Miss Landers who began every class with a sunny, "Good morning, class." The class always responded in unison, "Good morning, Miss Landers."

In one episode, the Cleavers invited Miss Landers to their home for dinner. They dined on the back patio. Meanwhile, unknown to Beaver, his pal, Larry Mondello, had charged Gilbert and Whitey, two other regulars in the Beav's posse, twenty-five cents each to perch in a backyard tree to witness the event. When Miss Landers stood from the dinner table, the revelation that she wore sandals was met with shock and amazement:

Gilbert: Look! She's got toes!

Whitey: Where?!

Larry: There! Coming right out of her shoes!

Busted for spying, Larry explained why they did it: "Gee, Miss Landers, none of us ever saw a teacher eat before."[83]

New law students share a similar fascination about their professors. In part because the 1L universe is so small, your first-year professors will become the center of it, at least early on. While it diminishes fairly quickly, at the beginning, law students often view their professors with something approaching veneration. At a social gathering during orientation many years ago, I was standing in the restroom at a urinal when a young man next to me exclaimed, "I can't believe it! I'm peeing next to Professor McClurg." I'm pretty sure he was serious.

So pervasive is the extent to which professors permeate the psyches of new law students that students commonly have

---

[83]   *Leave it to Beaver: Teacher Comes to Dinner* (ABC television broadcast Nov. 28, 1959).

dreams about them. A Torts student once reported a grisly nightmare in which I had him tied to a stake while peppering him with questions about the tort of battery. Each time he answered, I shouted, "Wrong!" and lopped off one of his limbs with an ax, saying "Is that a battery? Is that a battery?" Obviously, the dream was far-fetched. Law professors would never ask such easy questions.

Who Are These People?

Whether cast in terms of "know your boss" or, as some students might say, "know your enemy," it's worth knowing a little about those who become law profs and what makes them tick. Who are these people you can't escape even in your sleep, these maestros who will stand before you and orchestrate so much of your existence: your schedule, leisure time, success or failure, your very sense of self-worth?

Well, as it turns out, they're just that: just people, like Miss Landers. In the very first days of my career as a law professor, the dean invited me to his house with a group of other professors to watch a football game on television. It was my first ever social encounter with a group of law professors. Except for the interviewing process to become a professor, my only brushes with law profs had been as a student. I was nervous— intimidated I might not be able to keep up with their deep thoughts and brilliant discourse.

When I arrived, I planted myself on the sofa in front of the television next to a dapperly dressed, gray-haired eminence who had been teaching law for decades. That's when something happened that forever changed my perspective of law professors. On the television screen, Alabama was playing an SEC rival, I forget which. Alabama had the ball. The quarterback took the snap and handed the ball to a running back, who slipped through the middle of the line for a modest gain. The play prompted the oracle seated next to me to plunge his index finger into his cupped, orifice-imitating hand and cackle, "The old Ex-Lax play—right up the hole!" (Ex-Lax is a chewable laxative.) Hm, a joke I might have made in the sixth grade. I relaxed and enjoyed the game. Just regular people.

Here's some information about law professors, based on limited available data:

- Most of the nation's more than 11,000 full-time law professors are white males, although law schools have made substantial progress in diversifying their faculties in recent decades. In the early 1970s, women and minorities together comprised only 8 percent of law school faculty members. Today, 37 percent of law professors are women and 20 percent are minorities (with substantial overlap between those two groups).[84] Given that most women and minority professors have entered the profession recently, they're more likely to be younger and untenured.

- Professors of Legal Research and Writing are disproportionately women. Due to the fact that these jobs traditionally have not been tenure-track positions (with lower salaries as a result), this subset of law faculty jobs is sometimes referred to by law professors as the "pink ghetto." Currently, 72 percent of full-time legal writing instructors are women.[85]

- According to a 2008–2009 report, forty-two percent of law professors held a Juris Doctor or an advanced law degree from just nine "elite" law schools, with 20 percent coming from Harvard or Yale.[86]

- Law review membership and other academic honors, such as Order of the Coif (top ten percent of the class), are common credentials for law professors.

- Many law professors hold advanced law degrees such as an LL.M. or S.J.D. in addition to their J.D. degree, and a growing number have Ph.D.s in other disciplines.

- Disproportionate numbers of professors have held one or more federal judicial clerkships, a prestigious judicial assistant position.

---

[84] James Lindgren, *Measuring Diversity: Law Faculties in 1997 and 2013*, 39 HARV. J.L. & PUB. POL'Y 89, 140 (2016) (citing ABA SECTION OF LEGAL EDUC. & ADMISSIONS TO THE BAR, DATA FROM THE 2013 ANNUAL QUESTIONNAIRE: ABA APPROVED LAW SCHOOL STAFF AND FACULTY MEMBERS, GENDER AND ETHNICITY: FALL 2013 (2014)).

[85] ASS'N OF LEGAL WRITING DIRS. & LEGAL WRITING INST., 2015 NATIONAL SURVEY RESULTS 69 (2015) [hereinafter 2015 ALWD SURVEY].

[86] *See* ASS'N OF AM. LAW SCH., STATISTICAL REPORT ON LAW FACULTY 2008–2009 (2009).

- Most law professors have some previous practice experience in either the private or public sector.[87]

- Politically, Democrats dominate the ranks of law professors, comprising 82 percent of the total.[88]

Decades ago, an ABA committee used strong language in criticizing the tendency of law faculty to replicate themselves when hiring new professors: "Were we biologists studying inbreeding, we might predict that successive generations of imbeciles would be produced by such a system."[89] This inbreeding criticism continues today.[90]

I'm happy to report that the caliber of law faculties is extremely high, in all likelihood much higher than you encountered in undergraduate school or other graduate programs. This is true at all law schools because far more qualified candidates exist than available positions. Perhaps you've heard the adage, "Those who can *do*, those who can't *teach*." Applied to law profs, a more accurate statement of the second part would be, "those who are incredibly well-credentialed and extremely lucky teach." Law professor jobs are highly coveted. Becoming one is a very competitive process.

Beginning law profs do lack one important credential: they generally have no classroom experience or training. To teach first-graders to spell "cat" or add 2 + 2, teachers are required to take courses in educational theory and do internships working in classrooms. Not so for law profs teaching complex material and analytical skills to adults. The only training new law professors receive is an optional two-day new teacher workshop

---

[87]   *See* Richard E. Redding, *"Where Did You Go to Law School?" Gatekeeping for the Professoriate and Its Implications for Legal Education*, 53 J. LEGAL EDUC. 594, 601 (2003) (study of all law professors hired between 1996 and 2000 showing that 87 percent had some practice experience).

[88]   Lindgren, *supra*, at 149. Lindgren counted "only five schools among the top 100 that now have percentages of Republican-leaning faculty that approach or exceed their percentages in the full-time working population (George Mason, Notre Dame, Pepperdine, Virginia, and Northwestern)." *Id.* at 144.

[89]   AM. BAR. ASS'N, LAW SCHOOLS AND PROFESSIONAL EDUCATION: REPORT AND RECOMMENDATIONS OF THE SPECIAL COMMITTEE FOR A STUDY OF LEGAL EDUCATION OF THE AMERICAN BAR ASSOCIATION 82 (1980).

[90]   Tracey E. George & Albert H. Yoon, *The Labor Market for New Law Professors*, 11 J. EMPIRICAL LEGAL STUD. 1, 38 (2014) (study concluding that law schools have "continu[ed] to hire tenure-track professors who share the same credentials and experiences as tenured faculty. . . .").

sponsored by the Association of American Law Schools. It's a "learn while you earn" affair.

When I was first hired as a law professor, the school assigned me to teach Family Law. Not only did I know little about Family Law, I knew nothing about how to teach it or any other subject. I defaulted to trying to imitate the professor who taught me Family Law back in law school. Big mistake. At my first class, after ten minutes of brain-death inducing lecture on the ecclesiastical history of domestic relations law dating from the twelfth century, I saw a woman in the back of the room roll her eyes and nudge the person next to her.

That image burned in my brain for the rest of my scintillating lecture. Fortunately, because I was so nervous, the students' pain was short-lived. Orating like Socrates on speed, I covered twenty pages of notes in about thirty minutes and ended twenty minutes early (by comparison, I now cover seven or eight pages of notes in fifty minutes). Starting at the next class I reverted to just being myself. That worked much better, although I still recall a comment on my initial set of student evaluations that said: "Is there a fund to send this guy back to Florida?"

A Kinder, Gentler Law School Nation

Prior to starting law school, you may hear horror stories about law professors. Some famous print and screen accounts of law school portray law professors as sadistic ogres. There was some truth to these stories back in the day. A funny story still circulates at my current school about a now-retired professor. A former student approached him at a party and said, "Professor, you don't seem to like law students." "That's true," the professor said. "Then why do you choose to teach?" the student asked. "The exterminator doesn't have to like termites," he replied.

Those days are gone. When I ask students to name their biggest surprise about law school, a common answer relates to professors defying the stereotype of being cruel dictators bent on humiliating students. Several answers tracked the sentiments expressed in this comment:

The biggest surprise has been the attitude of the professors. After reading Turow's *One L*, which was recommended by many friends as an accurate depiction of first-year life, I expected professors to create a clear barrier between themselves and the students. I anticipated a class environment based heavily in fear, with an undertone of student humiliation, but I have found that the professors actually enjoy what they do (or are great actors). In all classes, there is a relaxed feeling in the dialogue and discussion. This certainly has not taken away from the fear—but for me it has shifted the fear from a fear of public humiliation to a fear of disappointing. In discussions with my classmates, everyone seems to share the same view— that the desire to be prepared and understand the material is not to avoid being humiliated in class, but to live up to the expectations that we place on ourselves and that the professors place on us.

Law schools are getting nicer all the time. In fact, many older professors would complain that legal education has become too nice, with professors going out of their way to be easygoing and friendly to students. Part of this attitudinal drift may be motivated by the desire to get good student evaluations, which both feed the ego and play a role in promotion and salary decisions. Also, with students paying high dollars for tuition and with so many law schools competing for the same pool of applicants, law school administrations feel pressure, which they pass on to the professors, to achieve customer satisfaction. In law school-speak, it's called being "student-centered."

A larger explanation for the shift toward "feel good" legal education is attributable to the fact that the old school Socratic traditionalists are retiring and being replaced by a new breed of Gen-X and Gen-Y professors who grew up in a world environment emphasizing affirmation and self-esteem building. That young law professors have a different view of law school teaching than their predecessors is routinely driven home to me whenever I attend the annual Faculty Recruitment Conference as part of an interviewing team. Most people become law professors by registering for and attending this conference.

At one recent conference, we interviewed twenty-five prospective law professors. A stock interview question is: "What kind of teaching style do you see yourself adopting?" The answer from nearly every candidate was "soft Socratic" or "modified Socratic," often followed by a qualifier that while the candidate would call on students, he or she wouldn't "put them on the spot," "embarrass them," or "intimidate them." Some candidates said they would rely on volunteers, rather than cold-call on students. One candidate summed up his teaching goal by saying: "Hey, let's all leave the classroom feeling good about ourselves!" That is an exact quotation I captured in my notes.

While this may sound like a glad tiding for law students, there's a downside. Tossing out softball questions to volunteers or letting unprepared students "pass" on questions is less stress-provoking, but it's also much less intellectually rigorous and, ultimately, more boring. The classes you will remember best will be those where your professors challenge you to figure out legal problems and defend your positions. Moreover, as mentioned in the previous chapter, the real world of practicing law is anything but kind and gentle. As Professor Michael Vitiello observed: "Treating our students gently is not kind. Instead, by abandoning the demanding form of the Socratic method, we fail to prepare our students for the rigors of practice."[91] But then, Vitiello is an old guy like me.

The Quirkiness Quotient

At their best, law professors are highly skilled, hard-working intellectuals dedicated to perfecting their craft and advancing the welfare of their students. At their worst, they can be arrogant, bitter, insecure prima donnas who sometimes forget they have one of the best jobs in the world. In between those extremes, we're all a bit quirky. Not necessarily quirky in a bad way. We just tend to move to the beat of a different drummer, like maybe Keith Moon or John Bonham (deceased wild and crazy drummers from The Who and Led Zeppelin, respectively). This grand tradition started early on. Judge and jurisprudential

---

[91]   Michael Vitiello, *Professor Kingsfield: The Most Misunderstood Character in Literature*, 33 HOFSTRA L. REV. 955, 959 (2005); *see also Robert M. Lloyd, Hard Law Firms and Soft Law Schools*, 83 N.C. L. REV. 667, 667 (2005) (arguing that law schools have turned "soft" with the result "that law schools are doing a poor job of preparing students for [the hard world of] practice").

scholar Jerome Frank once described Christopher Langdell, the father of the case method, as "a brilliant neurotic."[92]

Why do so many law professors tend to be a bit . . . er, unusual? In part, it's because academia overall attracts highly intelligent people who don't fit comfortably into normal corporate or other business environments. It's not a matter of whether they *can* do it. They just don't want to. But the nature of the job also encourages people to let out what might otherwise remain hidden eccentricities in other employment settings. Most beginning law professors arrive at their first jobs behaving as and appearing to be normal people. But unlike the rest of the working world, law professors are subject to very few workplace rules or restrictions.

There's the oft-repeated tale of the new law professor who arrived for the fall semester fresh from a corporate law firm wearing a dark blue suit, starched white shirt, silk rep tie, and shiny wingtips. By the end of the year, he was walking around in a pink unitard and cape, with a tattoo of the great Judge Learned Hand covering his shaved scalp and sticks of smoking incense in his ears. Now here I am writing books about law school. Who would have thought?

Seriously, law professors can dress as they wish, say what they want to whomever they want, and come and go pretty much as they please. They enjoy more or less complete autonomy over their lives, a luxury enjoyed by few other workers. Once a law professor achieves tenure, he or she is virtually untouchable. Small wonder they let their inner-selves show through more than most other workers.

Lawhaha.com, my legal humor blog, collects, among other items, funny memories of law school. One category is "Those lovable, quirky law professors," which includes tales about a bald, white professor who raps in class, a professor who acts like nothing unusual has occurred when a tooth flies out of his mouth and bounces off a table during a lecture, a professor who begins class teaching the wrong course from the wrong book, a professor who runs into a door and teaches an entire class with blood streaming down his face, and a distinguished professor who

---

[92]   Jerome Frank, *A Plea for Lawyer-Schools*, 56 YALE L.J. 1303, 1303 (1947).

stalks the classroom for an entire hour with toilet paper hanging out the back of his pants.

As with all people, their uniqueness is part of what makes law professors interesting cats.

Theoretical Versus Practical Professors

Which would you find more appealing? Learning "rules of law" and how to apply them or studying the history, policies, and jurisprudential theories that shape those rules?

One difference among law teachers that affects students is whether they teach primarily from a practical or theoretical standpoint. Law can be taught from a variety of theoretical perspectives. Among the more popular are economic theory, feminist theory, and critical race theory. The difference in a subject taught through a theoretical or policy-oriented lens compared to a practical approach is so dramatic that it can seem like a different course.

As an inexact rule of thumb, the higher a law school's ranking, the more likely the professors will lean toward theoretical classroom teaching. Conversely, law professors at lower-ranked schools tend to focus on teaching the substance and application of law. The perceived missions of law schools play a role in forging this rough dichotomy. Schools perceived to be "elite" see it as part of their mission to develop students into future legal scholars, policy-makers, and others who will shape the law. Lower-ranked schools, many of which are regional schools, are more likely to see their primary mission as training students to become competent lawyers. Of course, you'll get a mix of theoretical and practical teaching at all law schools and from most individual professors.

In my experience, most, although certainly not all, students, prefer practically oriented teaching.[93] Black-letter law and

---

[93]   One dated study identified three general types of law professor: the "Socratic Trainer," the "Caring Teacher," and the "Anti-Socratic Practitioner." The Anti-Socratic Practitioner was described as a teacher who "recognizes that the purpose of law school is to prepare students for the practice of law" and who emphasizes practical skills and "[h]ow-to knowledge." A group of seventy-seven law students at a Midwestern law school were asked to rank their image of an ideal professor. First-year students ranked all three personae relatively equally. Third-year students, however, had a much different notion of the ideal professor, ranking the Anti-Socratic Practitioner a clear first. Fifty percent of third-year students chose the Anti-Socratic Practitioner as their ideal professor, 40

exposure to the "real world" of practicing law seem more meaningful and relevant to what they're trying to accomplish than legal theory. I felt similarly as a law student. Most of my professors were very theory-oriented. In some courses, my class notes for the entire term were fewer than ten pages. My classmates and I appreciated the professors who taught us actual law. One reason adjunct law professors—practitioners hired to teach particular courses—tend to be popular among students is that, in addition to being notoriously easy graders, they approach their classes from a real world perspective, supplementing class presentations with heavy doses of "war stories."

In hindsight, I came to appreciate my theoretical professors. For most lawyers, law school will be the only time in their professional lives when they will be afforded the luxury of being able to think *about* the law. Practicing lawyers spend every day of their careers immersed in the practical application of law. For many, the real world they craved to learn about as law students gets old very quickly. Enjoy your law school opportunities to explore the origins, philosophies, and policies of law.

Is It Important What Your Professors Think of You?

Here's something you need to know about law professors: they watch you, notice things about you, form opinions about you, and in many cases share those opinions with others. In other words, law professors behave the same way toward students as students behave toward them. If there were a ratemystudents.com website similar to the popular ratemyprofessors.com, it might be heavily trafficked.

I suppose it would be nice if law professors, being professionals, could rise above forming opinions of their charges, but that's too much to ask. We're human beings. Just like professors make impressions on students, both good and bad, students make impressions on professors, both good and bad.

---

percent the Caring Teacher, and only 5 percent the Socratic Trainer. *See* Douglas D. McFarland, *Students and Practicing Lawyers Identify the Ideal Law Professor*, 36 J. LEGAL EDUC. 93, 96–98 (1986).

Does it matter what your professors think of you? Well, yes and no.

Why it isn't important: anonymous grading.

Suppose you're convinced a professor does not like you. Maybe he happened to stroll by one day while you were indicting him in the hallway to your classmates as the worst professor in the history of legal education. (These things do happen, so be wary of what you broadcast within the small confines of a law school.) Adding to your already high stress level, you're now saddled with the fear your professor will exact revenge in calculating your grade. Relax.

The main reason why it's *not* important what your professors think of you is that law school grading is anonymous. All law schools require students to use anonymous exam numbers, rather than names, on exams. The numbers are issued each semester by the registrar's office. I remember being suspicious as a law student as to whether professors had some way of matching exams with particular students, but they don't. The system really is anonymous.

What students don't realize is that professors don't want to know the identity of exam-writers. Students look at anonymous grading as protecting students, whereas professors look at it as protecting professors (against claims of favoritism, being punitive, discrimination, etc.). In truth, anonymous grading probably works more to the detriment of students than to their benefit. It's much easier to assign a low grade to a cold anonymous exam number than to a living, breathing person, particularly if it's a student the professor has come to like and respect. Human nature is such that professors would be inclined to give such students the benefit of the doubt when grading their exams. To the contrary, I can hardly imagine a professor intentionally grading an exam more harshly because the professor didn't like the student.

Two exceptions to anonymous grading exist that affect 1Ls: legal research and writing courses and grade bumps. According to the 2015 survey of legal research and writing program directors, 32 percent of legal writing programs do not grade any major writing assignments anonymously, while the rest grade all or at least some major writing assignments anonymously.[94] Maintaining anonymity in legal research and writing classes is difficult because students are sectioned into smaller groups than in other first-year classes, submit more than one draft of the same writing assignment, and often meet with their professors individually to discuss those drafts.

The other exception has to do with grade bumps. Many professors raise or "bump" grades based on classroom participation/preparation. Some profs also lower grades for the same reasons. In most cases, such changes are limited to one grade step (e.g., from a *B* to a *B+*). Because evaluating the quality and consistency of class participation and preparation is a subjective undertaking, there is room for a professor's impressions of students to enter into the calculus, consciously or unconsciously. Grade bumps usually are submitted by the professor by student name along with the list of anonymous exam grades. The registrar then adds in the bumps before posting the final grade.

Why it is important: references, research assistant positions, and other helping hands.

While your grade will not be affected by your professor's opinion of you, professors can impact your life in other ways, often without you knowing it.

• **References.** In my second year of law school, I decided I wanted to become a law clerk to a federal judge on graduation. It became my single-minded goal. Federal clerkships involve working closely with a judge doing tasks such as researching and drafting court orders and opinions. They are highly sought-after positions. I was fortunate to land a clerkship with U.S. District Judge Charles R. Scott, Middle District of Florida.

Federal judges receive tons of applications from qualified people. My law school credentials were good, but most people who apply for federal clerkships have good credentials. How did I get the job? According to Judge Scott, a strong letter of recommendation from Professor W.D. MacDonald, for whom I worked as a research assistant, tipped the balance in my favor. Four short paragraphs, just 110 words, literally changed my life.

---

[94]   2015 ALWD SURVEY, *supra*, at 11.

The letter opened the door to the clerkship and the clerkship opened the door to becoming a law professor.

Like all law professors, I write many recommendation letters for students. Whom do professors recommend? Any student they believe in. You don't have to be an *A* student to get a strong recommendation. Even a student without high grades can obtain a good recommendation if the professor likes and respects the student. I recently wrote a strong letter for a student who received a *D* in Torts that helped her land a summer job. Why? Because she impressed me with her work ethic and attitude.

Students don't realize how often professors' opinions of them are solicited without their knowledge. Professors commonly receive inquiries about students from judges, lawyers, and other professors who are considering hiring the student, even when the student didn't list the professor as a reference. Scholarship award committees seek nominees or recommendations from professors. Admissions directors ask professors' opinions when choosing students to serve as fall orientation leaders. Academic support deans may seek professor input when hiring students for tutoring positions. Bar examiners send forms to professors seeking their evaluation of former students who worked for them. FBI agents conduct in-person interviews of professors for any student applying for a government job that requires a security clearance.[95] Accordingly, the impressions you make on your professors can sometimes impact you without you even realizing it.

- **Research assistant positions.** Most law professors hire research assistants, which are good gigs. They pay. They're flexible, allowing students to work on their own time. The assignments help sharpen research and writing skills. Research assistants receive one-on-one skills-training and mentoring. Sometimes their research assignments involve interesting,

---

[95] These interviews can be amusing because the agents are required to ask the same questions about everyone, even when they sound preposterous. An FBI agent recently showed up at my office to ask questions about a graduate who had landed a choice position in the U.S. Department of Justice. She was a top student, editor of the law review, and an all-around stellar person. It was impossible to keep a straight face when the agent asked questions such as, "Has she ever participated in an attempt to overthrow the United States government?" I said, "I don't know much about her personal life, but that would really surprise me!" We both laughed.

cutting-edge legal issues. A certain prestige factor is associated with the position.

And if you do a good job, you could end up with one of those killer recommendation letters like I got from Professor MacDonald. The most meaningful job recommendations come from people who are closely familiar with a person's abilities and work habits. In law school, the professor-research assistant relationship is one of the primary avenues for a professor to gain that kind of insight about a student.

The work assignments vary widely depending on the professor and the professor's confidence in the particular research assistant. They often involve assisting the professor in preparing articles and books for publication (e.g., researching, drafting, cite-checking, proofreading). Numerous research assistants, for example, have assisted me in writing each edition of this book.

Unfortunately, like many other privileges in law school, research assistant positions usually go to students with high GPAs and class ranks, although this is not always true. If you're interested in working as a research assistant for a professor, be a proactive early bird. Approach professors during the second semester and ask whether they anticipate hiring any research assistants for the summer or the next year and, if so, whether you can apply.

• **Other helping hands.** Beyond references and research assistant positions, you never know when you might need a helping hand from a professor. Students frequently need law school advice, of course, but that's only the beginning. Sometimes they need legal advice. Sometimes they need life advice. Sometimes they just need a sympathetic ear. Many professors, used to playing dual roles as teacher and therapist, keep a box of tissue handy in a desk drawer.

Personal issues on which law students seek guidance and advice run the gamut. A few years ago, a third-year student I'll call Terrence asked to meet with me. When he came into my office and asked to close the door, I knew something was wrong. He sat down and unloaded a heavy burden he had been carrying around for three years. The bar application deadline was the following week. Everyone in his graduating class except him had completed and submitted their applications. He said he was afraid that an incident in his past would lead, at best, to a full-blown fitness hearing and, at worst, to the bar refusing him admittance. He even contemplated moving to another state before realizing he'd run into the same obstacle.

Terrence had impressed me more than once as being not only a good student but a good person. He received good grades and was a member of the law review. Most important, way back as a 1L, he demonstrated his integrity and good heart when he approached me after Torts class more than once, troubled by legal doctrines that led to unjust results. I offered to help Terrence draft an explanation of the incident to submit with his bar application. I thought that, framed properly, the incident could be explained. It worked. His bar application sailed through without any questions asked. Would I do the same thing for every student? No. I did it for Terrence because I believed in him.

The overarching point of this section is that your professors can be an important link in your legal education and your development and future as a lawyer. Apart from tangible assistance, getting to know some of your professors will make you feel more a part of your law school community, which will make law school a more enjoyable and fulfilling experience overall. It's a good, comforting feeling simply to walk down the hall and have a professor greet you by name. Researchers have suggested that the high student-teacher ratios in law school and the consequent disconnectedness between professors and students is a significant cause of distress and discontent in law students.

Five Easy Ways to Get to Know Your Professors

I was able to write the recommendation letter for the student who received the *D* in Torts and help draft the bar application for Terrence because I had come to: (1) know them; (2) like them; and (3) respect them. Most fundamentally, a professor can't help you if he or she doesn't know you. Professors often have to decline requests by students for letters of recommendation simply because they don't know the student.

Students can't remain completely anonymous—never participating in class, never asking questions after class, never coming for office hours, etc.—and then expect profs to come up with glowing endorsements of them. What's to recommend? That their breathing never created a disturbance in class? That they appeared to be conscious when the professor looked in their direction? Many such students may actually deserve good recommendations, but professors can only go by what they know.

When I was in law school, I was too shy to get to know my professors except for the professor I worked for as a research assistant. I always envied my classmates who did get to know them. I'd see a group of them sitting with a prof at an outdoor picnic table at lunch and hear them in the profs' offices when I walked down the halls. At law school parties and other social events, they'd hang around the profs, chatting and yukking it up. If I re-did law school knowing what I know now, I would make it a point to get to know my profs.

Not all professors are easily accessible or approachable by students. Some professors, truth be told, want little to do with law students. Teaching as a visiting professor at a top-tier law school, I had lunch with another visiting professor. He made a comment that stuck with me: "Being a law professor would be the greatest job in the world if it weren't for the damn students." But most profs don't think that way.

Here are five easy ways to get to know your professors:

1. Introduce yourself as early as possible. Due to a psychological phenomenon known as "primacy effect," people tend to best remember the first things they see or hear in a list or series of events. Trial lawyers are well-acquainted with primacy effect and the corollary principle of "recency effect" (people also tend to better remember the last items in a series), and carefully structure their presentation of evidence based on these phenomena.

At the beginning of a school year, the profs don't know any of the students. If you make it a point to introduce yourself to your first-year professors at that time, they'll be more likely to remember you once school starts, when you will become just one of the madding crowd. Mixers during law school orientation provide a good opportunity to introduce yourself early. If you can't catch up with a prof during such an event, stop by the professor's office during the week before classes begin.

2. **Volunteer in class.** Professors take note of and appreciate the students who volunteer in class. We need your help to make the whole Socratic thing work. Being known as a class participator also gives professors something concrete to say about a student seeking a recommendation. For 1Ls, except for their course grade, it's about the only specific thing professors can comment on because they haven't had a chance to work with any first-years on an individual basis. As students move through law school, professors get to know them in other contexts, as research assistants or in connection with law review, moot court, or other student organizations. Chapter 8 discussed the benefits of class participation. Getting known by your profs is one of the biggest ones.

3. **Stop by your professors' offices to ask questions.** Most professors post office hours during which they are available to meet with students, but surprisingly few students take advantage of them. If a professor hasn't posted office hours, don't hesitate to inquire about them. Many professors have an open-door policy, meaning that students are free to stop by any time the professor is in the office. If you feel intimidated about volunteering in class or going to visit professors in their offices, approach the professor after class and ask a question about the day's discussion. It's common for a few students to gather around the lectern after class to ask clarifying questions or continue discussion about the topic of the day.

4. **Email the professor a topical news article pertaining to the course material.** One easy, low-stress way to initiate contact with a professor, while also demonstrating you have your eye on the ball, is to email the prof a topical news article relevant to a subject covered in class. You can send the article with a simple note such as, "Dear Professor Kingsfield: I don't know if you saw this, but it reminded me of what we were discussing in class today."

5. **Give the professor a compliment if it's sincere and deserved.** Professors find it rewarding to be appreciated by their students. If your professors are doing a great job, let them

know. Don't worry about being seen as a brownnoser. Professors can tell the difference between sincere appreciation and phony-baloney attempts to kiss up.

Five Easy Ways to Make Your Professors Wish You Had Chosen a Different Career Path

It doesn't take special effort to get professors to like and respect you. It does, however, take a whole lot of regular effort. Professors like and respect good students. It's that simple. By good students, I don't mean students at the top of the class, although they usually will be included. I mean students who are diligent, committed, and hardworking. Good students come to class regularly, well-prepared, on time, and act like the professionals they are on the road to becoming. Referring back to Chapter 4, good students are best defined by the student types of Mr./Ms. Reliable and The Earnest Hard Worker.

If you're already in law school and suspect your professors of favoring some students, it might be true. But take an honest, objective look at those students. My guess is most of them will be "good students" as defined above.

But some students also act in ways that can make professors *not* like them. Here are five common ways students get on professors' nerves:

1. Coming to class late, being unprepared, web-browsing during class, etc. Yes, I know these sound obvious and that we've already discussed them. Of course, professors don't like these things. But what students don't realize is that some professors *take it personally* when students do them. Caught up in their ivory-tower worlds, professors' courses occupy positions of supreme importance in their lives. Disrespect shown by a student toward a professor's course is sometimes internalized as disrespect for the professor, even if not intended that way.

More generally, if your conduct leads the professor to conclude that you're a Slacker (see student types in Chapter 4), there's a chance you will be written off as a lost cause unless you do something to redeem yourself.

2. Acting belligerently or with a sense of entitlement. There's no quicker way to turn off a law professor than by approaching him or her about a law school issue displaying an air of belligerence or entitlement. Hard-nosed approaches will backfire faster than you can say res ipsa loquitur, if indeed you can say it at all. "You can catch more flies with honey than vinegar" are words to live by when dealing with law professors. You can influence professors more effectively by acting respectfully than by being confrontational.

This advice applies in all law school contexts, but a classic example involves students who want to meet with professors about an exam or writing assignment grade. Students who visit a professor to discuss a grade generally fall into one of four categories:

- Students who sincerely want to learn where they went wrong and how to do better next time.

- Students who arrive with the hope they can cajole the professor into changing the grade.

- Students who performed well on the exam or assignment, but who want to bask in their glory or make sure the professor knows they did well.

- Angry students who come to express outrage at the grave injustice that has been dealt them and to demand redress.

Of these four groups, professors have a genuine interest in talking only with the students in Group 1. Most professors are more than happy to try to help students who want to help themselves. Students in Group 2 are easily identified by the fact that they quickly lose interest in actually reviewing the exam or assignment once it's made clear there is no chance of a grade change. As for Group 3, professors are always happy to run into the students who did well, but don't really want to waste time engaging in unnecessary reviews with them. If you did well, just be happy about it and move on.

Then there's Group 4, whose methodology wins the award for "Most Likely to Cause a Law Professor to Shout *Get the Hell Out of My Office!*" Approaching a professor with a mindset of entitlement, especially if tinged with belligerence, about an exam or any other law school issue is the worst possible approach. It will practically guarantee you will not get what you want.

3. Whining and complaining. When professors give assignments or issue class policies about attendance, punctuality, etc., most students just do the assignments and follow the policies. But a few—some of whom qualify as Nattering Nabobs of Negativism (see Chapter 4)—prefer to waste time whining and complaining about them. In the words of the old Nike slogan, if a professor gives you an assignment or tells you to follow a class policy, "Just do it!"

4. Making excuses. Everyone has problems. Most people accept and deal with them. Others use them as excuses for not fulfilling their commitments. Professors respect students who accept responsibility for their actions, instead of blaming someone or something else (e.g., the professor, law school administration, traffic, their classmates, landlord, distant cousin, pet snake).

Having said that, some problems—health issues or the death of a close loved one are good examples—do unavoidably interfere with law school commitments. The key is to address these types of issues with professors as they are occurring, not after the fact. Most law professors, for example, have strict attendance requirements. You will get a certain number of "free" misses before your grade goes down. If you go over your allowed absences in a course due to illness, don't wait until the end of the semester when your grade gets lowered to raise the matter. Contact your professors while the issue is ongoing. A contemporary explanation of a problem will be more credible and, more important, can get you help when you need it.

If you're late or get caught unprepared, apologize to the professor after class. Leave out the excuses. Just say you are sorry it happened and that it won't happen again.

5. Bad-mouthing staff, classmates, professors, or your law school. Students who smear their law school or the people in it are not popular with professors or other students. Because whispers become shouts in the claustrophobic halls of law schools, even privately intended denigration can end up reaching a wider audience. A few bitter students go further, taking their grievances public by posting them online.

Learn Your Professors' Individual Styles and Expectations and Adapt to Them

I sent an email to my colleagues asking for input about the top traits of successful law students. Here's what one wrote back:

> Truth be told, my first reaction to [your] query was that the top trait of successful law students is that they do not waste their time or money on books telling them how to succeed in law school. I literally beg first-years to stay away from all manner of outside advice, and instead to follow what their teachers tell them to do in each of their courses.

Ouch, that can't be good for book sales. I don't agree with the first part or I wouldn't have written *1L of a Ride*, but I couldn't agree more with the second part. While most good law school advice applies across the board, the fact is that law professors, like students, are individuals. They have different teaching styles, preferences, and expectations. We touched on this earlier.

Ultimately, you want to do exactly what your individual professors tell you to do in their courses, even if it conflicts with other advice. Why? Because your professors will be the ones evaluating you—not the external advice-givers. So, for example, if your Civil Procedure professor instructs you to tell her everything you know about a subject area if it comes up on the exam, do it, even though this runs contrary to the standard exam advice to *not* engage in a general brain-dump.

The above is a real example. At one law school where I taught a number of students came to me questioning my advice to stay focused on the issues in writing answers to essay questions and not to discuss law that is irrelevant to the specific issues raised. "Professor X," they said, "told us she wants us to write down everything we know about the subject." I told them that couldn't possibly be what she meant. Professors often say one thing while students hear another. But when I asked Professor X about it, she said they were right. She wants her students to tell her everything they know about a subject. Who's right? She is for her exams because she's the one grading them. It doesn't matter what others think. Tailor all law school advice to your individual professors as necessary.

CHAPTER 10

TOP FIVE HABITS OF SUCCESSFUL STUDENTS: A C.R.E.D.O.

Assuming you're on the road to being a *successful* law student, you'll be spending most[96] of your non-sleep, non-classroom hours during the first year studying and doing study-related activities. Accordingly, we'll spend a substantial portion of the book learning how to study and prepare for exams. Law school's mass of complex material, unique teaching methodologies, and single-exam format impose different and far more intense study demands than students are used to from previous educational experiences.

Later pages are filled with specific study and exam advice, with chapters devoted to case-briefing, note-taking, outlining, exam preparation, essay exam mistakes, and tips for tackling law school multiple-choice questions. This chapter approaches academic success from a wide-angle view.

Every student begins law school at the same starting line. Within weeks, days even, some students pull ahead while others fall behind. By the end of the year, at law schools all across America, the class is divided into GPA and class rank strata that include a top, middle, and bottom. What factors determine which group students end up in?

Your LSAT Score Does Not Predetermine Your Fate

One answer is innate ability. Not everyone enters law school with the same chance of landing in the top of the class. Empirical studies show a correlation between LSAT scores and first-year grades, between undergraduate GPAs and first-year grades, and between a combination of LSAT scores and undergraduate GPAs and first-year grades.

---

[96] Most, but not all. Pay attention to Chapter 20, discussing how to live a balanced life as a law student.

However, the LSAT correlation is not as strong as most people believe. Correlation is measured by a coefficient for which 1.00 represents a perfect correlation and zero shows no correlation beyond one attributable to random chance. The Law School Admission Council (LSAC), the good folks who administer the LSAT, conduct validity studies of the LSAT. The most recent study covered 2013–2014.[97]

For 2014, the mean correlation between LSAT score and first-year grades was 0.39. The correlation varied widely among schools, from a low of 0.19 to a high of 0.56. Speaking very generally, variables are not considered to be "highly correlated" unless the coefficient reaches or exceeds 0.70, although the context of what is being considered is important in evaluating the strength of correlations.

While the LSAT correlates with success for many students, it does not reliably predict the success of any individual student. The LSAT measures a limited range of skills, primarily the abilities to read, comprehend, and analyze complex text. While these abilities are important, other key ingredients to academic success in law school are not measured by the LSAT.

Grit and Grind

In Memphis, we love our NBA team, the Grizzlies. Without any superstars, they've made the playoffs for seven consecutive seasons. Their motto is "Grit and Grind." Its origin is credited to tenacious, defensive-minded guard Tony Allen who was asked to explain his exceptional performance in a surprise win over the Oklahoma City Thunder in 2011. "All heart," he said. "Grit. Grind." When Memphisport.com asked Grizzlies fans to define "grit and grind," one fan captured it perfectly: "The intrinsic spirit of struggling to beat whatever's stacked against you— persistence in the face of any obstacles."

In 2016 Professor Angela Duckworth captured the essence of grit and grind in a bestselling book, *Grit*. Based on more than a decade of research, she explains how and why "grit"—a combination of perseverance and single-minded passion—is as

---

[97]   LISA C. ANTHONY ET AL., LAW SCH. ADMISSION COUNCIL, LSAT TECHNICAL REPORT SERIES: PREDICTIVE VALIDITY OF THE LSAT: A NATIONAL SUMMARY OF THE 2013 AND 2014 LSAT CORRELATION STUDIES 6 tbl.2 (2016).

important as native intelligence in predicting success.[98] Duckworth began her research studying cadets at the West Point military academy. Despite elaborate efforts to compile a success predictor called the "Whole Candidate Score" (based largely on traditional indicators such as SAT scores), the academy could not accurately predict which cadets would make it through training and which would drop out.

Then Duckworth came up with her "Grit Scale," a test to measure the degree to which a person approaches life with grit. Cadet scores on the Grit Scale bore "absolutely no relationship" to the Whole Candidate Scores, yet turned out to be "an astoundingly reliable predictor" of success at West Point.[99] She repeated her work with salespeople, high school students, spelling bee competitors, and other groups, always with the same result. Grit trumped talent alone.[100]

Throughout my teaching career, time and again, I've watched grit prevail and lack of grit fail. I've seen students with high LSAT scores flunk out and students with below-average LSAT scores reach the top. Two students with 148 LSAT scores come to mind. They both became editors of the law review and graduated in the top 10 percent of their class.

When I asked a group of 1Ls what advice they would give to a close loved one starting law school, I received this reply from a student who wrote the top exam in Torts:

> Do not let below-average undergraduate GPA or LSAT scores discourage you from attending law school. Admittedly, I fell somewhere slightly below average in both, and I nearly decided that I shouldn't come to law school for fear that I wouldn't be able to pass. I spent the first month in constant worry of not being able to compete with classmates who had great LSAT scores. I ended up in the top five of my class after the first semester. My advice would be that if you want to go to law school, use below-average

---

[98]   ANGELA DUCKWORTH, GRIT: THE POWER OF PASSION AND PERSEVERANCE (2016).

[99]   *Id.* at 9–10.

[100]   Notably, grit *and* talent prove to be a winning combination almost every time. *Id.* at 9–10 (observing that when "the talented . . . stick around and try hard . . . they do phenomenally well").

entrance numbers as MOTIVATION in proving your scores wrong, not as reasons you won't pass!

How did this student defy the predictors that said he wouldn't succeed? Read on.

A C.R.E.D.O. for Success

Keeping with the essential goal of this book to offer practical advice that can be implemented by any student on day one, I thought long and hard about the habits—as opposed to innate gifts—that successful law students have in common. I observed the behaviors of top students, particularly my many excellent research assistants over the years. I thought back to my own law school experience. I consulted other law professors. From all of that, I came up with a list of five habits shared by successful students. Top law students invariably are: (1) Consistent; (2) Rigorous; (3) Efficient; (4) Diligent; and (5) Organized. Put these habits together as an acronym and you have a C.R.E.D.O. for success in law school.

It's true that the C.R.E.D.O. habits are part of the intrinsic or at least ingrained personality of some people, but you have the power, with effort, to adopt and adhere to the C.R.E.D.O. habits even if they're not part of your default personality. *I urge you to do so.* Make a conscious decision at the beginning of law school to follow them and stick with it.

As you read the descriptions of each habit below, consider whether the attribute is a natural part of who you are. Be honest with yourself. Identify your C.R.E.D.O. strengths and weaknesses. Take note that the habits overlap to a large extent. For example, students who are consistent are more likely to be organized. Those who are organized are more likely to be efficient, etc. When you identify a weakness, make a point to pay special attention to it from the beginning. It's hard to change habits midstream.

Consistent.

Time for a pop reading-comprehension quiz. Identify the recurring theme in the list below.

The most successful law students:

1.   Read *every* assignment.

2.   Attend *every* class.

3.   Take good notes in *every* class and fill in gaps as soon as possible.

4.   Brief *every* case.

5.   Outline *every* course.

If you answered "consistency," congratulations! You can now brag to people that you aced your first law school test. Successful law students are consistent from beginning to end.

They don't skip a reading assignment because they were out late the night before. They don't miss a class unless they're ill or have a true emergency. If they do miss class, they still read the assignment and make sure to get good notes from classmates. If they have advance notice and the professor allows it, they arrange for the class to be recorded. They don't stop briefing their cases when they hit "The Wall" of the first semester, which occurs somewhere between the seventh and tenth weeks. They recognize that the material covered at the end of the semester is just as important and as likely to be tested as the material at the beginning (probably more so). They don't give up after the first semester because they're disappointed by their grades. They understand that law school is a marathon, not a sprint. Their consistency gives them a definite edge over their classmates who are less consistent, even classmates who are more gifted intellectually.

Of all the mistakes new law students make, being inconsistent in reading assignments, briefing cases, attending class, outlining, periodically reviewing the material, and conducting other study activities is one of the most fatal. Why? Because a law school exam—remember, there's usually only one per course—is only three or four hours long, yet covers an entire semester of material. For a three-credit course, that's forty-two class hours. A four-credit course has fifty-six class hours. Do the math. How do professors work forty-two or fifty-six hours of material into a three- or four-hour exam? They don't. They can't.

Instead, they usually pick out a handful of issues and package them into the essay questions on which your outcome in that course will depend. Many law professors also use multiple-choice questions, in part because they allow for broader course coverage, but multiple-choice questions usually make up only a portion of a first-year exam.

Here are two concrete examples to consider. I went back and studied my Torts I and Torts II exams from a recent year. I always split exams between essay questions and multiple-choice questions, with each section weighted to count for roughly 50 percent of the exam. In Torts I, the essay section was a single, lengthy issue-spotting/problem-solving question, yet it only addressed four issues. Perusing my class notes, I estimated that the four issues were directly covered in just seven out of the forty-two class hours. Thus, any student who missed one or more of those seven classes missed coverage of a substantial portion of the exam material.

In Torts II, I gave my students four shorter essay questions instead of one large one. I calculated that the material addressed in those questions was directly covered in only eight of the forty-two class hours. Of course, with respect to both exams, background material necessary to comprehend the exam issues consumed more class hours.

This is the way it always works. While short essay questions and multiple-choice questions allow professors to broaden course coverage on the exam, the bottom line is that missing law school classes or assignments is the legal education equivalent of playing Russian Roulette.

Here's an interesting factoid. I dug up the grade and attendance records from a previous year's Torts class of seventy students. I added up the absences of the students who received the top seven grades (i.e., the top 10 percent) and the absences of the students who received the lowest seven grades (the bottom 10 percent). The top seven students had only a single absence among them; that is, six had perfect attendance and one student missed one class. The lowest seven students had a total of twenty-three absences.

I repeated the experiment with a different year's class. The results were almost identical. The top 10 percent of the students missed only one class among them, while the bottom 10 percent totaled twenty-four absences.

To have a chance of succeeding at the highest level, you must be consistent in your studying and preparation from the first day to the last day.

Rigorous.

Rigorous is a word with several definitions. Here, it's used to mean "scrupulously right" or "exacting." Legal language is precise. Loose language or vague definitions of legal tests don't cut it. Similarly, partial or incomplete statements of rules won't suffice. More broadly, partial or incomplete *understanding* of what you're learning isn't good enough.

A rigorous understanding of the law will come, in large part, from following the other C.R.E.D.O. components. Going back to consistency, if you miss one day of a two-day discussion of a doctrine, your understanding of that doctrine is going to be less than rigorous.

The starting point for rigorous understanding of the law is getting it down correctly in the first instance in your class notes and then course outlines. Without the "rigorously right" raw material, you won't be able to accurately state and apply the law on the final exams.

Part of being able to apply law effectively on exams comes from a natural analytical gift that some folks are fortunate to possess, but if you can train and police yourself to capture the law accurately and precisely in your notes and outlines, you can gain ground on many other students, even those with superior analytical skills. Note-taking is addressed in Chapter 12 and outlining in Chapter 13.

It's difficult to offer meaningful comparative illustrations of rigorously right and amorphously wrong statements of the law since most readers probably have not yet have started law school and, thus, lack a foundation to recognize the difference. But let's give it the old college try using a simple example from the law of intentional torts.

Suppose the professor is defining the tort of assault in class. She explains that "an assault is a volitional act intended to cause imminent apprehension of a harmful or offensive bodily contact to another person, and such apprehension results, directly or indirectly." This one sentence contains several important words and phrases constituting what we call "operative language." They include the elements of a "volitional act" (as opposed to an involuntary act), "intent" (specifically a subjective intent to cause an imminent apprehension of a harmful or offensive bodily contact), and the requisite consequence (i.e., imminent apprehension of a harmful or offensive bodily contact results, directly or indirectly). Within these elements, all of the following words have legal significance: "volitional," "intended," "imminent," "apprehension," "harmful," "offensive," and "directly or indirectly."

If one were attempting to define the tort of assault on an exam, leaving out or mischaracterizing any of the above terminology would result in a non-rigorous—i.e., wrong—statement of the law. As an example, students often equate "apprehension" with "fear," but they are not technically the same thing under the law. A person can apprehend a bodily contact from another without being in fear of it, in which case an assault would still occur. Suppose a 98-pound weakling came up to former basketball star Shaquille O'Neal on the street, shook his fist and said, "I'm going to sock you, Shaq!" Shaq is more than seven feet tall and weighs more than 300 pounds. It is unlikely he would be afraid of the 98-pound weakling, yet he could still apprehend that a harmful or offensive bodily contact was imminent. Thus, the elements of the tort of assault would be satisfied.

Here's another example, involving a non-rigorous, *incomplete* statement of the law. When you take Torts, you'll learn that, as a general rule, landowners owe no duty to protect unknown trespassers from dangerous conditions on their property. An exception exists, however, with respect to child trespassers, to whom landowners owe higher duties. The dominant test nationwide for when a duty is owed to protect a child trespasser comes from section 339 of an influential treatise known as the *Restatement (Second) of Torts*, with which you will become very familiar. Section 339 provides:

§ 339. Artificial Conditions Highly Dangerous To Trespassing Children

A possessor of land is subject to liability for physical harm to children trespassing thereon caused by an artificial condition upon the land if

(a) the place where the condition exists is one upon which the possessor knows or has reason to know that children are likely to trespass, and

(b) the condition is one of which the possessor knows or has reason to know and which he realizes or should realize will involve an unreasonable risk of death or serious bodily harm to such children, and

(c) the children because of their youth do not discover the condition or realize the risk involved in intermeddling with it or in coming within the area made dangerous by it, and

(d) the utility to the possessor of maintaining the condition and the burden of eliminating the danger are slight as compared with the risk to children involved, and

(e) the possessor fails to exercise reasonable care to eliminate the danger or otherwise to protect the children.

Suppose you had a Torts essay exam question involving a child who was injured trespassing on the site of a chemical factory located three blocks from an elementary school when she went swimming in an unguarded, unfenced pool of sulfuric acid that looked like clear water. Which of the five factors from section 339 would you need to apply on the exam to analyze the problem fully and correctly? *All of them.* Not just two or three factors, or even four.

Section 339 is what is known as a "multifactor legal test," which are common in the law. The five factors—(a) through (e)—are *all* part of the test. (Note that they're joined by the conjunctive *and*, not the disjunctive *or* as is true of many legal tests). The only way a student would be able to apply all five factors would be if he or she had written them all down in her notes and/or outline and studied the complete test prior to the exam.

Sounds simple enough, you say. Well, yes and no. Even though section 339 appears in full in our casebook, and even though we go over the test in class, factor by factor, and even though I tell my students to make sure they get the complete test in their notes, and even though I let students bring in a "cheat sheet" to the exam on which they can write down all the legal rules and tests we covered, whenever I include a child trespasser issue on an exam, half the class will fail to accurately set forth and discuss the entire five-factor test. Some discuss section 339 in general terms. Others discuss some but not all of the factors. Some students fail to mention section 339 at all. Because the individual factors are not terribly difficult to apply, the students who are able to state the test "rigorously right" in their exam answer can usually address the issue well.

(As an aside, note that it is unlikely all of the factors of section 339 or any other multifactor legal test will be *in issue* in an exam question or require equal discussion. In the hypothetical given, for example, factor (b) would not require extensive discussion because it's fairly obvious that an unguarded, unfenced pool of sulfuric acid that looks like clear water is a condition a landowner should realize involves an unreasonable risk of death or serious bodily harm to trespassing children. Factor (b) could be addressed and dispensed with in a single sentence, but it *would* have to be addressed, because it's part of the test.)

Another way to describe the quality of being rigorous is to say that good students recognize the importance of *paying attention to detail* in capturing the law. They're not just in the ballpark. Not just close enough for rock and roll. They get the law right.

Some law professors use partial or complete open-book exams. Depending on the professor, this may include allowing students to bring in their casebooks, relevant rule books (such as, in Civ Pro, the Federal Rules of Civil Procedure), notes, outlines, or something like my cheat sheet. Thus, it may not be necessary to memorize all of the rules with precision, but one would still have to know and understand them in advance to be able to readily access and accurately apply them. It's too late to begin figuring out the law or even where to find it during an exam. There's not enough time.

Efficient.

So much to do, so little time to get it all done. Such is the life of a law student. With a typical load of four or five doctrinal courses and a time-consuming legal research and writing course, the plates of full-time students quickly fill up and begin overflowing. Part-time evening-division students have it even harder. They take fewer courses, but often have to juggle full-time jobs and families along with law school.

As a consequence, it should come as no surprise that all successful law students possess or develop efficient time-management skills. They establish schedules for getting things done and adhere to them. They do all the things they need to do, but don't waste time on things they don't need to do. Being efficient can enable students to succeed at a higher level than inefficient students who labor harder and longer. Think of efficiency as the ultimate and only officially approved "shortcut" method for law school success.

Efficiency in law school is a skill that takes some time to develop. At the beginning, everything is so new and confounding that students can't help being inefficient. The learning ladder, however, is climbed fairly quickly. Within a few weeks, you'll find yourself becoming much more adept at, for example, reading and briefing cases.

The *E* in C.R.E.D.O. is tied closely to the *O*. People who are more organized tend to be more efficient in how they allocate and apply their time. More on organizational skills below. Let's concentrate on some tips for improving your efficiency:

• **Don't waste time during the day.** Given that time is such a precious commodity, it's unfortunate that many students waste much of it during the school day. First-year law students sometimes complain that class schedules are not designed efficiently in that there are too many gaps between classes. They don't realize schedules are sometimes set up this way on purpose as a way to encourage ("compel" might be a better word) students to stay on campus during the day, rather than just attend their classes and flee the building. As a result, you're likely to have free hours available each weekday. Use them productively rather than fritter them away.

Study habits and preferences vary by personality. I hated studying late into the night. I realized this at the very beginning of law school. When I studied late, I'd end up dreaming about law and working in my sleep, waking up tired. After a few weeks of law school, I began developing an awareness of how much time I wasted during the day. My friends and I began each morning playing ping pong in the student lounge. We'd shoot the breeze between classes, even when there were lengthy gaps between the end of one class and the start of another. At lunch, we'd hang out and talk some more, probably gossiping and griping. One day it occurred to me that if I became more efficient during the day, I'd have more free time at night.

So I changed course. I began using every spare minute of the day productively. Within a couple of weeks, I had refined my system to the point where, by the time I left to go home (i.e., when many of my classmates were just getting ready to start studying), I already had most of the assignments for the next day read and briefed. I missed spending more time with my friends at school, but the payoff came each night. I found myself with plenty of time to work on my legal research and writing projects and still have time to just hang out and relax. Those long nights of working out legal problems in my sleep ended. I had found a time-management plan that fit me perfectly.

The point of this story isn't to persuade you to adopt my plan. It worked for me, but it might not work for everyone. Some people prefer studying at night. My purpose is to encourage you to think about how to organize your days so you can use your time more effectively. Each hour wasted during the day has to be made up at night.

• **Don't let diligence work against you by taking on unnecessary tasks.** It's hard for a professor to tell enterprising students to stop "wasting" time in the pursuit of extra legal knowledge, but sometimes I do. Some super-studious and/or inquisitive types (see entry for Curious George/Georgettes in Chapter 4) go above and beyond the call of duty in ways that, while admirable, can actually be detrimental because time is such a limited resource.

A classic example is students who look up the note cases in their casebooks. Most casebooks have main cases called "principal cases," which are followed by notes that reference additional cases, sometimes dozens of them. After all these years, I'm still impressed when a student comes up after class and begins discussing details of one of the note cases that he or she took the time to look up and read in its full version. Impressed, but also a bit troubled.

If the professor hasn't instructed you to look up a note case, she's not going to expect you to know its content. Thus, although you might gain a bit of extra knowledge, it's essentially wasted knowledge. Or more apropos to the discussion, it's wasted time. It could even be harmful knowledge if your extra reading gets you looking at the legal problem in a way different from how the professor and principal cases covered it. Truth be told, I've used the same Torts casebook for more than twenty years and still haven't looked up all of the cases in the notes.

- **Prepare for *every* class, but don't over-prepare for *any* class.** As repeated throughout this book, consistent, diligent class preparation is essential in law school. But some well-intentioned students actually spend too much time preparing for class, especially in briefing cases. Students who focus obsessively on case briefs not only take away time that could be better spent, they sometimes lose sight of the big picture. They end up lost in a forest where they can only see the trees around them (i.e., unnecessary details of individual cases) rather than the bigger picture.

It always saddens me when failing students show me their lengthy case briefs to prove how hard they worked. I page through them, saying sincerely, "Wow, you really put a lot of work into these," but also thinking, "Wow, you really wasted a lot of time on these overly long and excessively detailed briefs, time that you probably could have used more profitably."

As discussed in Chapter 11, case-briefing is *essential* for 1Ls, but the law of diminishing returns applies to case briefs. A brief that takes an hour to write may not be significantly more helpful than one that takes twenty minutes. It could be less helpful if it contains too many irrelevant details. Because cases vary in complexity, it's impossible to state a rule for how long a case brief should be, but as a general guideline, they shouldn't exceed one typewritten page. Half a page will be sufficient for many cases.

An important time-saving tip for efficient case-briefing is *know your professors*. We discussed this earlier. Professors approach classes and case analysis differently. By learning your individual professors' expectations for class preparation, you can save time on your case-briefing. In all courses, you want to be sure to get the rules and basic reasoning out of the cases, but the importance of other details can vary by professor. Consider this comment offered by a recent top student who was editor-in-chief of the law review. He said he briefed every case all the way through law school. No surprise there. But he also emphasized:

> Students should try to get a sense of what each professor is looking for from the class discussions, and modify their case-briefing style by professor accordingly. For example, Professor X would often want details on the parties, while Professor Y only cared about the rules. Professor Y *never* asked what the lower courts did, while other professors asked about that in *every* case. Figuring these things out was very helpful, not only as a 1L, but in upper-level courses with the same professors. I knew that when I had X for Evidence, I'd better know a lot more about the facts than I would for Y's Biz Org class. In short, students can save a lot of time preparing for class by getting to know their professors.

Do not misconstrue the above advice. *Class preparation and case-briefing are crucial to success.* But so are lots of other tasks we perform in our daily lives that can be done more efficiently and, hence, effectively. It all comes back to the fact that time is a scarce, fixed resource that needs to be allocated wisely.

One reason some students give up on case-briefing is because they never learned to do it efficiently. Rather than compromise, they go directly from spending an hour per brief to not doing them at all. Brief all of your cases, but don't spend disproportionate time on any one brief. Let this be your mantra: Prepare for *every* class, but don't over-prepare for *any* class.

• **Don't read far ahead.** Reading ahead in your assignments seems like an effort that would earn you a grade of *A* under the "D for Diligent" part of the C.R.E.D.O., but that kudos would be offset by the *F* you would earn under "E for Efficient." Reading far ahead is a waste of time because you will have to go back and reread everything to remember it, making the first reading wasted time and effort.

Some students, for example, try to read ahead on weekends for the entire next week, but as you'll see from data cited in the note-taking chapter (Chapter 12), people forget 40–70 percent of what they learn by the second day. Generally speaking, you're best off reading an assignment the day before the class. Even then, you'll want to refresh your memory by skimming it over before class. (An exception to this advice exists for part-time evening-division students, most of whom work full-time day jobs. They usually don't have any choice except to study on weekends.)

DO NOT carry this advice to the extreme and try to read your assignment for the first time right before class starts, as some students do. You won't have time to comprehend what you're reading or prepare case briefs and, often, won't have allotted yourself enough time to even finish the assignment. The first class you attend without having completed the reading will be your first step down the academic ladder.

• **Read and follow instructions on assignments.** Efficient law students read and follow the instructions for their assignments. Like the brick house-building pig in *The Three Little Pigs*, they spend a little more time up front and benefit from that investment later. Students who don't exercise the care to carefully read and follow instructions from their professors can end up squandering enormous amounts of time redoing assignments. Worse, often they won't even be granted the opportunity to correct their mistakes.

Legal research and writing courses offer the most opportunities during the semester for students to follow or not follow instructions, so I turned to a director of a legal writing program for help on this one. I emailed him the above paragraph and asked if he knew of any specific examples to demonstrate my point. Here are two attention-getters he sent back:

1. In the spring semester of the course, students must research and write an appellate brief. Students work on their brief for most of the semester, spending dozens of hours on it. The brief assignment covers two issues. I divide the class into two groups. One group works on Issue 1, the other on Issue 2. Students are told their issue and the issue list is posted on the TWEN course site. Despite this, at least one student a year researches and writes about the *wrong* issue. If they're "lucky" enough to figure this out before they turn in the final draft, all of their work will have been wasted. They have to start over and redo the entire brief. If they don't figure out the mistake before turning in the final draft, they get an *F* for the assignment no matter how good the brief is.

2. Each year, one or more students use the wrong ID number on their assignments. Students are assigned ID numbers at the beginning of the year and told to use the numbers in lieu of their names. Some simply make up their own number or use an incorrect number. Later, when I'm assigning final grades and can't find a grade for a pre-assigned ID, I simply mark it as an *F*. When grades are posted, offending students must then go through all the hoops to get the grade changed. They could have avoided all the distress and headaches associated with this time-consuming process simply by reading and following the instructions.

• **Limit your study aids.** Some students go overboard in trying to read too many study aids. Study aids can be extremely helpful, but one per course is, at most, all students need or can realistically handle time-wise. In addition to draining precious hours from your day, using more than one study aid for the same course can cause confusion because different study aids will present the material differently, and all of them are likely to present it differently from how the professor presents it.

The key to using study aids efficiently and effectively is to identify the best study aid for each course before investing in any of them. Quite often, a "gold standard" study aid—one that is widely recognized by students and sometimes even the professor as the best—exists for each course. As recommended in Chapter

2, find out either from the professor or upper-level students which one that is, get it, and stick with it.

Diligent.

I use "diligent" in the sense of being hardworking and staying on task from day one. The most frequently expressed reason I've heard from dismissed law students as to why they were unsuccessful is:

> I didn't understand [choose one: how much work was involved/what I was up against/the demands of law school] until it was too late.

For any of the advice in this book to help—but particularly the study advice in the ensuing chapters—*you need to follow it from the very beginning.*

To be successful, commit yourself to being diligent before you ever cross the threshold of the law school's front door. (More overlap: diligence overlaps with consistency, as well as rigorousness.) While the first semester of law school may seem like an eternity when you're in the midst of it, you'll be shocked at how quickly it passes. You cannot afford to get even one class behind. If you don't follow any other advice in this book, believe this: *You can't catch up.* No, really. You can't catch up.

As mentioned, many 1Ls are cursed by their previous educational successes. They arrive at law school having excelled in high school and undergraduate school without having had to expend tremendous energy.

When first-semester law school grades are distributed, they're genuinely shocked to find they are now only "average," or worse, hanging on to their status as students in good standing by the barest of decimal point margins. How could this be, they ask? In my experience, the answer in most instances is: they weren't sufficiently diligent.

Consider this comment from a student asked whether the first year turned out better or worse than expected:

> Much worse, unfortunately. I honestly thought that law school would be a breeze, difficult, but not more difficult that what I had already accomplished. I was so wrong that in retrospect it's a little amusing. Law school was a hit upside

the head for me. Having gone through high school, straight to college (where I graduated early), then straight to law school, I figured I was invincible.

Do not doubt that hard work can make up for other academic deficiencies. Take to heart the following comment from a student asked to list one thing she wished she had known when starting law school: "You don't have to come from a family of legal scholars to do well in law school. Hard work is truly the great equalizer."

Organized.

On the second day of law school in a fall semester, a student came to my office after Torts and said she missed class because she forgot it met on Wednesday. I smiled and said, "Make sure you get someone's notes because the stuff we covered was important." She assured me she had it covered, thanked me, and left.

I wanted to tell her that I doubted very much that she had it covered because the material was complex, especially for a beginning law student. I wanted to tell her that her Torts grade might already be in jeopardy because she missed the critical class at which we delved into the fundamental element of "intent" that underlies all of the intentional torts, a subject we would be studying for the next five weeks and which is always tested on the exam. I didn't say any of it because it was too late. She had already missed the class. She missed it because she wasn't organized enough to keep track of her class schedule.

Last but certainly not least in the C.R.E.D.O. of successful law student habits is "Organized." Being organized is a fitting habit to conclude the C.R.E.D.O. because it's entwined with all of the other C.R.E.D.O. factors. Being organized makes it easier to be consistent, rigorous, efficient, and diligent because successful application of those habits depends on having a well-plotted plan of attack. Organization, of course, is an asset in the pursuit of any endeavor, whether it's planning a vacation or preparing your tax return. It's especially critical in law school because of the sheer volume of material and activities that need to be ordered and managed.

Other things being equal, law school is one place where being a bit "anal retentive" or "obsessive" can be a benefit, assuming you're obsessing about the right things. In Chapter 2, I talked about the Myers-Briggs Type Indicator (MBTI), a personality inventory grounded in Jungian psychological type theory that measures preferences for different personality indicia, specifically: Extraversion vs. Introversion, Sensing vs. Intuitive, Thinking vs. Feeling, and Judging vs. Perceiving. I explained that your "type" is a combination of four letters, one from each pairing. I suggested you take the MBTI and consider looking into Martha and Don Peters' book, *Juris Types*, explaining how the MBTI applies to law student learning styles.

If you take or have previously taken the MBTI, look at the last of the four letters in your personality type and see if you're a "J" or a "P." While Ps possess some advantages over Js in law school (Js need to work harder at accepting ambiguity, delaying decisions until all the evidence is in, and listening in class for more than "the answer"), Js usually have the advantage with regard to being organized. The natural preference of Js is to organize, plan, and order the world around them. In general, they are more methodical. To the contrary, Ps prefer flexibility and open-endedness to planning and deadlines. They often find themselves scrambling at the last minute to finish tasks.

These preferences frequently carry over to education and work environments, where Js benefit from their organizational and planning skills and attention to detail. If you are the type of person who often forgets or loses things, is frequently late, and is always finishing tasks at the last minute, the chances are excellent that you're a P. Be conscious of this preference and recognize that, while a P preference carries other benefits in educational settings, you'll have to work harder on organization, planning, and scheduling than your colleagues with a J preference.

Alright, enough with the psychoanalysis, especially since you're going to need a whole lot more of it after the first year. Kidding. Let's turn to two concrete organizational suggestions. I'll give you several others related to study techniques and exam preparation in later chapters. These are big picture organizational tips that are easy to follow if you commit yourself to doing so consistently. They not only will improve your chances of success in law school, but save you time, headaches, and unnecessary emotional trauma.

- **Keep track of your schedule religiously.** To even begin resembling an organized person, you need to keep detailed track of what's going on in your life. Your law school life will be ridiculously busy. Added to all of your existing family, social, and (for part-time students) employment obligations, will be: class times (regular, rearranged, and make-up classes), reading assignments, room assignments, study group sessions, deadlines for legal research and writing assignments, review sessions, skills workshops, luncheons, student organization meetings, computer research training, application deadlines for scholarships and summer jobs, and, of course, your exam schedule.

Almost as important as documenting events, you want to block out specific times for study activities (e.g., "Work on Contracts outline," "Do practice exam for Civ Pro") and even recreational activities and errand-running (e.g., "Lunch with Matt and Lisa," "Work out").

I never owned a day planner before attending law school, but started using one religiously the first week I got there. In preparing this book, I found in my attic the moldy day planner I used in my first term at the University of Florida College of Law. For the first three weeks I found, along with all of my reading assignments and regular class times, dated entries like these:

5 pm library tour

Buy Bluebook (Uniform System of Citation)

Buy supplement and highlighters

Study group meets at carrels 2 pm

Legal research lecture Rm 190, 4:10 pm

Get photos taken and fingers printed for FL bar application

Study group meets 7 pm

10:20 Lexis instruction

Dickey Betts concert 2 pm

9:00 pm poolside party at Viscaya

Torts-Contracts class switch

Exercise 1 due in legal research

Fla. Bar exec. dir. 1–3 pm auditorium

Torts meets for two hours—12:40 in Aud. 1:50 in 190C

No study group tonight. Call to confirm cancellation.

Poker game tonight

Extra K [Contracts] class 1:50 in 190A

Later in the term, I found entries blocking off time for things like: "Study Property," "Work on memo," "Finish reading *Legalines*," "Review Civ Pro notes," and "Make case index for Con Law."

Maybe these calendar entries will cheer you up. I laughed out loud at the fact that I apparently was able to work in a pool party, rock concert, and poker game in those first three weeks of law school. So much for my stories about trudging twenty miles through the snow—in Florida!—to get to law school. But, hey, that's part of the beauty of being organized: it frees up more recreational time.

It's comforting to know that some things never change. In response to a request for organizational tips, here's what one of my research assistants, a top student, wrote. Notice the striking similarities in her approach to the one I adopted decades earlier:

My helpful hint for being organized with so much going on is to write everything down and block off time periods. My calendar breaks down each day of the week into hours so that I can block off class times and then also I'll block off each hour or so for a certain purpose (example: "update Civ Pro Outline" or "read *Glannon's* on res ipsa loquitur"). I even have workout time blocked off a few days a week. I realized I might be somewhat OCD after looking back at this. I found that having a plan of what I was going to study and when I was going to do it helped me get it done with much less stress. I did this especially on the weekends because I'm the kind of student who will sit down and work all day, but you have to take a break sometimes or you will quickly go insane. So with my list I would, on Saturday mornings and/or afternoons, do what I had planned, and then I would have the rest of the day to do something non-school related.

As I mentioned back in Chapter 2, I still use old-fashioned day planners with real paper and a lot of modern law students do the same because it's easier to map out and visualize one's life on a paper planner than on a phone screen. Whatever instrument you choose, just make sure you keep it with you at all times and keep it current and complete.

• **Organize your course materials.** Your main "course material" for your doctrinal courses (most likely all of your first-year courses except Legal Research and Writing) will be your casebook, along with any other required books. But professors often supplement the casebook with extra materials such as additional cases, statutes, Restatement provisions, or law review or news articles. In Legal Research and Writing (see Chapter 18), you'll have more materials to manage, such as research exercises, writing assignments, and the research for your writing assignments (e.g., cases, statutes, regulations).

Of course, you'll also have self-generated materials such as case briefs, class notes, and course outlines.

You need to keep all of this stuff organized, so you can lay your hands on each item when you need it. Electronic materials should be kept in folders organized by course. Paper handouts or print-outs should be kept in a binder notebook with tabbed dividers by course.

Bring necessary course materials to each class. At least once a week, I experience a moment in Torts that provides me with enough information, if I stopped to gather it, to divide the class into two groups I could label *Most Likely to Succeed* and *Less Likely to Succeed.*

How is that possible? At the beginning of Torts, I distribute a package of materials to supplement our casebook readings called, not very creatively, the *Supplemental Materials for Torts I* (or Torts II). The Supplemental Materials comprise about fifty pages of state-specific tort statutes, key sections from the *Restatements* of the law of torts (influential treatises), extra cases, problems, and a hodge-podge of other stuff.

At the beginning of the course, I tell students orally and in writing to bring the Supplemental Materials to *every class* because they won't always know in advance when we'll be referring to them. I also caution them that everything contained in the Supplemental Materials is fair game for the exam.

Every few days we'll come to a point during a class where I say, "Get out your Supplemental Materials and go to page *x*."

The *organized* students—the students who are more likely to succeed—promptly access the Supplemental Materials and turn to the proper page. The *unorganized* students—those who are less likely to succeed—sit looking around for the nearest organized student whose shoulder they can glance over, because they forgot to bring the Supplemental Materials. They're not bad people or even bad students. They're just not well-organized.

If you start out organized, it's a snap to stay that way. On the other hand, if you start out disorganized, you may never be able to pull everything together and your performance will suffer accordingly.

* * *

As we prepare to launch into chapters discussing study, exam-prep, and exam-taking strategies, pause and take stock of the C.R.E.D.O. habits. Keep them in mind as you read the forthcoming advice. Note how much of it ties in with the C.R.E.D.O. habits.

If you look up the definition of "credo," you'll find something like "a statement of the beliefs or aims that guide someone's actions." Make the C.R.E.D.O. your credo. Write it on sticky notes and post them on your refrigerator and study carrel. When the going gets tough and you're tempted to slack, remember the words of Tony Allen, the Grindfather: "All heart. Grit. Grind."

CHAPTER 11

CASE-BRIEFING

Case-briefing is the grunt work of law school, one of the most tedious, time-consuming, unglamorous—and certainly most underappreciated—aspects of being a good law student. A "case brief" is a synopsis of a judicial opinion that captures the key elements. Most first-year professors will expect you to come to class having not only carefully read the assigned cases, but having prepared a written case brief for each of them. Some first-year professors demand that students prepare briefs, although such demands are difficult to enforce.

Nearly all students begin their law school careers as diligent case brief writers, but as the first semester wears on, some students stop briefing their cases. In the second semester, the number of consistent case-briefers dwindles further. The trend accelerates in upper-level courses.

Students who stop preparing case briefs try to compensate by substituting online briefs or "book-briefing," a technique in which students use underlining, highlighting, and marginal notes in the casebook to track the case in a brief-like form. I confess that I resorted to book-briefing cases in some upper-level courses when I was a student, but I prepared a written brief for every case in every course in my first year. You need to do the same.

Why Case-Briefing Is Essential to Success

Learning to read and analyze a case is crucial to understanding law and legal method. Indeed, it is a principal goal of the case method. By reading, I don't just mean decoding the words. That will be hard enough at the beginning given that the law has a language of its own. In addition to your new vocabulary, which will—I am not making this up—include the word "enfeoffment," you'll come upon familiar words that have different meanings in law than in ordinary usage. A new student reading a property law case might think "legal issue" means the procedural or substantive issue of law in the case, which it might, but it's also legalese for "children."

Far more challenging when reading a case than understanding the legalese, which you'll pick up quickly, is *comprehending* what the words are actually saying—sentence by sentence, paragraph by paragraph, and, finally, as a whole. As you'll learn within about five minutes of tackling your first assignments, the principal reason preparing for law school classes takes a long time is because judicial opinions require careful reading *and* rereading. But even reading a case several times is not by itself going to enable you, the novice legal reader, to fully process and understand it.

In evaluating the utility of case-briefing, students tend to focus on the usefulness of the final product—the briefs themselves—but the *process* of composing case briefs is more important. Case-briefing forces you to identify what's important, separate it from the rest, and assemble it into an organized framework. The combined mental and physical process of extracting the case elements and writing them down in your own words will help you better understand and retain what you read. Just as important, it will call your attention to the parts you don't understand.

In short, case-briefing teaches you to analyze law. You won't accomplish the same goals as well through book-briefing, and certainly not by substituting online briefs, which are widely available. In addition to requiring little mental processing, online or other "canned briefs," as law profs call them, are not always accurate.

This is no time to overestimate yourself. No matter how smart you are or think you are, beginning 1Ls simply are not equipped to read, deconstruct, and digest complex judicial opinions without composing case briefs.

Even law professors, who, unlike you, are expert legal readers, essentially brief the cases they assign to students in their own class notes. They don't just read the cases, mosey into class and start talking about them. They extract all the essential ingredients from the case and put them into writing in their course notes in their own words.

The problem is that these benefits of case-briefing are intangible. That, combined with the time-sucking nature of preparing case briefs, leads many students to give up on case-briefing too soon. The benefits of case-briefing, though unseen, are real. But you don't have to trust my opinion. Trust the students quoted below. I wrote to three students, each of them ranked number one in their respective class, and asked if they briefed all of their cases as a 1L. Here are their responses:

- I briefed all my cases in all my classes during my entire 1L (and most of my 2L) year. I know many people who relied upon "online briefs" but these were not typically the highest-ranked students. In my opinion, briefing cases during the 1L year cannot be overemphasized.—*Number 1 in 3L class*

- The first semester I personally did my own briefs for about 95 percent of the cases. The second semester I prepared my own briefs for about 75 percent of the cases. For the remaining cases, I would use online briefs to which I would add my own details.—*Number 1 in 2L class*

- I briefed every single case that I read as a 1L. That is not to say that I don't read online case briefs, or even incorporate some of the lines from those case briefs into my own. But I never *just* read an online case brief, nor do I copy-paste an online case brief into my own or print off an online case brief. I read the case, make notes in my textbook as I gather the reasoning that I believe is relevant, THEN read the online case brief, THEN make my own case brief. It sounds like a lot, but it doesn't take much time when you get efficient at it. While everyone is different, the three guys I study with, who pretty much followed the same process as me, all did well (top 10, 15, 25 percent).—*Number 1 in 1L class*

Note from the above that even top students sometimes consult online briefs as a way to supplement their understanding of cases and to bolster their own briefs. Nothing wrong with that. We did it with printed canned briefs back in the day. The key is that you stick to *supplementing* and not resort to *substituting*. Students who make a habit of preparing their own briefs are demonstrating the essential C.R.E.D.O. qualities of Consistency and Diligence.

Does this mean that all students who don't brief their cases are destined to flunk out of law school? No. I asked students who had read an earlier edition of *1L of a Ride* what changes they would make in subsequent edition. One student replied:

> I disagree with your emphasis on case-briefing. My GPA is not stellar, but I am certainly not on academic probation and my grades are above the 2.5 required to compete for law review. I think that less time spent case-briefing and more time spent working on hypos and old exams, and also reading study aids, is time better spent. I feel that the professor will tell me what they want to see on an exam during lecture and that by case-briefing I am merely reinventing the wheel. (Ironically, I see *1L of a Ride* advertised on casebriefs.com, which is where I go to get the majority of my case briefs for your class and all of my other ones.)

I loved having this guy as a student. He qualified as both a Lightning Rod and Class Joker under the student types outlined in Chapter 4, so it didn't surprise me that he would be a straight shooter. But his comment about professors telling him what he needs to know misses the point of case-briefing.

He's correct that many students who don't brief their cases succeed in law school. He's also right that, as emphasized in the C.R.E.D.O. chapter, some students spend too much time on case-briefing and not enough on other things like working through examples and old exams. Balance is the key to most things in law school and life. Also, while the student's 2.5 GPA was respectable, the students quoted above had GPAs in the stratosphere (3.7 to 3.9 range). Briefing your cases certainly will not guarantee you will come out as a top student, but *not* briefing them will ensure that you won't.

In terms of more tangible benefits of case-briefing, the end-results—the actual briefs—are also useful. Briefs can be helpful in class, especially if you get called on. They aren't a full-proof security blanket because professors often will ask about parts of the case you didn't understand or didn't think were important enough to write down. But that's okay. If a professor knows you're prepared, which she almost always will if you've made a brief, you'll sail through Socratic questioning unscathed.

Briefs also are helpful in composing course outlines, although don't make the common mistake of simply incorporating your briefs as part of your outlines. This point is covered in Chapter 13, the outlining chapter.

Finally, briefs can be useful in exam preparation as a refresher for what was covered throughout the semester. However, because briefs are prepared before you attend the classes in which the cases are covered, you don't want to rely too heavily on them unless you make a practice of editing them during or after class, which many students do. Your professors invariably will emphasize different aspects of the case and/or present the material differently in class than you conceptualized it.

Like most other skills in life, case-briefing takes some practice to develop. Your early briefs will be terrible. Expect it and don't let it alarm you. They'll be too long and filled with unnecessary details while at the same time omitting important elements of the case. I still remember the first case brief I composed in law school. It was for Contracts. Our casebook contained no topic headings (an experimental approach that proved to be a major fail), so I was clueless even as to the general subject matter I was supposed to be looking for. I studied the opinion long and hard, then began writing longhand in a spiral notebook. My final product was anything but "brief"—more than two pages of rambling, unrelated fragments, most of them copied directly from the case. I knew it was junk, but had no idea how to improve it.

Within a few weeks, however, my case briefs began undergoing transformation, becoming more compact and accurate, almost day by day. Without realizing it at the time, I was learning how to analyze law. The case and Socratic methods were working. This will happen to you. Have faith.

Early inefficiency and overly long briefs are what tempt too many students to give up case-briefing. Stick with it. Tweaking one of the efficiency rules from the C.R.E.D.O. chapter, *Brief every case, but don't over-brief any case.*

Casebook Structure and Organization

Understanding how casebooks are structured will give you a head start in reading and processing the cases. Casebooks are divided by topic, with broad topics subdivided into more refined subsections. For example, many Torts casebooks begin with a section on "Intentional Torts." That section may in turn be broken down as follows:

- A beginning subsection addressing "intent," the crucial element common to all of the intentional torts;

- Separate subsections for each of the seven basic intentional torts (assault, battery, false imprisonment, intentional infliction of emotional distress, trespass to land, trespass to chattels, and conversion); and

- Separate subsections covering the main "privileges" or defenses to intentional torts (consent, self-defense, defense of others, defense of property, recovery of property, and necessity).

Within each subsection heading, the casebook will offer one or more judicial opinions that stand for and elucidate fundamental rules or principles regarding the topic. Most of these opinions will have been heavily edited by the casebook authors. An appeal may require the court to resolve numerous legal issues, but casebooks generally use opinions to address a single issue, excising portions covering extraneous issues. Other non-essential content also will be trimmed or summarized, including analysis of case precedent, non-essential background facts and procedure, dissenting and concurring opinions, and case citations.

This is all good news for law students. It means, for example, that instead of having to read a fifty-page opinion, you only have to read a five-page opinion. The extent of the editing depends both on the editing skill and philosophy of the casebook authors, as well as the nature of the course. U.S. Supreme Court cases, for example, are usually longer, even after extensive editing, than other cases, in part because it's often necessary to include portions of concurring or dissenting opinions. Thus, in 1L courses where Supreme Court cases play a large role, such as Civil Procedure and Constitutional Law, the opinions in your casebook will tend to be longer.

Principal (or "main") cases usually are followed by notes, many of which discuss additional cases. Unless they tell you otherwise, it's safe to assume your professors do not expect you to brief or even look up the full versions of the note cases (also called "squib cases"), although you certainly will want to study any assigned notes carefully. Professors may devote significant class time to discussing selected notes. Also, the notes often contain clearer, more comprehensive explanation of the law than the case itself.

How to Read and Brief a Case

I can't give you a concrete formula for how to read a case. The ability to read and synthesize judicial opinions is developed through repetition and by modeling the case analysis conducted by your professors in class. I can give you some good tips though.

Place the case in context.

Before you begin reading a case, place it in the proper spot on your big-picture canvas of the course by paying attention to where the case falls within the casebook's table of contents and section headings. Every case is put in a casebook at a particular place for a reason. A tort case that falls under the broad table of contents heading of "Intentional Torts" and the subheading of "Intent" is inserted to teach you something about the element of intent common to all intentional torts. Even if the case involves the tort of battery, it's not there to teach you about battery. Nor is it there to teach you about tort damages or negligence law or any other topic. Cases intended to teach you about those topics will be grouped under their own relevant headings and subheadings.

When students fail to contextualize the case—i.e., figure out where it fits in the context of the particular reading assignment as well as the broader topics being covered—they're unable to make discriminating choices when reading the case about what is important and what isn't. Even a judicial opinion that has been substantially edited for a casebook can touch on several points. Contextualizing the case within the framework of the book will help you get your bearings before you begin reading, which in turn will make it easier for you to identify the correct issue when you come upon it. It also will help you tailor your briefs more efficiently.

Don't skim.

Judicial opinions can't be skimmed by novices. You need to read every word. As Legal Writing Professor Leslie Burton wrote me in an email:

> When you read, you can't just *read*. You have to read every word. You have to read every sentence. Then you have to reread and analyze to make sure you understand. I once had a class of students who clearly hadn't understood the statute that they had read for homework. When I explained in class how to interpret the statutory language, one student complained: "But that would mean that we would need to read every word." Yes, that's right.

The devil is in the details in law, so you need to pay attention to them. One problem for new students is they're not sure what details to focus on. While all details must be read, not all of them are important. Getting a feel for distinguishing which details are important (e.g., what was the court's holding?) and which ones aren't (e.g., what was the Court of Azzize and why did it have three Zs in its name?) takes practice.

Realistically, as you progress through law school, you'll learn that some portions of some judicial opinions in some courses can, in fact, be skimmed. Sometimes it depends on the length of the opinion and the manner in which it has (or hasn't) been edited. Sometimes it depends on the professor. You'll learn that some professors focus on the details of every assigned case, while some rely on the cases only to get the basic legal principles out of them. I still recall spending hours reading a sixty-page opinion in Corporations only to come to class and learn that the professor was interested only in the one-sentence holding that corporate officers owe a fiduciary duty to shareholders.

Some professors never even mention the cases they assign. My Secured Transactions professor assigned tons of reading from the casebook each class, but never breathed a word about any of the cases in class. After a couple of weeks, my mates and I decided it was pointless to continue reading the casebook assignments. Instead, we took furious notes, studied Article 9 of the Uniform Commercial Code (which is the subject of Secured Transactions), and bought a study aid. But don't get your hopes up. It's unlikely you'll run into that type of professor or course in the first year. Secured Transactions is what is known as a "code course," meaning the bulk of the law in the area is derived from a code, or book of statutes, rather than from cases. Most first-year doctrinal courses are heavily dependent on case law.

In any event, you won't be in a position to skim *any* portion of *any* case until *after* you've mastered the art of case-analysis.

Resolve confusion as you encounter it.

Research shows that higher performing students stop and clarify their confusion about portions of a case as they read it before moving on, while lower performing students are more likely to just plow ahead, leaving their questions unanswered. If you read a paragraph that doesn't make sense to you, go back and reread it before moving to the next one.

Highlight.

Highlighting with markers is a helpful tool for law students. I highlighted my books extensively as a law student and still do it as a professor. I find that the physical process of highlighting helps me absorb and retain material better. Highlighting also facilitates quick review of the material, as when you're refreshing your memory of the reading right before class. If you're called on in class, highlighting makes it easier to track down the relevant excerpt of the case to answer the question.

Many students use different colored highlighters for different components of the case. For example: green for facts, yellow for procedure, purple for reasoning, and pink for the case holding.

Not long ago, I had a student who made no marks of any kind in her casebooks. When I asked why, she said she wanted to be able to recoup more money for the books when she resold them after the semester. Bad cost-benefit analysis. She was academically dismissed at the end of the first year. Your success, in which you're already investing many thousands of dollars, not to mention your blood, sweat, and tears, is worth far more than a few extra bucks come book resale time. Mark those books up!

Of course, highlighting is not a panacea. I'm not suggesting the academic difficulties of the student referred to above were attributable solely to a lack of highlighting. Some students think if they apply heavy-handed highlighting and underlining to a case, they've done an excellent job of studying the case, but that is not necessarily true. You can highlight every line of a case in a color pastiche worthy of being hung in a gallery, yet still come away without a real understanding of it. That's why you need to brief it!

Abbreviate.

With respect to both case briefs and outlines, developing a shorthand for oft-repeated words and terms will increase your efficiency. Traditionally, for example, law profs and students abbreviated "plaintiff" with a pi symbol (π) and "defendant" with a delta symbol (Δ). Why didn't we just use P and D? Because we didn't have computers and those two letters can end up looking like each other when handwritten. P and D are fine if you're using a computer. "Contract" is abbreviated "K," while "contracted" can be shortened to "K-ed." Similarly, "reasonable" can be shortened to "R" and "reasonably" to "R-ably." Terms can also be abbreviated. "Fee simple absolute" can be "FSA," "intentional infliction of emotion distress" can be "IIED," and so on.

The Essential Components of a Case Brief

Different advice-givers offer different formats for case briefs, which can be confusing to law students. But don't worry. There is no single correct format to use for case-briefing. If you peruse different recommended templates for case-briefing, you'll see that while they may use different section headings or put them in a different order, they all seek to capture the same main points about a case. When you get to the case-briefing exercise below, for example, you'll see that the three students whose briefs are included as examples all used somewhat different formats in briefing the sample case.

Regardless of the specific format, when reading a case, especially when starting out, you want to identify and include in your brief these components:

The relevant facts.

Law means little except in relation to facts. A change in a single fact can change the outcome of the case. As the famous English jurisprudential scholar Blackstone said, for every case resolved on a point of law, one hundred will be resolved on the facts. I will never forget my professor in Business Organizations who drilled the importance of the facts into us in a most unforgettable manner. "It's all about the *blanking* facts! It's the *blanking* facts!" He would scream this at us several times per class hour, except he didn't say "blanking." He used the F-word. Even back then, it struck us as an unusual classroom technique, but we definitely got the point.

The trick is separating the relevant facts from the irrelevant ones. Well-written judicial opinions will do much of the work for you in this regard. A skilled judge will focus on the relevant facts in setting forth the case in the written opinion. Further aid will come from the casebook authors, who may edit out unnecessary facts or even summarize the key facts for you.

Nevertheless, the cases in your casebooks (as well as questions on your exams) often will contain both material and immaterial facts. Distinguishing them will be part of the broader challenge of learning to conduct legal analysis, which will be especially difficult at the beginning of law school because you will lack the necessary foundation. This is one reason case briefs are longer early on and get shorter as students progress. At the beginning, you'll be more likely to include unnecessary facts in your briefs.

The amount of relevant facts to include in a brief will vary by the course and individual case. The relevant facts of many cases in Torts and Criminal Law are often simple and few in number as compared to the relevant facts of Contracts and Property cases, which can involve complicated business transactions. In tort cases, for example, the dates of events usually are not important, whereas they often are in contract cases. Of course, these are just general propositions. Everything depends on the particular case. In some tort cases the dates are crucial and in some contract cases they're not.

The procedural history/posture of the case.

The procedural history and posture of a case is the portion of the opinion explaining how the case ended up before the appellate court that wrote the opinion in the casebook. Under U.S. law, a party who desires to appeal an adverse ruling in a trial court must identify a particular error alleged to have occurred during the trial or pretrial proceedings. It's not a ground for appeal simply that the party lost and wants a second bite at the apple.

Trying to understand the procedural posture of a case may feel overwhelming starting out because you'll lack knowledge of the procedural mechanisms of the U.S. litigation system. The problem is exacerbated by the fact that the course designed to impart much of that knowledge—Civil Procedure—sometimes is not included as part of the first-semester curriculum and even when it is, the course is taken contemporaneously with the other first-year courses.

To give you an edge, below are the *Top Five Most Commonly Alleged Errors on Appeal* you will encounter in reading appellate court opinions in civil cases (as opposed to criminal cases), which will make up most of your first-year reading. Understanding these five errors will put you several steps ahead in the first weeks of law school.

PRODUCT WARNING: If you have not started law school yet, studying the five errors may cause drowsiness. In extreme cases, eye-glazing can occur. If you experience these symptoms, stop reading, tab this page, and return to the five errors when you begin reading your initial casebook assignments.

Top Five Most Commonly Alleged Errors on Appeal

1. ***The trial court erred in granting the defendant's motion to dismiss (sometimes called a demurrer) before trial.*** All lawsuits are commenced with the filing of a complaint by the plaintiff. The complaint outlines the grounds for the lawsuit and essential facts supporting those grounds. The rules

of civil procedure provide that if a complaint is defective on its face, the defendant can file a motion to dismiss the complaint (and, hence, the lawsuit).

A variety of grounds exist for dismissing a complaint. One of the most common is a generic assertion that the complaint fails to state a valid claim. If the defendant moves to dismiss the complaint and the court agrees that the complaint is deficient, the court will dismiss the complaint without a trial. Plaintiffs who have had their complaints dismissed may appeal on the basis that the trial judge committed error in granting the motion to dismiss.

2. *The trial court erred in granting a motion for* *summary judgment before trial.* Similar to a motion to dismiss, a motion for summary judgment is a mechanism for disposing of a case without a trial. The motion can only be granted when no material facts are in dispute and the moving party is entitled to judgment as a matter of law. If material facts are in dispute, the case must go to trial so that the fact-finder (either the judge in a bench trial or the jury in a jury trial) can resolve the disputed facts.

Unlike a motion to dismiss, which is based solely on the content of the complaint, a motion for summary judgment can be supplemented by external facts established by documents, affidavits, depositions, and answers to written questions called interrogatories. But again, those facts can't be in dispute. Alleged error in granting a summary judgment is a common basis for an appeal.

3. *The trial court committed an error during a trial* *that led to an adverse jury verdict.* When the jury returns a verdict for one party, the losing party may appeal if the party can point to an error in the trial. While a variety of errors can occur during trials, two of the most common trial errors asserted as grounds for appeal are that the evidence was insufficient to support the verdict and that the trial court gave improper instructions to the jury.

The first ground—that the evidence was insufficient to support the verdict—is self-explanatory. The argument often arises in conjunction with the more specific assertion that the trial court erred in denying the losing party's motion for directed verdict made during the trial, which is discussed separately below.

The second ground—that the trial court erred in giving or failing to give a particular jury instruction—requires elaboration. As it is often said, in a jury trial the "jury is the judge of the facts and the judge is the judge of the law." This means that the jury determines what actually happened based on the evidence it hears and the judge determines the appropriate law to govern the case. When all the evidence has been received, the trial judge instructs the jurors as to that law by reading them written "jury instructions." These instructions are often contentiously fought over by the parties. If the judge gives a jury instruction that a party believes is wrong under the law or refuses to give an instruction that a party believes is required by the law and that party loses, the party may assert that alleged error in an appeal.

4. *The trial court erred in granting or denying a motion for a directed verdict during trial.* A motion for a directed verdict is a motion made during a trial by either the plaintiff or defendant (usually the defendant) in which the moving party argues that, even viewing the evidence in the light most favorable to the other side, no reasonable jury could find in the non-moving party's favor. If the judge agrees, the judge will grant the motion, directing a verdict in favor of the moving party, hence, "taking the case from the jury."

The party against whom the directed verdict was issued may appeal arguing that the granting of the motion was in error. Conversely, if the judge denies the motion and the jury returns a verdict adverse to the moving party, the moving party may appeal on the ground that the judge erred in refusing to grant the directed verdict.

5. *The trial court erred after trial in granting or denying a motion for new trial or judgment notwithstanding the verdict.* After a verdict has been rendered, it is common for the losing party to file a motion for a new trial or, less commonly, for a judgment notwithstanding the verdict (called "motion for j.n.o.v."). Such motions argue that the verdict was contrary to the evidence or that some other error

occurred that renders the jury's decision defective. If the judge orders a new trial or enters a j.n.o.v., the non-moving party may appeal, alleging error in that decision. Conversely, if the judge denies the motion, the moving party may appeal the denial as error.

Students face a dilemma in deciding how much procedural history to include in their case briefs. In some instances, the procedural history of a case may be complex, requiring a lengthy paragraph to explain it accurately. I recommend that you begin law school by including an accurate procedural posture for each case in your briefs, both to protect yourself in class in case the prof calls on you asking for such information, but also to start you on your way toward understanding litigation procedure.

This can be time-consuming, however, and often unnecessary for class preparation purposes over the long term because, as we've discussed, many professors are not interested in the procedural posture of cases when case-dialoguing. After you progress several weeks into the course, be more discriminating about how much procedural background you include in your briefs. If you have professors who rarely ask about the procedural history of a case, you can trim that section of your briefs in those courses.

The issue(s) in the case.

To have any chance of learning to analyze law properly, you will have to learn to "spot issues," in cases, on exams, and in the practice of law. Identifying the key issue in the case is the essential foundation on which any strong case brief is built. Some folks have an analytical knack for issue-spotting from the moment they start law school. Most others develop the skill over time.

"The issue" of a case is *the point* of the case, as in "What's the point?" For each case, ask yourself: Why is this case in this book in this section under this subsection? What are the casebook authors trying to teach me by including it? Thinking about these questions can help you pinpoint the issues.

Students frequently confuse the *procedural issue* in the case, such as those listed above, with the *issue of substantive law* they're supposed to be focusing on. Such mistakes are perfectly understandable and in one sense aren't even mistakes because courts often explicitly state the issue in procedural terms, as in: "The issue in this case is whether the trial court erred in granting the defendant's motion for directed verdict."

But that's not why the authors put the case in the book. That will be the technical procedural issue in a hundred cases you will read. The issue you're looking for is the underlying issue of *substantive law* that the court is taking time to explain and offer rules and reasoning regarding. It may be that your professor also will want you to know the procedural issue, but come exam time, you'll be tested on the substantive law.

How do you spot the issue of substantive law? Not infrequently, you'll be lucky and the court will expressly state: "The issue in this case is . . ." followed by the substantive legal issue. But courts often do not expressly identify the issue, leaving it readers to infer the issue from the court's discussion of the holding, rules, and reasoning.

Sometimes you will have to think beyond the narrow issue raised by the case facts and infer a larger issue from the holding. For example, in studying the tort of intentional infliction of emotional distress, you might read *Slocum v. Food Fair Stores of Florida, Inc.*,[101] in which a stock clerk told an elderly woman who asked for the price of an item, "If you want to know the price, you'll have to find out the best way you can . . . you stink to me." The woman allegedly suffered great emotional distress and a heart attack because of the statement.

You will learn that to make out a claim of intentional infliction of emotional distress, the plaintiff must prove "extreme and outrageous conduct" by the defendant as one of the elements of the tort. The broad issue in *Slocum* was whether "mere insults" constitute extreme and outrageous conduct (the answer is that they generally do not), not the narrow question of whether it is legally permissible to inform a person that she smells bad. But, unfortunately, the *Slocum* court never came right out and said that was the issue, leaving it to students to infer the broader issue from the narrow facts.

---

[101]   100 So. 2d 396 (Fla. 1958).

Here's a great tip for issue-spotting. In addition to placing the case in the context of the subject headings as already suggested, study the notes following the case. Often these notes will identify the issue more clearly than the case itself. For example, the first note following the *Slocum* opinion as it appears in the popular Prosser, Wade, and Schwartz Torts casebook asks: "Why is the intentional infliction of mental disturbance by the *insult* not a tort in itself?"[102] This question essentially identifies the issue in the case for students. If you're struggling to figure out the issue, skip to the notes to see if they identify it for you, then go back to the case.

The rule(s) adopted by the court regarding the issue(s).

Ultimately, you usually will be looking to find one or more legal rules in a case. These are the rules that you will be expected to know and apply on the exam. The rules are intimately tied to the issue. One way to think about it is that the issue is the *question* of the case and the rule as applied is the *answer* to the question.

Generally, each case in a casebook will stand for one particular rule or an exception to a rule. If the case stands for an exception to a broader rule and you haven't already studied the broader rule, be sure to capture both the broad rule *and* the exception in your brief. The case-briefing exercise below provides an example elucidating this point.

As with issue-spotting, sometimes identifying the rule is simple while other times the rule can be elusive. The rule of the case is often bound up with the court's "holding" in the case; and, indeed, many people label the rule section of their briefs as the holding section. The holding is the court's resolution of the issue, which often incorporates the rule. Thus, one tip for rule-spotting (as well as issue-spotting) is to look for sentences that begin with words like "We hold . . . ."

Here's an example from a case you will read if your Torts professor covers the topic of defamation. In *Gertz v. Welch*,[103] the

---

[102]   Victor E. Schwartz et al., Prosser, Wade and Schwartz's Torts: Cases and Materials 60 (13th ed. 2015) (emphasis added).

[103]   418 U.S. 323 (1974).

U.S. Supreme Court, following up on *New York Times v. Sullivan* (the case used for the Socratic dialogue sample back in Chapter 7), was faced with the question of whether the First Amendment requires that the hard-to-hurdle "actual malice" test from *Sullivan* also be applied to private figure defamation plaintiffs. *Sullivan* and its progeny had thus far applied the standard only to public officials and figures. The Court, per Justice Powell, concluded it did not, stating:

> *We hold that*, so long as they do not impose liability without fault, the States may define for themselves the appropriate standard of liability for a publisher or broadcaster of defamatory falsehood injurious to a private individual.[104]

Well, that was easy. Thank you, Justice Powell. This is also a good example of how the holding often captures the main rule of the case. As a rule of thumb, the more modern the case, the more likely the court will clearly identify the holding.

Not all casebook cases will stand for specific rules. With some frequency, cases are included in casebooks to give general background about a particular subject area. These cases are harder to brief. In fact, some of them will not be brief-able under the traditional format.

The court's reasoning.

Life would be much easier for law students if courts labeled the different sections of their opinions like law students are advised to do in their case briefs. Certainly, this is true with regard to the court's reasoning, the last essential component of a good case brief. Identifying the court's reasoning can be particularly difficult because it may be scattered all over the opinion. Sometimes the reasoning will come before the holding, as a lead-in to it. Example: "*For these reasons*, we hold that . . . ." But often the reasoning will come after the holding, as a justification for it. Sometimes, there may be reasoning both before and after the holding.

The reasoning portions of opinions can sometimes be long. Because you're writing a brief and not a dissertation, you're looking for those nuggets of reasoning that *directly* support the

---

[104] *Id.* at 347 (emphasis added).

court's resolution of the case. *Why* did the court take the position it did in resolving the issue the way it did? Answer that question before you begin trying to write down the court's reasoning. Don't just copy from the opinion. Think about it first and then put it in your own words. As one of my research assistants commented on reading this section:

> I would emphasize the importance of *first* identifying and *second* putting in your own words the court's reasoning. The "why" of the case is what helped me the most in applying the law to different hypotheticals, both in class and on exams. Once I became effective at figuring out the "why" for the holding and/or rule of law, I found that briefing and understanding cases was easier.

A Case-Briefing Exercise

If you haven't started law school yet, here's an exciting chance to write your very first case brief using a real case: *Robinson v. Lindsay*, an opinion from the Supreme Court of Washington involving a lawsuit for negligence by a minor injured in a snowmobile accident against the driver of the snowmobile, who was also a minor. The case is included in the Prosser, Wade, and Schwartz casebook on Torts, used at more than 100 law schools. Here are the components of the exercise that you'll find below:

The case. The opinion issued by the Supreme Court of Washington, with a short prefatory explanation of the legal doctrine on which the case rests.

A case-briefing template. A template for writing your own brief of the case.

Sample briefs from real law students. Three sample briefs of *Robinson* written by three top law students, followed by a comparative analysis.

The case: *Robinson v. Lindsay.*

To make the exercise meaningful, you'll need a bit of background in the applicable legal doctrine. As explained back in Chapter 5, a tort is basically any civil wrong, other than a breach of contract, for which the law allows the recovery of money damages. Negligence law is the largest slice of the tort-law pie. Under negligence law, an actor is liable to the plaintiff if the actor owed a duty of care to the plaintiff, breached that duty, and such breach caused injury to the plaintiff. When a duty of care is owed under negligence law, it is usually a duty to use the degree of care that a hypothetical "reasonable person" would have used under the same or similar circumstances. Most adults are held to this same "standard of care," as it is known.

As with everything in the law, exceptions exist. Thus, people with physical disabilities are expected to exercise the degree of care that a reasonable person with the same disability would exercise. Professionals, such as doctors and lawyers, are expected to act with the degree of care customarily exercised by other professionals in the same specialty. Children, as we learn below, also get their own standard of care, but with an exception (so we basically have an exception to an exception at work).

Robinson v. Lindsay appears in the Prosser, Wade, and Schwartz casebook under the broad heading of "Negligence" and the subheading "The Standard of Care." Prior to reading the case, students know nothing about how children are treated under negligence law. Keep that in mind as you read the case and consider what the casebook authors and professor would expect a student to get out of the case. We'll also use this case for a course outline example in Chapter 13.

So here we go, beginning with the court's opinion:

ROBINSON V. LINDSAY
598 P.2d 392 (Wash. 1979)

■ UTTER, CHIEF JUSTICE.

An action seeking damages for personal injuries was brought on behalf of Kelly Robinson who lost full use of a thumb in a snowmobile accident when she was 11 years of age. The petitioner, Billy Anderson, 13 years of age at the time of the accident, was the driver of the snowmobile. After a jury verdict in favor of Anderson, the trial court ordered a new trial.

The single issue on appeal is whether a minor operating a snowmobile is to be held to an adult standard of care. The trial court failed to instruct the jury as to that standard and ordered a new trial because it believed the jury should have been so instructed. We agree and affirm the order granting a new trial.

The trial court instructed the jury under WPI 10.05 that:

> In considering the claimed negligence of a child, you are instructed that it is the duty of a child to exercise the same care that a reasonably careful child of the same age, intelligence, maturity, training and experience would exercise under the same or similar circumstances.

Respondent properly excepted to the giving of this instruction and to the court's failure to give an adult standard of care.

The question of what standard of care should apply to acts of children has a long historical background. Traditionally, a flexible standard of care has been used to determine if children's actions were negligent. Under some circumstances, however, courts have developed a rationale for applying an adult standard.

In the courts' search for a uniform standard of behavior to use in determining whether or not a person's conduct has fallen below minimal acceptable standards, the law has developed a fictitious person, the "reasonable man of ordinary prudence." That term was first used in Vaughan v. Menlove, 132 Eng.Rep. 490 (1837).

Exceptions to the reasonable person standard developed when the individual whose conduct was alleged to have been negligent suffered from some physical impairment, such as blindness, deafness, or lameness. Courts also found it necessary, as a practical matter, to depart considerably from the objective standard when dealing with children's behavior. Children are traditionally encouraged to pursue childhood activities without the same burdens and responsibilities with which adults must contend. (citation omitted) As a result, courts evolved a special standard of care to measure a child's negligence in a particular situation.

In Roth v. Union Depot Co., 13 Wash. 525, 43 P. 641 (1896), Washington joined "the overwhelming weight of authority" in distinguishing between the capacity of a child and that of an adult. As the court then stated (citation omitted):

> [I]t would be a monstrous doctrine to hold that a child of inexperience—and experience can come only with years—should be held to the same degree of care in avoiding danger as a person of mature years and accumulated experience.

The court went on to hold (citation omitted):

> The care or caution required is according to the capacity of the child, and this is to be determined, ordinarily, by the age of the child. . . . [A] child is held . . . only to the exercise of such degree of care and discretion as is reasonably to be expected from children of his age.

The current law in this state is fairly reflected in WPI 10.05, given in this case. In the past we have always compared a child's conduct to that expected of a reasonably careful child of the same age, intelligence, maturity, training and experience. This case is the first to consider the question of a child's liability for injuries sustained as a result of his or her operation of a motorized vehicle or participation in an inherently dangerous activity.

Courts in other jurisdictions have created an exception to the special child standard because of the apparent injustice that would occur if a child who caused injury while engaged in certain dangerous activities were permitted to defend himself by saying that other children similarly situated would not have exercised a degree of care higher than his, and he is, therefore, not liable for his tort. Some courts have couched the exception in terms of children engaging in an activity which is normally one for adults only. *See, e.g.,* Dellwo v. Pearson, 259 Minn. 452, 107 N.W.2d 859 (1961) (operation of a motorboat). We believe a better rationale is that when the activity a child engages in is inherently dangerous, as is the operation of powerful mechanized vehicles, the child should be held to an adult standard of care.

Such a rule protects the need of children to be children but at the same time discourages immature individuals from engaging in inherently dangerous activities. Children will still be free to enjoy traditional childhood activities without being held to an adult standard of care. Although accidents sometimes occur as the result of such activities, they are not activities generally considered capable of resulting in "grave danger to others and to the minor himself if the care used in the course of the activity drops below that care which the reasonable and prudent adult would use. . . ." (citation omitted)

Other courts adopting the adult standard of care for children engaged in adult activities have emphasized the hazards to the public if the rule is otherwise. We agree with the Minnesota Supreme Court's language in its decision in Dellwo v. Pearson (citation omitted):

> Certainly in the circumstances of modern life, where vehicles moved by powerful motors are readily available and frequently operated by immature individuals, we should be skeptical of a rule that would allow motor vehicles to be operated to the hazard of the public with less than the normal minimum degree of care and competence.

Dellwo applied the adult standard to a 12-year-old defendant operating a motorboat. Other jurisdictions have applied the adult standard to minors engaged in analogous activities. Goodfellow v. Coggburn, 98 Idaho 202, 203–04, 560 P.2d 873 (1977) (minor operating tractor); Williams v. Esaw, 214 Kan. 658, 668, 522 P.2d 950 (1974) (minor operating motorcycle); Perricone v. DiBartolo, 14 Ill.App.3d 514, 520, 302 N.E.2d 637 (1973) (minor operating gasoline-powered minibike); Krahn v. LaMeres, 483 P.2d 522, 525–26 (Wyo.1971) (minor operating automobile). The holding of minors to an adult standard of care when they operate motorized vehicles is gaining approval from an increasing number of courts and commentators. (citations omitted)

The operation of a snowmobile likewise requires adult care and competence. Currently 2.2 million snowmobiles are in operation in the United States. (citation omitted) Studies show that collisions and other snowmobile accidents claim hundreds of casualties each year and that the incidence of accidents is particularly high among inexperienced operators. (citation omitted)

At the time of the accident, the 13-year-old petitioner had operated snowmobiles for about 2 years. When the injury occurred, petitioner was operating a 30-horsepower snowmobile at speeds of 10–20 miles per hour. The record indicates that the machine itself was capable of 65 miles per hour. Because petitioner was operating a powerful motorized vehicle, he should be held to the standard of care and conduct expected of an adult.

The order granting a new trial is affirmed.

Brief the case yourself.

Before you look ahead, take a little time and brief the case yourself. Here's a form you can use:

Robinson v. Lindsay (Wash. 1979)

Facts: (thumb severed)
minor was injured in a snowmobile accident caused driven
by another minor

Procedural History: (held child to child standard of care)
Trial court gave wrong instructions to jury which led
to an adverse verdict for the plaintiff. The losing
party appealed for a new trial, on grounds of this
error. was ordered

Who won?:
The plaintiff won.

Issue: (specific to case)
operating a snowmobile
whether a minor engaging in an inherently dangerous
activity should be held to an adult standard of care

Holding/rule(s):
Yes
The petitioner should be held to an adult standard of
care since he engaged in an inherently dangerous
activity normally undertaken by adults.

Reasoning:
Such a rule protects the need of children to be
children, discourages immature individuals from
inherently dangerous activities, and protects the public.
※ Exception to reasonable person standard when
dealing with childrens behavior

Sample case briefs from three top law students.

To add authenticity to this exercise, I solicited help from
three top students. At the end of their first year, these students
ranked number one, two, and three in an entering class of

approximately 150 students. I asked the students to track down their case briefs for *Robinson*, which we had covered in the eighth week of their first semester.

Not surprisingly, being outstanding students (although they didn't know they would be at the time), *they had each briefed the case.* These are different students from those quoted at the beginning of the chapter, so we get reinforcement of the proposition that top students brief their cases. By the eighth week of the semester, I'm sure quite a few of their classmates had stopped briefing.

The three students submitted their briefs without alteration and gave me permission to share them. Their briefs illustrate the point I made earlier that case-brief formats can vary and still accomplish the same goals. The formats used are all somewhat different, yet each brief captured the essential elements of the case.

Student Brief No. 1

Facts. Billy Anderson (13 years old) was driving a snowmobile owned by Lindsay. Anderson had driven snowmobiles for about 2 years prior to the accident. He was pulling Kelly Robinson (11 years old) on an inner tube attached to the snowmobile. Robinson's thumb got caught in the tow rope and was severed. It was reattached but was not fully functional.

Procedural History. Trial produced a jury verdict for Anderson. A new trial was ordered because jury was not instructed to hold Anderson to the adult standard of care.

Issue. Whether a minor operating a snowmobile is to be held to the adult standard of care.

Holding. Yes.

Reasoning. Courts usually don't hold children to the adult standard of care. The standard is usually what is reasonably expected of children of the same age—a reasonably careful child of the same age, intelligence, maturity, training, and experience. But if the activity the child engages in is inherently dangerous (as it is here), the child should be held to the adult standard of care. This discourages immature individuals from engaging in such conduct/activities where the risk of harm is great.

Rule. When a child engages in an activity which is normally undertaken only by adults and requires adult qualifications, the child is held to the adult standard of care.

Student Brief No. 2

Facts. Snowmobile accident where plaintiff of 11 years of age was injured by a 13-year-old boy driving. The 13-year-old boy was driving a snowmobile, pulling the 11-year-old girl on an inner tube which was attached to the snowmobile with a tow rope. The girl's thumb got caught in the tow rope and was severed.

Alleged Error. The trial court instructed the jury to judge the 13-year-old boy's conduct against that of a reasonably careful child under the same or similar circumstances.

Legal Issue. What standard of care should the court use to judge the child's conduct?

Holding. Court overturns the trial court and holds that the 13-year-old boy should be held to the standard of care of an adult because he was partaking in an adult activity that was inherently dangerous (another chip in the "fault principle")— public policy must protect the general public over the interest of the children.

Rule. General standard of care applicable to children is that of a child their own age, experience, intelligence, maturity, list both training and experience would exercise under the same or the general similar circumstances. (Ultimately an objective standard, but rule and not purely objective . . . based on certain similar attributes of the the reasonable child.)   exception

Rule. "Adult Activity Exception"—When children partake in inherently dangerous activities, normally undertaken by adults, children should be held to the standard of care of an adult.

Reasoning. The "adult activity exception" protects the need of children to be children but at the same time discourages immature individuals from engaging in inherently dangerous activities. There would be great hazards to the general public if children were not held to adult standards when undertaking adult activities that are inherently dangerous.

Student Brief No. 3

Facts. Billy Anderson, 13, was driving a snowmobile, belonging to D, pulling P. P's thumb was severed when it was caught in tow rope.

Procedural History. Jury verdict in favor of Anderson, trial court ordered a new trial.

Legal Issue. Whether a minor operating a snowmobile can be held to an adult standard of care.

Alleged Error. Jury instruction to hold to adult standard.

Holding. Children involved in dangerous activities, usually reserved for adults, must be held to an adult standard of care.

Reasoning. Exception to the reasonable person standard when dealing with children's behavior. It would be a monstrous doctrine to hold a child to the same standard of an adult. The caution should be judged based on the capacity of the child. Held only to a standard of care of a reasonable child his age. However, when a child is engaged in an inherently dangerous activity, such as driving a motor vehicle, he should be held to an adult standard of care.

Rules.

Disposition. Affirm

Dissents/Concurrences.

Notes.

Comparing the student briefs.

All three sample briefs are of good quality, no surprise since they came from three top law students. Are they exquisite works of art? No, but case briefs don't have to be. In fact, the more perfect the case-brief composition, the more likely the student spent too much time on it. All three students got the job done.

Note one important quality all three briefs have in common: they're *brief* as case briefs should be. *Robinson* is a fairly simple case with simple facts. Not all briefs would be this short, but it bears reemphasizing that effective law students brief every case, but do so efficiently. They brief, but don't over-brief.

It's also worth mentioning, in part because it's the best brief of the three, that Brief 2 (as the writer told me) benefited from the fact that the student edited his briefs during or after class as part of his note-taking, as many students do. So, for example, when I made the point in class that the normal child standard of care is an *objective* standard (i.e., it compares the conduct of the child actor to how other similar "reasonable children" would have acted) even though it looks like a *subjective* standard (in that we tailor it to take into account the child's personal traits such as age and intelligence), the writer of Brief 2 inserted the point in his brief. Editing your briefs to fit the lecture is a wise strategy because it enhances their accuracy and completeness, making the briefs more useful as an exam prep tool.

Let's compare the student briefs, using my brief-formatting template:

Facts. The facts of this case, as is true of many tort cases, are fairly simple and straightforward. Brief 1 contains the most complete statement of the facts, but the two key facts—that the alleged negligent actor was a minor and was driving a motorized snowmobile—are included in all three briefs.

Procedural History. The procedural history of the case is stated most accurately in Brief 1. The procedural history in Brief 2 (designated as "Alleged Error") is incomplete and in Brief 3, even combining the "Procedural History" and "Alleged Error" sections, the result is incomplete and too vague.

The true procedural posture of the case is more complex than any of the students put in their briefs. The trial judge basically reversed himself, deciding he had erred during the trial in not giving the adult standard of care jury instruction that the plaintiff (called the "respondent" in the case) had requested. When the jury came back with a verdict for the defendant, the judge said he should have given the adult instruction and granted a new trial. This is unusual and somewhat convoluted, but note that the alleged error on appeal—the decision by the trial judge to grant a new trial—is included in my *Top Five Most Commonly Alleged Errors on Appeal* list, as is the underlying dispute over whether the jury instruction was in error.

I'm sure these smart students could have deciphered the full procedural history correctly if they had spent more time studying it, but I suspect they had already figured out that I rarely ask about procedural history after the first few weeks of the course. The students had learned the expectations of their professor—as I've recommended you try to do—and saved themselves a spot of time in preparing for class.

Who won? While not included in most case-brief templates or in any of the student briefs, it's a good idea to insert a separate section stating which party ultimately prevailed because it helps you see the forest for the trees. Very often in class, I'll ask "Who won?" during case-recitation dialoguing. You'd be surprised at the number of delayed or puzzled responses this simple question generates from even well-prepared students with full briefs.

Issue. All three of the students nailed the issue. Briefs 1 and 3 stated the narrow issue accurately and nearly identically; i.e., whether a minor snowmobile operator should be held to an adult standard of care. Brief 2 stated the issue more broadly in terms of what standard of care should be applied to children.

Holding/rule(s). Because the students had not yet learned the general standard of care applicable to children, it was important for them to get that general standard out of the case, as well as the exception to it that the court adopted and applied. Notably, all three briefs did include both the general standard of care applicable to children—even though it wasn't directly an issue in the case—and the exception for when children engage in inherently dangerous, adult-like activities.

Brief 2 did it best, stating the general standard of care applicable to children and the exception for inherently dangerous activities as two separate rules. Briefs 1 and 3 placed the general standard in their reasoning sections, but where they put it isn't as important as the fact that they got it in there.

Note that Briefs 1 and 2 basically quoted verbatim the court's definition of the child standard of care. That's good! Remember the R in the C.R.E.D.O. It's important to get legal rules rigorously right. The court defined the general standard of care applicable to children as "the same care that a reasonably careful child of the same age, intelligence, maturity, training and experience would exercise under the same or similar circumstances." Briefs 1 and 2 tracked that definition closely.

But not Brief 3. Compare the court's definition of the normal child standard of care to Brief 3, where the student stated the standard as: "The caution should be judged based on the capacity of the child. Held only to a standard of care of a reasonable child his age." That's too broad because it fails to include the several specific traits (age, intelligence, maturity, training, and experience) that judges and juries are supposed to consider in evaluating how a similarly situated, reasonable child would have acted. When I use child actors in negligence exam questions, I frequently will say something like, "Abby was an unusually bright child." I am looking for the students to pick up on the fact that Abby's conduct would be judged against that of a reasonable, unusually bright child, not a reasonable child of average or below-average intelligence.

Significantly, all three briefs accurately stated the court's holding/rule that when a child engages in an inherently dangerous activity, the child will be held to an adult standard of care rather than the normal child standard of care.

Reasoning. Only Brief 2 captured the two essential reasons given by the court for its holding, which are that the exception to the child standard of care is intended to protect the public and to discourage immature individuals from pursuing dangerous activities. Brief 1 got one of the reasons. Brief 3 omitted both.

Sizing up your brief.

How does your brief stack up to the examples? Did it contain the essential components of the case as reflected in the sample briefs? Go through this checklist, looking at whether you:

1. Included the two most relevant facts: that the defendant was a child and the accident occurred because of the defendant's carelessness in driving a powerful motorized vehicle.

2. Took a shot at describing the procedural history. As explained, the procedural history in *Robinson* was tricky even for law students, so don't worry if you missed this. You wouldn't have much to go on in trying to figure it out.

3.   Stated the issue correctly, either broadly in terms of what standard of care should apply to children or narrowly in terms of whether children should be subject to an adult standard of care when they engage in inherently dangerous, adult-like activities.

4.   Included the general rule regarding the standard of care applicable to children.

5.   Included the exception to that rule when children engage in inherently dangerous activities.

6.   Identified the court's two principal reasons for the holding: deterrence of children from engaging in dangerous activities and the need to protect the public when they do.

Also pay attention to anything you included in your brief that *doesn't* appear in the student briefs. Think about why you included the information. In retrospect, does it still seem important to you? If you got all or most of the points listed above, congratulations! If you missed some, don't fret. Like I said, case-briefing is a skill that takes time to develop. Consider this exercise your first baby step on the road to becoming an expert case analyzer.

CHAPTER 12

NOTE-TAKING

When students ask me to reveal the deep dark secrets of successful study strategies for law school, they're always surprised by the simplicity of my answer: read every assignment, brief every case, attend every class, *take good notes in every class*, and prepare course outlines. The C.R.E.D.O. chapter (Chapter 10) covered the importance of consistency in reading assignments and attending class. The previous chapter addressed case-briefing and the next one tackles outlining. Here we take up note-taking.

As shown by dozens of educational studies, taking notes furthers two important goals: encoding and storage of information. With regard to encoding, the process of taking notes enhances attention, idea-processing, organization, and retention of classroom material. In other words, writing down lecture content leads to better learning of the content than simply listening to it, even if one never reviews the notes. Thus, while students think it's a blessing when professors give them copies of their PowerPoint slides or notes, which some law professors do, they're missing out on one of the primary benefits of note-taking: the encoding function. One note-taking study showed that students who took and reviewed their own notes on a lecture performed better on a test than students who were given a copy of the lecturer's notes to review.[105]

Numerous studies also support the storage function of note-taking. Students who take notes and review them before tests perform better than those who don't. Who knew? Certainly, given the volume and complexity of material presented in a law school course and the long time lapse between its delivery and the exam—fifteen weeks from the first week's material until the exam—"storing" key classroom content is essential to success in law school. Using a computer analogy, your brain could be seen as the computer's temporary memory and your notes as the hard

---

[105] Judith L. Fisher & Mary B. Harris, *Effect of Note Taking and Review on Recall*, 65 J. EDUC. PSYCHOL. 321, 323 (1973).

drive on which you're able to store the information permanently. Without good class notes, you'll have little hope of remembering what you will need to know to perform well on a law school exam.

As said earlier, casebooks are not designed to teach or explain the law per se. While cases selected for inclusion in casebooks usually stand for particular rules or principles, the rules won't necessarily be clearly identified or articulated, nor will the case cover all of the satellite doctrines or exceptions to the rule or show how the rule is or should be applied to fact patterns different from the one involved in the case. These are areas that will be, or at least should be, fleshed out in class.

Study aids can help fill these gaps, but are not sufficient standing alone. The same case can be viewed and interpreted through different lenses. Professor Fleener might approach a case from a historical perspective, while Professor Tweener may approach the same case from a law and economics standpoint. Even professors who approach the case from a plain vanilla, black-letter law approach may emphasize, define, and organize rules differently than the study aids.

The only approach that matters to you is the one taken by the professor who will be grading your exam and that professor's approach can only come from one source: class presentations. Accordingly, it's critical to work diligently at capturing the law and its application as they emerge during class presentations. Carrying out this mission will be much easier to do in some courses than others, as professors and their teaching styles vary greatly. The amount of effective notes a student is able to take in a course depends greatly on the particular professor.

Most law professors will attempt to present the material in a clear ("clear" being a relative term when it comes to law), organized fashion designed to facilitate student understanding and effective note-taking of the material. Some professors, however, look down on what they see as "spoon-feeding" the law to students, based on a belief that developing analytical skills requires students to bear the burden of figuring out the law on their own. Recall that a hallmark of the traditional Socratic method was to ask questions without providing answers. Other professors may spend more time discussing the policies behind rules than the rules themselves. Attempting to take meaningful notes in courses taught by such professors can be frustrating.

And then there are those professors who are simply unclear or poor communicators. They deliver jumbled lectures and engage in confusing questioning and question-answering not for pedagogical reasons, but because they are inexperienced, unorganized, unprepared, or simply have brains that work that way. Needless to say, effective note-taking in classes taught by such professors also will be difficult. Students will be forced to fill in the blanks on their own through other means, primarily study aids.

Let's assume you're in a class conducive to effective note-taking. How do you become a successful note-taker? Effective note-taking consists of more than just trying to write things down. It's a four-step process that includes: (1) effectively processing the material as you're hearing it; (2) selectively capturing the key material while omitting unnecessary content; (3) filling in gaps after class before they fade from memory; and (4) conducting subsequent periodic review.

You Have to *Process* Material to Understand It

Your first challenge is to be an effective "encoder," which requires attentive listening. Yes, of course this sounds obvious, but it is much easier said than done, especially for a generation that has grown up with many more distractions than previous ones, including wi-fi in the classroom. I've already admonished you in Chapter 6 to avoid the temptations of multitasking on your computer in class, which is the biggest attention-distracter, so we won't rehash that here.

Listen to your *classmates* as well as your professors. Unlike other educational disciplines, in law school, due to the Socratic method, notes-worthy comments often will come from your fellow students. If a professor asks a question and a student gives an answer to which the prof gives thumbs-up approval, that's essentially the same thing as the professor saying it.

Also, class discussions are often one long complex chain, with professors chiming in clarifications and the like as it moves along. You can't effectively tune out and then tune back in without missing important links in the chain. To test this proposition, rent a movie with a complex plot. Stop listening at intervals to check a sports score, shop for shoes, and send a few text messages, then tune back in to see if you still know what's going on in the movie.

Capture the Best, Leave Out the Rest

Due to the Socratic and case methods, it can be hard to get a handle on what you should be writing down during class, especially in the early days of law school. Instead of straightforward lecture, most of your classes will be filled with back and forth colloquies between the professors and students. Which parts are important? As one student wrote when asked to name his biggest surprise about law school:

> The biggest surprise is the note-taking. It is not your usual note-taking, and I doubt that there is any real way to prepare for it. Law school classes are just not your usual lecture-based discussions, so you are left wondering whether you should write down the banter between teacher and student or just the hypotheticals, etc. People who are used to undergraduate lectures and things written on the board or shown on PowerPoint are in for a rude awakening.

Some law students write down too little, while some write down too much. It's easy to understand how capturing too little of the material could be a problem. If you don't record what you need to know in your notes, you'll forget it and won't have it available to study for the exam.

Students have a harder time understanding how they can write down too much. Isn't more always better? No. Students who try to write everything down in class spend too little time actually processing the information. You're not training to be a stenographer. You're trying to learn and understand law. You can't learn it without thinking about it. Note-taking research shows that when the presentation pace is quick and the informational density high, fast and furious note-taking competes with the mental resources needed to process the information.[106]

Handwritten Versus Computer Notes

This leads us to an important decision faced by new law students: whether to handwrite class notes or type them on a computer. A new trend in legal education in this regard is a seemingly backwards one. Until the past couple of academic years, at least 90 percent of my students used computers to take notes in class. Then suddenly one fall (which could be a great title for either a romantic comedy or disaster movie about the first year of law school: *Suddenly One Fall*), the majority of my new Torts students showed up carrying pens and pencils instead of computers.

What happened?

In 2014, a study emerged from Princeton University titled *The Pen Is Mightier than the Keyboard: Advantages of Longhand over Laptop Note Taking.*[107] The study gained publicity in news articles and subsequent currency in academic circles. Some law professors and academic support deans began advising students to abandon computers for note-taking. (The research may also have persuaded more law professors to prohibit computers in class.)

Through a series of experiments, the study found that college students who took notes in class by hand retained knowledge better than students who took notes on a computer. In the first experiment, students watched and took notes during 15-minute TED talks, then took a test on the content shortly thereafter. Not surprisingly, the hand-writers captured fewer words than the computer users in their notes.

The two groups performed equally well answering factual questions regarding the lecture content, but the hand-writers did better on conceptual questions. A second experiment was conducted, similar except that the computer-users were

---

[106] *See* Gilles O. Einstein et al., *Note-Taking, Individual Differences, and Memory for Lecture Information*, 77 J. EDUC. PSYCHOL. 522, 522–23 (1985).

[107] Pam A. Mueller & Daniel M. Oppenheimer, *The Pen Is Mightier Than the Keyboard: Advantages of Longhand Over Laptop Note Taking*, 25 PSYCHOL. SCI. 1159 (2014).

instructed to not take verbatim notes, an instruction they largely ignored. The results were the same: roughly equal performance on factual questions, but worse performance by the computer-users on conceptual questions. A third experiment allowed all of the note-takers to review their notes a week later and the hand-writers again performed better on a test.

The authors speculated that the primary explanation is that students who write by hand process material more effectively and selectively than students who type their notes, some of whom try to create verbatim transcripts of the class. Taking verbatim notes, they said, likely leads to "shallower processing" of the material.

The insight is not new. Many others have made the same observation without the benefit of the study. All the way back in the first edition of *1L of a Ride,* I quoted this ringing endorsement of handwriting class notes from a student who finished number one in her class:

> I do not find computers helpful in the classroom setting, although I'm sure I don't speak for most students. I never use mine in class. I know I am in the minority here, but I have always written much faster than I type. Even after becoming more proficient on the keyboard, I continue to retain much more information when I write. I have talked to a number of people who notice a similar difference in their retention of material when they write as opposed to type. For example, our Civil Procedure class last year did not allow laptop usage. Despite the difficulty of this class, some of my classmates did better in Civil Procedure than in their other classes where laptops were permitted. As a result, these students have made the decision to no longer use laptops to take notes in class and have indicated to me that they are already noticing an improvement in retention. Additionally, I think there is a lot of merit to the argument that laptop usage in class gets in the way of students engaging with the material.

I also related a story from early in my career when I worked as a law clerk to a federal district court judge. In that role, I sat through many trials and got to know the court reporters who transcribed them. During one jury trial, I asked the court reporter what she thought about the testimony of a key witness. She said she didn't remember anything about it. Surprised, I said something like, "How could you not remember any of it? You took down every word verbatim!" She said she never thinks about what's being said because it would interfere with her recording it accurately.

Too many computer-equipped law students do the same thing in trying to transcribe every word spoken by the professor. Not only does attempting to transcribe the class interfere with your actually hearing and processing the material (i.e., the encoding benefit of note-taking), it results in you writing down stuff you don't need. This clutter, in turn, often gets transferred to course outlines (see next chapter), reducing their effectiveness.

Having said that, while I don't dispute the results of the Princeton study, I also don't put complete stock in it with regard to law school note-taking. Taking a test about a short lecture almost immediately after hearing it (as in the first two experiments) or one week after the lecture (as in the third experiment) is much different from taking a comprehensive exam covering fourteen weeks of material, which is what happens in most law school courses under the single-exam format.

My concern is that students who hand-write class notes simply don't take down enough of the actual rules to remember them many weeks or even months later. During the past couple of years—the ones in which computers were largely absent in my Torts courses—I frequently articulated legal rules that were not in the casebook reading, but which many students were not writing down. I worried about where they planned to capture those rules from.

Also, perhaps countering the Princeton study, note-taking research shows that college students take down fewer than 50 percent of principal lecture points.[108] Studies also show a correlation between the quantity of notes taken and better test performance.

---

[108]   *See* Alan C. Eggert & Robert L. Williams, *Notetaking in College Classes: Student Patterns and Instructional Strategies*, 51 J. GEN. EDUC. 173, 195 (2002).

Computerized notes also are easier to add to, edit, and reorganize. Moreover, much of the content of your course outlines (see Chapter 13) will be inputted from your class notes. On the other hand, many students report a strong benefit in having to type their class notes from their handwritten notes when preparing outlines as a form of periodic review, an important component of law school success discussed below.

So what's the verdict? As usual, there is no one-size-fits-all answer. In earlier editions, I endorsed using a computer to take notes in class, but qualified it with the same advice I share on almost every learning issue: *Students have different learning styles and should do what works best for them.* Take note, for example, that the top-of-her-class handwriting student quoted above said, "I have always written much faster than I type." That's important. I'm the opposite. I'm a terribly slow handwriter. In the past, I blamed it on being left-handed; now, on being old and decrepit. If were starting law school today . . . um, sorry, had to shake off a PTSD flashback . . . I would use a computer. But that's me.

If you decide to take notes on a computer, make a pledge to avoid taking them down verbatim. If you take notes by hand, be sure to write your heart out when it counts. A middle-ground approach might also work. One of my research assistants said she varies her approach depending on the professor's teaching style:

> If the professor walks through the material slower, uses a lot of hypotheticals, and engages in a lot of class discussion, I am more likely to handwrite my notes. If the professor moves at a fast pace and sticks to Power Points, I am more likely to type my notes to keep up.

Keep in mind that your professor may make the decision for you by banning computers in class.

What *Exactly* Should You Try to Write Down?

We know now that in taking notes you don't want to write too much and you don't want to write too little. Like Goldilocks, you want to get it *just right*.

Generalizing is always fraught with danger when it comes to law professors, but whether you're writing by hand or using a computer, for most first-year courses *your primary goal* will be to record anything resembling a legal rule, test, principle, or doctrine, including sub-rules, exceptions to rules and sub-rules, and exceptions to exceptions. Whenever a professor begins a sentence with "The rule is . . ." or "The test is . . ." or other words to that effect, write it down.

It's not sufficient to get general principles, which nearly all students will do successfully. The most successful students are those who capture—and understand—the more specific subordinate rules. A group of note-taking researchers categorized lecture points on four levels, with level-1 ideas being the most general and levels 2–4 representing subordinate ideas clarifying, defining, and describing the general ideas. They found that 91 percent of students listening to the lecture captured the level-1 ideas in their notes, but the percentages declined with each level of increased specificity. The students recorded only 60 percent of level-2 ideas, 35 percent of level-3 ideas, and 11 percent of level-4 ideas.[109]

Law school exams emphasize and reward specific analysis over general analysis. For example, if a Torts essay question involving intentional torts presents a fact pattern in which A shoots B, 100 percent of the class is going to recognize that act as a tortious battery. To give you some idea how much recognition and understanding of general issues and principles count as compared to specific issues and rules, when I give an issue-spotting/problem-solving intentional torts essay question worth 100 points, mere recognition of a simple battery in the question facts usually counts for only a few points. More specific identification and analysis of subordinate issues, such as whether the tortfeasor had the requisite intent to commit a battery or a legal privilege to do so, count for much more, usually in the neighborhood of 15–20 points. So don't just write down the "big rules." Record the small ones too: the distinctions, the exceptions, etc.

---

[109]   *See* Kenneth A. Kiewra et al., *Qualitative Aspects of Notetaking and Their Relationship with Information-Processing Ability and Academic Achievement*, 14 J. INSTRUCTIONAL PSYCHOL. 110, 113 (1987).

To enhance understanding of a rule, include in your notes, if it's not already contained in your case briefs, the *core reasoning* underlying the rule. Understanding the "why" of a rule will make it easier to remember and apply it. As an example, you'll learn in Torts that a tortious battery can result from an intentional *offensive* touching of a person even if it doesn't cause physical harm. From one of our cases, my students learn, and we discuss in class, that the reason the law allows recovery for merely offensive batteries is to protect human dignity. In fact, offensive batteries are what we call a "dignitary tort." Understanding this reasoning allows students to answer questions they might otherwise miss.

In class I pose a hypothetical in which Student A kisses Student B after she falls asleep while studying for an exam. Student B finds out about the kiss later and is extremely offended. Does B have a valid claim for battery even though she was asleep and had no contemporaneous awareness of the kiss? Students who understand the reasoning behind allowing recovery for offensive batteries (and write it down so they don't forget it) can correctly answer that she would have a valid claim because a person's sense of dignity can be just as offended if they find out about an offensive bodily contact after the fact.

You should also strive to capture in your notes (either during or after class) the essence of the professor's primary hypothetical fact patterns posed in class. Remember that your goal is to learn to analyze and apply law, not simply memorize it. An added benefit is that professors often base exam questions on hypotheticals used in class or closely related to hypotheticals they used in class.

What can you safely leave out of your notes? Frequently, in Socratic case-dialoguing a turning point occurs where the dialogue shifts from fleshing out the assigned case and corresponding rules to a more generalized discussion of the issues marked by "What do you think?"-type questions. At this point, you usually can relax and enjoy the discussion without worrying about having to write much down. Most professors expect 1Ls to analyze and solve legal problems on the exam, which usually does not require extensive policy discussion. But

1L profs do use policy questions, so, again, generalizing is always risky.

In addition to extended policy discussions, you're usually safe in omitting discussion of off-topic tangents, anecdotes by the professor, statistics offered by the prof to back up points, and cases and statutes the professor mentions offhandedly, but which are not part of the assigned reading.

Comparing Two Students' Notes

Before we move on to other note-related tips, let's take time out for a real example to highlight what we've covered so far. Below is a comparison of class notes taken in a Torts class by two students we'll call Jane and Roger regarding the privilege of self-defense to the tort of battery. The privilege of self-defense, where applicable, operates to negate what would otherwise be an actionable tortious battery (i.e., an intentional harmful or offensive bodily contact on a person).

I'll spare you further legal explanation because the class notes below, particularly Jane's, do a good job of explaining the doctrine. Jane's class notes are on the left and Roger's on the right. Jane did a great job capturing the salient information. Roger did an okay, but not a great job. I'm sure some other students took far worse notes, but Roger's notes suffer from omissions and errors. Jane finished second in her class of approximately 150 students after her first year, whereas Roger finished somewhere in the middle. In other words, the comparison below is between the notes of a "top student" and an "average student." My added comments are bracketed and in bold on Roger's side of the ledger. I inserted spacing as necessary to make the same basic points line up side-by-side.

Jane's notes	**Roger's notes**
Self-defense	**Self-defense**
Test of the Privilege of Self-Defense (another objective test):	Reasonable Belief—If a reasonable person would believe that they were threatened with a battery or false imprisonment, they have a privilege regardless of
Were the circumstances such that a reasonable person would believe	

that they were threatened by a battery? Was the amount of force reasonable under the circumstances? Was it proportionate to the threat against you?

a mistake. This is because the court believes in the "first law of nature is self-preservation."

Hypo: A, a person who has martial arts training, is walking alone at night in a dangerous part of town. B comes up behind A and grabs A's shoulders from behind. A throws an elbow and shatters B's face. Turns out B is A's best friend playing a practical joke. B sues for battery. A claims self-defense.

[Roger got the basic rule down, but missed the "set-up" hypothetical (see Jane's notes on left) that formed the basis for most of the discussion. Getting the professor's hypotheticals down in your notes helps you understand how legal rules are *applied*. Note how the hypothetical that Jane captured involving A and B fleshes out the meaning of objective reasonableness (i.e., how would a reasonable person have acted under the same circumstances?), which is the test for a valid assertion of self-defense. The circumstances are what dictate whether conduct is reasonable, yet Roger—because he didn't take down the hypothetical—may have missed this crucial aspect, as we'll see below.]

What makes A's belief reasonable according to the facts? Under those circumstances—WHY?

Dangerous neighborhood
At night
Alone
B came up behind

Reasonable Belief: if a reasonable person under

[Critically, self-defense allows room for

these particular circumstances would believe that they were threatened by a battery, they have the privilege of self-defense to protect themselves.

> * Mistake: Self-defense is a privilege to prevent threatened battery and allows for a reasonable mistake.

>> Why? Self-preservation is the first law of nature

>> Why not make him wait and turn around? B/c it might be too late!

>> * You don't have to wait and determine that the force is absolutely necessary.

reasonable mistakes in the decision to use force against another. Roger mentioned "mistake" in his basic statement of the rule at the beginning, but did not explain what it meant. Jane, as we see on the left, elaborated on the mistake concept and the policies behind it.]

Hypo: suppose that A turns around and unloads a gun into B.

> Unloading a gun into a person who grabs your shoulder would not be considered reasonable force.

Reasonable Force: if a reasonable person under the particular circumstances would believe that the amount of force used was proportional to the amount of force threatened.

Reasonable amount of force— You are allowed to use the amount of force reasonably necessary to prevent the battery. You can use proportional amount of force to prevent the battery. You can however threaten to use more force than you are actually allowed to use.

[Again, we see that Roger got the basic rule down that not only must the *decision* to use force in self-defense be reasonable, the *amount* of

You are allowed to use the amount of force proportionate to the force that is threatened against you.

Note: You might be privileged to threaten more force than is proportionate against you. You can threaten more force than you can actually use.

> A turns around and threatens B with a gun would be reasonable force.

Deadly Force—Force that threatens death OR serious bodily injury.

> The only reason you can use deadly force is when a reasonable person would believe in your circumstances that you are threatened with deadly force.

> Because we want to restrict it, there is the old rule "the Retreat Rule." Now it's a minority rule. Doesn't have the relevance that it once did because of the modern use of guns.

force must also be reasonable. But we also see that Roger again omitted the hypothetical showing how this principle would be applied.]

Deadly force—threatens death or serious bodily injury. You must prove that he believed that he was threatened with deadly force. **[Oops. Roger misstated the rule regarding when it is permissible to use "deadly force" in self-defense in a manner that could prove fatal to his understanding of the entire doctrine. Note that he says that the actor must prove "he believed" he was threatened with deadly force. Because the privilege of self-defense is an objective rather than a subjective test, it's not enough for the actor to prove he personally believed deadly force was** necessary. The test is whether a *reasonable person under the same circumstances* would have believed the use of deadly force was necessary. Since this same rule of objective reasonableness under the circumstances applies to the use of any force in self-defense, Roger's misstatement calls into question his understanding of the basic rule, even though he wrote it down correctly at the beginning of his notes. Roger's failure to capture the earlier hypothetical and explanation involving objectively reasonable mistakes may have led to this later error. Moreover, the absence of the earlier explanation in his notes would make it less likely that Roger would detect the contradiction and error when later reviewing his notes.]

Retreat Rule—if a person can safely retreat from the use of deadly force, they are required to do so to avoid defending with deadly force.

    Never from a dwelling

    Never if the retreat would be unsafe (and if you are threatened with

Traditionally we had the retreat rule, a person must retreat if they can before using deadly force. It is now seen as the minority rule. You are not required to retreat from your home ever.

[At common law, before a person could use deadly force in self-defense a gun, you really can't retreat safely)

Only applies to the use of deadly force

(except in his dwelling), he had to retreat *if he could do so safely*. Roger got the basic rule down, but left off the italicized qualifier. What would Roger do if the exam involved a person confronted on the street by an assailant with a gun? Would he know the actor had no duty to retreat, even in a jurisdiction following the retreat rule, before responding with deadly force? Jane would because she got the entire rule down.]

From this example, we see the difference between good notes and average notes. Jane went beyond the general rules and captured many of the subordinate rules. Roger tended to stop after he got the general rules. Jane recorded the class hypotheticals. Roger didn't. Jane stated the rules more rigorously right than Roger. Jane also got more of the core reasoning behind the rules than Roger.

Fill in Gaps Quickly

Note-taking is a two-part endeavor: taking initial notes in class and filling in the gaps shortly thereafter. For a variety of reasons—the density of the material, professors who talk too fast, slow handwriting or typing, daydreaming—you're not going to be able to accurately capture every important point in your notes during class even if you're a good note-taker. As discussed, it's not even desirable to attempt to capture every point. So it's important that you clarify any confusion and plug any holes in your notes shortly thereafter, preferably the same day.

Dr. R.L. Kaplan, a neurologist, points out that most college students mistakenly think that after learning new information, they gradually forget a little bit of it with each day that passes. Not so. Memory curves developed by psychologists more than 150 years ago show that the greatest memory loss occurs within hours—not weeks or even days—after learning the material. By the second day, people forget 40–70 percent of what they learned. For law students, this means that the material you learned in Property class on Monday is already being flushed from your memory by Tuesday. According to the memory curves, within thirty days after taking notes, students will have forgotten 95 percent of the material.

Thus, to the extent possible, you should update your notes daily or, at a minimum, weekly. Add details to the basic rules you wrote down to ensure they are complete and accurate. Fill in the professor's hypothetical fact patterns that you weren't able to get down in class. Resolve any points on which you were confused. Not only will it be easier to do this while the material is fresh in your mind, it's essential to do it because learning law is like building a brick house, with each brick being laid on top of the ones that precede it. The bricks on top are only as strong as the foundation below.

Tools for filling in gaps and clearing up confusion include: (1) study aids; (2) student outlines for the same course and professor from previous semesters (more about these in the next chapter); (3) CALI (Computer-Assisted Legal Instruction) exercises; (4) study groups; and (5) your professors. Most professors are happy to help students who are struggling to understand material *provided* the students have already tried to help themselves. As I write this, I'm shaking my head from an email I just received from a student asking me to clear up a question about an assigned case we covered last week because "my notes are kind of confusing me." I wrote back: "Have you tried reading the case?" The clear holding of the case directly answered his specific question.

If you have to miss class, make sure you get that material covered by borrowing a classmate's notes. If you have advance notice, check with the professor to see if the class can be recorded. As discussed in the C.R.E.D.O. chapter, you cannot afford *any* gaps in coverage.

Conduct Regular Periodic Review

Assuming you have managed to listen well, record good notes during class, and fill in any holes afterwards, you should sleep well at night, knowing that you're doing a good job of laying the major groundwork in your exam preparation. The final step in the note-taking process is periodic review. With only a few days between the end of classes and your first exams, you can't wait until the end of the semester to start reviewing the material. The importance of periodic review cannot be overstated.

At the beginning of their second semester, I asked a class of first-year students what they intended to do differently in the second semester than in the first semester. A large number of students said they intended to engage in more frequent periodic review of their notes and, closely intertwined, start working on their outlines earlier and do a better job of keeping them updated. Composing course outlines is, in fact, one of the best forms of periodic review. Course outlines are covered in the next chapter.

Consider Using a Computer Note-Taking Tool

Many law students use—and some swear by—computer note-taking programs such as Microsoft OneNote or Evernote to facilitate the organization of and ready access to their class notes, case-briefs, and other course materials. If you have an interest in a note-taking program, familiarize yourself with it prior to starting law school. You don't want to be trying to figure out a new computer program at the same time you're struggling to understand personal jurisdiction. Also remember that some professors ban computers in class, which will thwart your use of computerized note-taking, although the programs can still be useful for managing your notes outside of class.

CHAPTER 13

OUTLINING

I didn't listen. I didn't make outlines. I thought if I studied hard enough I wouldn't need them. That was a big mistake.

> —1L's lament about what he would do differently if starting over

One major factor distinguishing legal education from other disciplines is the sheer amount of material covered, which can become overwhelming because of the single-exam format. Professors usually start out slowly, knowing that students need to become acclimated to the nomenclature and basic procedures of the law. The snail's pace at the beginning lulls some students into a false sense of security, prompting thinking along the lines of, "Hey, this isn't so bad. We're only covering one case per hour in each class!"

One week into a fall semester, a 1L came to my office and said, "Professor, everyone kept telling me I'll be working day and night in law school, but this Saturday I was sitting there looking for something else to do. Am I missing something?" I told her to enjoy it while she could because the pace would start quickening soon.

Within a few weeks, the reading assignments get longer. The concepts get harder. Professors begin covering material at a faster pace. The demands of Legal Research and Writing kick in with a vengeance. It all comes at students relentlessly, without a break. Before they know it, students are mired up to their ankles, knees, and finally necks in a quicksand of dense material.

Must I Really Make Outlines?—Yes!

Only one answer exists for administering this huge inventory of knowledge: preparing an outline for each course. Most law students do prepare course outlines. Certainly most successful students do. Many students prepare two outlines for each course, a comprehensive main outline and a secondary capsule outline they use for review immediately before the exam.

Some students attempt to rely solely on outlines prepared by students who took the course in earlier years. These are abundantly available. It sounds like a good plan on the surface. Why go through all the work to prepare an outline if someone else has already done it for the same course taught by the same professor? Especially if you can lay your hands on a really great outline composed by a top student, it seems like a no-brainer. And, in fact, you probably can obtain great outlines prepared by top students. Every law school has its share of famous, ridiculously thorough student outlines for particular courses that get passed down from class to class. Back at the University of Arkansas at Little Rock, for example, every 1L coveted a copy of "Bob's Bible," a student outline for the late legendary Professor Robert R. Wright's Property course that was so complete it even included Professor Wright's jokes.

But it's *not* a good plan to rely on outlines prepared by others. The reason the students who made the great outlines came out on top was because they *made* the great outlines, not because they *had* the great outlines.

As with case-briefing, the process of constructing outlines is more important than the final product. Making outlines is what forces you to organize, synthesize, and, hence, really learn the material. Assembling them will help you discover the framework of the subject into which all of the rules you've learned fit. Composing an outline and updating it throughout the semester also requires the periodic review of the material so essential to law school success. Moreover, because people have different learning styles and process information differently, even excellent outlines prepared by someone else are not likely to present the material in the manner or form in which you learned it.

Similarly, resist the temptation to rely exclusively on commercial outlines, even those keyed to particular casebooks. Commercial study aid outlines are not adequate by themselves because they will not contain all of the material the professor covered and will include a lot of material the professor didn't cover. Just as important, they will not present the material in the same way—either substantively or structurally—as the professor presented it and expects to hear it back on the exam.

It's easy when reading exams to spot the students who relied heavily on outlines other than their own. They state legal doctrines in formulations foreign to the professor or discuss cases the professor doesn't or no longer covers.

Having said all that, let me emphasize that both previously prepared student outlines and commercial outlines can be extremely helpful *supplements* for filling in gaps in your own outlines. But that is their only valid use.

If you're going to invest the time in doing outlines—and they take a lot of time—you might as well do them right. I've known academically dismissed law students who produced 150-page outlines for my courses that were a waste of paper. Without the right content and schema, outlines are not only unhelpful, they can be a trap because students often mistakenly assume they're doing a good job if they're pouring tons of time into making long outlines.

Below are ten sound outlining suggestions. Effective outlining goes hand-in-hand with effective note-taking and case-briefing. Thus, several of the outlining tips overlap with suggestions given in those chapters. Understand that, as with every law school study strategy, there is no one single right way to do an outline. Content is more important than format.

Immediately following the ten tips are excerpts from the Torts outlines of three top students addressing *Robinson v. Lindsay*, the case from the case-briefing chapter.

Ten Tips for Preparing Outlines

1. Collect the raw material by briefing all your cases and taking good notes in class. A good outline can't be constructed without the raw material to put in it. For most courses, your outlines essentially will be an organized version of your class notes and portions of your case briefs (not the whole things—see below), beefed up in some places and streamlined in others. Think of outlines as the third step in exam preparation, with case-briefing and class notes being steps one and two. It's not feasible to skip or slack off on the first two steps and produce effective outlines. Use study aids, previous student outlines, and—if they work for you—study groups to help you fill in gaps.

2. Never try to outline a topic before you attend the class where the topic is covered. Usually, diligence pays dividends, but sometimes being overly diligent can work to your detriment. Some eager students go astray in trying to outline a topic before attending the classes where it will be covered. This cannot be done successfully. In outlining, pay attention to what the professor emphasizes in class about the reading material, not what you thought was important when you read it. A fellow Torts professor and I used to joke that we'd probably get *C*s if we took each other's exams because we emphasize different doctrines in class and present some of them differently.

Not only will professors be likely to present a case differently than you briefed it, they'll add extra material not covered in the case. An example seen below in the student outline excerpts regarding *Robinson v. Lindsay* is the addition of the relevant rules from the *Restatement of Torts*. These were not contained in the case, but were included in class discussion of the case.

3. Begin your outlines around the third or fourth week of the semester. You can't wait until toward the end of the semester to start an outline. There won't be enough time. The beauty of gradually assembling good outlines week by week is that by the time you get to the end of the semester, you will have already done most of your studying for the exam. At the same time, however, 1Ls can't effectively begin an outline at the very beginning of the first semester because they lack an understanding of both the process of legal analysis and the subject matter. Start your outlines around the third or fourth week of classes.

At the beginning of their second semester, I asked a class of Torts II students: "What, if anything, do you intend to do differently in the second semester than in the first semester?" The most common answer was to start outlining earlier and engage in more periodic review. Here's a sampling of the replies:

- Outlining as the classes progress! While I did not wait until the last minute for this, I felt that I did wait longer than I should have. The outlining process is very helpful for exams, but is very overwhelming when left for too long.

- Outline earlier in order to gain a more united rather than divided understanding of the material. It will also alleviate stress.

- I intend to use Fridays and Saturday to compile, clarify, organize, and consolidate the previous week's notes into a working outline. Waiting until six weeks before exams last semester to outline was a grave and very stressful mistake.

4. Keep your outline updated on a weekly basis. Some of the above comments touch directly on this point. You want to input material in your outline while it's fresh in your mind. As discussed in the previous chapter, memory fades quickly. You also don't want to fall behind and leave yourself with too much ground to make up. If you follow the recommendation in the note-taking chapter to update your notes daily, you'll be in good shape to update your outlines on weekends.

5. Organize outlines by tracking the headings and subheadings in your casebooks or course syllabi. The organization (as distinguished from the formatting) of an outline is nearly as important as the content. Rules can only be fully understood when placed in the proper context and framework. You could memorize every rule in an entire subject area and still perform poorly on the exam if you didn't know where and how they fit in the overall scheme of things.

Organize your outline by *topics* (not cases) in the same chronological order they're covered. If your professor moves straight through the book starting at the beginning, simply track the table of contents and section headings in your casebook. Some casebooks are more clearly organized and include more helpful and detailed headings than others. If your casebook includes only broad topical headings, it will be up to you to develop more specific subheadings within them. Even with casebooks that have detailed tables of contents, you'll be required to add your own narrower subheadings.

Some professors prefer to skip around in the book, which can make outline organization more difficult. If a professor does that, you're better off outlining the topics in the order the professor covers them, rather than in the order the book covers them.

Many professors will provide a course syllabus with subject headings. Assuming the syllabus subject headings are reasonably specific (and that the professor does, in fact, follow the syllabus), you can use them as an organizational guide in structuring your outline.

Topic areas should be organized as an inverted pyramid with the broad topics on top and moving down to increasingly narrower topics. Similarly, within topics, the broad rules go on top, moving down to narrower sub-rules and exceptions. See the *Robinson v. Lindsay* outline examples below.

Whatever you do, don't try to reinvent or redesign the law in your own organizational schema. Just about every year a student comes along who decides that he can re-conceptualize the law in a way better than legal scholars (including his professors) have ever done before. I once had a student who decided that the entire course in Torts could be reduced to a flow chart. When he showed it to me, I didn't know whether to bust out laughing or refer him to psychological counseling. It looked like the schematic for the Starship Enterprise, with hundreds of lines and arrows and circles and boxes going in every direction. The student flunked the course.

6. Emphasize rules, sub-rules, exceptions to rules and sub-rules, and exceptions to exceptions. Most law school exams will test your knowledge of specific legal doctrines and rules and ability to apply those doctrines and rules. For a sample, see the sample intentional torts essay question and answer in the Appendix. While some professors include policy-type essay questions on first-year exams, they do not usually count as much as questions testing your understanding of and ability to apply black-letter law. As such, your outlines should focus on incorporating "the law" of the course with accuracy and precision in a sound organizational framework. This includes all rules, sub-rules, exceptions to rules and sub-rules, and exceptions to exceptions, as well as the core reasoning and policies behind them (i.e., the "why" of the rules).

7. Include case references, but not full case briefs. Do not make the common mistake of simply incorporating your case briefs into your outlines. Extensive recitations of case facts and procedure not only are unnecessary, they'll clutter up your outline and distract you from what you need to be concentrating on. *Lead with rules in your outlines, not cases.*

Students frequently ask if they need to know the names of cases for the exam. With typical law school ambiguity, I tell them, "It depends." You definitely should know the names of the "big cases" that stand for big principles. To the extent legal doctrines are closely associated with well-known cases, integrate coverage of those cases into your outlines. If that doctrine is raised on the exam, you'll be able to discuss it more cogently and intelligently by knowing the case.

Even with regard to lesser known cases you study, it can be helpful, although not essential, to know the names. Tying specific rules to specific cases in your essay exam answers informs the professor you know your stuff. To facilitate recall of case names and also to remind you of the context in which you learned particular rules, I recommend including in your outlines the names and very short descriptions of cases *following* the statement of the rules emanating from the cases. See the *Robinson v. Lindsay* outline examples below.

8. Incorporate the professor's hypothetical fact patterns. In Chapter 12, I recommended attempting to record in your class notes the primary hypothetical fact patterns your professors use in class. These hypotheticals should also be incorporated into your outlines alongside the pertinent rules. Exams are about applying law, not simply reciting it. It is not uncommon for the same hypotheticals, or something close to them, to show up on exams.

9. Err on the side of including too much, rather than too little, material. How long should a good outline be? No precise answer exists because many variables are involved, including the particular course, the way it is taught, and your outline formatting choices. One of my research assistants said that when she started law school, she inherited a large batch of student outlines ranging from 18–127 pages in length. She said her own outlines average about seventy pages per course. Over the years, students have told me their Torts outlines run from 35–75 pages.

Outlines that are too short will lack essential details. Several years ago, I presented a workshop on course outlines with Professor Lillian Aponte Miranda, a colleague when I taught at the Florida International University College of Law. Professor Miranda had the good idea to use her law school outline from Constitutional Law as a sample for the students to look at. When she projected a page from the outline onto a screen, the students were shocked. They couldn't believe how detailed it was. Good outlines are detailed because the law is detailed.

Of course, outlines that are too long cease to be useful outlines and become unwieldy treatises. But if you're not sure whether to include something in an outline, go ahead and stick it in there. Material can be deleted with ease. It's much more difficult to go back and add what you left out.

10. State rules completely and precisely. One reason good outlines tend to be lengthy is because they set forth legal doctrine completely and with precision. That is, they get the law rigorously right (see the C.R.E.D.O. chapter). Here's a comparative example involving the definition of the two types of tortious intent, an essential element of all of the intentional torts and a concept most law students encounter at the beginning of the first semester. Compare these two outline approaches to defining the terms, one complete and precise and the other incomplete and imprecise:

Complete and Precise Definition of Tortious Intent

Two kinds of intent. Two kinds of intent under tort law: "desire intent" and "belief intent."

Desire intent—Person acts with the desire or purpose to inflict the requisite consequence of the tort (e.g., for battery, a harmful or offensive bodily contact).

Belief intent—Person acts believing to a "substantial certainty" that the consequence will follow, even if he doesn't desire the result. (Hypo: throwing rock into crowd of people, but "not wanting to hit anyone.")

Incomplete and Imprecise Definition of Tortious Intent

Two kinds of intent: desire and belief.

Don't laugh. I've seen lots of outlines resembling this second example. Students who compose short and sweet outlines of this type may very well understand the two kinds of intent at the time they keyboard in the words. The problem is that come exam time—many weeks and hundreds of rules later—they're not likely to remember the important details they need to know to apply the concepts.

Sample Outline Excerpts from Three Top Students

It's difficult to give meaningful outlining examples to incoming law students for two reasons: (1) they don't know anything about the law, so the content of the examples may not make sense to them; and (2) because good student course outlines are well-organized, integrated wholes, short excerpts fail to convey the big picture. But let's give it a shot anyway.

We'll stick with a topic you already know something about: *Robinson v. Lindsay*, the case used for the case-briefing exercise in Chapter 11, and the issue of standards of care for children under negligence law. Recall that negligence law imposes a duty on actors to use reasonable care in their conduct. When they fail to use such care and cause injury, they have breached their duty (an essential element of negligence) to the plaintiff. The nature and amount of care expected from an actor is called the "standard of care." For ordinary adults, the standard is "reasonable care under the circumstances."

You'll recall from *Robinson* and the case-briefing exercise that the law treats children differently from adults under negligence law by creating a special, lower standard of care for them. Thus, the child standard of care is an exception to the normal adult standard of care. But we also learned that there is an exception to the exception when children engage in inherently dangerous activities. In those situations, the child will be held the adult standard of care.

Organizationally, these rules would fit in a Torts outline under the following topic headings:[110]

Negligence >

   Breach of Duty >

      Standards of Care >

         Exceptions to Normal Standard of Care >

         Children >

See how the topics move down from general to specific?

Before we get to the student outline excerpts, below is how I might outline the topic in my course. Note that my sample contains additional details not included in the *Robinson* opinion, such as variations of the exception to the child standard of care as contained in the *Restatements of Torts*. These are details that would be picked up in class and from the notes following the case.

Child standard of care: A child must "exercise the same care that a reasonably careful child of the same age, intelligence, maturity, training and experience would exercise under the same or similar circumstances."

Objective standard (a "reasonably" careful child) even though it is tailored to particular child's traits (e.g., smart child will be held to higher standard than a child of low intelligence).

Exception for inherently dangerous or adult activities: When a child engages in an "inherently dangerous activity" such as operating a motorized vehicle, child is held to adult standard (*Robinson v. Lindsay*—13-year-old defendant driving snowmobile injured another child.)

Restatement standards for exception: *Restatement 2d* standard is activities "normally undertaken only by

---

[110]   In a full outline, there would be additional subheadings and content between these headings.

adults and for which adult qualifications are required";
new *Restatement 3d* standard is "dangerous activity
that is characteristically undertaken by adults."

Reasons behind exception: To protect society and
discourage children from engaging in dangerous
activities.

Consistent with tip number 7 above, note how I led with the
rules and only briefly mentioned the *Robinson* case, rather than,
as many students mistakenly do, lead with the case and bury the
rules within the case discussion. Come test time, most professors
aren't going to give a whit about the specifics of *Robinson*. To
test the rules from *Robinson* in an essay question, the professor
most likely would use a fact pattern involving a child actor
engaged in a dangerous activity. Note also that, consistent with
my previous advice, I quoted the precise language of both the
general child standard and also the variants of the exception
from the *Robinson* case and the Second and Third *Restatements
of Torts*.[111] This ensures that the rules in the outline are
"rigorously right," the R in the C.R.E.D.O.

I contacted three top law students, one each from three
different classes, and asked if they could send me the portion of
their Torts I outline pertaining to the child standard of care.
Because all three are top students, I didn't have to bother with
the preliminary question of whether they had made an outline.
I felt sure they had. Their outline excerpts are reprinted below.
For reading ease, I didn't use abbreviations in my sample, but a
student normally would abbreviate many words and terms in an
outline. I left the students' abbreviations intact.

Student No. 1

I. CHILDREN

    a.   (Exception) RULE: child must exercise the same
    care that a reasonably careful (objective) child of the

---

[111]   This is an example, of which there are many, where competing legal tests exist
addressing the same issue. One jurisdiction might follow the *Robinson* "inherently
dangerous activity" standard while another might follow the *Restatement (Second) of
Torts* standard, which does not impose a dangerousness requirement. When a professor
covers multiple legal tests for resolving the same issue, you need to know all of them
unless told otherwise.

same age, intelligence, maturity, training, and experience would exercise under the same or similar circumstances (subjective evaluation)—overall obj rule

b. Different from adult standard because child standard specifically refines the reasonable person (child). The child actor is compared to a similar reasonable child (lower standard than adults). Child of high IQ would be held to higher standard

c. **Exception to exception** for inherently dangerous activities, two approaches:

   i. Inherently dangerous approach: An exception exists when a child engages in an inherently dangerous activity, such as operation of mechanized vehicle, OR activity normally undertaken by an adult, the child should be held to an adult standard of care to protect society and discourage children from engaging in such activities

   ii. Restatement 2nd; Adult Activity approach: child rule should not apply when actor engages in an activity which is normally undertaken only by adults, and for which adult qualifications are required

      1. Case law has led to ruling that any motorized vehicle would hold child to adult standard of care

   iii. 3rd Restatement: would apply adult standard to children engaged in dangerous activity that is characteristically undertaken by adults (incl. firearms)

d. Reasons: discourages immature individuals from engaging in inherently dangerous activities AND protects the public from activities which are capable of causing grave danger to others and the minor

e. Robinson v Lindsay: 13 year old was pulling girl on tube behind snowmobile, lost thumb; ct reasoned that kid needed to be held to higher (adult) standard bec doing an inher. dangerous activity

Student No. 2

i.   Standard of care for children

1.   Generally, it is the duty of a child to exercise the same care that a reasonably careful child of the same age, intelligence, maturity, training, and experience would exercise under the same or similar circumstances.

   a.   Exception: when a child engages in inherently dangerous activities, he will be held to an adult standard of care. (*Robinson v. Lindsay*—child operating snowmobile held to adult standard)

      i.   This exception is in order to protect the public and to discourage children from engaging in dangerous activities.

   b.   Restatement 3d of Torts says—"dangerous activity normally undertaken by adults"; Restatement 2d says—"in an activity which is normally undertaken only by adults, and for which adult qualifications are required"

Student No. 3

i.   **Robinson v. Lindsay**

1.   11-year-old girl's thumb cut off while riding behind snowmobile.

2.   **Second Exception: Children's Normal Standard of Care:** "same care that a reasonably careful child of the same age, intelligence, maturity, training, and experience would exercise under the same or similar circumstances."

   a.   It's objective because it is the "reasonable child."

   b.   **Exceptions**

      i.   RST—if it's an adult activity or inherently dangerous, adult standard.

Note how closely the first and second student samples track my own. They both include: (1) an accurate statement of the general standard of care applicable to children; (2) an accurate statement of the exception, including its variant forms from the Second and Third *Restatements of Torts*; and (3) the two reasons underlying the exception. The third student sample is a bit too skimpy, omitting some important details, but it's hard to quibble with his approach since the student wrote the top exam in Torts I.

Take note of an important attribute shared by all three student outline samples: they focus on the rules, including exceptions (which are also rules). Each of the students mentioned *Robinson v. Lindsay*, as I did in my sample, but only with a brief notation, just enough to give the rules a contextual anchor. The third student's excerpt, which begins with the case name, is contrary to my advice to lead with the rules rather than the cases, but only mildly so. Just as I recommend, the student devoted only a single tagline to the case. He didn't get enmeshed in the case details.

Three excellent students + three excellent outlines = three excellent grades in Torts.

* * *

Like so many skills in law school, composing effective course outlines is a technique perfected through practice. Don't just assume you're doing your outlines right. Get some input from your professors or academic support personnel. Within a couple of weeks after starting your outlines, ask your professors if they would be willing to take a look at your outline for their course to see if you're on the right track. Make it clear you're not seeking a line-by-line review to ensure you have all the law right. That's asking too much. Rather, explain that you just want to make sure you're following an overall sound format and approach. Not all professors are willing to look at outlines, but many will do so if asked. Doing this early could save you untold hours of wasted time if you're going down the wrong road.

CHAPTER 14

A SHORT COURSE IN LAW SCHOOL EXAMS

How fearful it is to go through the first semester with only one shot to make the grade. I just didn't realize how much that would freak me out.

—1L's "biggest surprise" about law school

Like many other aspects of law school, the exam and grading processes are unique among educational programs. Upcoming chapters give advice about preparing for and taking law school exams. This chapter goes behind the scenes for the inside dope about: (1) legal education's dreaded single-exam format; (2) the diabolical types of questions concocted by professors; (3) the misunderstood "mandatory curve" grading policies that exist at most law schools; (4) and the avoidable, but inevitable, self-torture students engage in by conducting post-exam autopsies.

The Single-Exam Format

As the opening quotation suggests, one of the most stressful aspects of law school is the single-exam format. New law students express both surprise and dismay when they learn that, except in their legal research and writing courses, their entire academic fate in a course typically rests on a single in-class examination at the end of the semester. Asked what they thought people should know and understand about legal education, several students targeted the single-exam format:

- The exam preparation period is probably the most difficult tribulation a law student will ever go through. Remember, each exam counts for 100 percent of the grade. In the second semester, I was literally sitting in a room for almost sixteen hours a day every day for about two weeks reading and studying. That's enough to drive anyone crazy. The exams themselves are an emotional and mental sledgehammer. Despite a whole semester's work

243

trying your best to learn the law, and those final few grueling weeks studying every hour of waking life, the exams are such that they leave you feeling as if you know nothing and that all your efforts have been in vain. This is particularly true the first semester.

- Studying for exams is such an extreme process it almost defies explanation. It is an intense period—beginning months before the actual test—of condensing tons of hours' worth of reading, thinking, and listening into digestible bits of information that can be instantly recalled in order to properly identify and competently analyze a number of complex issues. First-year students in particular struggle with even figuring out what it is they are supposed to learn.

- I always start my preparation four to six weeks before exams, depending on how many exams I have. Every semester, my husband makes fun of me for this. . . . I have tried to articulate to him the amount of information I need to comprehend and often memorize for each exam. I even try describing it to him using quantitative measurements, as in "I have X number of pages of outlines to memorize" or "I have X number of cases to grasp." It's impossible to convey this to someone who has never been through it.

In a survey in which law students were asked to rank the importance of twenty-four suggested changes to legal education, "more feedback on academic process" finished second only to smaller classes.[112] Of all the alleged deficiencies in legal education, the single-exam format is the one I have the hardest time defending. Particularly because so much rides on grades in law school, it seems unsound and unfair to evaluate a student's knowledge and understanding of fourteen intensive weeks of complex material based on a single exam.

The authors of the *Best Practices for Legal Education* report noted that effective student assessment tools must be *valid*, *reliable*, and *fair*, and concluded that law school's single-exam format fails all three criteria.[113] Flaws in the single-exam format

---

[112]   WHITMAN ET AL., *supra*, at 56–57 (discussing this survey).

[113]   BEST PRACTICES FOR LEGAL EDUCATION, *supra*, at 177.

include the time-crunch factor (the system favors students who can read, think, and write quickly), lack of comprehensive course coverage (one exam can't fairly cover 42–56 class hours of material, which are the number of classroom hours in a three- and four-credit course, respectively), and the absence of feedback to students during the semester (students have no way to gauge their progress until after the final examination, when it's too late).

Why do law schools use the single-exam format? What are the justifications for not giving students more bites at the apple, including different-sized bites from different angles, during the semester? We've discussed in other contexts how legal education, rooted as it is in tradition, is slow to change and this is another good example.

Part of the explanation for the single-exam format is historical. In the earliest days of American legal education, exams were administered weekly and even daily. The transition to the modern format came as a response to Christopher Langdell's case method back in the 1870s. As discussed, the goal of the case method is to train students to analyze and apply, rather than simply memorize, law.

To test these abilities, law professors developed the modern "issue-spotting/problem-solving" essay question, described below. The knowledge and training in legal analysis required to tackle this type of exam can be acquired only over time. New students aren't capable of effectively analyzing legal problems until they not only learn the law, but become acclimated to legal analysis. Students must acquire a capacity to think like a lawyer before they can write an exam like a lawyer. Of course, this doesn't explain why the single-exam format is used throughout all three years of law school.

Additional justifications include a legitimate concern that incorporating other exams, such as midterms, into the semester distracts students from their ongoing course work. It's true. When students have a midterm in one course, their attendance and class preparation suffer in other courses.

A practical explanation for why most law professors don't give exams during the semester, one that professors might be reluctant to concede, is that they simply don't want to take on the job of grading them. This is one more drawback of the large student-faculty ratios in law school classes. Grading law school exams, if done diligently, is a substantial burden. It can take several weeks to properly grade final examinations in a large class. A three-hour law school essay exam can generate answers exceeding five thousand words.

Unlike in other educational disciplines, law professors do not rely on teaching assistants to grade papers. And contrary to popular perception, most law professors (albeit not all) work hard. They put in long hours preparing for classes, doing administrative work such as serving on law school committees, and researching and writing scholarly articles or books. In legal academia, tremendous pressure exists to "publish or perish."

I know, go ahead and get out the world's smallest violin. Poor oppressed law professors. I'm not trying to justify the practice, just explain it. The bottom line is that it takes an unusual professor who is willing to devote a large chunk of time in the middle of a busy semester to grading a midterm exam or paper.

With that said, be aware that new ABA accreditation standards are in the process of being implemented that will require all accredited law schools to establish "learning outcomes" for students and assess whether students are achieving those outcomes.[114] How schools interpret these standards could have an impact on the single-exam format. While it seems unlikely that the assessment standards will result in the elimination of the all-or-nothing (or nearly all-or-nothing) final exam, they will probably result in more midstream feedback in at least some of your courses, which may

---

[114]   The new requirements are found in an amalgam of standards: Standards 301, 302, 314, and 315. Standard 301 requires schools to establish learning outcomes designed to achieve the core goals of legal education. Standard 302 mandates that, at a minimum, these learning outcomes must include: (1) knowledge and understanding of the law; (2) legal analysis, research, and communication; (3) professional and ethical responsibilities to clients and the legal system; and (4) other professional skills such as negotiation and document drafting. Standard 314 requires schools to use both formative (along the way) and summative (at the conclusion) assessment. Standard 315 requires that achieving and assessing learning oncomes be an ongoing process. STANDARDS & RULES OF PROCEDURE FOR APPROVAL OF LAW SCH. 301, 302, 314, 315 (AM. BAR ASS'N 2016–2017).

or may not be graded. It's difficult to predict the future impact of the assessment standards because, at least for now, they are clear in their intent to not impose specific rules and to leave their interpretation and implementation to individual schools.[115]

In the meantime, some schools already require or at least encourage multiple testing instruments during a semester and some admirable first-year professors voluntarily supplement the final exam with graded midterm exams, papers, quizzes, or class projects. If you have professors who do this, be sure to express your appreciation to them. Additionally, rest assured that most 1L professors offer ungraded practice exams with answer rubrics during the first semester.

Types of Law School Exam Questions

Law school exams don't resemble any exam students have seen before. In other educational disciplines, a student who has studied diligently and consistently can go into an exam feeling reasonably confident in her ability to perform well. That's not necessarily the case in law school. Consistent with the goals of legal education previously discussed, law school exams do not primarily reward memorization of the law, but the ability to engage in sound, organized analysis of it. While students obviously have to know the law in order to apply it, simply knowing the law is not sufficient to perform well.

Issue-spotting/problem-solving essay questions.

The classic type of law school exam question is the "issue-spotting/problem-solving question." I've included a sample from Torts as an Appendix to give you an idea of what one looks like.

These notoriously complicated and convoluted questions involve often elaborate hypothetical fact patterns in which various actors interact in ways that raise legal issues among them. As the name suggests, students must first spot the issues, then solve them through cogent legal analysis. An issue-

---

[115] Interpretation 314-2 to Standard 314, Assessment of Student Learning, specifically states: "A law school need not apply multiple assessment methods in any particular course. Assessment methods are likely to be different from school to school. Law schools are not required by Standard 314 to use any particular assessment method." STANDARDS & RULES OF PROCEDURE FOR APPROVAL OF LAW SCH. 314, Interpretation 314-2 (AM. BAR ASS'N 2016–2017).

spotting/problem-solving question may contain many issues or only a few, but the instructions don't tell students how many issues they are supposed to be looking for. Some issues might be easy to identify, but a question might also include tricky issues that only a portion of the students spot. Obviously, if a student can't spot an issue, she has no possibility of analyzing it.

If the exam isn't crafted well, which is sometimes the case, even well-prepared students may be left scratching their heads wondering what the professor wants them to discuss. Despite excelling in law school, I entered every exam with a lurking fear that I was going to read the exam and have no clue what the professor was looking for. The fear, shared by many students, proved to be unfounded, except one time. In my Corporations course, the exam content was so foreign that I actually went to the professor's office to make sure he handed out the correct exam.

Once students spot an issue, they must give a well-reasoned analysis of it by accurately stating the relevant legal rules and applying those rules to the facts of the question. In doing so, the student must address the relative strengths and weaknesses in each argument and offer a conclusion as to how each issue should be resolved.

Meanwhile, in the background, the clock is ticking away like a time-bomb. Although some professors give take-home exams, most exams are held within strict time limits, usually with one hour of exam time allotted for each credit hour of the course. The professor will usually write the ending time on the board as the last step before the exam begins. Unfortunately, some professors compose exams that can't possibly be adequately completed within that time frame, adding even more pressure.

Just about every aspect of this most popular of all law school exam question-types seems designed to induce extra stress.

Short essay problem-solving questions.

Also common are short essay problem-solving questions. As the label suggests, such questions are literally shorter in length than issue-spotting/problem-solving questions. They're also narrower in scope, often focusing on a single issue. Accordingly, short essay questions are less daunting than issue-spotting/problem-solving questions. Often, the question will expressly identify the issue, eliminating altogether the challenge of issue-spotting. Even if the question doesn't expressly identify the issues, they are easier to spot because fewer actors and actions are involved. For the same reason, answers to short essay questions present far fewer organizational challenges than questions raising multiple issues among multiple parties.

Policy questions.

Another oft-used type of essay question is known as a "policy question." Policy questions don't test students' ability to apply law to facts and solve legal problems. Depending on the question, they don't necessarily even test one's knowledge or understanding of specific principles of law. Rather, they focus on a student's ability to construct a thoughtful argument or analysis regarding a policy issue relevant to the course material. Here's a sample policy question that I once used on a Torts II exam:

> The U.S. rule regarding payment of attorneys' fees and litigation costs is that each side must bear its own fees and major costs, such as expert witness fees. Most other nations follow the "loser pays" rule, in which the losing party must pay the winning party's attorneys' fees and costs. Compare the two approaches as applied in personal injury cases and discuss their relative advantages and drawbacks to a legal system.

Be forewarned: Some professors will intentionally ask policy questions addressing issues never discussed in the course because they want to see how students apply what they learned to new situations. The story might be apocryphal, but I once heard of a policy question that asked simply: "What is law?" Most policy questions aren't that abstract, but by their nature, grading policy questions is very subjective. Will the professor reward you for thinking like he does about the policies? Punish you for thinking differently? Boost or lower your grade for taking an outlandish position? No way to know.

Don't get me wrong. Policy questions have value. Lawyers often are at the forefront as lawmakers and legislative advocates, and the abilities to think beyond the rules and analyze, critique, and advance the policies behind law are vital. My problems with pure policy questions—which I no longer use—is that they tend to benefit creative thinkers who are good writers over the students who worked the hardest, and are difficult to grade by objective standards. If your professor uses policy questions, I think it's perfectly appropriate to ask the professor what the grading criteria will be for them and for a sample question and answer to review. She might not provide them, but there's no harm in asking.

Don't let this section make you overly worried about policy questions. Although many law profs use them, they usually count for only a small portion of the exam.

Other types of essay questions.

Between the traditional "apply law to facts" essay questions and pure policy questions are a host of other essay questions—which can be long or short—limited in their content and format only by the ability of law professors to think creatively. In other words, there are no limits. A professor could ask you, for example, to draft a statute or answer a list of questions about a given fact pattern or put yourself in the role of the judge and write an opinion, or just about anything else. Such questions may be hybrids that combine legal problem-solving with policy discussion.

Multiple-choice questions.

Many, if not most, professors also use some multiple-choice questions. A blessing for students, you would think, and in some ways it is. For one thing, multiple-choice questions facilitate broader coverage of the course material. But law school multiple-choice questions, like everything else in law school, are different from anything students have previously encountered.

Most law school multiple-choice questions are styled after the format used on the Multistate Bar Examination (MBE), which comprises 200 questions and is given as part of the bar exam in every state except Louisiana. MBE-style multiple-choice questions require the ability to read, manage, and analyze complex text, and like the law itself, may lack clear right answers. They're difficult, which is one reason you can miss a large percentage of them and still pass the bar exam.

Chapter 17 more fully explains law school multiple-choice questions and offers strategies for addressing them.

Grading: The "Mandatory Curve"

While no current data exists (the last comprehensive survey of law school grading policies occurred in 2003), the vast majority of law schools have some type of mandatory "grade normalization" policy. Better known as "mandatory curves," grade normalization policies come in three basic varieties: (1) Curves requiring that certain percentages of grades be distributed within specified grade categories; (2) Curves requiring that the cumulative GPA for a course fall within a specified mean or median; and (3) Curves that combine mandatory grade distributions with a mean or median. The specifics of the policies vary tremendously. Some grade normalization policies are limited to first-year courses, but some policies include upper-level courses as well.

Below is an example of a first-year grade normalization policy combining both a mandatory grade distribution and a mandatory mean.

Mandatory Grade Distribution for 1L Courses:

In order to ensure fairness among the 1L sections and maintain rigor in grading, the following standards apply to the required 1L courses except for Legal Research and Writing . . . :

A– to A+ = 15% Maximum
B– to A+ = 40% Minimum
C– to C+ = 35% Minimum
F to D+ = 5% Minimum

Required GPA for each class = 2.70 to 3.10

A primary benefit of grade normalization policies is that they ensure fair, consistent treatment of students. Absent a grade normalization policy, a single outlying professor, either an unusually high or low grader, can unfairly shift the class rankings for an entire entering class. I taught at a school where my first-semester Torts grades fell right at the law school's institutional (but not formally imposed) first-year norm: a 2.67. The other first-year professors graded similarly, except for one. A professor teaching the other section of Torts awarded his students a cumulative GPA of 3.4. An analysis showed that this one professor unilaterally elevated the class rank of one section above the other at a statistically significant level. It can happen the other way as well. In a different year at the same school, a Civil Procedure professor gave his class a 2.2 cumulative GPA, unilaterally lowering the class standing of one section against the other.

Law students don't like grade normalization policies because they believe the policies force professors to give lower grades to students who deserve higher grades. They theorize, "If we're all writing A exams, why should we be punished by an artificially imposed curve?" The fallacy in that thinking is that students are not all writing A exams. Not anywhere close. They're not all writing B exams either. Truth be told, many law students are writing exams warranting lower grades than the students end up receiving. The only artificial forcing of grades I see on a regular basis, and hear professors complaining about, involves raising grades to meet the curve.

If law students better understood grade normalization policies, they would adore them. Law school grades have subtly drifted upwards over a period of decades, but during the past several years many schools have given official imprimatur to substantial grade inflation through their grade normalization policies. Today, it is common to find schools with mandatory first-year means of 3.1 to 3.3 grade points on a 4.0 grade scale.

The primary motivator behind these direct injections of GPA helium is the tepid legal job market. Higher grades, it is thought, allow a school's students to compete more easily in an employment arena with too many graduates applying for too few jobs. Some schools may also consider a high grade curve to be an effective marketing tool.

Most students welcome inflated grades, and who could blame them? But grade inflation may be coming back to bite law schools in the form of declining bar passage rates. Absent significant changes in application and enrollment trends, schools will be forced to confront the conflict between grade inflation and admitting students with lower profiles to fill seats. See Chapter 3 for a discussion of these issues.

To date, rather than readjusting grade curves downward to account for the lower credentials of incoming students, some law schools have reacted at the back end, by raising the GPA floor for academic dismissal. Traditionally, under a 4.0 grading scale, students had to maintain a 2.0 GPA (*C* average) to remain students in good standing. To offset high grading curves, some schools have simply raised the 2.0 academic dismissal floor to a 2.2, 2.3, or even 2.5, meaning a first-year student who earns *C*s— passing grades by traditional measures—can flunk out of law school.

You know by now that I'm old school, so it probably won't surprise you that I'm not a fan of gross grade inflation. I think it demeans legal education, which has always been known for its rigor, while also devaluing the high grades of students who truly earned them. Give credit to the student below for seeing value in law school's historically more honest evaluation of student performance:

> Although the soul-crippling uncertainty of the first semester is just awful, when law school does provide feedback, you know it is sincere. . . . Most of us were programmed to expect praise and reassurance for everything we did growing up, even if we couldn't actually draw, dance, catch a ball, or do any kind of math past long division. Now when I receive positive feedback, I know I actually deserve it. Law school does not always make us feel great about ourselves, but it helps us recognize our strengths while forcing us to address our weaknesses.

In the meantime, if you're at a school with a high grading curve, enjoy, but be wary of acquiring a false sense of security. In the past, it was rare for students with good grades to fail the bar exam. That may no longer be the case.

Exam Autopsies and Waiting for Grades

When "Time's up!" is declared after each exam, the sense of relief is huge . . . *until* the student walks out the door of the exam room and starts engaging in an exam autopsy with other students. Professors always tell students: "Don't talk about the exam when it's finished. There's nothing you can do about it. Just move on." But students never listen, and neither did we when we were students.

I still recall walking out of my first-year Criminal Law exam, feeling good, until I ran into a couple of classmates who started talking about a big conspiracy issue that I had missed. I stood there feeling like I had just wasted the three hardest months of my life, convinced I was going to flunk out of law school. In true law student fashion, I obsessed about this for the remainder of the exam period. As it turned out, I got an *A* on that exam. Once again, neurotic obsessiveness—a hallmark trait of law students—shows its limitations as a lifestyle.

What happened to me happens to most law students. One of my research assistants read the above and wrote:

> My first (but not last—slow learner!) taste of the crushing emotional devastation caused by the inevitable after-test chat was after my Contracts exam. We were all talking it up, asking each other how we answered this or that question, and someone asked me, "So was it a firm offer or an option contract? I wrote about both." We'd had an essay question on the sale of a racehorse with multiple issues, a major one being whether the seller had made a firm offer or whether it was an option contract, and I completely missed the distinction, writing instead about something else entirely. I literally spent the whole next day in bed under the covers thinking about *my* options, since it was obvious law school was not working out.

She got an *A* too. The moral of these stories is not that students always get *A*s on exams they think they botched, but that students rarely have an accurate idea about how they fared on a law school exam until grades are released. More often than you would imagine, the exam a student thinks she did the best on will be her worst grade and the exam she thought she bombed will be her best grade.

* * *

Despite the pain of post-mortem second-guessing, with each passing exam, the weight on a student's shoulders proportionately lightens. But then the waiting kicks in, and as rocker Tom Petty sang, "The wa-ai-ting is the hardest part."[116] Okay, that's not true. Studying for and taking the exams is the hardest part, but the waiting is still tough.

It usually takes several weeks for exam grades to be posted. Talk about cruel and unusual punishment. Needless to say, the delay in posting grades is both perplexing and irritating to law students. "Why does it take so freaking long?" they want to know. First, and most legitimately, it really does take time to diligently grade a stack of lengthy essay exams for a large class. Second, during the holiday break after the fall semester, law schools often close for a week or more, so there are no staff around to process grades even for professors who have finished grading and want to turn in their grades. Finally, and inexcusably, some professors turn in grades late.

---

[116] TOM PETTY & THE HEARTBREAKERS, THE WAITING (Backstreet/MCA 1981).

CHAPTER 15

EXAM PREPARATION

"At one-thirty, wild now with drugs and frustration, I rolled out and began to flail at the mattress: I was *trying* to destroy myself, I shouted; I was *insuring* failure." Drug rehab gone bad? Nah. Just another 1L freaking out the night before his first exam, in this case, Scott Turow, writing in his classic book, *One L*.[117]

Because of the single-exam format, law school exams, especially the first set, are likely to bring out a touch of insanity in just about every student, but you can reduce your stress while maximizing your chances of success in the final countdown days by following some easy, practical tips outlined in this chapter.

But hold on. Why is this chapter on exam preparation one of the shortest in the book when it seems like it should be one of the longest? Because—great news!—if you follow the advice in the preceding chapters, you already will have completed 90 percent of your exam prep by the time exams roll around. Indeed, Chapters 11 (case-briefing), 12 (note-taking), and 13 (outlining) could all accurately be denoted as "exam preparation" chapters. The C.R.E.D.O. chapter is the most important exam preparation chapter of them all. If you follow the C.R.E.D.O. from day one, you can feel confident that you will be very close to ready for your exams when the time comes.

This chapter is dedicated to that final home stretch: how to get ready for exams in the days immediately preceding and during exam week. Follow these suggestions:

Plot an Organized Study Schedule

Nowhere are efficient time-management skills more important than during exam prep. You need to map out a schedule that allows you to arrive at each and every exam fully

---

[117] SCOTT TUROW, ONE L: THE TURBULENT TRUE STORY OF A FIRST YEAR AT HARVARD LAW SCHOOL 167 (Grand Cent. Publ'g 1997) (1977). Turow went on to become a bestselling author of legal thrillers such as *Presumed Innocent*, which was made into a 1990 blockbuster movie starring Harrison Ford.

prepared. Usually (but not always), you'll be afforded at least a few days to study prior to the commencement of exams. This breathing space is called "reading week" or, back in the day, "dead week," although it's not always a full week.

Don't make the mistake—which some students do—of using all your free days before exams studying for the first exam. You need to spread your pre-exam study hours among your different courses to account for the fact that your exams will be stacked back to back, with perhaps only one free day between them. You'll often find that you need to start studying for your last exams first.[118] Indeed, one of my research assistants advises that students do all of their studying for exams "*backwards*; i.e., start the reading week by studying for your last exam first and proceed to study in reverse chronological order all the way through."

Begin by plotting all of your reading days and exam period days on a calendar grid so you'll be able to assess your available time from a big-picture viewpoint. Below is a sample prep grid for a twelve-day combined reading week and exam period:

Day 1	Day 2	Day 3	Day 4	Day 5	Day 6
Study Civ. Pro.	Study Contracts	Study Torts	Study Torts	**Torts Exam 9:00 am** Study Civ. Pro.	Study Civ. Pro.

---

[118] One benefit of being a 1L is that law schools intentionally schedule first-year exams with at least one free day between exams. In your second and third years, you might have exams on consecutive days.

Day 7	Day 8	Day 9	Day 10	Day 11	Day 12
Civ. Pro Exam 9:00 am	Study Property	Study Property	Property Exam 9:00 am	Study Contracts	Contracts Exam 9:00 am
Break			Study Contracts		

Note how the studying for the Civil Procedure and Contracts exams is front-loaded because of the one-day gap between those exams and the immediately preceding exams. This allowed me to allot a minimum of two full days to each exam. I built in a break after the Civil Procedure exam to take the afternoon and evening off to relax and recharge brain cells. Because of the gap in the preparation for Civil Procedure and Contracts, I included an extra half-day of study for those exams on the same day of the previous exams, but if you feel adequately prepared, you might want to consider taking breaks after the exam on all exam days. That's what I did back in law school. Whether you can afford yourself this luxury will depend on how prepared you are entering the exam cycle.

Divide your study time relatively equally among courses with the same credit hours. Sure, Property may seem harder than Torts, but a *B* in Torts is worth the same as a *B* in Property if the credit hours are the same. Also, the Torts prof might be a more rigorous grader or write harder exams. It's a fool's game to try to predict which exams will be the "hardest."

Seeing the above grid should help drive home the point about most exam preparation being accomplished during the semester through consistent class preparation, note-taking, outlining, and periodic review. Two days per exam is barely enough time to review and absorb your notes and outlines. It definitely is not enough time to begin learning the material for the first time.

Within each study day on your grid, break your tasks down more specifically. For example, a "Study Torts" day might be broken down more specifically as follows:

Study Torts

1.   Read case briefs once.

2.   Read outline twice.

3.   Review Torts flashcards with study group.

4.   Work through one practice intentional torts and one negligence essay question.

There is no single correct way to allot your study time. I asked a research assistant, ranked number one in her class, to summarize her exam prep schedule from the first semester. Here's what she wrote:

> I started about a month before the first exam and made a study schedule very similar to the one you included. I alternated one subject per day and studied anywhere from fifteen minutes to two hours depending on how much time I had. My studying consisted of reading over my class notes, rereading cases and other reading assignments, and doing practice questions. I looked at old exams, did problems in the textbooks, and did CALI exercises online. About a week before finals I increased my studying to two subjects per day (still alternating to give each equal weight). When dead week and exams started I upped my study time to about three hours per subject a day.
>
> I continued to study two subjects per day except for the day before an exam, when I studied only the subject that was tested the next day. I always took the evening of an exam off and did something else (like go out with non-law school friends or watch a movie). Starting so early really helped to decrease my stress level when exams rolled around. Since I had so much of my exam prep already done, I had a lot more free time and was able to stay rested.

While there are differences in the details, notice the common thread in our approaches: *thoughtful advance organization and time distribution.*

Do Practice Exams

One of the best exam preparation strategies is working through practice exams. If you were training to be a motorcycle mechanic, you wouldn't just study books on how to do it. You'd get your hands dirty disassembling and reassembling motorcycle engines. It's like that with every skill in life. People training to be pilots don't just read books about it before climbing into the cockpit of a Boeing 747. They study, practice with flight simulators, and start with smaller aircraft. Since many law school courses don't offer this kind of practice, you'll have to do it on your own.

Students spend tons of time memorizing the law and far too little time learning and practicing the *process* of law school exam-taking. Many students know all the law there is to know, but still don't excel on exams because they never learned how to take a law school exam. The best way to get a handle on that process is through practice exams.

Working through practice exams advances several goals. First, it helps you know what to expect, increasing your comfort zone. Second, doing practice exams also helps train you to spot issues, the crucial threshold step to good exam performance. Third, if you're working through old exams from your professors, you will get a feel for what to expect from that particular professor because professors usually are consistent in their approach to fashioning exams.

You might even get lucky enough to stumble on a question that turns up on the real exam. Many professors recycle exams over the years. While most don't release exams they have any intention of recycling, it can happen. I remember getting together with a group of classmates to go over old exams in preparation for my Civil Procedure II exam the following day. We started later than I wanted and I've already told you I wasn't much of a group studier, so I barely glanced at the exams before calling it a night and going home to bed. As soon as the exam was distributed the next day, I wished I had stayed longer. The essay question was the *exact same question* I laid eyes on the night before.

Many law school study aids contain practice essay questions. These can be helpful, but the best approach is to work with original source material: exams prepared by your professors. While there is similarity in the structure and format of law school essay questions, professors have their own styles for writing exams. Returning to the analogy above, if you were training to be a Kawasaki motorcycle mechanic, you'd be better off practicing on Kawasakis than Hondas even though substantial similarities exist between brands of motorcycles.

Most law professors make copies of old exams available to students. Don't hesitate to ask your professors about this. Unfortunately, unlike the practice exams contained in study aids, these sample exams may not include answers.

Be aware and beware that practicing with commercial exams or professors' old exams can be counterproductive and even harmful if the exams are not tailored to the material you have covered. As a top student explained:

> I took some [brand omitted] practice tests a couple weeks before the end of the semester and they stressed me out way more than they helped because we hadn't covered a lot of the material the practice exams tested. Also, some professors post old exams on TWEN about halfway through the semester and I had the same problem with those. We hadn't learned all the material yet, which made me frustrated and stressed when I didn't spot a lot of the issues.

Especially in your first semester, it's wise to actually "take" at least a couple of practice exams in a mock-testing situation. Treat them like the real deal. Time yourself. Try to replicate the entire experience. Remember: familiarity reduces stress.

I don't recommend writing lengthy answers to *every* old exam you come across because such a time-demanding approach will detract from your other exam preparation, *but do read* all sample exams made available by your professors to practice your issue-spotting skills. Each first-year course raises a limited number of issues ripe for essay testing, so you're likely to come across some of the same issues that will appear on the real exam even if they're packaged in different fact patterns.

If you're in a study group, reviewing practice or old exams can be one of the most productive group study activities. A group of students are more likely to spot all the issues on a question than any individual student. Reviewing exams with a group can help you learn from your oversights. If others identify an issue you missed, ask what facts in the question flagged the issue for them.

By all means, if your professors afford you opportunities to take one or more practice exams during the semester, which most first-year professors do, take full advantage of them even if the exams are not graded. I distribute two practice essay questions in Torts, one addressing intentional torts and one addressing the tort of negligence, along with a full model answer to each question. I've witnessed students go from writing *F* answers on the practice exams to *A* or *B* answers on the real exam, in part because they learned from their mistakes.

I've also watched far too many students unwisely squander the best opportunity they will have to learn how to take my exam by blowing off the practice exams because they were "too busy"— a classic case of penny-wise, pound-foolish. If a professor gives you a practice exam and answer, she's essentially telling you: "This is exactly how I want you to do it."

Get Exam Supplies

Most law schools provide students with essential exam-taking materials, but ask your professors to be sure. You don't want to show up without something you need. Extra supplies to consider include something to drink, pain-reliever such as Ibuprofen (in case your stress causes a headache, which happens), and foam earplugs. Available at any drug store, the latter are inexpensive, comfortable, and do a good job filtering out background noise. Some schools even hand them out, as do state bar examiners. As for drinks, be careful about consuming too many fluids during an exam because restroom breaks will cut into your exam time and professors or proctors look askew at students who take more than one restroom break during an exam.

Practice with the Exam-Security Software

As discussed in Chapter 2, most students take exams on computers. Some law schools require them to do so. To prevent cheating, students are required to use exam-security software, such as Exam4 or ExamSoft, during each exam. Depending on the settings chosen by the professor or school, the software blocks access to folders, programs, and the internet during the exam. It basically converts your computer into a word processor.

Don't wait until the last minute to register for and download the security software. Glitches can and do occur. If they do, you don't want to be worrying about having to resolve them right before an exam. One student came running frantically into my office forty-five minutes before her first law school exam, explaining that she just tried to download the exam software—which had been available to students for weeks—and got an error message. Fixing it entailed the IT department contacting the software company. They finally got it working—she hoped—as she raced off to the exam.

After you download the software, *practice* with it. Word-processing applications on exam-security software allow only for basic text entry and editing. While there are some similarities to Microsoft Word, there are many differences. Thus, for example, exam-security software has a spell-check function, but it's not autocorrect like on Word. Judging by the frequent misspellings on my exams, I doubt most students know it exists. These are things you want to figure out in advance of your exams.

Rest and Relax

Even during exams, you need to allot yourself time to relax and recoup. This includes getting normal sleep and also scheduling breaks for relaxation and exercise.

Studies show that sleep-deprived students perform substantially worse on tests. "Pulling an all-nighter" is not only ineffective, it impairs performance. Lack of sleep negatively affects attention, concentration, and memory. Cramming is a particularly bad strategy for law school success because of the huge amount of material.

If you're at the point where you feel the need to desperately cram all night for an exam, it might already be too late. The flipside is that if you've worked consistently and diligently throughout the semester, you won't have to study all night. It bears repeating. The bulk of exam preparation occurs long before exams begin, starting with the first week of classes.

Your best overall strategy for arriving at exams fully prepared is to follow the C.R.E.D.O. habits in Chapter 10 from the beginning of the semester until the end. If you read every assignment, brief every case, attend and take good notes in every class, compose outlines for every course, and engage in periodic review, you'll be rounding third base and heading for home when exam week arrives.

CHAPTER 16

LAW SCHOOL ESSAY EXAMS: FIFTEEN COMMON MISTAKES

Alright! Finally, the good stuff, the carefully guarded secrets to succeeding on law school exams. Well, kind of, sort of. Hate to be a buzz-kill, but the truth is no secret formula or system for acing law school exams exists. If anyone offers to share such a formula or system with you, follow these steps: (1) restrain yourself from falling on the floor laughing; and (2) politely tell them thanks, but no thanks.

My best advice for excelling on law school exams, as I've already said, is to apply the C.R.E.D.O. habits (Chapter 10) to all of the other advice in these pages. If you fail to consistently, rigorously, efficiently, and diligently pursue your studies in an organized fashion, no amount of exam advice in the world is going to put you on top.

But even following that advice isn't sufficient to ensure your best performance. Lots of diligent, hard-working students fail to maximize their potential on their first rounds of exams simply because they lack experience and understanding about what to do and what not to do.

Most first-year law school exams consist of essay questions or a combination of essay and multiple-choice questions. This chapter focuses on essay questions, while the next chapter addresses multiple-choice questions. These chapters are a perfect example of why you need to consider *1L of a Ride* to be a yearlong handbook, not just a book to be read before law school. These chapters will definitely be worth rereading as your first exams approach, including midterms or practice exams.

I've graded thousands of law school essay exams. Year after year, at law school after law school, students make the *exact same mistakes*. So I decided one effective way to explain how to do things right in answering essay questions would be to explain what students commonly do wrong. I'm sure other professors could come up with additional mistakes or reframe the entries on my list, but here are fifteen common law school essay exam mistakes:

1.   Failing to carefully read and follow instructions.

2.   Starting to write before analyzing the question and organizing the answer.

3.   Not managing time properly and efficiently.

4.   Issue-spotting: Not paying attention to the facts.

5.   Issue-spotting: Not recognizing "givens."

6.   Issue-spotting: Insisting on finding issues you just *know* must be in the exam.

7.   Issue-spotting: Ignoring issues raised by the facts because the issue would ultimately fail on the merits.

8.   Failing to structure exam answers in a rough IRAC (Issue, Rule, Analysis, Conclusion) framework.

9.   Leaving out the *relevant* rules of law.

10. Failing to use precise, accurate language in stating legal rules and analysis.

11. Giving a general dissertation on the law rather than answering the question asked.

12. Omitting or skimping on the analysis.

13. Doing the "Monster [Issue] Mash."

14. Being sloppy.

15. Writing too little.

The traditional issue-spotting/problem-solving essay question remains a popular testing tool in first-year courses, so we'll focus on that format in this chapter, but as discussed in Chapter 14, professors use other types of essay questions as well. Much of what is discussed here applies to any type of essay question.

To give us a vehicle for illustrations, below is an intentional torts practice essay question. It's a short, simple question designed for students who are only four or five weeks into law school.

Intentional Torts Practice Question

It was the night of the company holiday party at the Holiday Inn lounge. Jane was the office receptionist hired by the company six weeks earlier. Dick was the office boor who was attracted to Jane and tried to flirt with her every chance he got.

Throughout the evening, Dick followed Jane around, making eye contact with her whenever he had the opportunity. At one point, he decided to be daring. He approached her and, without saying a word, dangled a hotel room key in front of her. When she winked at him, he put his arm around her and pinched her. Unfortunately, Jane was not winking in response to Dick's advances, but because she had accidentally squirted the lime from her gin and tonic in her eye.

When Dick pinched her, Jane said, "Take your hands off of me, you jerk!" Hearing this, Moe, a coworker who was six-feet, four-inches tall and weighed 260 pounds, came to render assistance. Dick was just five-feet, seven-inches tall and weighed 130 pounds. Moe punched Dick in the face, breaking his nose. Moe drew back his fist to launch a second punch, but before he could act, Dick pulled out a pocket knife and said, "Don't move even one inch or I'll cut you into linguini." Moe froze, staring at the knife.

Dick then saw Sikorsky, the company president, standing nearby with his back to him. Figuring he could increase his leverage, Dick pointed the knife at Sikorsky and said, "Stay away or the boss gets it too." Sikorsky had a hearing impairment and was unaware any of this was going on. He kept talking to the person in front of him, chewing on a chicken wing. When he later found out about Dick's threat, Sikorsky was outraged.

In a later deposition, Dick said: "I didn't desire to cause any offense. I swear. I really thought Jane liked me."

This is an intentional tort question. Do not discuss negligence. Fully discuss all potential claims and defenses arising from this unfortunate sequence of events.

We won't discuss all of them, but issues in the practice question include the element of intent, the torts of assault, battery, and false imprisonment, and the privileges of consent, self-defense, and defense of others. (The Appendix provides a more fleshed out sample intentional torts essay question and a model answer.)

Fifteen Common Law School Essay Exam Mistakes

1.   Failing to carefully read and follow instructions. After thirty years teaching law students, I continue to be astonished at the number of students who self-destruct because they don't carefully read or follow the exam instructions. It happened the first semester I taught; it happened the most recent semester I taught.

On law school exams, instructions show up in different places: (1) most exams begin with a set of instructions applicable to the exam as a whole; (2) each essay question will have its own instructions applicable to that question, usually at the end of the question; and (3) a multiple-choice (or other objective) section is likely to have its own instructions at the beginning of the section.

Knowing it is impossible to be too clear when dealing with stressed-out 1Ls taking their first exams, I go out of my way to include specific instructions. Nevertheless, on every exam, some students do not follow them.

Look at the last paragraph of the Dick and Jane practice question. The two basic divisions of tort law are intentional torts and negligence (with strict liability forming a smaller third category). While intentional torts and negligence are separate areas of law, they can overlap depending on the facts. To simplify the lives of students and increase the coherency of their exam answers, I keep these areas separate in essay questions with this instruction: "This is an intentional tort question. Do not discuss negligence." For negligence questions, I say the opposite. Would you believe that students sometimes overlook this instruction and spend all or part of their time writing about the wrong subject area? It happens.

Because negligence is such a broad, complicated subject, I often include detailed instructions on negligence essay questions that eliminate certain issues from consideration. Every exam, some students overlook the instructions and write about the non-issues.

Oversights like these are killers on several levels. First, time is a precious commodity when taking law school exams. Every minute spent writing about a non-issue is one less minute students have for writing about the issues raised by the question. Second, students usually receive no credit for content addressing non-issues, no matter how brilliant their understanding of the law on those issues. Most law professors don't even read irrelevant analysis. We skim it, searching for the point where the student gets back on track. Some professors mark down for incorrect analysis.

Finally, blunders from not following instructions cast both the exam and exam-writer in a negative light. Picture your professor as a kind of forensic pathologist. Exam-writers are anonymous, but at every step of the way in reading an exam, the professor is picking up clues and drawing inferences about the writer, both positive and negative. Errors from misreading or not following instructions generate negative impressions that affect the grade the exam receives.

Why does it happen? Why do so many intelligent students fail to read and heed clear instructions? Often, it's because in the stress and rush of the moment they make the mistake of . . .

2. Starting to write before analyzing the question and organizing the answer. Poor law students. Law professors give them incredibly difficult exams and, sometimes, not enough time to adequately complete the exam. No wonder students feel the urge to begin writing answers before giving sufficient thought to what they're writing about. The temptation is understandable, but you must resist it.

Failing to fully digest the question and organize your answer before you begin writing leads to a jumbled mess. It also substantially increases the likelihood of your overlooking key instructions (see above) and facts and issues (see below).

Take time to carefully read and do a rough outline of the question on scratch paper before you begin writing. When you hear classmates pounding away at their keyboards while you're only halfway through studying the question, hold course! Don't panic and abandon the plan.

How much time should you spend reading the question and outlining the answer before you start writing? It's impossible to say with exactitude because it depends on the nature of the question and how much time has been allotted to it. As a general guideline, I recommend devoting at least 20 percent of the time allotted for the particular question (e.g., twelve minutes for a sixty-minute question; eighteen minutes for a ninety-minute question).

Tips for Quickly Analyzing a Question

Here are three tips for analyzing and organizing your answers on the fly:

Use a highlighter. Students are allowed to write on their exams. Use a highlighter to mark key facts as you read.

Make a rough outline as you read. On a piece of scratch paper, compose a rough outline as you read the question. Not a formal outline with Roman numerals, etc. Just jot down issues (including claims and defenses) as you spot them. Then take a few minutes to organize them. Address issues in the order they are raised by the question. It's always weird when students take the issues up in reverse order.

In addition to improving the organization of your answer, outlining the issues will prevent you from forgetting about them. Many have been the students who, on reviewing their exams alongside the model answer, say, "Doh! I spotted that issue when I read the question, but then forgot about it."

Use subheadings to separate party disputes and issues. If the question raises issues involving multiple parties, organize your answer under subheadings listing the parties, as in "A v. B." In addition to making your exam easier and more appealing to read, using subheadings will help force you to address all claims, defenses, or other issues between A and B before moving on to other parties.

Nothing wears out an exam-grading professor faster than students who take the alternative stream-of-consciousness, mash-up approach. Thanks to amazing new brain imaging software installed on student computers, I was able to record the actual thoughts of an exam-taking student who did not separate his analysis by parties in taking the Dick and Jane practice exam:

> Okay, first, I will discuss issues involving Jane v. Dick. [Writing] Alrighty, I'm done with Jane and Dick. Now I will move on to Dick v. Moe. [Writing] Sweet. I did an awesome job on those issues if I do say so myself. Time to move on to Sikorsky v. Dick, but, wait, I just thought of something I forgot to say about Jane and Dick. [Writing] You know, that makes me think of an interesting point to add about Dick and Moe. [Writing] . . . Phew, that was a grueling question. Time to wrap things up . . . but, first, I just had an *amazing* idea I need to tack on about Jane and Dick! [Writing].

New thoughts about prior issues you've discussed will often strike you as you proceed through the exam. Just be sure to go back and integrate them in the right places.

In addition to using subheadings to separate disputes between different parties, I also recommend using subheadings to denote distinct legal issues. Mistake number thirteen (Doing the "Monster [Issue] Mash") addresses this point.

3. Not managing time properly and efficiently. Because time is scarce on most law school exams, it's crucial that you efficiently allocate your time among the different exam components and monitor it as you progress through the exam.

Not infrequently, students will get so wrapped up in answering one question, or addressing one issue in a multi-issue question, that they run out of time before getting to the others. This is a mistake that can have disastrous consequences. When students run out of time, it's not usually because they spent their time profitably writing an exquisite answer to one question or one issue at the expense of others, but because they squandered time engaging in one of the:

Top Five Law School Essay Exam Time-Wasters

1. Engaging in a generalized brain-dump rather than focusing on the specific issues raised by the facts.

2. Going off on tangents analyzing non-issues, including "givens."

3. Writing lengthy introductions that simply restate the facts of the question or lengthy conclusions restating what has already been stated.

4. Restating legal rules that have already been stated once.

5. Spending disproportionate time on the first issue simply because it's first.

Numbers 1 and 2 are parts of larger mistakes discussed below. With regard to number 3, quickly cut to the chase when writing answers to essay exams. You don't need an introduction to your answer other than one sentence such as: "This question raises several issues that I will address in the order they appear." While you definitely want to discuss relevant facts as part of your legal analysis (see below), don't begin your answer by restating or summarizing the facts of the question as you would for the law office memorandum in your legal writing course. Similarly, while most professors will want you to offer your predictive conclusions as to the resolution of each issue raised in the exam, you do not need a concluding paragraph that summarizes or restates the conclusions you have already articulated in the body of your analysis.

Time-waster number 4 is similar to number 3 in that it involves avoiding repetition. Once you've stated a legal rule or test in an essay question, you do not need to restate it. For example, in the practice question there is more than one battery claim. The first is Jane's claim for an offensive battery against Dick for pinching her. In discussing that, it would be proper to state the elements of the tort of battery. But when you get to Dick's battery claim against Moe for punching him, it's not necessary to restate them. Simply refer back to the previous statement of the elements. You might say, for example: "The elements of battery have already been stated above," then proceed to identify and analyze the specific issues raised by the facts as to Dick's battery claim against Moe.

As for time-waster number 5, it seems to be a phenomenon of human nature to devote a disproportionate amount of time and attention to the first item in a list of items for no reason other than it's first. I see this happen in faculty meetings. No matter how insignificant the first item on the agenda, the faculty will discuss it to death at the expense of items that appear later on the agenda, even if they are more important. Thus, the law school's inclement weather policy (first item on the agenda) might get fifty-five minutes of discussion in a one-hour meeting, while a proposal to abolish grading (last item) gets five. Law students commonly do the same thing on exams. They'll spend far too much time belaboring the first issue at the expense of other important issues that come later.

Size up and apportion your time at the beginning of the exam and keep your eye on the clock. Some students calculate and write down specific starting and ending times next to each question before they begin. (This can also be done with the timer built into the exam-security software.) Your professor might include suggested time limits for components of the exam, but if not, it's up to you to figure out.

You want to allocate your time roughly in accordance with the points assigned to the various exam components. Most law school exams are three or four hours. If you have a three-hour all-essay exam with three equally weighted questions, you'd want to spend approximately one hour on each question. If the exam is half essay and half multiple-choice, with equal points for each section, split your time roughly equally.

If you do find yourself running out of time before you've had a chance to tackle a question or to address all the issues, use your remaining time to hit the high points. Jot down as many issues as you can. Simply mentioning an issue, even without analysis, can get you some points. Some professors, particularly inexperienced ones, will load up a question with too many issues, making it impossible to analyze them all adequately.

Finally, use all your available time on the exam. It kills me when I see people leaving exams early. Students devote hundreds of hours over a fourteen-week period to learning the subject matter of a course well enough to give themselves a fighting chance on a single exam. Why would anyone not take advantage of every available second? Are they in a hurry to grab lunch? Take in a movie?

If you finish early, it's almost always because you: (a) did not spot all the issues; or (b) did not fully analyze them. If you *think* you've finished early, use your leftover time to reread the questions and your answers. Maybe you'll spot an issue you overlooked. I remember walking out of a law school exam early and immediately realizing I missed a huge issue. If I had sat there a few more minutes, it might have come to me before it was too late. Or maybe you'll notice on rereading that you forgot to state an applicable rule in your answer or that your analysis on a particular point needs beefing up. At a minimum, you'll be likely to notice missing punctuation, misspelled words, and other typos you can correct.

4. Issue-spotting: Not paying attention to the facts. Issue-spotting is the all-important preliminary challenge for students on law school essay exams. If a student can't spot the correct issues, she has no chance of analyzing them. "How do I spot the issues?" is one of the most common questions law professors receive. Issue-spotting difficulties come in two forms: (1) overlooking issues that your professor wants you to analyze; and (2) finding or creating issues the professor is not looking for.

Unfortunately, there is no easy answer or magic formula to successful issue-spotting other than the broad generalization that the process is *always* rooted in the facts of the question. Mistakes 4–7 all relate to issue-spotting and can all be roughly grouped under the penumbra of not paying attention to the relevant facts.

Each fact in an essay exam question should be scrutinized from the perspective of, "Hm, why would the professor insert that fact? It must be there for a reason." Reading the question in this manner can help you spot more issues. Most facts are included for a reason: either to raise issues or exclude them.

Refer back to the penultimate[119] paragraph of the practice question for an example. Dick's statement at his deposition that he "didn't desire to cause any offense" to Jane is a fact of legal significance, but one which students frequently overlook, maybe because it's at the end. Dick's statement was included to raise the issue of whether Dick had subjective tortious intent to commit an offensive battery against Jane. The intent issue was worth more points on the practice exam than any other issue (generally, the more difficult the issue, the more points it will be worth).

But not all facts in a question have legal significance. Unfortunately, there are no reliable rules here. Many professors will include introductory narrative simply to set the scene; that is, to set up the question for the legally significant events that follow. This is the situation in our practice question. None of the facts in the first paragraph have legal significance, but nearly all of the remaining facts do. But sometimes the very first sentence of the question may be vitally important.

Some professors sprinkle legally irrelevant facts throughout the question. Sometimes they do this with a pedagogical purpose of challenging students to distinguish material from immaterial facts, but often immaterial facts are included simply to facilitate the story-telling aspect of the question. Reading samples of previous exams by your professors will help you size up their question-writing style in advance.

Almost as common as overlooking the legal significance of facts, but much less understandable, is simply not paying attention to facts of obvious significance. When grading exams, I commonly scribble in the margin: "Read the question!" The comment is born of frustration in reading student analyses that

---

[119] "Penultimate" means second to last. It's become something of a running joke in my classes that all students leave my course understanding the meaning of penultimate. It started years ago after I asked an assistant at a different law school to draft a flyer encouraging students to participate in the law review's summer write-on competition. (See Chapter 24 for information about law review.) Reading the flyer, I came to this bolded sentence: "Law Review will be the PENULTIMATE experience of your life!" "That makes me sad," I said. "Why is that?" the assistant asked. "They're so young. Law review shouldn't be the second-to-last experience of their lives." She thought it meant "super-ultimate." I tell the story each year, with the result that I now have an inscribed coffee mug from one class that says, "Professor McClurg: The PENULTIMATE Law Professor."

are off-base simply because the student failed to take note of facts of obvious significance.

An example comes from a recent Torts exam involving a defamation lawsuit against a newspaper. There are two types of defamation: libel and slander. Libel is written defamation and slander is oral defamation. Every student understands this simple rule. The defamation in the question was printed in a newspaper. It was libel. Nevertheless, I'd estimate that 10 percent of the class launched into a discussion of whether the defamatory words were "slander per se."

5. Issue-spotting: Not recognizing "givens." As a subcategory of not paying attention to the facts, students often analyze issues they don't need to be talking about because they aren't raised by the facts of the question. Often, this occurs with regard to what are called "givens." A given is an assumption either clearly stated in the question (an "express given") or one that is easily inferable from the facts (an "inferable given").

Often, express givens are inserted for the very purpose of preventing students from talking about the point. If an intentional tort question, for example, says that "A committed a battery against B," there is no need to analyze the elements of battery in connection with A and B because the question is already assuming they have been met. Similarly, if a negligence question states that "A negligently drove his car into B," you can assume A failed to exercise reasonable care while driving and do not need to discuss that point.

If something is a given, note it as such in your answer and move on to the real issues. For example, in the second illustration, an astute writer would say something like: "It is a given that A acted negligently in colliding with B, so there is no need to discuss that point."

Overlooking givens is problematic on several levels. It causes students to waste time writing about non-issues, tangles up the organization of their answers, and conveys to the professor that the student either didn't read the question carefully or didn't understand what he or she was doing.

Not all givens are expressly stated. Often they are inferences that can be readily drawn from the stated facts. For example, the elements of the tort of battery are: (1) a volitional act; (2) intended to cause a harmful or offensive bodily contact; and (3) such a contact results, directly or indirectly.

Suppose the question says "During an argument, A pulls a gun from his pocket, points it at B and pulls the trigger, shooting B in the abdomen."

Absent some privilege to shoot B raised by the facts (such as self-defense), this would be a battery. Unlike the example above, however, the battery is not an express given (the question doesn't actually say "this is a battery"), but satisfaction of the elements of a battery claim are easily inferable givens unless other facts call them into question. Accordingly, while you would want to state the elements of battery and briefly note that they are satisfied, you would not want or need to engage in a discussion of whether A pulling out the gun and shooting B was a volitional act (it was), whether A intended the shooting (he did), or whether the contact element was satisfied when the bullet entered B's abdomen (it was).

Extensive discussion of any particular element of a legal claim is necessary only if the facts put the element in issue. Thus, for example, to make the volitional act element of battery an issue, we would need facts suggesting that what occurred didn't involve a voluntary act, as in:

A and B, two friends, got into a dispute at a bar one night over which songs to play on the jukebox. On the way home, A was still mad and told B, "I have half a mind to shoot you." B told A to shut up and sleep it off in the backseat while he drove. A agreed. While A was asleep, he rolled over on a handgun in his coat pocket, causing it to discharge, hitting B.

See the difference? Here we have specific facts raising the volitional act element (as well as the intent element) as an issue.

Bottom line tip: Look for facts that specifically raise particular issues. If no such facts exist, the professor did not intend it to be an issue (with the unhelpful caveat: unless it's a poorly written question).

A related point bears mentioning. Essay questions sometimes require students to assume facts that are not specifically stated to fully analyze the issues. If the assumed facts are reasonably inferable from the stated facts, this is perfectly acceptable. For example, if the question states that a relevant event occurred at dusk and the amount of available light is important to resolving an issue (e.g., the possible negligence of a motorist driving without headlights), it is perfectly appropriate to say something like, "Assuming it was already dark . . ." or "Assuming it was still light enough to see at a distance . . ." Such assumptions are not only permissible, but necessary to completely and accurately analyze the issue. But you must *state* your assumptions. Don't just make assumptions in your head, even reasonable ones, without noting them in your answer.

Any assumed fact must be reasonably inferable from the given facts. I still remember the student from many years ago who was analyzing an intentional Torts question that said something like: "A shot at B, but the bullet missed him." The student came back with an analysis saying: "A shot at B, but missed him. However, assuming the bullet had hit B, it would be a battery." Then he plunged headfirst into an analysis of the law of battery. Assumptions that are *contrary* to the question facts are never reasonable.

6. Issue-spotting: Insisting on finding issues you just *know* must be in the exam. Students often come into exams hell-bent on finding particular issues in essay questions whether they exist or not. This occurs because every course has its own classic legal issues, issues to which professors devote substantial class time.

It's smart to be on the lookout for those issues, but a mistake to go further and insist, as some students do, that regardless of the facts of the question, a particular issue *must* be present. Once when I was teaching at a West Coast law school, I discovered a student was operating a gambling ring in which he set odds and accepted bets from other students as to which issues would be tested on their upcoming exams, including Torts. I recall learning, for example, that the odds of the negligence defense known as "assumption of risk" turning up as a major issue on my Torts exam were 4–1. Presumably, these odds were tied to the fact that we had spent two full classes on the doctrine.

I bet heavily against the odds, omitted the issue, and cleaned up. Ha! That'll teach the little punk. Kidding, but I did omit the issue. Again, it's wise to be on the lookout for issues to which the professor devoted substantial class time, but if the facts needed to raise an issue aren't in the question, the issue isn't there either. Don't force in a discussion of it.

On the other hand, if you're unsure whether a question is intended to raise a particular issue, err on the side of discussing it rather than leaving it out. The principal harm from discussing a non-issue is wasted time. The harm from not discussing something intended by the professor to be an issue is much more severe: no credit.

7.   Issue-spotting: Ignoring issues raised by the facts because the issue would ultimately fail on the merits. What if the question *does* contain facts that appear to raise an issue, but which you, with all your newly acquired knowledge, know is a red herring? Write about it! Don't think, "The professor's trying to trick me into thinking that's an issue, but I'm not falling for it." Do not confuse "exam issue" with "successful outcome on the merits."

Let's go back to the practice question for an illustration. Contrary to the popular understanding of the word, the tort of "assault" occurs when a person acts intending to create in another an *imminent apprehension* of a harmful or offensive bodily contact. No actual bodily contact is required. If a contact does occur, it's a battery.

In paragraph four, we find Dick trying to gain leverage in his dispute with Moe by threatening the boss, Sikorsky, with a knife. Sikorsky, however, has a hearing impairment and doesn't hear the threat. Because his back is turned, he also doesn't see the knife. Accordingly, Sikorsky was not in imminent apprehension of a harmful contact and no assault occurred even though Dick threatened him with a knife.

Some students read these facts and think, "Aha! McClurg's trying to trick me into thinking this is an assault, but I'm not falling for it." They omit discussing the potential assault claim. But I *am* looking for students to discuss it. That's why I put the facts in there. Assault is an issue in the question, even though the claim would ultimately fail on the merits. If the facts raise an issue, it's an issue.

8. **Failing to structure exam answers in a rough IRAC (Issue, Rule, Analysis, Conclusion) framework.** In law school, you will learn about what's called the "IRAC" method for analyzing legal issues. IRAC is a mnemonic that stands for:

ISSUE

RULE

ANALYSIS[120]

CONCLUSION

IRAC is not a mechanical formula, but simply a common sense approach to analyzing a legal issue. Before students can analyze a legal issue, of course, they have to know what the issue is. Thus, logically, step one in the IRAC methodology is to identify the issue (I). Step two is to state the relevant rule(s) of law that will apply in resolving the issue (R). Step three is to apply those rules to the facts of the question—that is, to "analyze" the issue (A). Step four is to offer a conclusion as to the most likely result (C). Exam answers to issue-spotting/problem-solving questions should be constructed keeping in mind a *rough* IRAC framework.

Here's an example using the practice question. When Dick pinched co-worker Jane at the party, Moe came to her assistance, punching Dick in the face and breaking his nose. Dick would sue Moe for battery (one issue) and Moe would assert as a defense the legal privilege of "defense of others" (another issue). Here's how the defense of others issue could be addressed in an IRAC format:

> [ISSUE] Moe will assert the privilege of "defense of others" in response to Dick's battery claim, arguing that he had a privilege to use force to defend Jane from Dick's offensive

---

[120]   The "A" portion of IRAC is often stated as standing for "Application," which is interchangeable with "Analysis." Legal analysis is applying the relevant legal rules to the relevant facts.

battery. **[RULE]** The privilege of defense of others allows one to use reasonable force to protect another from a threatened battery. Reasonable force is measured by a proportionality standard. The force used in defense must be proportionate to the force being defended against. **[ANALYSIS]** Moe may have been privileged to use some mild force in defending Jane from a physically harmless pinch, such as pushing Dick away. But smashing Dick in the face and breaking his nose to ward off a pinch at an office party was disproportionate, unreasonable force. **[CONCLUSION]** Because he used unreasonable force, the privilege will fail and Moe will be liable to Dick for battery.

Some students misconstrue the IRAC methodology as an inflexible formula, which it most definitely is not. Some even go so far as to set their answers up in the form of an outline with headings like "ISSUE: . . . ," "RULE: . . . ," etc. Don't do that! I inserted those words above only as a guide. An answer to an essay question should read like, well, an essay. IRAC is simply a structural way of thinking about legal analysis in a problem-solving context. It has no application to some types of essay questions, such as policy questions.

Moreover, even in problem-solving questions, IRAC cannot be applied with mechanical rigidity. It worked that way for the above issue because the issue was extremely simple. The more complicated the issue, the less likely you'll be able to fit your answer within a precise IRAC framework.

The issue may require more than one level of analysis. It may be necessary, for example, to first state the issue broadly, discuss and apply the general rules relevant to the issue, then move on to an exception to the general rules raised by the facts. Rules often must be intermingled with the application, rather than neatly separated from it. If a multi-pronged legal test is being applied, each prong or element may require a separate mini-analysis. Sometimes it might be more effective to state the conclusion before you give the analysis.

Nevertheless, even when IRAC cannot be mechanically applied, it is a useful framework for identifying the essential components of a sound legal analysis. In any complete evaluation of a legal issue, all of the IRAC components will be represented.

My goal here is to introduce you to IRAC and also to highlight below the two most common failings in executing it on essay exams, which are to omit the two middle parts: Rules and Analysis. Far too many students "IC" the exam, causing the professor to go "ICK!" when reading it; that is, they successfully identify the issue and offer a conclusion as to how it should be resolved, but leave out both the relevant legal rules and analysis.

Mistakes 9–12 below focus on those all-important middle parts. So let's hear a hearty rah, rah, rah for some helpful tips about the "RA" in IRAC.

9. Leaving out the *relevant* rules of law. It's unfortunate how many students, after spending a grueling semester learning hundreds of rules of law, neglect to include those rules in writing answers to essay questions on their final exams.

A student can't successfully perform legal analysis—applying law to facts—without articulating the relevant legal rules they are applying. What makes this omission so surprising, as well as a crying shame, is that so many students who fail to state the rules know them. They simply don't write them down. Frequently, when I point out to students during exam reviews that they failed to include the relevant rules of law in their answers, the response is along the lines of: "Well, I assumed you knew the law, so I didn't think I needed to include it."

Even average students can bolster the quality of their answers just by remembering to perform the essential step of inserting the relevant rule(s) after identifying the issue and before proceeding to the analysis (or depending on the nature and complexity of the question, weaving rule statements into the analysis). Before starting an exam, give yourself a memory prompt by making a note on your scratch paper: "Don't forget the R in IRAC."

10. Failing to use precise, accurate language in stating legal rules and analysis. Many students understand the law, but lose ground on their exams by expressing legal rules and analysis in overly broad or layperson terms, rather than in precise, accurate legal terminology, which is what professors are looking for. Remember the R in the C.R.E.D.O. You want to get things rigorously right. *Specific always trumps general on law school exams.*

An example from the practice question will bolster the point. As discussed above, tort law recognizes as a defense to a battery claim a legal privilege to use reasonable force to protect other people. The privilege is known as "defense of others." "Defense of others" is a term of art. It's the legal name attached to the privilege.

In the practice question, Dick harassingly pinched Jane at the office party. Jane cried out and chivalrous Moe came to her aid, punching Dick in the face. Because they are such easy issues, all students recognize Dick's potential battery claim against Moe and nearly all students successfully identify Moe's potential privilege to use force in defense of others. But compare the following two statements of the privilege issue from different students:

Student 1: Moe will raise the privilege of defense of others, asserting he had a privilege to use reasonable force to protect Jane from Dick's advances.

Student 2: Moe will argue that he is not liable because he was helping Jane.

Both students recognized the issue, but notice the difference—and it's a BIG difference—in how they framed it. Student 1 did it correctly, using rigorously right legal language. Student 2 did it incorrectly, framing the issue in mushy, layperson language. "Helping Jane" is not a cognizable legal privilege. Thus, even though both students spotted the issue, Student 1 would considerably out-point Student 2.

11. Giving a general dissertation on the law rather than answering the question asked. Note the repeated emphasis above on *relevant* rules. The R in IRAC refers to the specific rule or rules that will govern resolution of the particular issue being discussed. It does not envision a treatise-like brain dump of everything one knows that is somehow related to the general subject matter. This is an extremely common mistake. Professor Joseph Glannon estimates that 20 percent of his students fall prey to this error, which he labels "abstract expressionism."[121]

The only rules that should be discussed in answering an essay question are those needed to resolve the issues raised in the question. This will rarely include broad-based discussion of a large subject area. Once again, specific always trumps general. Generalized discussions of the law that don't answer the question asked are a waste of time.

12. Omitting or skimping on the analysis. Many students include the issue, relevant rules, and conclusion, but leave out the analysis, thereby "IRC-ing" their exams and irking the professors forced to read them.

Skimping on analysis is the most common exam deficiency of them all. Analysis is the meat of the answer. It's what separates the best from the rest. It's difficult to concisely explain in a vacuum how to analyze legal problems. Reading the sample essay exam question and answer in the Appendix will give you an idea of what a complete legal analysis looks like. Study the answer in light of these tips for conducting legal analysis correctly:

If you're not talking about the facts, you're doing it wrong. In its shortest definition, legal analysis is applying law to facts. Highlight the relevant facts in the question and make sure to weave them into your analysis. Facts dictate results. Change one fact and you'll often get a different result. Chances are good that if you're writing a lengthy block of text without discussing any of the facts in the question, you've substituted brain-dumping in place of legal analysis. But you can't just *state* facts. You must explain their legal significance in connection with the rules.

Explain your reasoning process. A simple way to think of legal analysis is as an "explanation." You're trying to explain to someone what the legal issue is and how it should be resolved under the rules of law. Too many students keep their reasoning to themselves. But professors, for all their superpowers, aren't

---

[121]   JOSEPH W. GLANNON, THE LAW OF TORTS: EXAMPLES & EXPLANATIONS 632–35 (4th ed. 2010).

mind readers. They can only evaluate what students actually explain.

Many students mistake conclusions for analysis. They're not the same thing. Analogize analyzing a legal issue to working through a math problem, such as: $2 \times 2 + 4 - 8 = 0$. Some students, presented with a fact pattern on a law school essay question, will begin and end their analysis with: "The answer is zero."

The professor needs to know what formula they used to get to zero. Other students will include some analysis, but leave out major portions, resulting in something resembling: $2 \times 2 = 0$. Because their analysis is incomplete, their work product is defective even when they reach the correct conclusion. As your math teachers taught you: "Show your work."

Avoid "he argues/she argues" analysis. Too many students, having been told that they "should argue both sides of an issue," default to what I call "he argues/she argues" analysis, which is not really analysis at all. He argues/she argues answers track this format: "A will argue w. B will argue x. A will argue y. B will argue z. . . ." As Professor Glannon notes, while students who take this approach leave the exam believing they have argued both sides, they, in fact, have not argued either side. Arguing both sides requires not just listing competing points of argument, but evaluating the relative strengths and weaknesses of those arguments under the applicable law.

Note also that many legal issues do not require arguing both sides. Some advice-givers get carried away in telling students they need to argue both sides, unintentionally misleading them. As often as not, legal issues on exams will have a clear resolution; that is, there will only be one side. "Arguing both sides" is appropriate only if there are two sides under the facts.

Specific trumps general. I'm not senile. I promise. I remember when I've already said something once. I remember when I've already said something once. Okay, well, maybe not always. In this case, however, I realize I've already told you this twice, but maybe third time's a charm: specific analysis is always superior to general analysis.

When you think you've finished your analysis, consider whether more is needed. Once you think you've fully analyzed the issue, try to go one step deeper. A single added cogent sentence can boost an exam answer above others.

13. Doing the "Monster [Issue] Mash." In October 1962, Bobby "Boris" Pickett had a number one *Billboard* hit with the novelty tune "Monster Mash." The perennial Halloween favorite features a mad scientist's monster that comes to life in the lab late one night and starts a new dance craze. The law school exam version of the Monster Mash is much less fun.

Legal issues are discrete and should be analyzed as such, even when they're interrelated. Discussion of each issue should be compartmentalized with a topical sentence introducing the issue, followed by a full-blown IRAC attack on that issue and that issue alone. Only when you have completed fully addressing that issue should you move on to another issue, which should also be compartmentalized, and so on.

Students often err by introducing several issues in a single paragraph, then trying to discuss them collectively. It can't be done. Instead of a coherent discussion of each issue, the result is one big monster mash of issues never destined to reach number one.

Here's a way to test yourself on this point. Look at your discussion of a particular issue. Visually cut it out with an imaginary pair of scissors. (Avoid real scissors. Hide all sharp objects during periods of exam stress.) The excised excerpt should be able to stand alone as a complete and coherent discussion of that issue without having to refer to other portions of your answer. If it doesn't, you may be dancing to the Monster [Issue] Mash.

This is why I recommended earlier that you use subheadings to denote not only separate party disputes (e.g., A v. B), but separate legal issues. Look at the model answer to the sample question in the Appendix for an example.

14. Being sloppy. This catch-all category includes a number of errors that can be grouped together as general sloppiness, including: using the wrong exam number or forgetting to include one, making repeated misspellings and grammatical errors, writing illegibly, not following procedural or formatting instructions, and resorting to too many abbreviations.

You want to present your work in its most favorable light and that includes overall appearance. Sloppy errors affect the overall impression your paper makes on that forensic pathologist professor we were talking about, who is already displeased even under the best of circumstances about having to spend his or her holiday or summer break wading into a thick stack of exams. Avoid these common sloppy errors:

Using the wrong exam number or forgetting to include one. Invariably, at least one student per class will lose or forget their anonymous exam number and make up a number when they get to the exam. Exam numbers are one of the first things a professor sees when grading an exam. They appear in a large, bolded font on the cover page printed via the exam-security software, as well as at the top of every page on both the left and right. If your number is nonconforming it can stick out like a beacon. Example:

Exam No. 321

Exam No. 324

Exam No. 8675309

This can create an instant bias against the nonconforming exam. Fair or not, the professor's thought process might be: "Everyone else got it right. How could this student be so lame as to forget or lose his exam number?"

Using the wrong exam number also entails extra hassle for the professor and registrar. Get your exam numbers right. It's one of the easiest challenges of law school.

Making repeated misspellings and grammatical errors. One of the most common questions students ask about exams relates to misspellings and grammatical errors. "Do they count?" I've heard that question a hundred times. Heck, yes, they count, but not in the way students worry about. Very few professors officially mark down exams for misspelled words or grammatical errors. But a paper littered with such errors obviously does not bolster the professor's estimation of the

content or the writer. Occasional typos or misspellings are
nothing to be concerned about, but some students misspell words
pervasively—sometimes several words in a single sentence.
Even if the content is good, it's hard to give high grades to such
an exam.

Be especially careful when spelling legal terms of art.
Because professors will be looking for these words, misspelling
them will be particularly glaring. "Assault" looks really bad as
"assalt." Spelling "Judge Hand"—a legendary judge famous for
his formula for negligence—as "Judge Hanks" can cause actual
physical pain to a professor. Defendants in defamation cases
may be liable for libel, but they are not being sued for "liable."

Spelling and grammar aren't things to obsess over during
an exam, but they are things to pay attention to. If you finish an
exam early, go back and reread your work product. Correct
typos, insert omitted words, and make other corrections. Good
writers spend more time editing and rewriting than composing
an initial draft. You won't have that luxury during an exam, but
you might have time for a quick proofread.

The exam-security software used by your school is likely to
have a spell-check function, but it's not autocorrect like Word.
Be sure to look for and figure out how to use it before exams
start.

Writing illegibly. In the old days, deciphering illegible
handwriting was one of the great scourges of grading exams. The
problem has largely disappeared because most students take
exams on computers and some schools require that all students
do so. If you do write an exam by hand, you need to ensure your
handwriting is legible. Indecipherable handwriting will hurt
you. Truth be told, some professors just skim past material they
can't read.

***Failing to follow procedural or formatting
instructions.*** Above I talked about the essentiality of following
substantive instructions. Here, I'm talking about less egregious
but still important procedural or formatting instructions. Many
exams contain specific instructions about "how to do things" in
terms of formatting or turning in your exam. When students fail
to follow these instructions, they stand out in an irritating way.

Using too many or undefined abbreviations. In their rush, some students resort to too many abbreviations in writing essay answers. It's permissible, and even advisable as a time-saver, to abbreviate the names of the actors you will be repeating in your answer, provided you spell out the names the first time and note the abbreviations you will be using. Thus, if you're writing about Greta Garbonski and Henry Flankenhocker, it's okay to say "Greta Garbonski (GG) will sue Henry Flankenhocker (HF) for negligence" and then use GG and HF from that point on.

Similarly, you can abbreviate unwieldy legal terms that you will be repeating. Follow the same rule as for proper names. In Torts, for example, it's fine to abbreviate "intentional infliction of emotional distress" as "IIED" or "res ipsa loquitur" as "RIL," provided you write the terms out the first time, followed by the abbreviations in parentheses.

15. Writing too little. This last mistake of writing too little subsumes some of the more specific errors already discussed. It's more of a general observation than a diagnosable stand-alone error. But it's worth pointing out and thinking about.

The exam-security software used by law schools spits out a cover page for each exam showing a word count for essay answers. Examining these word counts in relation to performance yields an important, if unsurprising, insight: students who write more tend to do better on law school essay exams. In the first edition, I mentioned an experiment in which I examined a batch of Torts exams and found that the average word count for the ten highest-scoring answers to a ninety-minute essay question was 1952, whereas the average word count for the ten lowest-scoring answers was 1163—a 40 percent difference. I've repeated the experiment since then with similar results each time.

The moral of this story, of course, is not simply to write more. An essay answer with Tolstoy-esque bulk is worthless if the content isn't accurate and on point.

Tracing the connection between low word-counts and poor performance, one can almost always point the finger at one of two causes: (1) missing issues; or (2) IC-ing the exam; that is, leaving out or skimping on the rules and/or analysis portions of IRAC.

While no definitive conclusions can be drawn from my anecdotal investigation, there is no disputing that thorough analysis of complex legal essay questions entails more discussion than most students devote to it.

Hey, Maybe I *Can* Guarantee You As After All . . . Nah

After rereading this chapter, I'm thinking I should change my mind about not being able to guarantee you As if you follow my advice. If you could truly avoid all of the above mistakes, you probably would get As. Of course, you won't be able to avoid them simply by reading this book. Several of the common mistakes involve skills that take time and practice to develop, but at least now you know what to be on the lookout for.

On the other hand, several of the mistakes *can* be easily avoided. You *can* make yourself be more careful about reading instructions. You *can* make yourself spend at least 20 percent of the allotted time for an essay question studying the question and organizing your answer before starting to write. You *can* make yourself remember not to leave out the relevant rules of law (assuming you know them). You *can* pay attention to time and allocate it efficiently during the exam. You *can* stay for the entire exam time. You *can* avoid most sloppy errors.

Did you notice any common threads in the mistakes? Specifically, did you notice how the C.R.E.D.O. habits carry over even to actual exam-writing? The only one not implicated, because it's too late for it to apply, is being *Consistent*. But note that avoiding common essay exam mistakes requires one to be:

Rigorous in stating legal rules and analysis with precision and completeness;

Efficient in assessing and allocating the allotted time; specifically, in avoiding the *Top Five Law School Essay Exam Time-Wasters*;

Diligent in reading the question carefully, following the instructions, staying for the entire exam period, and proofreading your work; and

Organized in outlining your answer before you begin writing, using subheadings to denote party disputes and issues, following an IRAC framework, and compartmentalizing your issue discussions to avoid the Monster [Issue] Mash.

Now that you're familiar with common essay exam mistakes, study the sample essay question and model answer in the Appendix. If you haven't started law school yet or are in its early throes, the exercise will be of limited value because the content will be foreign to you, but it's still useful for illuminating what to expect in a law school essay question.

CHAPTER 17

TACKLING LAW SCHOOL MULTIPLE-CHOICE QUESTIONS

Back when I attended law school, exams comprised exclusively essay questions. Today, many, if not most, professors also include multiple-choice questions on exams. Some professors rely solely on multiple-choice questions, although usually only in certain upper-level courses. My Torts exams are split roughly half and half between essay and multiple-choice questions.

A couple of good reasons exist for including a multiple-choice component on a law school exam. As previously explained, the use of multiple-choice questions allows for broader course coverage than essay questions only. A practical benefit of multiple-choice questions is that, depending on the format the professor uses, they can provide good practice for the bar exam, which is dominated by multiple-choice questions. The Multistate Bar Examination (MBE), administered in forty-nine states and the District of Columbia, is a six-hour marathon of 200 multiple-choice questions focusing mostly on first-year subjects. The MBE covers Civil Procedure, Contracts, Constitutional Law, Criminal Law and Procedure, Evidence, Real Property, and Torts. The state portion of the bar exam also often includes multiple-choice questions.

Multiple-Guess Mess: Questions Without Right Answers

Law school multiple-choice questions are unlike anything you've encountered in your prior educational experiences, primarily in that they can be frustratingly difficult even if you know the material well. This is because, like law school essay questions, they're designed to test not only legal knowledge, but reasoning ability.

Many law school multiple-choice questions follow the MBE-style. They are made up of a one- or two-paragraph fact pattern in which events of legal significance transpire among the named actors, followed by the "call of the question," followed by four or more answer choices. The "call of the question" is the part that tells you the issue you are to address. With some frequency, a series of two or three questions will be based on the same fact pattern. The succeeding questions in the series may add new facts or change the original facts. If they do, those new or changed facts apply only to that particular question unless otherwise specified.

The call of the question usually asks the reader to predict the most likely resolution of a legal issue raised by the facts. Thus, if the question facts describe actions and interactions between Bob and Jill on Bob's property, the call of the question might be something like "If Bob sues Jill for trespass, Bob will:"—followed by answer choices such as, "Win, because . . . ." or "Lose, because . . . ." Another common format in the call of the question asks students to assess the relative strength of legal arguments, as in: "If Bob sues Jill for trespass, his best argument will be . . . ."

The problem for students is that the answer choices do not always include a clearly right answer. The essence of MBE multiple-choice questions is perhaps best captured by an odd piece of advice I remember hearing for the first time many moons ago while taking a review course for the Florida bar exam: "Remember," the speaker said, "On the MBE you're not looking for the right answer. You're looking for the *best wrong answer.*" While that might be a bit of an overstatement as applied to all law school multiple-choice questions, the basic point is sound: you're looking for the *best* answer among the choices given, even if you think a better, more "right" answer exists that's not included.

Ten Multiple-Choice Strategies

Here are ten strategies for tackling these beasts:[122]

---

[122]   The most commonly cited law school multiple-choice strategies, including several of the suggestions in this chapter, are derived from MICHAEL JOSEPHSON, LEARNING & EVALUATION IN LAW SCHOOL (Ass'n of American Law Schools Annual Meeting, 1984).

1. Read the question carefully, evaluating every fact as potentially important and not assuming any facts not stated. The ability to comprehend and manage complex text is important to being an effective lawyer, which is why it's part of the skill-set tested on the LSAT, law school essay questions, and MBE-type multiple-choice questions. As with essay questions, read every sentence asking why particular facts were included, while recognizing that multiple-choice questions can also contain immaterial facts. Overlooking a single word can change the meaning of the question, including small words like "and" or "or." Don't assume any facts that are not given.

2. Pay attention to the call of the question. Pay close attention to the call of the question (sometimes called the "stem"). The call of the question is the part immediately preceding the answer choices, telling test-takers what they're supposed to analyze. Sometimes the fact patterns of MBE-style multiple-choice questions will set forth a scenario seemingly setting up one legal issue, only to surprise test-takers by asking about a different issue in the call of the question.

For example, a question may raise what appears to be an intentional tort issue, such as battery, but then the call of the question will ask about a negligence claim, as in "If Bob sues Jill for negligence . . . ." Students will be reading along thinking *battery, battery, battery,* and wrongly pick an answer involving battery or intent (battery is an intentional tort), overlooking the call of the question. Or the question may refer to multiple parties, one of whom is clearly a tortfeasor or contract breaker or other wrongdoer, but who is not part of the call of the question. It's not a bad idea to glance at the call of the question before studying the entire question so you'll know what to look for as you read.

3. Use a process of elimination. As on the LSAT, use a process of elimination to narrow down your answer choices. There always will be at least one and usually two answers that are clearly wrong. Mark those out and focus on the ones remaining. Here are some tips to help in the elimination process:

- Very few legal questions have answers that are true all of the time or none of the time. Thus, in answering multiple-choice questions, answers qualified by words like "always" or "never" will usually be wrong.

- Answers relating to a different topic area than the question seems to be focused on usually will be wrong. In the sample question at the end of the chapter, answers (a) and (e) are good examples of this. The doctrines of strict liability for harm caused by animals and implied primary assumption of risk are foreign to the question topic and are clear wrong answers.

- If two opposite answers exist, one of them usually is right. For example, suppose a question included these two answers: "(a) Dinkle will lose because of the doctrine of modified comparative negligence; (b) Dinkle will win because of the doctrine of modified comparative negligence." These are opposite answers and there's a good chance one of them would be the correct answer.

- Some professors will toss in humorous answers to questions. These answers will always be wrong.

- Several articles about multiple-choice strategies in general (not focused on law school) advise that the longest answer is often correct because the professor is trying to give a precise and accurate answer. This suggestion may have some validity in law school because right answers in the convoluted world of law often require qualifying phrases and other details to make them accurate. I haven't ever counted the words in the answers to my multiple-choice questions, but I do recall instances of writing longer answers to some questions to make them technically correct.

   4.   **Don't answer by your gut reaction.** Read all the choices carefully, eliminating the obvious wrong answers, before choosing a selection. It may be that one answer intuitively appeals to you the moment you read it before you've considered all the options, and that may be the answer you ultimately decide on, but don't choose any answer until carefully weighing all the options.

   5.   **Divide your time equally among the questions.** Unlike essay questions, which can vary in weight, multiple-

choice questions are usually worth the same number of points. Don't get bogged down on one question at the expense of others. Answer it and move on.

6. **Don't skip questions.** If you're not sure of the answer, pick one anyway. Don't leave it blank with the intention of returning to it later. Skipping questions poses two risks. First, you might forget you skipped it and start bubbling in answers for the other questions in the wrong spaces on the answer sheet. Second, students frequently skip questions and forget to go back to them. Every semester, a couple of students will leave some questions blank on my Torts exam. Since I don't penalize students for wrong answers, the most plausible explanation is that they skipped the questions and forgot to go back and fill them in.

7. **The devil is in the details.** The students who do best on multiple-choice questions are those who know the law best. I always tell my students that while I'm not trying to trick them, the multiple-choice questions are tricky in that students must have mastered the fine points of the law—not just the general rules—to do well.

As an example, in the sample question at the end of this chapter, many students, relying on the general rule that there is no duty under negligence law to aid or protect other people, will pick answer (d), which is a wrong answer. The students who get the question right will have learned and retained a narrow exception to the rule—that a person who, even innocently (i.e., non-negligently), creates a continuing risk has a duty to eliminate it—and will pick (b), the correct answer.

Thus, doing well on multiple-choice questions is directly tied to the case-briefing, note-taking, and outlining chapters. Many students assert "I've never done well on multiple-choice questions." To some extent, as we see in this chapter, it is true that test-taking strategies or "tricks" can improve performance on multiple-choice questions and it's also probably true that some people have an innate feel for them. But one big reason students do not excel on multiple-choice questions is that they don't know the law as well as the students who do excel.

8.   Don't be afraid to change your initial answer.
You've probably heard the conventional wisdom that you should not change your initial answers to multiple-choice questions because it's more likely you will change an answer from right to wrong than from wrong to right. I heard this advice my entire life, starting in elementary school.

Guess what? It's completely backward. Study after study, some of them dating back to the 1920s, shows that changing multiple-choice answers is more likely to increase, rather than decrease, test scores. For example, a study of upper-level accounting students showed that 95 percent of the students changed answers on their multiple-choice examinations (changing a total of 5.6 percent of the answers). Fifty-six percent of the answers were changed from wrong to right, while only 21 percent were changed from right to wrong. The remaining 23 percent were changed from one wrong answer to another wrong answer.[123]

9.   Answer all the questions. If time is about to run out and you haven't finished, pencil in an answer for every question. Unless you've been told otherwise by your professor, points won't be deducted for wrong answers. You're better off choosing the same answer for all unfinished questions (e.g., all (b) answers or all (c) answers), rather than randomly alternating. That should assure at least some right guesses. If you have enough time, skim the questions and eliminate any clearly wrong answers. Eliminating even one answer in a question will significantly improve your mathematical guessing odds.

In case you're wondering, I looked for, but didn't find any reliable research as to which answer to pick if you're completely guessing. Assertions—claimed to be based on "studies" that are never named or cited—can be found online saying it is better to pick one particular letter and best not to pick another particular letter. I'm not going to repeat them here because they may be spurious myths. You can find the magic letters online if you poke around a little bit, but hopefully, you won't find yourself in the position of having to resort to complete guessing.

---

[123]   *See* Marshall A. Geiger, *On the Benefit of Changing Multiple-Choice Answers: Student Perception and Performance,* 117 EDUC. 108, 110 (1996).

10. "How do you get to the Supreme Court? Practice." This takeoff on the old joke about how one gets to Carnegie Hall captures one of the best strategies for succeeding on multiple-choice questions, which is to practice by working through a large number of them. Unfortunately, your professors are unlikely to provide you with many multiple-choice questions as samples because, more so than essay questions, crafting valid, reliable multiple-choice questions is difficult and time-consuming. (Bad news: some professors draft really lousy multiple-choice questions and/or borrow questions from other sources without revising them to fit the material the professor covered or the way he or she taught it.)

Look for sample multiple-choice questions in alternative sources, such as CALI (Computer-Assisted Legal Instruction) exercises, available free to law students. Several law school study aids feature multiple-choice questions. The MBE itself is not released to the public, but some sample questions and older exams have been made available. You might be able to lay your hands on copies of bar review course prep books, which contain loads of MBE-style questions, although these books are harder to come by these days because the bar review companies offer financial incentives for course-takers to return them.

Don't get bogged down in fretting about the specifics of practice questions unless they were crafted by your professors. Some practice questions you encounter may be poorly drafted. Some will address the law differently than your professor did or focus on issues you didn't cover. Concentrate on the format and thought process involved.

Sample Multiple-Choice Question

To give you a taste of what to expect, here is a sample Torts multiple-choice question used on a recent exam, along with an analysis of the answer in case you're curious:

Caspid went out for a Sunday drive in his Bentley automobile. He decided to leave the city, crank up the music and just unwind for the afternoon. The farther out into the country he drove, the sparser the population became. Before long, he found himself driving down an empty winding road through the woods. Caspid was driving carefully around a curve when a 200-pound wild boar ran in front of his car. He hit the brakes, but could not stop in time. Caspid's car collided with the boar, killing the large animal and damaging the front of his automobile. Caspid got out of his car to survey the situation. He felt bad about killing the animal, but also about the crumpled front bumper on his Bentley. Shaking his head in disgust, he backed up, turned his car around, and headed back to the city. Ten minutes later, Dort was driving down the same road. He came around the curve and ran into the boar, which was lying in the road. This caused him to lose control of his car and crash into a tree. Dort sustained a head injury. If Dort sues Caspid, the most probable result will be:

(a) Judgment for Dort, because of strict liability for harm caused by animals.

(b) Judgment for Dort, because Caspid created an unreasonable risk that he had a duty to eliminate.

(c) Judgment for Caspid, because Caspid was not negligent in creating the risk.

(d) Judgment for Caspid, because the law does not impose an affirmative duty to help or protect others.

(e) Judgment for Dort based on implied primary assumption of risk.

Analysis. The correct answer is (b). Normally, under the law, one has no legal duty to act affirmatively to aid or protect others absent a special relationship with them. Such inaction is known as nonfeasance; i.e., a mere failure to act. For example, if Caspid overheard two men plotting to rob a convenience store and kill the clerk, he would have no legal duty to do anything to protect the clerk, not even a duty to dial 911. But the law is filled with exceptions and one exception to the "no duty to aid or protect" rule is that if an actor creates an unreasonable risk, even innocently, he has a duty to exercise reasonable care to eliminate or minimize the risk. Even though Caspid did nothing wrong in creating the risk (the question says he was driving carefully when the boar ran in front of his car), he had a duty to act reasonably to remove the boar from the road or warn approaching drivers.

* * *

Let's close with another practice multiple-choice question:

In reading this chapter, I learned that:

(a) Law school multiple-choice questions often don't include a clear right answer.

(b) Law school multiple-choice questions sometimes trip students up through the "call of the question."

(c) Law school multiple-choice questions usually contain one or two answers that are clearly wrong and can be easily eliminated.

(d) Law school multiple-choice questions are going to cause me to have nightmares for the next three years about being eaten alive by 200 of these little monsters on the Multistate Bar Exam.

(e) All of the above.

The correct answer, of course, is (e).

CHAPTER 18

LEGAL RESEARCH AND WRITING: AN INTERVIEW WITH FIVE EXPERTS

The insane amount of work required for the two-hour course in legal research and writing. . . . It was almost comical to me when teachers were urging us to spend hours every weekend working on our outlines for class, when I was barely able to use that time to keep up with my legal research and writing assignments.

—1L's "biggest surprise" about law school

You heard it here first. Legal Research and Writing will consume you. Legal Research and Writing is known as a "skills course." Your other 1L courses are all likely to be "doctrinal courses." While first-year doctrinal courses differ in content, they are extremely similar in format. Each will involve similar daily reading assignments of judicial opinions from a casebook, some mix of Socratic Q & A and lecture about those cases in class, and the same single-exam evaluation method at the end of the semester. Whether it's Civil Procedure, Contracts, Criminal Law, Property or Torts, the quest for first-year success will follow a similar path and require similar tools and strategies. Thus, nearly all of the advice in this book applies equally to each of the doctrinal courses in the first-year curriculum.

But Legal Research and Writing will be wildly different from your other first-year courses, generating a disproportionate amount of fretting and angst-letting. For every student gripe about doctrinal courses, I hear five about Legal Research and Writing.

That the subject commands such out-of-balance attention from students alone makes it a candidate for its own chapter, but there's a more pressing reason for giving extended, separate treatment to legal research and writing courses: *they are the most important courses you will take in law school.* Five legal writing professors from different law schools will explain why in more detail below, but the reasons are nicely summed up in this observation by Professor David Walter: "Because this is what lawyers do every hour, every day, every year of their careers—they speak and they write—and when they're not speaking and writing, they're listening and reading."

Legal research and writing courses are part of the mandatory first-year curriculum at all law schools. They usually extend through both semesters (as in Legal Research and Writing I and Legal Research and Writing II). Roughly a quarter of law schools require a third legal writing course in the fall semester of the second year.[124] Legal research and writing course packages travel under a variety of names, including Legal Research and Writing, Lawyering, Legal Method, Legal Skills and Values, and Legal Writing and Analysis. I'll just refer to the courses generically as "legal writing," while recognizing that all legal writing courses also teach legal research skills and most have an oral advocacy component.

The fundamental goal of legal writing courses is to teach students how to research and analyze legal issues and effectively communicate their analyses in writing. If the primary purpose of the other first-year courses is to teach students to "think like a lawyer," it could be said that the goal of legal writing is to train students to "write like a lawyer thinks." Legal writing isn't about how to construct sentences. It's about how to conduct and convey legal analysis in a written form.

As a teacher of doctrinal subjects, I know better than to give advice about an area that is so different from my own milieu. Hey, I didn't get to be a law professor for nothing. So I asked for help with this chapter from five experienced legal writing professors. The Q & A with these five experts is the highlight of this chapter. But before we get to it, here's an overview of some of the common components—and frustrations—of legal writing courses.

---

[124]   2015 ALWD SURVEY, *supra*, at 7.

An Introduction to Legal Writing Courses

Legal research.

Typically, legal writing begins with a research component, which usually includes exercises designed to train students to find and use different types of legal resources in the law library (e.g., case reporters, digests, legal encyclopedias). Depending on the school, the person teaching you legal research may be a member of the legal writing faculty, a law librarian, a student teaching assistant, a Westlaw or LexisNexis representative, or some combination of these folks.

Every law student recalls traipsing around the library on treasure hunts for research sources. As one student described it:

> I remember thinking to myself how stupid all us little 1Ls must have looked trekking through the library looking for all the old books while doing our physical research assignments and finding our way around. All the 2Ls and 3Ls were in there trying to study while we bumbled about muttering to each other or asking for their assistance. I remember looking forward to the day when I could watch all the neophytes do that as well.

Another student described legal research exercises more bluntly as "scavenger hunts straight from hell."

Law schools are still searching for the proper balance between old and new when it comes to teaching legal research skills. Should students continue to be required to learn the old ways of book research in a technological world where legal research is routinely performed online using computer databases such as Westlaw and LexisNexis? Schools differ in their answers.

Many legal writing directors believe it's important that law students first learn how to do legal research with books, similar to the belief that it's important that elementary school students learn how to do basic math before they are given calculators. Knowing how to do book research makes students more effective computer researchers because they better understand the sources with which they're working, which are the same whether the medium is papyrus or megabytes. Moreover, while law students enjoy the luxury of free access to paid legal research databases, lawyers have to pay substantial fees for those services (although many free legal research databases are also available these days).

Nevertheless, the trend is toward providing unlimited computer research training and access from the get-go, with only about one-third of law schools currently limiting computer research training and access in the first semester.[125] It should be noted, however, that this trend is explained by economics in addition to pedagogy, as law school libraries continue to slash their collections to save money.

"The memo."

You'll be stunned to find that something as innocent-sounding as a "memo" will be the source of so much tribulation and woe in your early law school existence.

Shortly into the first semester of legal writing, students begin working on their first legal writing project: an internal law office memorandum from an associate (you) to a fictitious partner analyzing the law as applied to a given set of facts. These memos, common in real-life law practice, ask you to explain and analyze the legal issues in a client's case so the partner can make informed decisions about the case, which may include the decision whether to accept the case or pass on it.

It's common to assign two such memoranda in the first semester, often denoted as the "minor memo" (the first one) and the "major memo" (the second one). Often, the minor memo will be a "closed universe memo," meaning the professor will provide students with all the necessary research, while the major memo will be an "open universe memo," meaning you will be required to do the research yourself. Other common first-semester writing assignments can include drafting a client letter (i.e., a letter from a lawyer to his or her client), contract, or pleading.

Non-law students around you will not be able to fathom your preoccupation with "the memo."[126] I asked students to explain why it is so all-consuming. The most common answer was the

---

[125]   2015 ALWD SURVEY, *supra*, at 12 (providing data).

[126]   When students talk about "the memo," they usually are referring to the major memo.

tremendous amount of work required compared to the disproportionately lower credit hours awarded in legal writing courses as compared to the first-year doctrinal courses (see below).

But there are other reasons. One student astutely noted that the memo is "the first opportunity we have to create something that is our own." Law school does not offer many outlets for creativity. It's not as if the law office memorandum throws the door open for prose stylists or performance artists. Strict rules regulate just about every aspect of the document, including structure, length, font size, and margin widths. But it is the first and often only opportunity students get in the first semester to create their own legal work product.

Along the same lines, the memo is a law student's "first turn-in homework." In other first-year courses, students simply read cases, day after day. Students prepare case briefs and outlines, but these are not turned in. Last, but certainly not least, the memo not only gets turned in, "It's graded!" Because students receive so little evaluative feedback during the semester in their other courses due to the single-exam format, it is no wonder they over-obsess about their memo feedback.

Filleted by feedback.

"You write well, but made a substantive error of malpractice dimensions." Ouch! This comment, scribbled by my legal writing instructor on the last page of my major memo assignment introduced me to the harsh realities of law school grading. Like many law students, I was used to As and praise in my previous educational experiences. Now I had a professor telling me I screwed up so badly I could get sued for it.

A large practical difference between legal writing and other first-year courses is that students get performance feedback during the semester, including grades. One can almost hear the self-esteem bubbles bursting when the first wave of legal writing feedback is distributed. Standing in class on those days looking out at rows of morose faces, I feel I should be delivering a eulogy instead of a Torts lecture. As one student put it:

As law students, the majority of us are used to receiving As and when you get that first draft of your first memorandum back with a *C–* on it (and believe me, this happens even to the students who finish at the top of the class), it can be discouraging.

She should know. She finished the year ranked second in her class.

The credit-hour crunch.

The single most iterated 1L gripe—and that's saying a lot—is that the workload required for legal writing is disproportionately heavy compared to the credit hours allocated. Usually, the workload for a law school course corresponds to the number of credit hours for the course. But students would argue we reversed everything for legal writing, requiring more work for fewer credit hours. Students complain that this allocation is completely arbitrary, but they're wrong. It's all done according to a highly scientific, mathematical formula:

$$x/y = 2 \text{ Credit Hours}$$

With x being the number of hours required to complete legal writing assignments (rounded to the nearest thousand) and y being the number necessary to make the answer equal two credit hours.

Just kidding. On the other hand, the real reasons for why legal writing courses get the short end of the credit-hour stick aren't much more satisfying. They include the fact that legal writing courses are, relatively speaking, newer additions to law school curricula. Some doctrinal professors, particularly older ones, think legal writing courses aren't as important as doctrinal courses. Related to that, territoriality and turf-protecting often come into play in faculty deliberations to increase credit hours for legal writing. Increasing hours for one first-year course usually entails reducing credit hours for another.

But the situation continues to improve. Most law schools have or are taking steps to alleviate the credit-hour disparity. In 2015, credit hours for legal writing averaged 2.57 hours in the fall and 2.47 hours in the spring,[127] an increase since the last edition of *1L of a Ride.*

---

[127]   2015 ALWD SURVEY, *supra*, at 7.

Citation style.

Another component of legal writing courses that students find frustrating is learning legal citation style. "Citation style" refers to the form and format in which legal authorities (such as cases, law review articles, and books) are referenced or documented.

The standard legal citation manual is *The Bluebook: A Uniform System of Citation* (20th ed. 2015). The *Bluebook* tells legal writers what citation information to include (e.g., volume, page number, date), what font to put it in (e.g., big and small caps, italics), when to use abbreviations and what they should look like, where to insert commas and periods, and many other details. It's somewhat similar to the MLA (Modern Language Association) style book you might have used in undergraduate school, except roughly one trillion times more detailed and complex. Look at the footnotes in this book for samples of *Bluebook* citation style.

The Bluebook is famously hyper-technical and obsessed with minutia. I had to laugh when reading a comment from a student consultant advising new students to pay attention to *The Bluebook* because an entire letter grade can be lost on a writing assignment "if you leave off just one comma!" The comment brought back memories of a humor column I wrote several years ago for the *American Bar Association Journal* satirizing a *Bluebook* rule that required a comma in a particular place under particular circumstances. An excerpt will give you a taste of what you're up against when dealing with *The Bluebook*. The setting for the column was a mock meeting of the board of *Bluebook* editors:

Irving: We need that ******* comma! Rule 15.2 means nothing without The Comma. I'll gladly die for it.

Frieda: *Accord.* [A *Bluebook* reference.]

Dan: *Accord.*

Wendy: Put down the gun, Irving. *The Bluebook* was meant to bring peace.

Irving: Not until I have proof of everyone's commitment to The Comma. I've decided to quit law school and become addicted to amphetamines so I can contemplate The Comma twenty-four hours a day.

Dan: I'm going to have Rule 15.2 tattooed on my thigh, right below the rules for Separately Bound Legislative Histories.

Frieda: I'll cut out my husband's entrails and form them into the shape of one huge comma.

Irving: What about you, Wendy?

Wendy: My parents died in a plane crash yesterday. I have to go to the funeral.

Irving: Doesn't The Comma mean anything to you?

Wendy: Alright, I'll send flowers.

While the *Bluebook* is the dominant legal citation manual, a small percentage of law schools use a different citation manual called the *ALWD Guide to Legal Citation* (5th ed. 2014). When the ALWD manual was first published in 2000, its simplified approach to legal citation style earned acclaim and popularity in some circles, but after a few years the scale tilted back to the old standard.[128]

Regardless of which manual is used, it's important to pay attention to learning citation style. Not only can bad citation skills lose you points on your assignments in legal writing and other courses with writing requirements, they can hurt you in the real legal world. If your school doesn't devote substantial attention to learning citation style in its legal writing program, make a point to study it on your own. If you join the law review, you won't have any choice but to master *The Bluebook*, but the opportunities to learn citation style are more limited for other students.

The second-semester appellate brief and oral argument.

In the second semester, legal writing usually includes a written and oral advocacy component. Typically, students are

---

[128]   The Association of Legal Writing Directors 2015 survey showed that among responding schools: 134 law school legal writing programs use *The Bluebook*, seventeen use the *ALWD Citation Guide to Legal Citation* (down from fifty-six in 2005), eleven use both, and nineteen leave the decision to the individual professor. 2015 ALWD SURVEY, *supra*, at 19.

required to research and write an appellate brief and make an oral argument to a panel of mock judges. The brief, which may run thirty pages, is excruciatingly time-consuming.

As for the oral argument, it's the most exciting, but also the most terrifying, event of the first year. It's exciting because the oral argument is often the first law school exercise in which students get to act and feel like "real lawyers" (meaning, in the minds of 1Ls, the lawyers they see on television, who, unlike real lawyers, are always in court). The terror aspect derives from a generalized fear of public speaking accentuated by the fact that oral arguments are also public interrogations. They're not monologues. The judges drill students with lots of questions, sometimes starting before students have finished their first sentence.

It's normal to be nervous about public speaking. Surveys show that public speaking ranks higher than death on lists of people's greatest fears. These surveys, according to a great Seinfeld monologue, mean that at a funeral, the average person would rather be the guy in the casket than the one delivering the eulogy. I was so nervous about my oral argument back in law school that I showed up on the wrong day! I arrived at school all spiffed-out in my suit, ready to go, and started freaking out when I couldn't find the correct room. Sweating buckets, I frantically searched the law school for my professor and the judging panel only to finally figure out my argument wasn't until the next day. At least I was a day early instead of a day late. I got a good laugh out of it once I was released from the coronary unit.

Looking back, the oral argument still stands out as one of the most memorable, albeit most nerve-wracking, events of law school. A student consultant, quiet by nature, wrote that the "mere thought of having to stand in front of others and argue makes you nauseous." To help her get through the experience, she wrote the reminder to "BREATHE" at the top of her notes. She did fine though, as most students do, in part because they put so much time into the preparation. Sometimes the quietest students shine the brightest in the oral arguments. So don't underestimate yourself. A great oral advocate may be lurking beneath your shy exterior.

Balancing legal writing workloads with other courses.

Take legal writing seriously and give it your best, but not at the expense of neglecting your other courses. Keep in mind that from a cost-benefit analysis, your doctrinal courses usually will be worth more credit hours, meaning they will weigh more in your cumulative GPA.

Don't procrastinate (once again, see the C.R.E.D.O. chapter). On days when assignments are due in legal writing, class attendance can drop off by a third or more. Professors find such major declines irritating and may take them personally. I know professors who intentionally test on material covered in class on days when there are large numbers of absences. At one school, in a faculty email exchange over this issue, a professor commented that the dismal attendance in his class on the due date of a legal writing assignment was "unfortunate" for the students because "[t]oday's materials will find their way onto my exam."

An Interview with Five Legal Writing Professors

Five experienced legal writing professors generously agreed to share their insights and tips for success regarding key issues common to all legal research and writing courses. Here's our all-star lineup, in alphabetical order:

Kimberly Boone is the director of the legal writing and moot court programs at the University of Alabama School of Law, where she graduated Order of the Coif and was a member of the law review. She worked several years in employment litigation before joining academia in 2000.

Chris Coughlin is the director of the legal analysis, writing, and research program at the Wake Forest University School of Law. She also holds appointments in the Wake Forest Graduate School of Arts and Sciences and the School of Medicine's Translational Science Institute.

Joan Malmud Rocklin is a legal writing professor at the University of Oregon. Prior to joining academia, she clerked for a federal judge in California and worked as a litigator at a corporate law firm in New York City.

Sandy Patrick is a Professor of Lawyering at Lewis & Clark Law School in Portland, Oregon, where she teaches legal writing and upper-division courses. Prior to entering academia, she clerked for a state appellate court judge, served as an assistant state attorney general in the appellate division, and practiced civil litigation in a large, international law firm.[129]

David D. Walter is the co-director of the legal skills and values program at Florida International University College of Law (FIU), with more than twenty-five years of experience teaching legal writing. Previously, he taught at Seattle University and Mercer University. He also teaches upper-level skills courses and directs the appellate advocacy, negotiation, and mediation programs.

Our five experts answered ten questions about legal writing courses, including many that bear a direct connection to success or failure in those courses.

1. For students who recognize they have writing deficiencies, is there anything they can do to help themselves succeed in their first-year legal writing courses before they begin law school?

COUGHLIN: If a student knows he or she has a writing deficiency, I recommend the following—not only to succeed in their first-year legal writing courses, but to succeed in law school and the profession. First, consider investing in a program such as *Core Grammar for Lawyers*, http://www.coregrammarfor lawyers.com/, an online, self-directed tool to help students learn grammar and punctuation for legal writing. Accept that learning basic rules of grammar, punctuation, and parts of speech may not be exciting or fun. No "instant gratification" is involved. One student who took it on himself to upgrade his writing skills after

---

[129]   In addition to their other credentials, Professors Coughlin, Malmud Rocklin, and Patrick are co-authors of *A Lawyer Writes* (2d ed. 2013), a legal writing book for first-year students. Check out their book for expanded discussion of some of the points they make in this chapter.

his first year of law school analogized his summer remedial writing activities to repeatedly sticking a fork in his knee.

The nature of the deficiency, along with the nature of the individual learning style, must be assessed. Each student is unique and learns differently, and there is no magic pill or process to cure all deficiencies. If the deficiency involves simply a lack of knowledge, step one above might be sufficient. If the deficiency is more serious, the student should consider being tested for a learning difference or disability. If the deficiency rises to the level of a disability, such as dysgraphia (which is a neurological disorder characterized by writing disability), the school may be able to provide reasonable accommodations to help the student succeed. Obviously, any such disability would need to be documented by a medical provider and that information communicated to the law school as soon as possible.

Regardless, a student must understand how he or she learns best. To do this, the student should look back on her educational career, and determine whether there is a common denominator in the teachers, environments, situations, and subjects in which she responded most positively and successfully. Everybody learns differently and everybody writes differently.

ROCKLIN: Learning to write well is a lifelong process that should start well before law school begins and continue long after law school ends. There are no quick fixes.

That said, I recommend that all students read William Strunk and E.B. White's classic *The Elements of Style*. We should probably all read it once a year. Another great book on writing is Richard Wydick's *Plain English for Lawyers*. Both books cover the basics of clear, concise writing.

Once the student gets to law school, if she is still concerned, she should go to her legal writing professor to discuss her concerns. Her professor may have some helpful suggestions, especially if the student has submitted a writing assignment and the professor has had a chance to review the student's writing.

Finally, the student should become a critical reader. During law school, students see a lot of writing—mostly appellate opinions. Some appellate opinions are well written. Others are not. The distinction between work that is well written and work that is not is whether you can understand it. If you can't understand what the writer is trying to convey, the writer has failed. So when you cannot understand what you are reading, ask *why*. What could the writer have done differently? If you find yourself blissfully gliding through your reading, ask *why*. What has the writer done to make the ideas easy to absorb? By asking why some writing is effective and other writing is not, you will begin to develop better judgment about your own writing.

WALTER: Even students with serious writing deficiencies can improve their writing. The first step, of course, is often the most difficult—recognizing that you, the writer, have writing deficiencies. Sure, Cs and Ds in English classes and other courses with major writing requirements are a good clue, but I've seen several writers with serious problems who received Bs and even As in undergraduate courses with extensive writing requirements.

Once the need for assistance is recognized, several avenues are available for students who want to improve their writing. First, there are plenty of professors and tutors in English departments, other departments, and college "writing centers" who are willing to help students correct those writing deficiencies—find them ASAP and ask for their help! Ask them to read samples of your writing. Ask them to look for organizational issues—do your sentences and thoughts flow together in a logical manner? Ask them to check for mechanics issues—are your commas in the right place, is your word usage proper, and is your grammar correct? Ask them to examine the "readability" of your writing—is your writing clear, do you use words precisely, and are you concise in your writing?

Second, as suggested above, find a good "style" book and give it a careful review. That should give you a better idea about some of the topics you'll see in legal writing.

Third, review and critique a few of your writings and the writings of others to evaluate your deficiencies—if you can spot the problems in your past writings or the writings of others, you have taken one more step toward improving your writing in law school and beyond. The idea here is to learn how to read very carefully and with a critical eye.

Even excellent writers will benefit greatly from following the steps outlined above.

2. Is it common for students to enter law school entertaining mistaken assumptions about the nature of "legal writing"? What are those misconceptions?

BOONE: One of the most common misconceptions is that being a strong writer in other fields or being an English major necessarily translates to being good at legal writing. This is not always the case. Different undergraduate majors both help and hinder you in legal writing. For example, English majors may love to write and know what it means to write in the active voice, but might have a terrible time learning to be more concise and direct. Math and engineering majors may sometimes forget to write in complete sentences, but they may pick up on legal analysis more quickly.

Students may also assume that they can use the same processes they used for college papers on their legal writing assignments. This will not work. The research is different, the citation style is different, and the analysis is new. Let's be brutally honest. Somewhere along the way, many of you wrote a paper shortly before (or even the night before) it was due. If you received a good grade, you may have made a habit of it.

Be forewarned that this will not work in legal writing for several reasons. First, good legal writing may look simple, but it usually requires long hours and multiple drafts to make complex ideas look simple. Second, you may not realize you are lost until you actually start writing. If you start assignments early, you'll have time to ask for help if you need it. And finally, as if you won't hear this enough, all of your law school classmates were at the top of their classes too. Your work will be judged in relation to other good students.

COUGHLIN: One misconception is that legal writing drains your creativity. The reason for this misconception is many legal writing professors require that students use a mnemonic (a specific order) to structure their legal arguments. For example, commonly used mnemonics in legal writing include "IRAC" (Issue, Rule, Application, Conclusion—pronounced similarly but not to be confused with IRAQ)—and "CREAC" (Conclusion, Rule, Explanation, Application, Conclusion).

In reality, using a mnemonic structure should not limit the creative process. Mnemonics are supposed to be flexible tools, not rigid formulas. They provide an effective starting point for drafting a legal analysis. The substance of your analysis—the way you frame your legal arguments and your unique application of the law—is necessarily creative.

To illustrate this point, think of the poetry form of haiku, a Japanese form of unrhymed poetry that is always three lines long, with five syllables in the first line, seven syllables in the second line, and five syllables in the third. While the haiku is written in a strict form, the writer has freedom within the substance of the poem to be creative. Likewise, while the legal writer may use a preset organizational structure, outstanding legal arguments build bridges between prior cases and new sets of facts, a skill that mandates creativity. As my colleague Professor Miki Felsenburg says to her students: "Bore me with your organization and thrill me with your analysis."

PATRICK: I agree with what Professor Boone said that one great misconception about legal writing is that researching and analyzing a legal problem will mirror the work students did for term papers in undergraduate school. This misconception arises in large part because new law students don't understand that legal writing is not just about "writing." It's about something much more complex—legal *thinking*. Committing sound analysis to paper requires far more skill than knowing the parts of a paragraph, how to use commas, or whether the period goes inside the quotation mark (it does). Legal writing requires students to find the law that governs a client's issue, discern the relevant parts of the law, weave those parts into a cohesive explanation, and apply it to a client's fact situation. Doing all of those things requires the student to mentally engage the material with critical reading, thinking, and questioning.

3. I commonly tell students that their legal research and writing courses may be the most important courses in law school and I'm sure you would agree. How would you explain to students why that is so?

ROCKLIN: Legal writing teaches the must-have skills to be a successful attorney. I promptly forgot most everything I learned in Contracts, Civil Procedure, and Constitutional Law within hours of taking the exams. On the job, though, that wasn't a problem. I worked for big fancy law firms and for government agencies but none of my employers expected me to remember much substantive law. My employers did expect me to know how to research the substantive law, synthesize it into a coherent explanation of the law that would apply to a client's problem, and then write my analysis in a clear and compelling way. I learned those skills primarily in my legal writing class.

PATRICK: From their first day of orientation, my students hear the proclamation that legal writing is the most important class they will have in law school. They initially hear those words from me (whom they might not believe), but soon hear them echoed by upper-division students, practicing attorneys, and prospective employers. Each year I invite guest speakers to class—upper-level students, law clerks, or attorneys. Invariably, without my solicitation, they confirm the notion that legal writing is the most important class in law school. Why? Because it teaches students the core skills for legal learning: how to assess law, think about law, and communicate law to someone else. Effective lawyering requires those skills. An attorney can know everything there is to know about tort law, but if he cannot assimilate law relevant to a client's issue and communicate his analysis, that attorney will not effectively represent his client.

WALTER: I do agree! I tell my 1Ls on the first day that legal writing courses are the most important courses in law school. Written and oral communication skills are so critical to everything lawyers do. In two American Bar Foundation studies, the lawyers polled overwhelmingly identified oral communication skills and written communication skills as the two skills/knowledge bases that are most important to lawyers. They ranked "knowledge of substantive law" as seventh in importance.[130]

The researchers also surveyed hiring partners to determine the most important skills students should learn in law school.

---

[130] *See* Bryant G. Garth & Joanne Martin, *Law Schools and the Construction of Competence*, 43 J. LEGAL EDUC. 469, 473 tbl.1 (1993).

The top three skills? Library legal research, oral communication, and written communication. Knowledge of substantive law came in a distant eleventh place.[131]

Why are oral and written communication skills more important than knowledge of the substantive law? Because this is what lawyers do every hour, every day, every year of their careers—they speak and they write—and when they're not speaking and writing, they're listening and reading.

4. The standard major assignment in most first-semester legal writing courses is the law office memorandum written from junior associate to senior partner. Why is the office memorandum still seen as the most effective or important vehicle for teaching legal writing to 1Ls as opposed to, say, drafting pleadings or legislation or some other type of assignment? Related to that question, I'm sure 1Ls often wonder what drives the content of legal writing courses. Any insights on that point?

BOONE: The *process* required to write the memorandum is what makes it a good first-semester tool. The office memo, at least as we teach it, requires the students to research two legal issues and analyze them objectively. We ask the students to write an interoffice memo (from associate to partner within the same firm) to train students to fully and objectively evaluate legal issues, rather than argue for or against a certain result. For example, in a civil suit, we may ask the student to evaluate two issues to help determine whether the firm (the student's fictitious employer) should take the case. Even with an assignment structured this way, most first-year students struggle with the notion that we aren't seeking a single "right answer." In other words, I could usually care less whether the student concludes the firm should take the case. I'm much more concerned with whether the student has thoroughly researched and analyzed the issues and fully explained the reasons both for and against taking the case.

The content of our legal writing course is driven in part by a desire to prepare students well for their first summer jobs. An

---

[131]   *Id.* at 490 tbl.11.

in-house memo is the type of assignment our students are most likely to be assigned in those jobs.

Learning to explain legal rules and apply them to a fact scenario also helps students develop the skills they will need to write effective exam answers.

COUGHLIN: While some students complain that the office memo is dated, it remains the optimal vehicle for beginning law students to develop the skills of legal analysis and argumentation. It is also important, of course, to learn to effectively draft pleadings and legislation, but those skills are more sophisticated, technical, and require knowledge of litigation and/or legislative processes. Such exercises are better taught after the students have completed Civil Procedure and/or a legislation or administrative law course or seminar.

Typically, most legal writing programs begin by assigning an office memorandum with a closed universe of research (that means that three or four cases are provided to the students and the analysis is limited to using those materials). The students must critically read and analyze the cases, extract the governing rules, and distinguish between relevant and irrelevant facts from the prior cases. These are fundamental skills all lawyers must develop.

Among other things, composing a law office memorandum teaches students two types of basic legal reasoning skills: (1) *rule-based reasoning*, where the student applies the language of a rule to a client's facts to predict an outcome; and (2) *analogical reasoning*, where the student shows that the client's case is sufficiently similar to, or different from, previous cases and that the outcomes in the previous cases either should or should not control the client's case.

PATRICK: Legal writing professors still use the legal memorandum as the primary vehicle for a writing assignment because it requires engaged analysis and exemplifies the type of assignments students will most likely be doing early in their legal careers.

Attorneys, particularly those in the private sector, will likely draft more legal memos than they can count during their first years of practice. In two years as an associate at a large law firm, I drafted three times more legal memos than I did pleadings, briefs, interrogatories, and other documents combined.

Legal memoranda are relevant to students for another reason: A memorandum assignment simulates what the students will be asked to do on most of their first-year exams. Most exams during the first year ask students to predict an outcome for a factual scenario and support their decision with the law they know. Although exams have certain differences from the office memo, both assignments ask students to assess a problem, discern and apply the relevant law, and communicate a cogent answer.

5. If you had to list just three hallmarks of an outstanding law office memorandum, what would be they be? Conversely, if you had to list three hallmarks of a poor law office memorandum, what would they be?

COUGHLIN: "The Outstanding Office Memorandum" is:

1.   A direct and precise response to the question being asked. The writer tells the reader up front what the specific issue is being analyzed, as well as the predicted outcome. The body of the memorandum—the analysis—does not go off on tangents but builds bridges between each point to reach a conclusion.

2.   A clear, concise response using plain English. As my colleague Professor Barbara Lentz puts it, if you wouldn't use the word when ordering at McDonald's, don't use it in your office memorandum. So just as you wouldn't say "Herewith my hamburger, french fries would be a most effective side dish and, accordingly, supersize me," when ordering at the drive-thru, do not use that type of language or sentence structure in your memorandum. For maximum clarity and effectiveness, use the KISS theory (Keep it Simple, Stupid).

3.   A response that shows all steps of the analytical process. An outstanding office memorandum can be thought of as a math problem in elementary school. Simply getting to the correct solution or prediction is not enough. You must show your work.

Conversely, "The Not So Outstanding Office Memorandum" is:

1.   A response that is overly formal in style. Students sometimes think that if they write formally their reader will not realize the writer did not take enough time or did not understand the analysis. When students are confused, they think that if they use eighteenth-century prose, the professor will not realize that they did not spend enough time to understand the links between the cases and/or build the necessary analytical bridges between the cases and their "client's" facts.

2.   A response that is written in the passive voice. While there are strategic uses of the passive voice (i.e., "mistakes were made" rather than "the defendant made a mistake"), consistent use of the passive voice is a red flag that tells your legal writing professor one of the following: (1) I haven't spent enough time on this memo. One can think back to Samuel Clemens' (Mark Twain) famous quote "I apologize for the length of this letter, but I didn't have time to make it shorter."; or (2) I don't understand this analysis, but if I use really complex language maybe my legal writing professor will think I am really smart.

3.   A response that is fraught with *Bluebook* errors, typographical errors, and formatting errors. Typically, there is a correlation between a lack of precision in analysis and a lack of precision in style. Errors with these "finer points" distract a reader from the analysis and limit the amount of confidence a reader has in the writer's prediction of the outcome.

PATRICK: I agree wholeheartedly with Professor Coughlin's comments regarding the hallmarks of a good memo, so let me concentrate on the hallmarks of a bad one. Local attorneys at large law firms in our city recently asked our Legal Writing and Analysis department to conduct a seminar instructing young associate attorneys on how to improve their writing. The partners articulated a fairly consistent list of problems with which associates struggle. Those problems mirror the hallmarks of a poorly written law office memorandum:

1.   Poor organization. Often neither the overall presentation of issues nor the component substantive parts

within each issue are presented in a logical, clear order that the reader can follow, absorb, and understand.

2. The legal substance of the memo is not clearly communicated to the reader. The paragraphs fail to signal their points, leaving the reader lost as to what each paragraph will prove. The law may not be fully explained. Additionally, the memo may be organized around cases instead of legal points, with the writer failing to show how the cases fit together. The application of the law to the client's facts often has leaps in logic, leaving the reader unclear about how legal precedent requires a particular outcome for the client's case.

3. The product is not professional. Often, because of time constraints so prevalent in law practice, memos are rife with errors—typographical errors, poor grammatical choices, inappropriate punctuation, and poor citation. The overall effect of the errors paints the attorney as either lax or incompetent.

Ironically, writing an outstanding memorandum does not take that much more time than writing a poor one. A little extra time spent organizing the research, mapping out the most logical flow of arguments, and polishing the final draft can transform a mediocre memorandum into a great one.

WALTER: First, the most important hallmark of an outstanding office memo is its selection and development of the law (i.e., relevant cases, statutes, regulations, and so forth). Accuracy is critically important because the writer is flying solo—no one else will be researching and analyzing the issues—so the writer must get it right the first time. If the writer fails to find or discuss a key case, or if the writer explains the case or the legal rule poorly, the attorney relying on the memo may give the client inaccurate legal advice. Thus, the writer's most important task is to find the appropriate law and explain it accurately.

The second hallmark of an outstanding memo is its organization. The large-scale organization of an outstanding memo will be perfect from beginning to end: from the memo heading, to the framing of the legal questions presented, to the brief answers to those questions, to the statement of the facts, to the discussion, and finally to the conclusion. The mid-scale organization of an outstanding memo also will be near perfect. For example, the discussion section will be organized into appropriate subsections, each one starting with a conclusion, followed by explanation of the law, application of the law to the facts, and ending with a mini-conclusion. Finally, the small-scale organization of an outstanding memo will be excellent, with nearly every sentence and idea leading to the next idea in a logical manner, like climbing a staircase step by step to reach the logical conclusion on the landing at the top of the stairs.

The third hallmark of an outstanding memo is superb application of the law to the facts; that is, clear explanation of the legal arguments.

6. Some students mistake functional writing (e.g., coherent sentences, good grammar, etc.) with good legal writing. They don't realize how important the analysis is or even what analysis is. How would you define "analysis" in a way that law students can understand what it means?

BOONE: Everyone can read the rules (cases, statutes, etc.) and most students can learn the rules well enough to predict accurate answers to many legal questions. But analysis goes further than that. Analysis is not about the answer. It's about the process of reaching that answer. Some have analogized it to long division: if you don't show all your work, you get no credit. For example, if you are asked to "analyze" what time it is, you would first explain to the reader the "rules" of time zones, identify the important facts about the time zone you are in, and apply the time zone rules to those facts to reach an answer.

COUGHLIN: Analysis is the process of evaluating the law on a particular topic. In a legal analysis, the writer will show how an established rule of law will function given a new set of facts (i.e., rule-based reasoning) or explain why a client's case is like or unlike a previous case and how those comparisons work to yield a particular result (i.e., analogical reasoning). In other words, it is deducing a likely outcome considering prior law and new facts. Analysis is where a student's creativity and brain power truly come to light.

Analysis is like the fixings in a sandwich. While two pieces of bread may be homemade and quite good, it isn't enough unless you add the meat, veggies, cheese, and condiments. Before all the fixings are added, there is no sandwich. There are simply two pieces of bread. Likewise, in your memorandum, the analysis is the fixings—it is the most important component of the memorandum.

ROCKLIN: In the typical fall-semester memo, there are three analytical components that distinguish functional writing from really good, insightful legal writing. The first analytical component involves separating the whole into its parts. Every legal analysis will begin with a governing rule. Almost all legal rules are made up of component parts known as "elements" or "factors." For example, the tort of negligence has four elements (duty, breach of duty, causation, and injury). Part of analysis is breaking down broader rules and principles into their constituent elements or factors and examining each of them one by one.

The second important analytical component is the explanation of the law. For each element or factor that is at issue to a client's problem, law students must coherently explain the relevant law. Doing so is difficult because students must pull together the law from numerous, disparate sources. But that's the analytical challenge: assembling a group of relevant disparate legal snippets into a seamless whole. This component of legal writing is analytical in that it requires students to understand both the whole and the parts and explain their relationship to the reader.

Finally, students must apply the law to a particular fact pattern in order to predict an outcome in the client's case. This part of the argument is analytical in the sense that students must think precisely about why the law will lead to one outcome and not the other and then articulate their thinking in a compelling way. Law professors commonly refer only to this last part—applying law to facts—as "the analysis." But please know that the first two parts are also analytical in their own way.

7. If we divide the process of composing a law office memorandum or other legal writing assignment into three parts—researching, writing the initial draft, and

rewriting/editing the final product—which part commonly gets the short end of the stick from students? In other words, which of the three steps do less successful students regularly not devote enough time and attention to?

ROCKLIN: Editing—it's key to a professional work product. A study by Anne Enquist of Seattle University showed that successful legal writing students spend approximately three-fifths of their writing time revising and proofreading, while less successful students divide their time more equally between writing the first draft and revising and proofreading it.

But to say "edit more" is unhelpful. One has to know *how* to edit. Effective editing requires first a big-picture understanding: What's my goal? If you understand your goal, you can step back from your project and ask yourself, does this work achieve my goal? For example, if you are writing an objective memo, the goal is to educate and inform. Understanding that goal allows you to step back and ask yourself, have I educated the attorney receiving this memo about all the relevant law? Have I done so clearly? Have I informed the attorney about the areas where the law favors our client and the areas where our client will struggle to make her case? Have I clearly explained why those strengths and weaknesses exist?

Second, effective editing requires you to understand the problems that typically get in the way of achieving your goal and actively look for those problems. Essentially, you have to create a checklist out of your legal writing class. Let's say in class you've discussed that a well-organized legal argument states a conclusion, explains the law, applies the law, and then concludes again. Well, have you done that? Be sure to go back and check. Let's say your professor has pointed out that your sentences tend to be wordy. Well, that needs to be added to your checklist, and with each memo you write, you'll need to check your sentences for wordiness.

Because editing often seems like such drudgery, I'd like to put in a personal plug for editing. Editing is about creating a synchronized, lucid solution to a complex problem. The reward and "fun" comes from seeing the improvement.

Let's say I want to build a machine that will squirt just the perfect amount of mustard onto a hotdog. The parts lay before me. I start trying to fit them together. I discover at the end of my first attempt that I've done pretty well, but the machine has a leftward tilt, so that all the mustard winds up on the conveyor belt to the left of the hotdog. I tinker until the mustard is hitting dead-on, but there's too much of it. I tinker a little bit more so that just the right amount of mustard is hitting the hotdog. Finally, for a flourish, I adjust the machine so that instead of the mustard running in a straight line, it has an S-shaped flow down the hotdog's spine. I did it! I created the perfect mustard-hotdog combination. To me, that's the pleasure in editing. It's the time when I sync up all the parts to create exactly the product I want to deliver. There's beauty in that.

PATRICK: Without a doubt, students spend the least amount of time revising and polishing the final product. Realizing that the revising and polishing steps can often take longer than the research and drafting steps is a secret to success.

The research phase is often the most enjoyable because students can wander mindlessly, breezily, through library stacks or online databases—working, yes, but minimally engaging difficult material. Research can be a delightful black hole, allowing students to save the thinking for later.

Once some thinking has occurred and the student has slogged through statutes and cases and mapped out some kind of tangible structure, students are willing to devote some time to hashing out that draft—what they hope will be the *only* draft. That draft is like painting the walls of a room; we all paint expecting immediate gratification and hoping that two coats will not be necessary. And maybe even that we can skip doing all that difficult trim work! Likewise, some students hope one slapdash draft will be enough.

When students finally finish the first two laborious stages (research and writing the first draft), they are spent—from both a time and a mental standpoint. They rationalize that the first draft is good enough, and submit it.

Early in my legal writing career, colleagues introduced me to Anne Lamott's book on writing, *Bird by Bird*. Lamott's ideas on fiction writing transfer quite easily to legal writing. In one chapter she accurately captures the three stages of composing a written document. The first draft is the "down draft," where the goal is just to get the words down on paper. The second draft is the "up draft"—you fix it up and "try to say what you have to say more accurately." The final draft is the "dental draft," where you "check every tooth, to see if it's loose or cramped or decayed, or even, God help us, healthy."[132] My students love this analogy, although sometimes they add their opinion that the final draft is called a dental draft because getting it done is worse than having a root canal.

Students who are willing to complete that third step—revising and polishing until they get a dental draft—usually are very successful.

WALTER: While all three aspects of the research and writing process often get the "short end of the stick," I think the legal research process gets "shorted" most often, causing great damage to students (and their clients) in the long run.

Here's what frequently happens. After the students are given the facts for the open memo problem (i.e., a memo where students have to do the research themselves), most of them begin their legal research. Some perform in stellar fashion, devoting the necessary hours in the books and online, carefully researching the issues, closely reading the cases, and finding nearly all of the relevant law. Many students, however, underestimate how long it will take to locate the relevant law, and some underestimate how frustrating it can be to find the law. In both instances, these students do not complete the research task. Unfortunately, and as surprising as it might sound, there are also a few students who never start their research, figuring instead that they'll simply rely on another student, or the professor, to tell them which statutes and cases are important.

Once the research phase ends and the drafting phase begins, the students typically discuss the law both in and out of class, and most students will then learn which cases and statutes

---

[132]   *See* ANNE LAMOTT, BIRD BY BIRD: SOME INSTRUCTIONS ON WRITING AND LIFE 25–26 (First Anchor Books 1995) (1994).

should be included in the memo. Even if a student did not do a great job during the research phase, the student *might* be able to earn a good grade on the draft and final project by "borrowing" the research and ideas of others, without going back and completing the research on their own.

Students know they have to turn in high-quality drafts and final versions of the memo to do decently in the course, so built-in incentives exist for these phases. In the long run, however, students who shirk quality research will earn lower grades in legal writing courses, as well as future courses, such as seminars, that require research. And because they never develop efficient research skills, they'll actually spend more time earning those lower grades than their classmates. But the bigger harm will befall the clients of these students, as less effective and less efficient researchers pass the short end of the stick to their clients.

8. One would assume a correlation exists between the amount of time spent on a major legal writing assignment and the result. But we all know students who fruitlessly pour in tons of time inefficiently. What are some of the ways time devoted to a major legal writing assignment is not time well spent?

BOONE: I don't think this should count as time devoted to the assignment, but apparently an amazing amount of time is spent worrying about the assignment and complaining about how hard (or how simple) it is to one's classmates. I would not want students to completely miss this chance to bond with their fellow 1Ls, but they should try not to waste too much time commiserating. Inefficient research and the quest for a perfect outline also take up untold hours. If students have been lost for hours or days in the research or the writing process, they should stop and ask for help. Finally, searching relentlessly for a very clever turn of phrase is probably not the best use of your time.

COUGHLIN: Many law students are competitive. Because many law schools grade on a curve, this population of students want to make sure they are on the top end of that curve. For many students, instead of focusing on answering the question asked by the assignment, they try to go above and beyond the facts and relevant authorities to find alternate areas and authorities to explore so as to make legal arguments that other students are not making. While students may spend inordinate amounts of time researching to come up with unique arguments that no one else may make, it is time that would have been better spent proofing and editing their papers or relaxing with a cup of coffee and newspaper.

While researching all arguments thoroughly is commendable, and spending time thinking about alternative arguments is helpful, students tend to go down tangents and waste a lot of time for minimal or no return. An analogy is going to the doctor and telling her that you have a runny nose, cough, and are achy. You would expect the doctor to say you have a cold and that you need rest and lots of fluids—not to send you in for a full-body MRI in search of any possible ailment.

In legal writing, to maximize time and effort, spend sufficient time researching, writing, editing, and proofreading so that you feel comfortable that you have done the best you can. The rest will take care of itself. Even if all the students use the same authorities, every student's thought process is unique. So, be strategic with your time. While you want to consider all viable arguments, don't create arguments that really aren't there.

PATRICK: Students become the most inefficient at two points in time: when they postpone thinking until *after* the research process and, similarly, when they start writing before they've developed a map of how the pieces of the legal argument should be arranged.

Research can seem like a productive time, but it can actually be a waste of time when students avoid critically reading and thinking about the sources *before* wasting time and resources printing them. Thinking during research makes the task a little more difficult, but understanding early on how each source will (or will not) contribute to the answer will certainly save the student a lot of time later in the process. I encourage students to use charts or diagrams along the way to see how the legal authorities relate to each other and how the authorities together answer the legal question.

Once the authorities are compiled, students too frequently want to jump into the writing without first organizing the law around the points they need to explain. Many students have never outlined assignments before writing them, and they utterly resist this step. Outlining or mapping the structure of the arguments saves the writer time and aggravation. Students normally find that once they understand the document's overall organizational structure and the organizational structure within each issue, the writing is not so difficult. To the contrary, students who try to figure out the organization as they write hit a lot of dead ends and usually must discard a lot of what they wrote along the way.

The most successful students quickly learn that producing a solid piece of legal analysis is a multi-step process. Skipping steps inevitably backfires and makes the student's effort less efficient.

9. Related to the previous question, research obviously is a key ingredient of successful legal writing, but ineffective or inefficient research can go on with no end in sight and little to show for it. Any tips for how students can improve the efficiency of their research? How does a student know when he or she has done enough research?

BOONE: To effectively research a legal issue, students must understand two things. First, if there were an easy answer to the question, they probably would not have been asked to research and write about that issue. Second, students must make sure they understand the question. For example, if I ask my students to predict how a California state court will rule on a particular issue, a student who answers only with law from other states has not answered my question effectively. The most relevant law would, of course, be California law. If you are thinking that this student simply failed to follow my instructions, you are partially right. My students don't intentionally disregard the instructions, but they often end up with poor research results because they got lost somewhere in the process. This tends to happen when the students are trying too hard to come up with the "perfect" case to answer my question. When there isn't one, they tend to start changing the question. They are, after all, going to be lawyers, right?

Seriously though, students can research much more efficiently if they keep in mind that there is usually no "golden egg" in the treasure hunt. Students often spend days looking for the "perfect" case to resolve their issue. They quickly discard cases that are fairly similar and provide good rules in the relevant jurisdiction, because they just know that there is a better case out there if they just keep looking. Surely, some court somewhere has addressed this exact issue before! These are great students, and they just know they can find THE answer—even if I have told them there is not one. Once they are completely exhausted and the deadline for the assignment is fast approaching, they realize that those cases they discarded might have been exactly what they needed. That leads us to another suggestion. Students should carefully track their research paths. This allows the exhausted student to avoid further frustration because he can at least go back and find those sources he discarded earlier.

A student has probably done enough initial research when he begins to see the same sources over and over again. When a student starts noticing that all of her sources seem to be citing each other, rather than citing sources the student has not yet seen, she is probably done with this round of research.

COUGHLIN: Take advantage of all training opportunities from Westlaw and Lexis. Not only will you enhance your research skills, you'll have the opportunity to win prizes and eat lots of free pizza.

But do not rely on computerized legal research as your only option. An understanding of print resources will provide you with a better idea of the scope of information you are researching. In addition, computerized legal research has the drawback of being only as good as your search terms. If your search term does not precisely appear in the document, you may miss a big case. You are more likely to get a wider breadth of relevant materials when you combine computerized and print research.

It is difficult to be efficient in legal research at first. Initially, the best way to begin is to use a flow chart and make sure that you document each step or source that you find for easy retrieval in the future. There are many such flow charts or decision trees for basic case law and statutory research skills that will be available in the legal research materials you receive in class or on the web.

As far as knowing when you are finished, a good rule of thumb, as Professor Boone said, is to continue with your initial research until you start seeing the same sources appear over and over again and the cases or sources begin to cite each other.

PATRICK: Efficient and thorough research requires a student to do four things: know the question being asked, follow a methodical process of reviewing sources, keep a trail of where you have been, and above all, think as you go.

Students, and even young lawyers, can be horribly inefficient at research because they do not adhere to those four mandates. Research can be deliciously mindless as one prints off stacks of cases to read later or as one follows tangential queries down a cyberspace rabbit hole. But once that illusion of productivity wears off and that young student or attorney realizes he is no closer to answering the legal question than he was hours or days ago, frustration and panic erupt.

Using a methodical process for research can foster efficient and thorough research. First, always know the exact legal question you are being asked to answer. Usually clients pose narrow legal questions; understanding the question before you delve into myriad sources can save time and energy.

Next, establish a logical method for going through the various sources of authority. Most research texts students will see in law school set out some sort of step-like process to use in research. Understand that process and use it consistently.

Keeping a trail of where you have been and the sources you have checked can be crucial for a successful research project, particularly in real-life practice. Whether in school or practice, finishing a research project at one sitting will not likely happen. In reality, a research project may take several days or weeks and may be interrupted by competing tasks. Keeping a detailed list of search terms, sources, queries, will prevent duplicative research efforts later in the project.

Finally, think as you go. Never print a stack of "possibly relevant" cases to read later when you have time. No one, not even an experienced attorney, can read and assimilate two dozen cases at once. I warn my students to print a source *only* after they know what part of the legal puzzle that source solves. Thinking as you go through the research process is more difficult (and sometimes not as much fun), but saving time and finding the answer efficiently is well worth the effort.

I also echo that research is finished when either your search efforts start to yield the same legal authorities time and again or you run out of time on the project.

10. I'm always all over my seminar students about typos, *Bluebook* errors, formatting mistakes, and other fine points. They think I'm just being an unreasonable nitpicker. You've touched on this, but could you elaborate about why these finer points are important when it comes to evaluating either a student's or lawyer's writing product?

COUGHLIN: The finer points mentioned in the question are essential. While my students may consider my strict attitude toward citation, formatting, etc. frustrating, they generally come to appreciate that precision and attention to detail make the difference in being invited onto the moot court board or law review, or getting a job offer.

Specifically, many times I take a point off the student's final grade for any *Bluebook* error. My philosophy is that these finer points represent the area of your writing product over which the student has the most control. You do not have control over your client's facts, and you do not have control over the state of the law. You cannot control what your professor, judge or senior partner will think of your legal argument because of personal bias or prior life experiences or simply because the law may be against you. You can control, however, citation, formatting, and proofreading.

If you are sloppy with these finer points, your reader will think that your analysis is likewise imprecise. If you are not precise with your typing, your proofreading, your citation, your punctuation, how then will your reader have confidence in your work? For example, when I was in practice, a colleague sent out a letter that was supposed to read "return receipt requested" but instead read "rectum receipt requested." One can imagine recipients having a difficult time placing confidence in the substance of a letter when the heading makes an illicit proposition.

ROCKLIN: You are being a nitpicker, and your students should thank you for it. Let's fast-forward to the question of how important these finer points are in the real world. Imagine you are a lawyer interviewing two job candidates. One candidate walks in wearing a suit and presents you with a crisp, clean resume. The other walks in wearing jeans, flip-flops, and presents you with the same resume content-wise, but full of typos. Which one would you hire? Whether we like it or not, those reading our work make judgments about our capabilities based on its appearance, just as people make judgments about us based on our appearance. Sloppy citations, punctuation, grammar, or formatting will make your reader skeptical about the quality of your analysis.

Because attention to these details matters in the real world, we pay attention to them in legal writing classes. Although legal writing grades are always more dependent on the legal analysis than on mechanics, they will ultimately be lower if the student doesn't pay attention to the "finer points" of grammar, typos, punctuation, and citation errors.

WALTER: The "fine points"—punctuation, usage, grammar, spelling, citation, and formatting—are very important to the overall grade on a legal writing memo and may be even more important in the real world. In my legal writing classes, I give a specific point value for the errors listed above, a value that is typically about 10–15 percent of the overall assignment grade. Committing too many of these errors will cost a student about one-third letter grade, dropping a *B+* to a *B*, for example.

For legal writing professors who use a more "holistic" grading system rather than a specific point system, I think that the grading penalty for such errors is likely to be even more severe. Why? Because of something called "heuristics." The concept of heuristics is pretty straightforward: when decision-makers are short on time or information, they often make judgments based on more observable factors, even if those factors don't necessarily lead to a purely rational decision. In other words, heuristics are a decision-making shortcut often based on appearances.

In practice, it might operate like this: A trial judge, looking over a three-foot tall stack of court documents so that she can make decisions on dozens of pending motions, begins reading the plaintiff's memo. It's full of typos, the cases are cited incorrectly, and some of the sentences don't make sense because of grammar and usage problems. Frustrated, the judge picks up the defendant's memo. It's perfect. There are no misspellings or typos, the cases are properly cited, and the memo is well written. The defendant could very likely prevail on the motion even if the law actually favors the plaintiff.

It works the same way in legal writing courses. Poor mechanics may cause the grader to undervalue the substance of the writing, giving a lower grade than the substance might otherwise dictate.

* * *

Despite all of the talk in this chapter about the importance of Legal Research and Writing courses, you may end up as one of the many students who don't appreciate the courses until they obtain their first legal job. Legal writing professors hear from these students all the time: "Professor, I really hated—er, well, sorry, not *hated* . . . I really *unloved* my legal writing courses while I was taking them,[133] but as soon as I got to my law firm job this summer, I realized what you said is true: they're the most important courses in law school. That's all I did all summer long: research and write!"

---

[133]   Tip for success: Never tell a professor you hated his or her course.

CHAPTER 19

THE BLEAK SIDE OF
LAW SCHOOL

Can't put it off any longer. I said in the Prologue I'd be honest about the good, bad, and ugly of law school, so it's time to share the news that being a law student isn't easy from an emotional well-being standpoint. One law professor offered this grim assessment:

> Law students get sick more frequently than others: headaches, stomachaches, colds, allergies. They have problems in their relationships with friends or family. They worry more than they work. They are continually agitated or lethargic. They gain or lose weight. They take up or increase their chemical crutches, such as caffeine, nicotine, alcohol, or cocaine. They often become angry and bitter—especially at their teachers, sometimes at their colleagues or at the profession—or they withdraw, dropping out, skipping classes, or simply avoiding getting to know their classmates. When called upon in specific stressful situations to use reserves of courage and confidence, they may be debilitated; and they often have no reserves to call upon.[134]

Well, that doesn't sound good. Let's see what she's talking about.

* * *

Just months before I started law school in 1978, a new book came out: Scott Turow's *One L*. It's the classic book about law school. *One L* tells the story of Turow's experience as a first-year law student at Harvard Law School. The book scared the heck out of me at the time. I didn't remember why until I recently reread it and realized that a dominant theme of the book was negative affect. I counted specific references to: anxiety, fear, stress, panic, vulnerability, self-doubt, shame and grief,

---

[134] B.A. Glesner, *Fear and Loathing in the Law Schools*, 23 CONN. L. REV. 627, 631 (1991).

wounded self-esteem, unhappiness, paranoia, embarrassment, oppression, and insanity. Turow's 1L story turned out to be my 1L story and the story of many law students since.[135]

This chapter explores the negative psychological impact of law school on students. However, it's important to emphasize at the beginning (*ab initio*, as we say in the law) that not all law students are overly anxious or depressed. Many students appear to be largely unaffected by the aspects of law school that cause other students high anxiety. Part of this may be explained by happiness research, which shows that from 40–80 percent of a person's happiness level is determined by genetics.[136]

If you're a laidback, happy person by nature and continue that way in law school, be thankful for it. Also be aware, however, that some "no sweat it" law students are laidback simply because they do not care enough about law school or succeeding in it (or don't understand what it takes to succeed) to undertake the workload with the same motivation as some of their "peace of mind"-challenged classmates. "Sad but true," as James Hetfield of Metallica sang,[137] many of the most successful law students are obsessive-compulsive worriers. So if you find yourself lying in a fetal position in the corner of the closet clutching your memo in despair, cheer up! It might actually be a good thing.

With that introduction, prepare yourself for some disquieting information about law students.

Anxiety and Generalized Psychological Distress

That a competitive, demanding professional degree program like law school would cause students to be anxious is no big surprise, but the issues are bigger than that. Studies have found that psychological distress in law students significantly outpaces not only the general population, but other graduate student populations, including medical students.

---

[135]   *See* Andrew Jay McClurg, *Neurotic, Paranoid Wimps—Nothing Has Changed*, 78 UMKC L. REV. 1049 (2010) (recounting my rollercoaster 1L experience).

[136]   NANCY LEVIT & DOUGLAS O. LINDER, THE HAPPY LAWYER: MAKING A GOOD LIFE IN THE LAW 33 (2010) (discussing research of genetic contributions to happiness levels).

[137]   METALLICA, SAD BUT TRUE (Elektra 1993).

As early as 1957 a study comparing law students and medical students found that law students scored higher on an anxiety scale, both in the first year and also at graduation.[138] A 1980s study of law and medical students at the University of Arizona found that the law students scored significantly higher than both the general population and the medical students in nearly every category of psychological dysfunction measured, including anxiety, depression, feelings of inadequacy and inferiority, hostility, and obsessive-compulsiveness.[139] A study of lawyers in Arizona and Washington found that 30 percent of male lawyers and 20 percent of female lawyers exceeded the clinical cut-off for generalized anxiety disorder, compared to 4 percent of the overall population.[140]

While law school attracts some people already inclined toward anxiety (overachievers and obsessive-compulsives), evidence suggests a causal relationship between law school and psychological dysfunction. A later study of University of Arizona law students found that law students begin school with psychopathological symptoms similar to the general population, but that those symptoms become substantially elevated during law school and stay that way after graduation. Researchers administered a battery of psychological tests to groups of law students before, during, and after their legal education. Depending on the particular symptom, 20–40 percent of the students reported significantly elevated symptoms above the normal population after starting law school for anxiety, obsessive-compulsiveness, hostility, interpersonal sensitivity, paranoid ideation, and psychoticism (social alienation and isolation).[141]

---

[138] Leonard D. Eron & Robert S. Redmount, *The Effect of Legal Education on Attitudes*, 9 J. LEGAL EDUC. 431 (1957).

[139] *See* Stephen B. Shanfield & G. Andrew H. Benjamin, *Psychiatric Distress in Law Students*, 35 J. LEGAL EDUC. 65 (1985).

[140] Connie J.A. Beck et al., *Lawyer Distress: Alcohol-Related Problems and Other Psychological Concerns Among a Sample of Practicing Lawyers*, 10 J.L. & HEALTH 1, 50 (1995).

[141] G. Andrew H. Benjamin et al., *The Role of Legal Education in Producing Psychological Distress Among Law Students and Lawyers*, 11 AM. B. FOUND. RES. J. 225, 236 (1986).

A 2004 study reached similar conclusions about 1Ls.[142] Researchers administered a battery of tests to entering law students at Florida State University to measure their state of happiness, life satisfaction, physical symptoms, and depression. Their scores were compared to a set of advanced undergraduate students at the University of Missouri who took similar tests. The comparison showed that the law students began law school as a contented, normal group, with higher positive affect and life satisfaction scores than the undergraduates. By the end of the first year, however, the law students showed significant reductions in positive affect, life satisfaction, and overall well-being, and increases in negative affect, depression, and physical symptoms.

The most recent data comes from the 2014 Survey of Law Student Well-Being to which approximately 11,000 law students from fifteen law schools responded. Using an anxiety screening tool known as Kessler 6, 37 percent of the respondents screened positive for anxiety (23 percent showing mild to moderate anxiety and 14 percent showing severe anxiety).[143] By comparison, in a national survey using the Kessler 6, only 13 percent screened positive for anxiety.[144]

Anxiety affects all law students to varying degrees because it's a normal reaction to stress. But a significant percentage of law students experience unhealthy anxiety, suffering both psychological and physiological adverse effects,[145] including alcohol and other substance abuse as discussed in the next chapter. The National Institute of Mental Health lists these common symptoms of generalized anxiety disorder:

---

[142] *See* Kennon M. Sheldon & Lawrence S. Krieger, *Does Legal Education Have Undermining Effects on Law Students? Evaluating Changes in Motivation, Values, and Well-Being,* 22 BEHAV. SCI. & L. 261 (2004) [hereinafter Sheldon & Krieger, *Does Legal Education Have Undermining Effects on Law Students?*].

[143] Jerome M. Organ et al., *Suffering in Silence: The Survey of Law Student Well-Being and the Reluctance of Law Students to Seek Help for Substance Abuse and Mental Health Concerns,* 66 J. LEGAL EDUC. 116, 137 (2016) [hereinafter Organ et al., *Suffering in Silence*] (reporting and explaining the survey results).

[144] *Id.* at 137 n.78.

[145] The American Psychiatric Association subdivides anxiety disorders into numerous categories in the Diagnostic and Statistical Manual of Mental Disorders (DSM-V). *See generally* AM. PSYCHIATRIC ASS'N, DIAGNOSTIC AND STATISTICAL MANUAL OF MENTAL DISORDERS 189–233 (5th ed. 2013) [hereinafter DSM-V].

- Restlessness or feeling wound-up or on edge
- Being easily fatigued
- Difficulty concentrating/mind going blank
- Irritability
- Muscle tension
- Difficulty controlling worry
- Sleep problems (difficulty falling or staying asleep or restless, unsatisfying sleep)[146]

Be self-aware. A person can suffer from anxiety without realizing it. Keep a lookout for worrying that is *excessive and prolonged* and that appears to be *impairing* your ability to function.

I once had a first-year student rush out of class thinking she was having a heart attack. I ran out after her and found her sitting on a bench clutching her chest. Her face was flushed and she was sweating and trembling. But it wasn't a heart attack. It was a panic attack. An overly sensitive Nervous Nellie/Ned? Not at all. She went on to be not only an outstanding law student, but a star at moot court, where she regularly stood before panels of judges who grilled her with tough questions. Law school anxiety does not prey only on the weak. The point of the story is she had no idea she was under such duress. Not only are we good at hiding distress from others, we often expertly hide it from ourselves.

Depression

Law students also suffer disproportionately higher rates of depression than the general population and other graduate students. On depression scales, 17–40 percent of law students in the second University of Arizona study mentioned above were found to suffer from depression.[147] By comparison, the Centers for Disease Control and Prevention (CDC) reports that 4.7

---

[146]   *Anxiety Disorders, Signs and Symptoms, Generalized Anxiety Disorder*, NAT'L INST. MENTAL HEALTH (last visited Feb. 10, 2017).

[147]   Benjamin et al., *supra*, at 247.

percent of all persons aged 18–39 (an age range covering the vast majority of law students) suffer from depression.[148]

A 2000 study of University of Michigan law students found that more than half of law students showed symptoms suggestive of clinical depression by the end of their first year and that these high levels remained throughout their law school careers.[149] The most recent law student depression data is found in the 2014 Survey of Law Student Well-Being, where 17 percent of the students who participated screened positive for depression.[150]

Symptoms of depression to watch out for include:

- Feelings of sadness, emptiness, or hopelessness
- Loss of interest or pleasure in activities normally enjoyed
- Social withdrawal
- Weight loss or gain
- Decreased energy
- Feelings of worthlessness or guilt
- Persistent irritability or anger
- Feeling "blah"
- Brooding
- Rumination about minor failings
- Difficulty concentrating
- Memory difficulties
- Insomnia or other changes in sleep patterns
- Recurrent thoughts of death or suicidal ideation[151]

As with anxiety, the gloominess pattern continues after graduation. A Johns Hopkins University study found that

---

[148]   *Mental Health, Depression, Depression Statistics* fig.1, CTRS. FOR DISEASE CONTROL & PREVENTION (last visited Feb. 10, 2017).

[149]   Alan Reifman et al., *Depression and Affect Among Law Students During Law School: A Longitudinal Study*, 2 J. EMOTIONAL ABUSE 93, 101 (2000).

[150]   Organ et al., *Suffering in Silence*, *supra*, at 116, 136.

[151]   *See generally* DSM-V, *supra*, at 160–71 (describing diagnostic criteria for major depressive disorder and persistent depressive order).

lawyers ranked fifth in the overall prevalence of depression out of 105 occupations.[152] When the data were adjusted to focus on the association between depression and the particular occupation by taking into account non-occupational factors, lawyers moved into first place.[153] The study of Arizona and Washington lawyers mentioned above found that 21 percent of male lawyers and 16 percent of female lawyers exceeded the clinical cut-off measure for depression, significantly higher than depression rates found in the general population.[154]

Self-Doubt

While feelings of low self-worth are not recognized as a separate psychological disorder, they have been tied to a host of other disorders, including anxiety and depression.[155] Law school may be the undisputed champion of causing talented people, people who have achieved at a high level their entire lives, to almost instantly begin questioning their self-worth.

As one student put it, "It seems that law school is *designed* to make the student feel unsure of himself and inadequate." Other students amplified the point:

- Law school is where smart people go to feel dumb. It is difficult having gone through life being at the top of the academic heap to deal with the stress involved in having to lower one's expectations for performance.

- I feel like I came here being a really good public speaker and writer. I've won awards for both. Somehow, law school has managed to turn that on its head. I'm apparently a bad public speaker and a mediocre writer at best.

- My biggest change in personality is a complete loss of self-confidence and feeling of self-worth.

---

[152]   *See* William W. Eaton et al., *Occupations and the Prevalence of Major Depressive Disorder*, 32 J. OCCUPATIONAL & ENVTL. MED. 1079, 1082 tbl.1 (1990).

[153]   *Id.* at 1085 tbl.3.

[154]   Beck et al., *supra*, at 49–50.

[155]   Mel Schwartz, *Low Self-Esteem: A Missed Diagnosis*, PSYCHOL. TODAY (July 23, 2013) (asserting that "marginal self-worth manifests through an array of dysfunction, including but not limited to depression, anxiety, ADHD, codependence, failed relationships" and under-lived lives).

"Cognitive distortion" is a psychological term used to describe a condition that occurs when a person internalizes neutral or mildly negative external stimuli as signs of severe personal failure.[156] Law school establishes optimal conditions for this to occur. Everything a student does is judged and never seems good enough. Every word uttered in law school classes is critically scrutinized, or at least may be interpreted that way by a student. Professors often critique student classroom comments even when they wholeheartedly agree with them. It's the nature of the beast. Some students shrug it off, but many take it personally and let it diminish their self-image. As Beck and Burns said:

> As part of his internal recurring, cognitive pattern, [the student] globalizes and catastrophizes. He views any evidence of substandard performance as . . . cataclysmic to himself, his friends and family. For instance, the student may evaluate his classroom performance as poor. When reciting in class, he fumbles, blanks out, or is told by his professor that he is wrong. He views his inadequate performance as conclusive evidence that all his classmates are superior to him (globalizing). He is convinced if he continues in school, he will humiliate himself, his friends and family (catastrophizing). He will be dropped or placed at the bottom of his class.[157]

A large part of the problem is that most law students have never before felt matched or over-matched by their classmates. Their previous educational experiences taught them they were the best. Now comes law school, filled with smart people and administered in a way that puts one's habits and skills on public display.

If you find yourself struggling, it's important to stop and recognize that most other students are feeling the same way, even the ones who appear to have it all together. Law school shook my confidence so deeply that it took until midway through the first year before I voluntarily raised my hand in class for the first time. Our Property professor was everyone's favorite, a

---

[156]   Phyllis W. Beck & David Burns, *Anxiety and Depression in Law Students: Cognitive Intervention*, 30 J. LEGAL EDUC. 270, 273 (1979).

[157]   *Id.* at 274.

great teacher with a good sense of humor. One day he asked a simple question. "What is the legal relationship of a bank and a bank depositor?" Several hands went up. "Bailor-bailee?" "Wrong." "Assignor-assignee?" "Wrong." "Mortagor-mortagee?" "Wrong." This continued until the class exhausted every possible combination of two words ending with "or" and "ee."

All but one. I thought I knew the answer. This was it. My moment of glory. I took a deep breath and stabbed my hand in the air.

"Mr. McClurg?"

"Lendor-lendee?"

"Wrong!"

Dang. The correct answer was debtor-creditor. Double "or"-words! Another law school mind trick. O for 1. In *One L*, Scott Turow described a similar crisis of confidence when he gave a wrong answer in Criminal Law. He said it made him feel "horribly embarrassed—worse than that, corrosively ashamed."[158]

Seek Help

If you're suffering from anxiety, depression, or any other type of psychological distress—*or think you might be*—seek help. Universities offer free, confidential counseling services for students. At my university, it's widely rumored that our law students are the counseling center's largest constituency. Good for them. I'm glad they're not deterred by the reasons that keep many students from seeking help. In the 2014 Survey of Law Student Well-Being, 42 percent of the participants said they thought they needed help with emotional or psychological issues in the past year, but only half of them actually received professional help.[159]

Call and make an appointment. Don't accept depression or severe anxiety as normal consequences of law school. There's no

---

[158]   TUROW, *supra*, at 103.

[159]   Organ et al., *Suffering in Silence*, *supra*, at 140. Survey responders listed the following as factors discouraging them from seeking help regarding mental health issues: perceived threat to job or academic status (48%); social stigma (47%); financial reasons (47%); perceived threat to bar admission (45%); belief they could handle the issues without help (36%); too busy/time conflicts (34%); privacy concerns (30%). *Id.* at 141.

shame in experiencing psychological distress or seeking counseling for it and no pride or honor in suffering silently. Simply unloading one's pent-up feelings to a neutral listener can be therapeutic.

Take to heart the comments of this student who, asked what single piece of advice she would give to a close friend or relative starting law school, said:

> Stay psychologically sound and watch for warning signs. I already had a graduate degree when I came here and was still overwhelmed by the culture of fear they promote and the massive inferiority I felt as a result. I only survived the first semester because I sought psychological counseling from the amazing university counseling center. The day I finally went, it was beautiful outside, and I wasn't feeling as bad. "You don't need help," I told myself. But I knew when I woke up the next morning at 4:30 (I could no longer control my sleep habits) with nervous anxiety, it would be no different. The anxiety gave way to major depression, and I started taking antidepressants shortly before finals. I was a new person.

Other options include talking to the dean of students or a professor you trust, or contacting your state's Lawyer Assistance Program (LAP). Originally formed to help lawyers with substance abuse problems, today LAPs provide confidential assistance to lawyers and law students regarding any type of psychological health issue. The deputy director of the Tennessee LAP told me that roughly one-third of all new clients are law students or bar applicants.

Each year, I talk to my 1Ls about psychological distress, confessing that I suffered from it as a 1L to the point where I almost quit law school. Each time, students contact me afterwards to say that simply having someone acknowledge the issue made them feel less alone. That's a good thing, but it's not enough. *Seek help.*

* * *

Hey, law school's sounding pretty awesome so far, isn't it? It might not be too late to get your deposit back. Just kidding. Grim chapter, I know, but don't worry. Law school isn't all gloom and doom. The research just makes it look that way. No one has ever studied the positive aspects of law school, of which there are many. Perhaps surprisingly in light of what you just read, surveys show remarkably high levels of student satisfaction with their law school experience. Eighty-five percent of the 17,820 students who responded to the 2016 Law School Survey of Student Engagement rated their law school experience as either good or excellent and 84 percent said they definitely or probably would attend the same law school if starting over.[160]

Sure, law school is a challenge, but it's supposed to be. It's obviously doable though, or we wouldn't have 1.2 million people with law degrees in America. I like this comment from a student asked whether her first year was better or worse than expected:

> I love law school. I love the material, the professors, and my classmates. Law school is definitely more challenging than I ever anticipated, but that's what makes it great. If it were easy, I can say in all honesty that I would be disappointed. It's supposed to be hard because it means something. I wouldn't have it any other way.

Recognize that the studies showing higher rates of psychological dysfunction in law students do not predict an outcome for any individual student and also take comfort in the fact that law school inflicts its most visceral impact on students in the first year. There's an old law school adage that still has some currency today: "In the first year they scare you to death, in the second year they work you to death, and in the third year they bore you to death."

While research shows that law student psychological dysfunction continues into the third year and even past graduation, the most intense whirly rides of anxiety and emotion occur in the first year, especially the first semester, when there is so much uncertainty. After that, things settle down and life falls into a more or less normal pattern. Stressors undergo a fundamental reprioritizing. Panic over the Socratic method and exams is replaced by external worries about finding a job and paying back student loans. These external pressures are

---

[160]   2016 LAW SCH. SURVEY OF STUDENT ENGAGEMENT, *supra.*

significant, but in terms of day-to-day law school, many 3Ls do in fact seem more bored than afraid.

Although my first year was marked by heavy stress, by the third year, I was loving law school so much I didn't want to leave. Loved it so much that I decided to come back and stay forever. As you're counting the days until you become a 3L, let's consider some strategies for managing stress and maintaining well-being.

CHAPTER 20

MAINTAINING WELL-BEING

To the extent law school is responsible for causing emotional distress in law students, one doesn't have to look far for plausible explanations: the heavy emphasis on early grades and corresponding fear of failure or disappointment, lack of feedback due to the single-exam format, the competitive environment, high student-teacher ratios, the Socratic method, a brutal workload, being constantly immersed in an adversarial legal system, the emphasis on objective analytical thinking over values and emotions, strains on personal relationships, burdensome debt, worries about getting a job, and, of course, for 1Ls, general fear and uncertainty about what to expect.

Stress isn't inherently bad. In proper doses, it can be a good source of motivation. As a law student, for example, I felt pressure to not sound stupid in class in front of my peers. That made me work harder in preparing for class—not a bad thing. Some degree of law school stress is inevitable and unavoidable, just as "military stress" is unavoidable for service members, "relationship stress" for partners, and "parenting stress" for parents.

While some law students are more prone to stress than others, *all* students have control over lifestyle choices that can bolster or impair well-being. This chapter discusses a dozen strategies for maintaining well-being and reducing stress. Some of them relate to finding and keeping a proper balance between law school and the rest of your life. Lawyers are famously poor at maintaining a healthy work-life balance, a failure thought to contribute to emotional distress, alcohol and other substance abuse, family problems (see Chapter 23 about the impact of law school on outside relationships), and even suicide. The same issues affect law students.

Take Care of Yourself Physically

The first year of law school is part academic test and part endurance test. It will tax your mind and body to the limits. As one commentator said, "Physical and psychological exhaustion are, I think, programmed into the first year."[161] As the first semester progresses past the halfway mark, classrooms start sounding like tuberculosis wards as more and more students begin showing up sick. The reasonable apprehension about missing class keeps students coming to class—and spreading germs—when they'd be better off at home in bed.

One student consultant shared this tale, which is at once funny, disconcerting, and a revealing statement about law school:

> During the second semester, it seemed like everyone in our class was coming down with the flu. When I felt that familiar achy, feverish feeling one morning, I cried. Literally, I cried because I knew there was no way I could skip class or slow down. So I struggled through that day and the next and finally went to the health clinic on campus. When the nurse practitioner asked if I had been exposed to anyone who had the flu, I said, "Well, three people who sit next to me have it." She asked if they had been coming to class and I said, "Yeah. I mean, we are in law school. You can't miss class." She got this very frustrated look on her face and said emphatically, "Well, if that's the case then maybe we should make the entire law school get flu shots next year so you don't infect the whole campus!"

I felt guilty when I read her story, knowing I'm part of the problem in repeatedly emphasizing how important it is to not miss class. Let me modify that advice here: If you're ill and contagious, stay home and get a classmate's notes or arrange to have the class recorded.

In the meantime, there are things you can to do to keep yourself healthy both physically *and* mentally.

Exercise. Exercise is a proven stress reliever and promoter of physical and mental well-being. Indeed, a list of the benefits from regular exercise resembles a cure-all prescription for many of the ailments suffered by law students. Exercise reduces

---

[161] Stephen C. Halpern, *On the Politics and Pathology of Legal Education: (Or, Whatever Happened to that Blindfolded Lady with the Scales?)*, 32 J. LEGAL EDUC. 383, 388 (1982).

depression and anxiety and increases energy, strength, and stamina. It improves mental acuity, enhances the immune system, promotes better sleep, and raises self-esteem.

Join the university's fitness center. Memberships usually are available at low cost to students or included as part of student fees. Use the stairs instead of the elevator at law school. Do bicep curls with your Contracts and Property casebooks. Just find a way to work exercise into your routine. A large portion of your new life will be sedentary: sitting in a classroom or at a desk or study carrel. Asked to name one thing he wished he knew prior to starting law school, a student said: "I wish I would have known how wide my backside was going to get from sitting around studying all the time."

Maintain a proper diet. With all of the time demands imposed by law school, it's common for students to fall into a snack food/fast-food diet. Law schools don't help matters. For all the free pizza they provide to students for various luncheon events, they might as well install Pizza Hut franchises in law school libraries.

Everyone knows that a poor diet threatens physical health, but a growing body of integrative science now links dietary habits to mental health. A 2011 study of more than 5,000 men and women concluded that people with better quality diets were less likely to be depressed, and that consuming unhealthy foods was associated with increased anxiety.[162] Another study found that the favorite diet of many law students—processed and fried foods, refined grains, sugary products, and beer—was associated with higher depression and anxiety scores.[163] A group of international researchers went so far as to suggest that "diet is as important to psychiatry as it is to cardiology, endocrinology, and gastroenterology."[164]

---

[162] Felice N. Jacka et al., *Association Between Habitual Diet Quality and the Common Mental Disorders in Community-Dwelling Adults: The Hordaland Health Study*, 73 PSYCHOSOMATIC MED. 483 (2011).

[163] Felice N. Jacka et al., *Association of Western and Traditional Diets with Depression and Anxiety in Women*, 167 AM. J. PSYCHIATRY 305 (2010).

[164] Jerome Sarris et al., *Nutritional Medicine as Mainstream in Psychiatry*, 2 LANCET PSYCHIATRY 271, 271 (2015).

You *do* have time to eat well. You just have to make a habit of it. Listen to this student:

> It didn't take long for me to develop tunnel vision about my studies and forget to tend to my daily health. I relied on caffeine and Goldfish to hold me over while at school and usually grabbed takeout on my way home. I still have to remind myself that it takes less than thirty minutes to go to the grocery store and that, yes, I do have thirty minutes to spare.

Avoid germs. Law schools are breeding grounds for bacteria and viruses because students often force themselves to come to class even when they're sick. Many illnesses are spread through hand-to-mouth contact. Wash your hands frequently. Carry and use an anti-bacterial hand sanitizer. Take it from the CDC: "Keeping hands . . . clean is one of the most important steps we can take to avoid getting sick. . . ."[165]

Beware of Alcohol and Other Substance Abuse

Lawyers like to drink. Alcohol flows freely whenever and wherever they gather socially. Several studies have documented alcohol problems in the legal profession. One researcher estimated that at least 15 percent of lawyers are alcoholics,[166] compared to 6–8 percent of the general population.[167] The most comprehensive data comes from a 2016 survey conducted by the Hazelden Betty Ford Foundation and ABA Commission on Lawyer Assistance Programs.[168] More than 11,000 lawyers completed the Alcohol Use Disorders Identification Test (AUDIT), which screens for "hazardous use, harmful use, and the potential for alcohol dependence." Results indicated that one in five respondents (20.6 percent) engaged in problematic drinking. Participants who did not rate as "problematic

---

[165] *Handwashing: Clean Hands Save Lives, Show Me the Science—Why Wash Your Hands?*, CTRS. FOR DISEASE CONTROL & PREVENTION (last visited Feb. 10, 2017).

[166] Patrick J. Schiltz, *On Being a Happy, Healthy, and Ethical Member of an Unhappy, Unhealthy, and Unethical Profession*, 52 VAND. L. REV. 871, 876–77 (1999) (collecting and reporting on these studies).

[167] *Alcohol Facts and Statistics*, NAT'L INST. ON ALCOHOL ABUSE & ALCOHOLISM (last visited Feb. 10, 2017).

[168] Patrick R. Krill et al., *The Prevalence of Substance Use and Other Mental Health Concerns Among American Attorneys*, 10 J. ADDICTION MED. 46 (2016).

drinkers" had lower depression and anxiety scores. Although the data are less extensive, in addition to alcohol issues, drug misuse is also believed to be prevalent among lawyers.

Law students enjoy alcohol as well. The 2014 Survey of Law Student Well-Being found that more than half of respondents got drunk at least once in the previous thirty days and 43 percent engaged in binge drinking at least once in the prior two weeks.[169] The results suggested that perhaps 25 percent of the participants warranted screening for alcoholism.

Law schools and bar associations may contribute to the problem by maintaining and fostering activities that emphasize the consumption of alcohol. In addition to teaching students "to think like a lawyer," law school culture could be accused of teaching students "to drink like a lawyer."

Following a Torts class discussing the potential liability of individuals and businesses for providing alcohol to persons who then drive drunk and cause injury, a student asked if he could speak with me privately. Because first-semester grades had just come out, I was expecting a sad story about his Torts grade. Instead, he said: "Professor, I didn't want to bring this up in the class discussion because I didn't want the class to turn against me, but I don't understand how or why law schools encourage so much drinking."

He described a social event promoted by the student government organization in which the local bar association offered free drinks at a bar during a happy hour. "Everyone just came for the free drinks," he said. "Because they were free, people were pouring them down as fast as they could." He went on to describe ugly scenes at other law school social events where some students get "falling-down drunk." "You'd never recognize them from class, Professor," he said.

The 2014 Survey of Law Student Well-Being also found evidence of drug abuse among law students, although apart from marijuana use, the percentages are much lower than for alcohol.[170] One common type of law student drug misuse comes

---

169   Organ et al., *Suffering in Silence, supra,* at 128. These percentages were somewhat lower than for undergraduate students as measured in a different study. *Id.*

170   *Id.* at 133–36.

in the form of using Adderall and other stimulants commonly prescribed for attention deficit disorder to boost alertness and stamina, especially around exams. According to one source, so common is the use of Adderall that students can be heard excitedly announcing, "I found someone to sell me the 15 milligrams for four bucks instead of five. Only seven bucks for 20 milligrams!" In addition to obvious health concerns, taking prescription drugs without a prescription is illegal.

Excessive drinking or other substance abuse is problematic for law students on several fronts. First, alcohol is a depressant, so while it might provide short-term stress relief, it actually feeds depression. A close association between depression and heavy alcohol use is well-established by research. Second, the adverse consequences of an arrest for drunk-driving or other substance-related illegality are enhanced for law students, who have a strong interest in maintaining a good reputation and clean record. State bar organizations conduct thorough background checks of applicants. Misconduct in law school that might have been excused as youthful indiscretion had it occurred in undergraduate school will be more carefully scrutinized and harshly judged.

Drinking too much in public carries its own risks. Not uncommonly, intoxicated students embarrass themselves in front of their colleagues, unwisely pose for party pics that get posted online,[171] and even become victims or perpetrators of sexual assaults. You can count on the fact that any untoward behavior at a law school social gathering will be widely circulated among your peers.

Alcohol and other substance abuse reportedly are involved in 50–70 percent of all disciplinary actions against attorneys.[172] Small wonder that every state bar organization maintains a Lawyer Assistance Program for substance abuse and other

---

[171]   Here's a useful tip: Before allowing anyone to take a picture of you in a social setting, set aside any alcohol containers so they do not appear in the picture.

[172]   Carol M. Langford, *Depression, Substance Abuse, and Intellectual Property Lawyers*, 53 U. KAN. L. REV. 875, 902 (2005) (stating that an ABA survey of California and New York lawyers "determined that 50 to 70 percent of all disciplinary cases involved alcoholism").

mental health problems. If you need help, don't hesitate to seek it.

Don't Fall Behind

This piece of advice sounds *so* familiar to me, but I just can't place where I've heard it before. Oh yeah, I remember. It was in Chapter 3 . . . and Chapter 10 . . . and Chapter 13 . . .

One of the surest ways to ratchet up your anxiety level, and one of the most dangerous pitfalls to avoid in law school, is falling behind. Not only are consistent students who stay current more academically successful, they can justifiably feel more confident and less stressed-out because they don't have to go to bed every night worrying about how far behind they are.

Once you fall behind in law school, it is impossible to catch up. There are no restful gaps in law school semesters that one can use to get up to speed. Every day brings new cases, new concepts, and new rules in each course. Weekends are usually needed for outlining, periodic review, or working on legal writing assignments. Dismal as it might sound, my greatest joy of the Thanksgiving holiday in my first year of law school was that I had two full, extra days to study. The risk of falling behind is exponentially higher for part-time evening-division students. Chapter 22 addresses the unique challenges they face.

Don't fall behind. Don't fall behind. Don't fall behind. A few more repetitions can't hurt. Follow the C.R.E.D.O. and you won't have to worry about it.

Maintain a Support Network of Positive-Minded Classmates

We all need the support of loved ones when we're going through an ordeal and law school can be quite the ordeal. It's well-established in academic literature that social support promotes well-being. Being involved in a happy intimate relationship, for example, has been shown to have positive effects on overall well-being—all the more reason to pay attention to and take care of your preexisting relationships when you arrive at law school (see Chapter 23).

Unfortunately, your non-law school loved ones aren't going to be able to help with all of your law school travails because they can't truly understand what you're going through, no matter how hard you try to explain it. To the contrary, there may be times when they seem overtly unsupportive because they feel neglected and jealous of the time you're devoting to your new endeavor.

This is where your law school buddies can be a lifeline to well-being. They'll give you someone to vent to, borrow notes from, ask clarifying questions of, laugh, cry, mourn, and celebrate with. Hold on to them for dear life and treat them well. You'll need them and they'll need you.

In forming your inner circle, seek people who are optimistic about life, even if cynically so. Nattering Nabobs of Negativism, described in Chapter 4, should be avoided. A 1L shared this tale of an encounter she had with a Nattering Nabob:

> The other day I made the mistake of muttering "Good Morning" to one of my peers. Apparently, this is all the carrot one must dangle for a Nattering Nabob of Negativism to launch into a soul-sucking tirade, against legal writing instructors, Emanuel Outlines, exams . . . I was cornered for ten minutes by this person, with whom I'd never spoken before, while she drained the lifeblood out of me with her incessant complaining.

If you get trapped by a Nattering Nabob of Negativism, tell them you've enjoyed talking with them and wish you could stay longer, but are running late for a root canal you've been looking forward to, then sprint in the other direction.

Use Study Aids to Bolster Confidence

As discussed back in Chapter 3, one of the greatest law student fears is not understanding the material. It's scary to feel like you're in the dark about what you're supposed to be learning. The case method and nature of casebooks preclude your textbook from being a reliable place to turn for answers and the Socratic method of teaching can interfere with your professors being an in-class source of understanding.

These are key reasons why supplemental study aids are popular in law school. In undergraduate school, you didn't buy extra books to explain the book assigned for the course. In law school, you'll probably have to, at least for some courses. In addition to helping you learn the law for exam purposes, study aids can bolster your confidence and sense of self-efficacy by flipping on light bulbs in your murky confusion.

Study aids are more necessary in some courses than others, due either to the complexity of the material or the professor's presentation style (e.g., talks too fast, is a non-linear thinker, intentionally "hides the ball"). Even clear, well-organized professors won't be able to explain everything in class thoroughly, in part because imparting information is not the sole goal of first-year classes and in part because there's just not enough class time.

One of my research assistants recommended reading the relevant sections of reliable study aids *prior* to attending classes on the theory that it allows one to enter the room with more confidence, already possessing a mental framework for processing the material covered that day.

In other chapters, we discussed finding help in "canned briefs" (pre-prepared printed or online case briefs) and course outlines composed by students who took the same course taught by the same professor in the past. Most professors despise both practices, but both of these sources can be helpful if used properly; that is, if used as a *supplement* for understanding the material, but not as a replacement for your own diligent case-briefing and outline preparation.

Establish Contact with a Faculty Member You Like and Respect

In their study documenting elevated psychological distress in law students, Benjamin and colleagues noted that one cause might be the high student-teacher ratios that exist at most law schools. They speculated that the resulting distant relationship between law students and faculty is "related significantly" to student dissatisfaction.[173]

---

[173]   Benjamin et al., *supra*, at 249.

Having a faculty contact can make you feel more comfortable, connected to, and at home in your law school environment, as well as give you a person to turn to for advice and other help. Chapter 9 gives specific suggestions about how to get to know your professors.

Live Frugally to Minimize Debt

Early on, as part of your pre-arrival trip planning, I urged you to pay particular attention to developing a plan for financing your legal education. Piling up debt is a major source of anxiety—justifiably so—for law students, especially in an uncertain job market.

I was fortunate to escape law school with minimal debt, in large part because of cheap tuition, a luxury modern students no longer enjoy even at public law schools. But my law school mates and I also maintained an extremely low cost of living. Five of us shared a ramshackle house, so rent was cheap. We didn't use the air conditioning even though it's hot as Hades in Gainesville, Florida for much of the year. We never ate out, so food was cheap. For lunch, I took a can of tuna and piece of bread to school on most days. We picked our entertainment based on cost. Our big nights out were backyard parties or pitchers of cheap beer at happy hour. We didn't take vacations. Our cars were falling apart. We didn't buy clothes. This isn't a sob story. To the contrary, we were probably happier then than we've ever been.

I'm convinced that even in the era of rising tuition law students could shave a substantial percentage off their loan debt by living more frugally. Compare my Spartan law school existence to the lifestyle of many current debt-ridden students: they live alone without roommates, drive nice cars, eat out frequently, drink $5 cups of coffee like water (which they also buy instead of turning on the tap), enjoy $15 martinis, take vacations, belong to health clubs, etc.

Witnessing the lack of money consciousness of some law students reminds me of a time when my daughter was a child. She was barraging me with one of her gazillion requests to buy her something. It might have been "Baby Uh-Oh," a doll that soiled its diaper. I remember that being a must-have item among the toddling set at the time. Whatever it was, I said in my best

Ward Cleaver voice: "Honey, that costs money. We don't have money to buy everything you want." She said innocently, "Daddy, just go to the machine that gives out the money." Some students view the student loan spigot the same way my kid viewed the ATM machine, as if it were free money.

Students can—and should—scrimp in all areas of consumption, but the easiest way to cut expenses substantially is through shared living. Students sometimes mention their woes to me, and they often involve finances. One student recently complained about the size of her student debt. I asked if she lived by herself or with roommates, mentioning she could save a lot of money by living with roommates. She said, "Oh, I don't really like living with roommates." A couple weeks later another student told me his debt fears were tearing him apart, causing him to not be able to sleep at night and making him think about dropping out of law school. "Do you live by yourself or with roommates?" I asked. "Myself," he said. "I don't like living with roommates."

Get over it! Most people would prefer not to live with roommates, but living communally is the single most effective way to cut student debt-load. Students can't control the direct costs of education (tuition, books, fees). They can only control their consumption expenses, and housing is the largest consumption expense of all.

If you're moving to a new city to attend school and are in search of roommates, check with your law school admissions office. They sometimes provide formal or informal roommate matching services. Also, most law schools set up Facebook pages for incoming students on which students can post items such as roommate solicitations.

Here's another possibility: attend law school where your parents live and request if you can move back in with them. You may shriek at the thought. Your parents may shriek even louder. Poor things. Just when they thought they were rid of you. But what if you could save fifty thousand dollars in room and board—and debt—over three years? It's definitely worth thinking about.

A ton of information about budgeting and managing student debt is readily available online. The Law School Admission

Council (LSAC) website is a good place to start, but the admissions or financial aid office of your law school is the best direct source.

Make a point of getting up to speed and staying current on federal legislation and other programs designed to reduce the burden of student loan debt, such as the federal REPAYE program (Revised Pay As You Earn), which gives anyone with federal student loans the option of capping monthly payments at 10 percent of disposable income and forgives graduate degree loan debt after twenty-five years (twenty years for undergraduate loans). And keep your fingers crossed for further federal help to materialize.

In the meantime, steps have been taken to support students who come to law school with the goal of practicing public interest law, such as working for a non-profit organization or government agency. Too often, high loan debt prevents students from pursuing these internally rewarding, but lower-paying jobs. The federal Public Service Loan Forgiveness (PSLF) program forgives the balance on federal student loans for persons working in qualified public service legal jobs after 120 qualifying payments (i.e., ten years). Qualifying jobs include full-time employment by any federal, state, local, or tribal entity or any non-profit organization.

In addition to the federal legislation, at least twenty-four states and the District of Columbia and more than 100 law schools maintain loan repayment assistance programs, or "LRAPs," for law graduates who take public service legal jobs. If you're interested in a public service legal career, be sure to investigate and compare these programs. The details vary widely from state to state and school to school.

Don't Give Up Your Primary Hobby/Interest

To maintain a balanced life, all law students need a healthy outlet for their energy outside of law school, something they really enjoy doing. One of the cool things about law students is how multi-faceted and talented they are. On my entering-student questionnaire, I ask students to list their outside interests and talents. The answers always leave me impressed. As a conversation point, when I run into students outside of class, I'll sometimes ask, based on their questionnaires: "So do you still like to [play Frisbee golf/write poetry/build cabinets, etc.]?" More often than not, the answer is something like, "No, I had to give that up when I started law school. There wasn't enough time."

Wrong answer! There *is* enough time to continue a recreational pursuit if you develop and implement effective time-management skills. Maybe not to the same degree you engaged in it prior to law school, but enough to enjoy the benefits of it. If it's something you're good at, so much the better. Because law school can inflict such a beating on one's sense of self-worth, it's comforting and confidence-boosting to partake in a hobby you know you're better at than your classmates and professors.

Nearly every day for my entire three years of law school, I carved out an hour or so in the evening to sit around playing my acoustic guitar and writing songs. It helped me stay sane and took my mind off my troubles. Whether your passion is a musical instrument, chess, rugby, or bird-watching, make a pact with yourself not to give it up.

Treat Yourself to a Day Off

Related to the above, all work and no play makes Jack and Jill Law Student not only dull boys and girls, but candidates for early mental health intervention. Set aside at least one day or night (or both) a week to relax and unwind. If you have a significant other, this is vital not only to you, but to your partner and to you both as a couple. Don't feel guilty about it or look at a night off as wasted time. Look at it as recharging your batteries so you'll be more effective when you get back to work the next day.

Make it a point to leave law school behind during these R & R breaks. This is much easier said than done, particularly if your time off involves socializing with law students. If you end up sitting around talking or complaining about law school the entire time—as many students do during social activities— you're not really spending time away from law school, which defeats the purpose.

Make it a contest: every time a person mentions anything about law school, they have to pay a penalty of some type. I held an end-of-the-year party at my house for my Torts students. One of the student party organizers came up with a game in which each student was issued three clothespins on arrival. If a student mentioned anything about law school, anyone who overheard the statement could take one of their clothespins. The students with the most clothespins at the end of the party received prizes.

Of course, being law students, the contest got intense and competitive. All afternoon, I heard cries of "Gotcha!" and "Darn!" as students snatched clothespins back and forth. Particularly amusing were the lengthy legal debates as to whether certain comments were or weren't actually about law school. Watching that game unfold reminded me of the extent to which law school permeates the souls of poor 1Ls.

Never Forget: The Number of Excellent Students Far Exceeds 10 Percent

Most students, even if they deny it, arrive at law school hoping they can be one of the top students in the class. When Professor Lawrence Krieger, who researches law student well-being, asked his first-year class how many of them wanted to be in the top 10 percent of the class, 90 percent of the students raised their hands. As Krieger noted, herein lies a major obstacle to law student well-being. If the "want" to be on top is perceived as a "need," most everyone in the class is going to end up perceiving themselves as a failure.[174]

Just because you're not in the top 10 percent doesn't mean you're not an excellent law student or won't be a great lawyer. Law school exams measure a limited range of skills. They don't measure oral facility, resourcefulness, dedication, heart, grit, integrity, or even necessarily the amount of knowledge a student has acquired.

This isn't to suggest grades aren't important. They are. High grades open more opportunity doors than lower grades, especially early on. But recognizing that grades are important and that it's worth doing your best to improve them is different

---

[174] *See* Lawrence S. Krieger, *What We're Not Telling Law Students—And Lawyers—That They Really Need to Know: Some Thoughts-In-Action Toward Revitalizing the Profession from Its Roots*, 13 J.L. & HEALTH 1, 11 (1999).

from letting grades define who you are as a person. People come to law school to get a professional degree and a license to practice law. No one sits down and says, "I think I'll go to law school to see if I can rack up three more years of good grades!"

Compete only against yourself. If you work diligently and consistently, your grades will improve. Hard-working, reliable students will earn the respect of their classmates and professors regardless of their class rank.

Cling Tightly to Your Values

On the questionnaire I give to incoming students, I ask why they came to law school. A substantial percentage of students give sincere answers about wanting to help people, often targeting specific groups such as children, the elderly, or the disabled. Very few students, however, end up pursuing those goals once they become lawyers. What happens to them?

Research by Kennon Sheldon and Lawrence Krieger suggests one plausible explanation.[175] Sheldon and Krieger conducted a study of law students at two law schools to test a number of hypotheses about declines in law student well-being. They grounded their research in self-determination theory. Self-determination theorists study the connection between human motivations and optimal well-being. In short, self-determination theory hypothesizes that people are happier when they are motivated by autonomous, rather than externally coerced goals and values.

As applied to law students, Sheldon and Krieger hypothesized that 1Ls experience a decline in autonomous motivations and an increase in externally controlled motivations, and that this change is accompanied by a shift from internal to external values. They further hypothesized that these changes lead to lower levels of happiness and life satisfaction. Their study results supported their hypotheses.

Here's a plain-language example to illustrate their points: Sarah arrives at law school with the goals of enjoying the learning process, getting a degree, and becoming a lawyer who

---

[175]   *See generally* Sheldon & Krieger, *Does Legal Education Have Undermining Effects on Law Students?*, *supra.*

will help people with mental disabilities. Sheldon and Krieger's hypotheses predict that the coercive environment of law school, with its emphasis on external rewards, will cause Sarah's motivations and values to change. Her autonomous motivation to simply enjoy learning will decline, replaced by external motivations such as achieving high grades. Her personal value to serve people with mental disabilities will be replaced by extrinsic values such as enhancing her image and obtaining a lucrative job. Significantly, the more successful Sarah is in law school, the larger the threat that law school will reconstruct her values because of her wider opportunities. As Krieger explained, these shifts can lead to an overall lowering of well-being:

> Scientific research for the past 15 years has consistently shown that a primary focus on external rewards and results, including affluence, fame, and power, is unfulfilling. These values are seductive—they create a nice picture of life but they are actually correlated with relative unhappiness. Instead, people who have a more "intrinsic," personal/interpersonal focus—on personal growth, close relationships, helping others, or improving their community—turn out to be significantly happier and more satisfied with their lives.[176]

Sheldon and Krieger's hypotheses bear spooky similarities to my own experience. I attended law school with dreams of becoming a great civil rights lawyer. My hero was Clarence Darrow, the Chicago criminal defense lawyer known for championing unpopular causes. He was my hero because he was my mother's hero and she told me stories about him when I was growing up. Before I even knew what a lawyer was, I knew that there was this great man out there, this *lawyer*, who always stood up and fought for the underdog.

Somewhere along my law school journey, I took a wrong turn and got lost. I either forgot or sublimated my dream. I allowed the culture of law school to inculcate a new value system in me, one in which prestige, high salaries, expense accounts, and other perks became the most valuable prizes of becoming a

---

[176] LAWRENCE S. KRIEGER, THE HIDDEN SOURCES OF LAW SCHOOL STRESS: AVOIDING THE MISTAKES THAT CREATE UNHAPPY AND UNPROFESSIONAL LAWYERS 4 (2005).

lawyer. Success as a law student, just as Sheldon and Krieger predicted, made matters worse. With high grades and law review membership, all signs pointed in one direction. On finishing a judicial clerkship, I found myself interviewing only at prestigious, high-paying firms. I didn't apply to a single civil rights firm. On receiving an offer from a highly regarded commercial litigation firm, I accepted the job even though I didn't enjoy the interview or think I wanted to work there.

Everything turned out fine in the end. I love being a law professor. But I still regret never having made an attempt to be that civil rights lawyer I dreamed about. Words to live by from Shakespeare: "To thine own self be true."

Complicating this advice is that, much more commonly than in other graduate programs, too many law students come to law school for the wrong reasons, such as "What else am I going to do with an undergraduate degree in Things that Happened in England in 1208 A.D.?" or "I figured it would be a decent way to make a living." They aren't equipped to be true to their selves because they haven't figured out who they are or what they want in life. The well-being of these students is more at risk than people who pursue a legal education because they really want to be there. It's one thing to tolerate the workload and stress of law school if you have a good reason and strong motivation for being there, but quite another if you have no clue why you're there or arrived with only a vague goal of improving your career options. Anecdotal evidence suggests that the happiest lawyers are those who genuinely wanted to be lawyers before they got to law school.

The Three Gratitudes

Filming the *1L of a Ride Video Course* in 2015, I first heard of a practice called "the three gratitudes" from my friend, Professor Nancy Levit, who researches and writes books about law student and lawyer happiness and well-being.[177] She discovered it in the works of happiness researcher Sonja

---

[177]   In addition to the previously cited *The Happy Lawyer: Making a Good Life in the Law*, Professor Levit and co-author Douglas Linder are the authors of *The Good Lawyer: Seeking Quality in the Practice of Law* (2014).

Lyubomirsky.[178] Although several studies exist, the precise origin of giving gratitude as a happiness increaser are unclear. Oprah, for example, has been keeping and touting the benefits of a "gratitude journal" for twenty years.

It's a simple practice that even busy law students have time to engage in. At the end of each day, stop and think of three things you're grateful for. Recite them out loud. "I'm grateful for. . . ."

They don't have to be big things. To the contrary. It would be difficult to come up with three extraordinary gratitudes every day that weren't repetitive. The goal is to come up with new gratitudes to make you appreciate the small, ordinary good things in life that are easy to overlook and take for granted. Singer-songwriter Carrie Newcomer wrote a poem called "The Three Gratitudes" that lists big things like her father's health and her daughter getting a new job, but also small things like getting decent coffee at the airport and the fact that her car is still running despite its high mileage.

After watching Professor Levit explain the practice and offer her own three gratitudes in the well-being module of the video course, I started practicing it myself. It's too easy to focus on the negatives in life that stress and press on us.

Happiness research suggests that you want to practice proven happiness-increasers such as giving gratitude for a sustained period (maybe six weeks) to open up and train neural networks in the brain. When it starts to become a chore, take a break and resume the practice at a later point.

Good Advice, but Will You Follow It?

Hearing advice and following it are two different things. That's a particular problem with the recommendations in this chapter, some of which constitute "lifestyle advice" as applied to law students. Admittedly, some of my tips for maintaining well-being fall under the "I didn't need to buy a book to tell me that" category. Will couch-potato readers start an exercise regimen because it's suggested above? Will law students with drinking

---

[178] *See* SONJA LYUBOMIRSKY, THE HOW OF HAPPINESS: A NEW APPROACH TO GETTING THE LIFE YOU WANT (2008).

issues become teetotalers because of the alarming statistics regarding law student/lawyer alcohol abuse? Will 1Ls keep up with their hobbies because a law professor said it's a good idea?

Maybe, but I'm not counting on it. My goal in this chapter is more modest: to alert you to reliable strategies for reducing stress and increasing well-being. It's up to you to make the choices.

CHAPTER 21

WELCOME *BACK* TO THE JUNGLE: THE PERILOUS SECOND SEMESTER

In a way I kind of feel as though the first semester was like me going into a burning building to pull somebody out of the fire. I wanted to go and was happy to do it, and after coming out I was glad I did it, but felt like I wouldn't want to do it again. Now for the next semester I feel as though there is somebody else in the house and the fire has gotten worse. I groan and make myself go in again, and part of me wants to go back in, but in the back of my mind I'm aware of how tired I am from the first time and am a little more worried about whether or not I will get out of the building alive this time.

—1L's comment about starting the second semester

All of the advice in this book applies equally to the first and second semesters. This chapter focuses on some issues and obstacles unique to the second semester. Knowing and understanding those obstacles will lessen the blow of smacking into them face-first, and also make it easier to navigate around them.

The second semester, particularly in the opening days and weeks, is one of the most daunting challenges in all of law school. How students respond to it is a crucial determinant of their long-term success. This is the juncture where, for reasons described below, students make judgments and decisions about themselves and law school that play a large role in determining and defining their ultimate "law school selves."

The Second Semester Has Upsides

It may seem counterintuitive that many law students find the second semester more difficult and dispiriting than the first.

With three months experience under their belts, one might think the second semester would be a "been there, done that" relative breeze. In the first semester, students are lost in a maze of uncertainty and burdened by the anxiety of stumbling through it blindly. Beginning law students must acclimate themselves to an entirely new educational world. They spend forever preparing for class only to arrive feeling unprepared because the professors are asking questions they hadn't thought about. Some live in paralyzing fear of the Socratic method. A new vocabulary converts reading a single paragraph of a case into a marathon love-making exercise with a law dictionary. The first semester is when students, many of whom arrive at law school in search of "the right answer" to every question, are dragged kicking and screaming to the realization that legal doctrine is frustratingly ambiguous. All of this must be accomplished in strange surroundings full of strangers. Aggravating matters, students have little clue if they're doing things right because of the feedback vacuum.

These conditions are vastly improved come the second semester. Students know how to prepare for class. They're efficient at reading and briefing cases. The Socratic method is much less intimidating. To their pleasant surprise, students saw that no one got tortured or executed for giving a wrong answer in class. The physical environs are familiar. Many of those strangers from the first semester are now good friends and at least some of the professors are known quantities. Students know what to expect on law school exams. After receiving their first-semester grades, they finally have the feedback they craved. They've made it through the first crucible of law school. Full-time students are one-sixth of the way to becoming lawyers. Part-time students are one-eighth of the way home.

So what's not to like about the second semester? Plenty. It's true that all of the reasons listed above operate to alleviate some major causes of stress and anxiety in students. But the second semester brings its own set of new problems. Before considering them, let's take a glimpse at the state of mind of 1Ls returning after the holiday break for their second semester. For a couple years, I polled my Torts students at the start of the second semester with this question:

What is your dominant feeling as you begin the second semester?

- Excited

- Tired

- Bored

- Depressed

- Rested and ready

Very few students selected "Excited" or "Rested and Ready." The most common answers by far were "Tired" and "Depressed." A couple of students even picked "Bored," definitely not a good sign with more than two years of law school still to go.

I decided to probe more deeply into student sentiments about starting the second semester. Just before classes began, I asked a section of Torts students to comment on, among other things, their: (1) state of mind; (2) motivation level; and (3) happiness level in comparison to the first semester. The responses showed that, while some students felt better off in the second semester, a significant segment were less happy and less motivated. In between was a large group of students who were ambivalent.

Students expressing positive feelings about their state of mind, motivation level, and happiness level emphasized many of the improved conditions listed above: more efficient study skills, a larger comfort zone from knowing what to expect, new friendships, increased confidence from having made it through the first semester, and excitement about being on their way to becoming lawyers. Here are some sample positive responses:

- Overall, I am happier than at the start of the first semester. I am one-sixth of the way through! If the second semester goes as fast as the first, the three years should fly by. I feel engaged by all of my professors and am genuinely happy to be *learning*. (Cheesy, I know, but it's true.)

- I am definitely happier! I know now that I made the right decision in coming to law school. I have met many great friends and am very impressed with the law school and the professors. I learned that law school wasn't as horrifying as I was told it would be, and after a semester of it, my confidence is really boosted.

- I might actually be a little more motivated now that I know what to expect. I was so nervous at the beginning that I couldn't concentrate on anything else. Now that I know what to expect from the finals, I feel like I have more of an opportunity to improve my study skills and just my performance in general.

Unfortunately, those feel-good vibes were offset by a strong current of discontent among many students. Note the similarity in the responses of the three students below to my questions regarding, respectively, state of mind, motivation level, and happiness level:

Student 1:

1. My general state of mind as I start this semester is unmotivated.

2. I am definitely less motivated at the start of this semester than I was at the beginning.

3. I am also unhappier than I was during the first semester.

(The student added a post script: "Though this sounds depressing, I'm not depressed. Just struggling a little at the moment.")

Student 2:

1. Unhappy and sullen.

2. Much less motivated—I'm already convinced I failed out of school, so the last thing I want to do is continue to work hard.

3. The same amount of light unhappiness, but it's for different reasons. In the beginning it was fear and anxiety. Now I just feel defeated.

Student 3:

1. I generally feel depressed to be quite honest.

2. I am less motivated now than when I started the first semester.

3. I am a bit unhappier than when I began.

Potential Pitfalls of the Second Semester

Difficulties in the second semester that contribute to feelings like those described above are largely overlooked in giving advice to first-year students. I make an effort to give my students relevant advice as they progress through law school, but until composing this book had never thought deeply about the special challenges of the second semester. Let's take a look at them.

Ignorance can be bliss.

The uncertainty of the first semester is a substantial strain on 1Ls, but removing the veil from law school can be problematic as well. In the second semester uncertainty about law school is replaced by a disquieting *certainty* that the journey toward a law degree can be an exhausting, onerous slog. In his 1709 *An Essay on Criticism*, eighteenth-century English poet Alexander Pope coined the phrase "A little learning is a dangerous thing." Law students might modify it to say a little learning can be a depressing thing. Look at how some 1Ls weighed in on their newfound awareness in response to the questions about starting the second semester:

- Now I know exactly what I'm walking into. First semester there was a bit of excited anticipation, etc. Now I know I'll be in the library for the next four months.

- In some ways I'm happier because I really enjoy the process of learning and have really enjoyed school, but in other ways I am unhappier because I now know how hard I will have to work this semester.

- The hardest thing to me about starting the second semester is knowing that I have to go through the whole exam process at the end again, and not only one more time, but five more times.

The thrill is gone.

The realization that law school is going to be a long haul is worsened by the fact that much of the excitement and adrenaline that fuels students through the first semester evaporates. Students arrive at law school brimming with anticipation and energy. Seeing and feeling it is one of the great pleasures of being a 1L law teacher. But like romances that lose their dizzying effects once the newness wears off, law school can seem like more of a chore than an adventure after the ebullience of the first semester subsides.

Students start the second semester with a hangover effect of physical and emotional exhaustion from the first semester. The holiday break is just long enough to remind students what it's like to live like a free person, but not quite long enough for students to fully recharge their batteries. In the words of bluesman B.B. King, "the thrill is gone."

Be prepared for this letdown at the beginning of the second semester. Know that it's completely normal and, happily, transitory. Within a week or two, most students bounce back to their old selves. While many never quite regain that exhilaration that comes with newness, they do get their second wind.

The double-edged grade blade.

Depending how they turn out, first-semester grades can be either a major boost or impediment to starting the second semester. You've heard the aphorism, "Be careful what you wish for." It applies to law school feedback big-time. We've discussed how most students begin law school with at least some hope of finishing near the top of their class, but also the mathematical reality that only a small percentage of students can fulfill that dream.

For those who performed well, first-semester grades can infuse new energy and confidence. It shows up in class. Every year, in the early days of the second semester, students who never raised their hands the first semester start volunteering in class. When they do, I smile inside, thinking: "Ah, good for you. You must have done better than you expected."

But for every student whose confidence gets a jolt from grades, three or four others get their egos electrocuted. Making lower-than-hoped-for grades is particularly demoralizing for the students who worked their tails off in the first semester. It undermines spirit and confidence to work harder than one has ever worked before and come up short, at least (or perhaps especially) in one's own eyes. Many students just don't see a connection between their hard work and the results. One student responded to my second-semester questions with the following thoughtful comments, adding that he wrote them mostly for his own benefit:

> You are told when you come to law school that, more likely than not, you will not be the best of the best. That's fine. From my personal experience, everyone lies if they tell you they do not wish in their heart that when grades are posted they will be perched towards the top of their class. Reality dictates that many of us will be disappointed—seriously disappointed in some cases. Personally, I did "fine" this semester. I had grades that I am proud of and one in particular that I am not happy with. I am, at the moment, your everyday Average Joe law student. Middle of the pack or a notch or two above.

> I have many deep and close friends here, and I know that I worked very hard the previous semester. I know that I worked harder than some of my dearest friends. I know that several of them did better than me—some did tremendously well. It's difficult to describe the frustration that causes. You are happy for the individuals who did well, yet you are mystified and deeply frustrated that the hundreds (thousands?) of hours that you worked did not provide the reward you sought.

How students respond to first-semester grades is crucial to their remaining law school existence, as well as their post-law school lives. Far too many students define themselves by their first-semester grades. If they received average grades, they tell themselves: "Well, I guess I'm only an average student." Then many of them proceed to behave that way by not working as hard from that point on.

It bears repeating: Law school is a marathon, not a sprint. Suppose you really were a serious marathon runner. A marathon is roughly twenty-six miles. The one-sixth mark—that is, the equivalent mark of finishing one of the six semesters of law school for a full-time student—would be 4.3 miles. Suppose you came to that point of the race and realized you were in the middle of the pack. Would you give up? Of course not. With so much ground remaining and so much time and terrain to gain on the competition, you wouldn't tell yourself, "Well, I guess I'm just an average marathon runner. I might as well slow down."

It's *way* too early to give up after just one semester. For people who continue working hard, grades generally go up. For people who start working less, grades generally go down. I've seen it happen a hundred times. Think back to the student mentioned in Chapter 9 for whom I wrote the strong recommendation letter even though she received a *D* in Torts I. One reason I was willing to go to bat for her was because after she received the *D* she came to me and said she intended to work even harder in the second semester. She got a *B−* in Torts II, a five-step increase.

Law school exam-taking is a learning process for most students. It's true that some people in each class have a knack for it from the start. It's also true that a small number of students never get the hang of it. But for most students, as with any new skill, it's a matter of improving through repetition. You're only at the one-sixth mark of the race at the beginning of the second semester. Don't give up!

Getting back in the groove.

A universal challenge of starting the second semester is simply getting back into the routine of daily classes and class preparation. After going and going like the battery bunny on meth for three months, students finish that last exam of the first semester and everything suddenly stops. Many students report they can't enjoy the break at the beginning because they feel guilty about not studying. Then, just when they readjust to an unstructured lifestyle full of leisure time, it's time to get back to the grind.

Included in my "starting the second semester" survey was this question: "The hardest thing for me about starting the second semester is [fill in the blank]." The dominant response was getting refocused to do it all over again. Look at the commonality—indeed, near identicalness—of the following responses:

- The hardest thing for me about starting the second semester is getting refocused to do it all over again. The first semester felt so draining both emotionally and physically. It is hard to adjust to getting back and getting refocused.

- The hardest thing for me about starting the second semester is getting back into the mindset (you have to get into a certain mindset, I think, to get into the habit of briefing, etc.).

- The hardest thing for me about starting the second semester is feeling like I'm back at the beginning. I felt so good about finishing that first semester, and even though I was unsure about my grades I was still pretty proud of myself for making it. Now I feel like I have to start all over again. But I'm sure once I'm back in the swing of things, the semester will begin to fly by just like the first semester did.

And in that last sentence we find the saving grace of this challenge. This too shall pass. Students *do* get back into the swing of things and, once they do, the second semester flies by just like the first one did and like the third, fourth, fifth, and sixth ones (and seventh and eighth for part-time students) will.

Key to your success is forcing yourself back into the groove *at the very beginning.* Don't squander the opening weeks of the second semester moping or dawdling. If you'll forgive the mixed metaphor, you'll get back in the swing of things quicker if you come out swinging. The C.R.E.D.O. (Consistent, Rigorous, Efficient, Diligent, Organized) from Chapter 10 applies to each semester of law school. It's important to be consistent from the get-go in the second semester, just as in the first semester. Warm-up class sessions are even less likely to occur than in the first semester. Profs generally come in and start teaching new law in the opening minutes of the first class. Hit the ground running or you can lose ground quickly.

Increased competitiveness.

Even if they don't admit it (perhaps even to themselves) most law students are competitive. And even if they aren't competitive by nature, law school forces them to become that way because the entire process is structured around competition. The competition for high grades and class rank is intense. Many schools have a first-year oral argument competition. To get on law review requires successful participation in a summer write-on competition. Students compete to land limited slots for on-campus interviews by potential employers. Just about every undertaking in law school, including writing the best exam in each course, carries the potential for an individual award.

Before you start law school, you may hear stories about how competitive law students are, to the point where many are alleged to be "cutthroat." In general, my experience as a professor has been that law students are quite supportive of one another. Of course, like all human experiences, the level of competition in law school varies depending on the particular group and individuals. I frequently observe students going out of their way to help and support their classmates, sometimes to astonishing degrees, but also hear occasional ugly stories of ruthless competitiveness.

To the extent competitiveness is an issue with which to be concerned, it gets worse in the second semester. Much of it relates back to that first set of grades having been issued. In the first semester, everyone is in the same boat, struggling to stay afloat. The shared experience creates a communal bond. But once first-semester grades have been issued, there may be a feeling—both among some high achievers and some lower-than-hoped-for achievers—of "Hey, you're in *that* boat and I'm in *this* boat." Reading this assertion, a research assistant commented:

> This is definitely true. One thing that surprised me in law school was its clique-ish nature. Very early on groups of people became friends and always hung around each other. This became even more pronounced in the second semester after grades came out. It seemed that students in each clique

generally received similar grades, thus reinforcing their companionship—seemed like everyone was in their own boats now.

Some students with high grades may consider themselves superior to their classmates and project, or be perceived to project, that image to others. In turn, some lower-performing students may resent the students at the top, particularly if they flaunt their success. As one disappointed student wrote:

When first-semester grades came out, I literally watched my classmates high-five and fist-pump each other and say their grades out loud. It reinforced a feeling of inadequacy that I had to talk myself out of. I vowed that if/when I get the grades for which I am striving, I will never tell a single soul at the law school.

Meanwhile, students who may not have appreciated the importance of class rank and GPA in the first semester become all too aware of it as the second semester progresses and they see the top-ranked students landing most of the on-campus job interviews.

To say this is unfortunate would be an understatement. The fact is you and your 1L mates are all in the same boat. There's not much meaningful practical advice I can give you on this issue other than to put you on notice that over-competitiveness is not an attractive quality. If you do well your first semester, follow the vow of the student above. Keep it to yourself. People will respect you all the more for it. If you brag about your high grades, people will despise you, with justification. A professor at another law school told me about a student who received an *A* on her memo assignment in Legal Research and Writing, then proceeded to carry the memo around on top of her stack of books, with the *A* clearly showing, for three weeks until the professor had a "little chat" with her about it. "Her classmates were about to crucify her," she reported.

Heavier workload.

A major cause of second-semester stress at many schools is an increased workload. Some schools add an extra course in the second semester. Professors may move at a quicker pace, which means longer reading assignments and more rules to memorize.

Some students voluntarily take on too many extra activities, such as participating in student organizations, which I cautioned against doing as a 1L back in Chapter 6.

And then there's the appellate brief and oral argument, one of the heaviest burdens of 1L existence. As discussed in Chapter 18, most students' second semester load in Legal Research and Writing will include having to write an appellate brief and engage in an oral argument before a mock appellate court. No reason to rehash the subject, except to note that these requirements add substantially to second-semester workloads. It takes more time and effort to research and write an appellate brief than to compose the law office memoranda assigned in the first semester. Additionally, the oral arguments consume tremendous prep time and emotional energy. Some schools make it into a competition, adding to the pressure and workload.

Second-guessing life as a lawyer.

One obstacle some students face in the second semester is the global issue of wondering whether they made the right choice in sacrificing so much in time and financial resources in coming to law school. Should I be here? Is this really what I want to do with my life? In the first semester, students are excited and struggling to keep up, with little time to ponder their career choice. In the second semester, nagging doubts kept at bay may creep into their consciousness.

Most students come to law school with very little understanding of what lawyers actually do. For many, their exposure to the law has been limited to glamorized media accounts. Marketable title? Collateral estoppel? Who cares about those? When do we get to do those awesome television cross-examinations that extract confessions just in time for the last commercial break? And what's up with all these very un-*Law and Order*-like cases? Where's the intrigue, the suspense, the romance?

Instead of inspiring students about practicing law, professors may unintentionally dampen student enthusiasm, although not intentionally. Many people become law professors to escape the practice of law. While I try to enthuse my students about the institution of law, I feel an obligation to be candid about the sometimes hard reality of actually practicing it.

But good news. Several studies show that most lawyers *are* satisfied with their career choice. The most prominent of these is the *After the JD* project, which tracked the careers of 5,000 lawyers for ten years. The researchers released their data in three waves. The first wave, reporting survey data collected two to three years after graduation, showed that 80 percent of the lawyers were either "moderately" or "extremely" satisfied with their decision to become a lawyer. The report found no evidence of pervasive unhappiness in the legal profession. The second wave, surveying the lawyers as they approached a decade of practice, found similar results, with 76.2 percent of the lawyers indicating they were moderately or extremely satisfied.[179] That figure held steady in the third wave survey, conducted after a decade of practice.[180] (Interesting side note: The study found that public interest lawyers are the most satisfied, despite the fact that salaries in public interest law are typically low.[181])

If you have doubts about your career choice, stop and ask why. First, understand that it's normal and appropriate to reevaluate such a life-changing decision as going to law school. Unfortunately, a fully informed evaluation isn't possible prior to actually attending. The second semester is a good time to pause and size things up. Some students decide they simply don't like law school, the law, or the prospect of being a lawyer—or all three—and withdraw. There's nothing wrong with such a decision if it's made for the right reasons.

If you feel quite certain you don't want to be a lawyer, it's better to cut your losses by figuring that out sooner rather than later. I'll never forget the student who showed up at my office the Monday after her law school graduation and asked if I would

---

[179] *See generally* Jerome M. Organ, *What Do We Know About the Satisfaction/Dissatisfaction of Lawyers? A Meta-Analysis of Research on Lawyer Satisfaction and Well-Being*, 8 U. ST. THOMAS L.J. 225 (2011) (reporting the results of the *After the JD* project and also discussing several other studies of lawyer satisfaction).

[180] D. Benjamin Barros, *Review of* After the JD III, *A Law Professor's Take*, *supra*.

[181] *Id.* at 1 (reporting the following percentages of lawyers by group who are moderately or highly satisfied: "public interest (87.6%), legal services/public defender (86.1%), large firms of 251+ lawyers (80.4%), and state or local government (78.5%)"). The least satisfied group are lawyers working in a business under people who are not lawyers (63.4%). *Id.*

write a letter of recommendation for her to enroll in a graduate program in social work. Surprised, I asked what prompted her decision. She said she knew from the beginning that she didn't want to be a lawyer, but felt pressure to complete her legal education so she wouldn't be seen as "a quitter" by her family or in her own eyes.

The key in making this assessment is to be sure you're looking at the long-term prospects for happiness in the legal profession, rather than the frustrations or stress of the moment. Law school itself will pass, more quickly than you realize. In my first year, I did not enjoy law school, but I did like the law itself. I loved that every case was different. I was awed by the power of law to affect people's lives. I found—and still do—the mental challenge of solving the law's many puzzles to be stimulating. When students come to me second-guessing whether they want to be a lawyer, the first question I ask is: "Do you enjoy the law itself?" If the answer is a clear no, I suggest that maybe law isn't the field for them. But if they answer yes, I usually encourage them to hang in there.

Take heart in the fact that many students absolutely *love* law school and many lawyers *love* the practice of law. Here are some glowing endorsements of law school and the prospect of becoming a lawyer I received from second-semester students in response to a question about their career choice:

- I'm excited! I know this is what I was meant to be!

- I love the career. I do love the law. I'm surprised with how much I actually enjoy reading the cases, even the cases that I'm reading for the appellate brief.

- I have always wanted to be a lawyer, since I was in sixth grade. I cannot see myself in any other profession, so I feel like this is the right career choice for me. Also, I really enjoy talking about the law and politics, and I enjoy being in law school where I don't have to feel like a dork if I get excited to talk about something related to the law, like the difference between assault and battery. I feel that being a lawyer is a respected profession, and even though as you know, we are always made fun of, when someone finds out I am in law school, there is definitely a respect there.

Related to questions about whether they want to be lawyers, some 1Ls get stressed when people around them ask *what kind* of lawyer they want to be and they don't have an answer. In response to my career-choice question, one student said he was happy he came to law school, but added: "I just wish that when everyone asked what kind of lawyer I want to be I had an answer. When I answer with 'I don't know,' they look at me like I have been wasting my time. That is really getting annoying."

Certainly, it's a good question to start thinking about, but there's no reason 1Ls should know what kind of lawyer they want to be because they haven't been exposed to enough types of law or to the real world to develop informed opinions. Many lawyers' career paths end up being determined purely by fortuitous circumstances, such as where they happen to land a job. My older brother was one of the most prominent bankruptcy attorneys in the country, listed in that field in the *Best Lawyers in America* book. I once asked him how he ended up as a bankruptcy lawyer. He said when he took his first job at a large law firm, he was assigned an office that just happened to contain the law firm's set of *Collier on Bankruptcy*, a multi-volume treatise that is the bible of bankruptcy law. Other lawyers started coming into his office asking him bankruptcy questions simply because he had the set of *Collier*'s in there. He said he started looking up answers to the questions and the next thing he knew he was a bankruptcy lawyer!

Don't feel rushed to pick a specific career path. I didn't figure out my permanent path until six years after graduating from law school. Unless you came to law school to be a specific type of lawyer, keep your mind open to all options and trust you will find your way. In the meantime, when someone asks what kind of lawyer you want to be, just say, "A great one! But I need to do more exploring before deciding on a particular type of practice."

Summer job anxiety.

Students feel pressure in their second semester to land summer legal jobs at law firms, often called "summer associate" positions. In many cases, this pressure arises from pressing financial needs, but it also stems from an expectation that getting a summer legal job is something that all 1Ls absolutely must do.

Certainly, there are benefits to obtaining a summer legal job. Income is an obvious one. Big law firms pay summer associates handsomely, but these jobs are limited in number and reserved for top-performing students or students from elite law schools. Small firms pay less, but are a good way to get some experience and get your foot in the door. While not an ironclad rule, it is true that many firms hire permanent associates from the ranks of former summer associates who performed well.

I tell my students not to worry too much if they can't land a paying summer legal job after their 1L year. For one thing, they don't have a great deal of control over the situation. The job market is tighter than it used to be. Also, many law firms simply don't hire students after their first year because they haven't learned enough yet to be of value.

If you need money, consider non-legal jobs as a way to get a hiatus from law school. Many students can earn more waiting tables than by clerking at a law firm, while also getting a refreshing break from the law. If you don't need the money, summer school is a good option. Getting a couple of courses out of the way in the summer will lighten your burden during the regular academic year. It's even possible to graduate a semester early if that's your goal. Interning for a government agency or non-profit organization is a good way to network and get some experience, although these are unpaid positions.

One thing you absolutely should *not* do is work for free at a law firm or other for-profit organization. I've had several students report to me that in applying for summer jobs, firms have offered to let them work without pay. Gee, what a great deal . . . for the law firm. Not only is it exploitative, such "intern" arrangements most likely violate federal labor law. According to the U.S. Department of Labor, "if the interns are engaged in the operations of the employer or are performing productive work . . ., then the fact that they may be receiving some benefits in the form of a new skill or improved work habits will not exclude them from" being classified as employees subject to the minimum wage and overtime requirements of federal law.[182]

---

[182]   U.S. Dep't of Labor Wage & Hour Div., Fact Sheet #71: Internship Programs Under the Fair Labor Standards Act (2010).

If you have the resources (don't do it on borrowed money), consider a summer abroad program. Law schools sponsor summer abroad programs in every corner of the world. I've never had a student attend one who didn't come back reporting that it was a great experience.

* * *

I want to close with a reminder of why you should keep this book handy throughout the year rather than just reading it before law school and setting it aside. A student, one of my favorites, who worked very hard the first semester but did not get the grades she hoped for, sent me this message shortly after the start of her second semester:

> I just read the chapter on the second semester and it was just what I needed to read. My grades are not where I want them, and I am not one of those people who complain about *B*s, if you know what I mean. I was gravely disappointed, but I own those grades 100 percent. The chapter was particularly helpful in encouraging me not to waste energy on past grades about which I can do nothing and to focus on this semester—something I do have control over. It really captured the emotions I wasn't expecting to feel when I started this journey, but every good journey requires overcoming adversity to get what you want, right?

Good for her! She wrote me again at the end of the year to report that her Torts grade increased from a C− to a B, a four-step boost. Nice! Be sure to come back and reread this chapter after the first semester.

CHAPTER 22

"NIGHT" AND OTHER NONTRADITIONAL STUDENTS

Too often overlooked in law school prep books are nontraditional students, especially those dwellers of the night. Most law students attend law school full-time during the day and graduate in three years, but about 13 percent[183] of law students are enrolled in one of the nation's seventy-nine ABA-accredited part-time evening-division programs and graduate in four years.[184]

This chapter focuses on these "night students," as we'll call them for convenience, but a good portion of it applies to all nontraditional law students, full- or part-time, day or night. "Nontraditional student" can carry different meanings, but it's used here to describe students who are older and have not followed a direct route from college to law school. Most day students are "traditional" students in their early twenties. Most night students—the largest subset of nontraditional students—are significantly older. The 2016 Law School Survey of Student Engagement found that 52 percent of part-time student respondents were over the age of thirty compared to 15 percent of full-time students.[185]

Night law students face the same rigors as day students, but with some huge extra challenges thrown in. They take the same curriculum taught by the same professors. They use the same casebooks, read the same cases, and do the same legal research and writing assignments as the day students. The only difference is they take fewer credit hours per semester, 10–11 hours compared to 15–16. Their classes typically are held three or four nights a week, three or four hours per night.

---

[183] Robert Morse, *Methodology: 2017 Best Part-Time Law Programs Rankings*, U.S. NEWS & WORLD REP. (Mar. 15, 2016) (reporting that in fall 2015, about 13% of the 113,394 J.D. students were enrolled part-time).

[184] *Id.* Some part-time programs offer classes on weekends. In addition to formal part-time programs, approximately 4 percent of day students have part-time status.

[185] 2016 LAW SCH. SURVEY OF STUDENT ENGAGEMENT, *supra*.

Some part-time, evening students start law school concerned they will get a lesser legal education because it's "night school." Not true at all. The 2016 Law School Survey of Student Engagement found that part-time students were just as satisfied with their legal education as full-time students.[186]

Contrary to what you might guess, classroom experiences at night are usually more energized and exciting than day classes. A primary reason is that, unlike many traditional students, night students, being older, are less afraid to express their opinions and mix it up in class discussions. They don't worry about being labeled as "gunners," as do many younger students. If they have something to say, they raise their hands and say it. This is true of nontraditional day students as well. The other reason for the high-energy level is that night students typically consume copious amounts of caffeine prior to class.

The extra challenges for night students center around the fact that, as one student put it, they are "spinning more plates in the air." Most of them work outside of law school, a majority in full-time day jobs. Because they are older, night students also are more likely than day students to have spouses and kids, which is also true of nontraditional day students.

When most day students are leaving campus for the day, night students are just arriving. Many of them have been up since the crack of dawn getting kids ready for school, rushing off to full-time jobs, then hurrying to law school. It's a grueling schedule. As one student described it: "I didn't see my house in the daylight for almost three and a half years. Getting up at 4:45 a.m. to go to work, leaving work and going straight to school, and getting home at 11:00 p.m. was brutal on my mind, body, and my wife."

Not all night students have hours that extreme, but it's an around-the-clock challenge trying to keep those plates spinning. And we haven't even mentioned the studying part yet. Oops, where is that supposed to fit in?

I've taught more than a thousand night law students at three law schools and, like many professors, have a special fondness and respect for them. They come from all walks of life:

---

[186] 2016 LAW SCH. SURVEY OF STUDENT ENGAGEMENT, *supra.*

social workers, police officers, doctors, nurses, teachers, business executives, homemakers, you name it. The life experiences they bring with them add tremendously to the classroom experience. Their ability to manage so many different roles—employee, parent, and law student—never ceases to amaze me.

For help with this chapter, I called on former night students of mine from three law schools (in Little Rock, Miami, and San Francisco) for their insights about this unique slice of legal education. Their comments, in response to survey questions, illuminate both the extra challenges faced by night students (and nontraditional students generally), but also the benefits. That's right. There are "cons" to being a night student, but there are also some significant "pros." We'll start with the cons, so we can end on an up-note.

The Ultimate Time-Bandits

The biggest obstacle faced by night law students is finding enough hours to successfully attend law school while still managing the rest of their busy lives. Night students are particularly at risk of falling behind in their studies—the law school kiss of academic death—so we'll focus on strategies for maximizing time management and efficiency.

Figure out and resolve employment conflicts in advance. Employment conflicts are the most common reason for part-time students not succeeding in law school. I've sat through countless readmissions committee meetings listening to part-time students explain how their job didn't allow enough time for them to succeed, along with their "new plan" for reducing employment hours, etc. The "new plan" needs to be worked out before you set foot in the door.

Talk to your employer. Don't try to hide that you're going to law school. Work out an arrangement that will allow you get out of work in time to get to class without having to drive like a tortfeasor before you even learn what that is. If possible, shorten your work hours. Cutting them from forty to thirty hours per week, for example, can make a big difference.

Be sure to plan ahead for exams and save your vacation days for that period. You will need blocks of time both to prepare for them and do your best when you take them. Working all day before taking a mind-numbingly complex law school exam the same night is a recipe for disaster. You need to approach each exam with a fresh, rested brain, in part because you'll be competing against other students who are not working or only working part-time.

Develop a specific scheduling plan and stick to it. Nowhere is an efficient, organized scheduling plan more important than when you're a night law student. Learn from the student below, who finished number one in her class overall, not just among the night students. It's a long comment, but I included it in full, so you could take note of and learn from the high level of specificity in her day-by-day scheduling plan:

> At our school, we were in class Monday, Tuesday, and Thursday nights when we were 1Ls. Monday night was Legal Writing and Research, and Tuesdays/Thursdays were Contracts and Torts (an hour and a half of each on each night). So dividing time was simple. I'd spend Saturday and Sunday preparing for Monday and Tuesday classes, and Wednesday preparing for Thursday's classes. Legal writing assignments were reserved mostly for Friday night and Saturdays.
>
> Here's how the breakdown worked:
>
> Monday night: Go to Legal Research and Writing. After class, skim whatever assignment we got in that class so I would know how much time I would need to devote to it over the weekend.
>
> Tuesday night: Go to Contracts and Torts.
>
> Wednesday night: Read the reading assignments for Thursday night's Contracts and Torts classes.
>
> Thursday night: Attend classes.
>
> Friday night: Meet up with a couple of friends in the library and work on the legal research assignment we were given on Monday night. (NEVER leaving the library until it was done.)
>
> Saturday morning: Outline class notes every other week. (The off-week Saturdays were my one day to sleep late.)

Saturday afternoon: Read in depth the legal writing assignment and draft whatever was required for the next Monday night's class.

Sunday afternoon and evening: Finish up the legal research assignment for Monday night and read the Contracts/Torts assignments for Tuesday night.

If Sunday's reading was light, I'd get a jump on the reading I normally did on Wednesdays, and vice versa. Friday night legal research was a must every week, as was Saturday for legal writing. Many times there was not a heavy-duty legal writing assignment, so I might have a few free hours.

If things were going on at home, I'd go to the library at school to do my reading. I carried my books with me everywhere. If I had a ten-minute break at work, I'd read. During my lunch hour, I'd read. Because I would take every free minute to get my reading assignments done for my various classes, I could usually block off Saturday evening for fun, Sunday morning for family (or church for those who attend), and Sunday evening for family time. It was tough, but doable.

Impressive! She was a student of mine long before I wrote the first edition of *1L of a Ride,* but she could have been a model for the C.R.E.D.O. chapter as applied to part-time evening students. Her most important piece of advice?

DO NOT PROCRASTINATE. I can't say that enough. When you are working full-time and raising a family and spending all your nights in class and are expected to be prepared, you simply cannot skip your reading for the week. *If you get behind, you'll never catch up.*

There's that same old song again.

"Everybody's working for the weekend."[187] Poor night law students. For them, the chorus to this eighties rock hit about anticipated weekend fun would have to be changed to "Everybody's working *on* the weekend." While many night students manage to squeeze some time for class preparation and legal writing assignments in during the week, it's not enough time to do all the work. If you can't stomach the thought of

---

[187]   *See* LOVERBOY, WORKING FOR THE WEEKEND (Columbia 1981).

sacrificing weekends for law school, reconsider your decision to attend as a part-time night student.

Asked for time-management suggestions, one night student said, "I mostly got my school work done during the weekends. You just learn that your decision to go to law school came with the additional decision to give up weekends. Those two days are the only times you can fit in school work." Another said, "I would go out either Friday or Saturday night, but I was always home at a reasonable hour so I could get an early start the next day. I would sit at home all day on Saturday and Sunday and read or write. I was never 'off' during that first year."

Steal minutes where you can. Efficient night students learn to steal time whenever and wherever they can. "I would carry my books everywhere," said one student. "If I was getting my nails done or cooking, I was reading for Torts. If I was waiting for a doctor's appointment or waiting for class, I was reading Contracts." Other students mentioned reading cases while doing the laundry, at their kids' soccer games, or on the bus.

Some jobs and employers allow students to get some studying done during the work day. Obviously, a lot depends on the flexibility of the particular job and employer. If you're working purely to earn extra money to go to law school (as opposed to working in a career-type job), look for a job that offers that kind of flexibility. One student suggested fudging workplace rules a bit: "If you have an office door, shut it and read when your boss isn't looking."

Second-Class Citizenship

Everywhere I've taught night students, they've complained about being treated as second-class citizens by the law school. The complaints are justified. For economic reasons (not to intentionally disregard night students), most services and institutional structures within law schools are set up to benefit full-time day students.

Important law school offices such as admissions, financial aid, career placement, and the registrar are staffed by 9–5 workers. Elective courses are fewer at night because it's expensive to double-up on course offerings. Courts operate during the day, which means night students are prevented from enrolling in litigation-based clinical courses, the most common type of law school legal clinic. Outside speakers brought in by student organizations or the law school usually present during the lunch hour. Law review, moot court, and other student organizations typically schedule their activities during the day, making it difficult for night students to participate. In terms of law school social activities, most are organized by day students. While many of the activities occur at night or on weekends, the day students rarely make it a point to include the night students.

No wonder night students can feel left out, unappreciated, and under-loved. As a result, an unfortunate divide can arise between night and day students, which one former night student described as follows:

> One of the hardest parts is that the law school atmosphere makes part-time night students feel like second-class citizens. When I began law school, the financial aid person went home at five. Night students get off work at five and start getting to school around five-thirty for classes that begin at six. So if we needed to do anything with financial aid, we had to try to find a way to take off work because we were *never* accommodated. Likewise, school clubs and organizations would meet at lunch during the day, effectively cutting all night students out of every social and support activity that existed. I was working a fifty-hour-a-week job when I began law school. I took my vacation from work so I could attend orientation week. I remember one particularly derisive day student cracking the comment to me, "Well, it must be nice to only take three classes when the rest of us have to take five." I replied, "Yeah, and I'd trade my fifty-plus hours a week that I work full-time for your extra two classes in a heartbeat!" All of this caused us to feel like we were never really a part of the school.

Law schools have an obligation to provide important services to their evening-division students at feasible times, and schools have made progress in that regard. If you're at a law school that's falling short in those areas, pursue the issues with the administration or Student Government Association (SGA).

Elect a SGA class representative who pledges to push for improvements.

Toll on Outside Relationships

The next chapter is devoted to issues that can arise in outside relationships due to law school, so we won't go into the matter in detail here. Read that chapter carefully. To give you a preview (hopefully not a portent) of what's to come, consider these soul-searching comments from a former night student whose marriage ended in divorce:

> I was only married a year before I started law school and neither one of us was prepared for the toll it would take on the relationship. We got into bad habits and we got into them quickly because law school can overwhelm you from the start. Communication with my spouse devolved into a sort of short-hand speak (to save time, of course), which only led to miscommunication and one misunderstanding after another. Plus, my spouse felt constant rejection as she went to bed alone practically every night—leading to her understandable resentment.

> On the other side of the coin, I felt pressure from all sides (work/school/marriage/her family/my family). More often than not, my feelings of resentment came from feeling under-appreciated. I remember feeling guilty for going to law school, and being angry about feeling guilty. Dealing with the competing forces in my life was draining and I didn't have the tools at the time (and neither did she) to actually give a voice to the concerns so we could deal with them together.

He went on to explain that he and his wife grew further apart until divorce resulted, and identified poor communication as the main culprit. Take heed of his closing remarks: "Part of the artistry of being an effective attorney is being a good communicator. Start now and start at home."

Older but Wiser

Time for some good news. While nontraditional law students face special challenges, they also enjoy some unique benefits. Too many fresh-out-of-college students go to law school for the wrong or uninspired reasons. Older students tend to be there because they really *want* to be there. Sometimes they seek a law degree to further an existing career, but many have simply worked in other fields, figured out what they don't like, and made an informed decision that they'd rather be lawyers. Motivation is a powerful force.

As one student who started law school at age forty explained:

> I think I had a much more serious perspective on things than many of the day students. Oh, I played as hard as they did, but my play time took up much less time than theirs because the rest of my time was filled with family, work, and school. My experience gave me focus that I would not have had when I was in my early 20s. It also gave me a wider world view, which helped me see more facets of the issues we were covering in our classes.

A related advantage of being an older student is that most nontraditional students don't have either the time or inclination to engage in nonstop law school talk, obsess about grades and class rank, or become enmeshed in law school drama or the social scene. One former night student commented, "Having been out of school for ten years, I had sowed my wild oats and partied while in undergrad and grad school, so I was ready to settle down and study (for the most part!) in law school."

Easier Relationships with Professors

This point had not occurred to me, but that's why I ask students for help. It surprised me that several former students commented on the unique nature of relationships between night students and their professors. More than one student said that professors seem to go a bit "easier" on night students, as in this comment responding to a question about the pros and cons of being a part-time student:

> PRO: Some professors will cut you more slack in class and respect you more for taking on such a heavy load. (Ex.: PROFESSOR: Ms. Smith, what were the facts in *Blank v. Blank*? ME: I'm sorry, professor, but I didn't get that far in the reading. PROFESSOR: It's the first case. ME: I know.)

There's probably some truth to her observation, but don't think that night students get a free pass. While law professors do respect and are sympathetic to the plight of night students, most hold them to the same high standards as day students. I mentioned earlier that I expect students to be on time. When they aren't, I give them "the evil eye" or call them out as a deterrent.

While teaching a night Torts course at the Florida International University College of Law, a student walked into class late. He was a busy surgeon and medical school professor, but I treat everyone the same. I stopped class and said, "Dr. Bailey, you're late." "I'm sorry," he said sincerely. "I was in the middle of a kidney transplant operation and couldn't get out in time." Whoa, what's the comeback to that? I said something like, "Well, alright then . . . but don't let it happen again." And we all had a good laugh. Dr. Bailey and I went on to become friends and co-author a chapter in a medical textbook.

Another student commented that night students know that if they get called on once, "they may be able to slack," but added "unless they were lucky enough to take McClurg and get to *Palsgraf v. Long Island Railroad* and get grilled for two days." Perhaps the moral of these stories is "Avoid McClurg!"

No, the real moral is that night law students usually are held to the same high standards as day students, so prepare yourself. If you enter an evening-division law school program thinking it will be like an M.B.A. or other graduate school night program, you will be in for a rude awakening.

One interesting professor/student dynamic is that, because they tend to be older, many with successful careers, night students aren't afraid of their professors. As one student observed:

> I think older students can talk to the professors more easily because it's easier to see them as contemporaries. I remember a day student having an issue about a class, but she was reluctant to approach the professor. She couldn't see the professor as just another person in the world, one that would want to help her succeed. Older students just aren't as fearful of professors.

Professors recognize this "more equal footing" aspect as well, as noted by this student's comment: "I was only twenty-three when I started and quickly realized that the older students in my night classes had a lot more insights into a lot more topics. The professors seemed to realize this too. The jerky professors didn't seem to be nearly as jerky to the older students."

More Collaborative

All 1L classes form close bonds and make deep friendships, but night students have a unique bond. It's not that their friendships are better or deeper than friendships among day students, just different. A plausible explanation is their shared circumstance of being in survival mode the entire time in law school.

Night students work hard to achieve academically, but are less competitive than day students and more likely to adopt a collaborative, less clique-ish approach to their studies. One student described how she and her night comrades would work together in the library every Friday night on their legal research assignments before heading to the local pub to wind down. "No man was left behind," she said. "No one enjoyed their beer until everyone could enjoy their beer."

Other than time-management issues, comments about bonding with classmates dominated the answers of the former night students I surveyed. The below comment sums up the sentiments expressed by several students:

It seemed to me that the younger/day students had a certain "me-centric" approach. This was in contrast to the older students. I never had a problem obtaining notes or assistance from a classmate. It was as if we were all in the hull of a ship—a dark, dimly lit ship littered with delivery pizza boxes and empty coffee cups—all rowing in essentially the same direction, and all dependent upon each other. While we were weighed down by our common familial and personal sacrifices, we also had the bond of understanding those sacrifices in a way no one else could appreciate.

A Parting Note to Nontraditional Day Students

While this chapter has focused on night students, nontraditional day students face some of the same hurdles, plus an added one. Some older day students have told me it's difficult for them to integrate socially with their younger classmates.

One student asked me for suggestions on how to make friends with his younger classmates. It broke my heart when he explained that he, a non-smoker, had taken to hanging out in front of the law school building where the smokers indulge their habit in the hope that some of them would talk to him.

If you're an older day student, the extent of your social and other relations with your younger classmates will depend a lot on you and your personality. Compare the above student to this happy fifty-five-year-old day student who managed to seamlessly merge with the "kids" in her class:

> At fifty-five, I was the oldest person in my graduating class, but, as the saying goes, you're as young as you feel. I think that having a young attitude together with a sense of humor about my age helped a lot. I jokingly referred to myself as "the old lady." I respected the young students and treated them as peers and they responded similarly. It may have helped that some of my interests were in sync with some of theirs. They were particularly impressed that I love to home-brew beer—an essential food group, of course, for law students. At the same time, there were occasions they seemed to welcome having a classmate who could impart some nonjudgmental, no strings-attached "motherly advice." Those very few students who were dismissive toward me acted stuck up toward others as well. The vast majority of my classmates were friendly and accepting. Like any other law school peers, we discussed school and exchanged outlines and notes, and supported each other in the extremely stressful law school environment. Some of the young students invited me to their parties, and I went, and we all had fun! I came to dearly love some of those "youngsters," and we remain close friends today.

Making friends in law school, as discussed early on, is easy because everyone is living the same life: same classes, same professors, same fears, same workload, etc. But it's understandable young adults in their early twenties might not know how to interact with substantially older classmates. You may be the one who has to take the initiative to establish contact.

* * *

In sum, the main challenge for nontraditional students juggling jobs, family, and law school is that there are only 86,400 seconds in a day. You'll need to efficiently use all of them. If I had to rank the C.R.E.D.O. factors for night students, I might put *Efficient* and *Organized* on top. Your key to success will be not only working hard, but maximizing your input (effort and time) to output ratio. To accomplish this will require a highly organized schedule. Look again at the detailed weekly study plan quoted earlier, from the night student who graduated number one in the entire law school. Don't let yourself fall behind.

CHAPTER 23

LAW SCHOOL AND OUTSIDE RELATIONSHIPS

Law school can take a toll on outside relationships, one reason most law schools offer special sessions during orientation for married students or students with families. It is commonly said that law students suffer higher divorce rates than the rest of the population, although no data exist to support that assertion. But even if law school doesn't kill outside relationships, there's no question it can add stress and conflict to them. Several factors contribute:

- Law schools train students to be argumentative and analytical with the result that even well-meaning students may approach relationships in off-putting ways.

- Law students can wear down the people around them with nonstop talk about the law and law school.

- The workload and all-consuming nature of legal education can cause students to neglect loved ones.

- The close relationships law students develop with each other in a world only they understand can leave non-students feeling excluded and sometimes jealous.

- The stress of law school can spill over into outside relationships, causing friction.

- The time demands of law school may cause students to not uphold their share of household responsibilities, including childcare.

- The high cost of legal education combined with the fact that the student is not generating income can cause money issues.

This chapter looks briefly at each of these potential relationship disrupters so that you and your loved ones can recognize them in the event they come creeping into your lives. The chapter includes perspectives from both law students and their partners, collected via surveys conducted at three law schools. Although the comments focus on partner relationships, most of what is said below applies to all close family and friendship relationships.

Symmetrical Versus Asymmetrical Relationships

First, some good news for readers whose partner is or will also be a graduate student. Research shows that graduate students in "symmetrical" relationships have an easier time than students in "asymmetrical" relationships. As used by family relationship researchers, symmetrical relationships are relationships in which both partners are in graduate school; asymmetrical relationships are those where only one partner is in graduate school.

Several studies have found that students in symmetrical relationships have better quality marriages. In one study, graduate student couples scored higher on marital satisfaction tests.[188] Another study found that relationships in which both spouses were enrolled as college students "ranked significantly higher in quality of marriage than couples in which only one spouse was enrolled."[189] Another researcher found that graduate students in symmetrical relationships are more stable and satisfied with the relationships, while those in asymmetrical relationships "tend to be more volatile, conflictual, and dissatisfied."[190]

What accounts for the difference? Partners in symmetrical relationships are more likely to share the same goals, interests, and lifestyles, all of which makes them more compatible.[191] Importantly, they *understand* each other better. They understand the academic pressures of exams and deadlines, erratic schedules, late-night studying, and other hallmarks of being a graduate student. Both partners are excited about what

---

[188]   Rebecca Groves Brannock et al., *The Impact of Doctoral Study on Marital Satisfaction*, 3 J.C. COUNSELING 123, 127 (2000).

[189]   Gerald R. Bergen & M. Betsy Bergen, *Quality of Marriage of University Students in Relation to Sources of Financial Support and Demographic Characteristics*, 27 FAM. COORDINATOR 245, 248 (1978).

[190]   Michele Scheinkman, *Graduate Student Marriages: An Organizational/ Interactional View*, 27 FAM. PROCESS 351, 355 (1988).

[191]   *See id.*

they're doing and working toward. They are more likely to be on equal footing, both intellectually and financially. It's easier being dirt-poor when you're struggling together toward similar objectives.

Not so with many asymmetrical relationships. While the graduate student is soaring through an adventure filled with intellectual stimulation and dreams of better days, the non-student may be grinding away at a nine-to-five job—often an unfulfilling one—to support both of them. Whereas grad students need to spend much of their nights and weekends with noses in books or eyes locked on computer screens, non-students, like other normal human beings, want to get out and do things. When the non-student says "Let's PAR-TAY!" they don't want to hear back, "Sorry, have to STU-DAY!" Asymmetrical relationships also may be marked by feelings of inequality that can be manifested at several levels: in finances, educational attainment, and household responsibilities.[192]

Sources of Law School Relationship Conflict

Even for law students in symmetrical relationships, law school relationship experiences are no walk on the beach. Let's examine some major sources of potential conflict in relationships with law students.

Law students become overly argumentative and analytical.

Law school will literally train you to argue. Court cases are set for "argument." Not discussion, consideration, or presentation, but argument. In the U.S. Supreme Court, the proceedings in every case begin with the Chief Justice saying: "We will hear *argument* today in [case number followed by case name]."

The Socratic method requires students to argue and defend, not simply recite, their positions. Many answers to professor questions will be followed up by "Why?" Why, why, why? Every day for three years. In between being questioned in class, students will be practicing for and delivering their oral argument in the second semester of Legal Research and Writing.

---

[192]   *Id.* at 357–59.

For students who end up participating in moot court, arguing becomes the focus of their lives. One insight into the relative importance that the U.S. legal system places on resolving disputes peaceably rather than adversarially is that only one national law student competition exists in negotiation skills compared to scores of competitions that champion argumentation skills.

Skillful arguing is one of the most valuable tools of a lawyer's trade, but it does not rank highly on lists of traits considered helpful to successful relationships. To a law student, the simplest assertion may be an invitation to a challenging response. If a mate complains, "You don't give me enough attention," a law student might reply:

> First, we must define the word "attention." Attention comes in different degrees and forms and can reasonably mean different things to different people. Let's assume A asks B for more attention. In response, B dumps a vase of water onto A's head. Would B be giving A attention? In one sense, yes, and yet the act probably would not fall within the scope of the requester's original intent. And what about "give"? Does one really give attention? "Give" suggests a conveyance and since attention is not personal or real property, it cannot be conveyed. To discuss this intelligently, we first need to clarify the operative terms.

At this point, the non-law student may simply give up and leave the room or perhaps pick up on B's idea and pour water on the law student in rebuttal.

Several students recognized that their escalating propensity for argument had infiltrated their relationships:

- After my first year of law school, I was arguing with my wife in the car. I was pretty aggressive in my arguing and she got rather upset. She said, "Is this what they teach you in law school?"

- Much to the annoyance of my wife and family, I always present the other side of issues we are talking about, whether the subject is politics, sports, or whatever. I do this even if I don't agree with the side I'm arguing. They all say all I want to do is argue.

- I will argue with members of my family about anything. If they use an incorrect term, or write something on Facebook that is wrong, I will correct them. I don't like to—no, I *won't*—let an argument go. If I lose the argument on the facts, I will argue about the terms they used when making their arguments. This is a sad development.

Even more frustrating to outsiders will be the fact that law students become *really good* at arguing, making it impossible for anyone to win a debate with them even when the student is wrong. Law students are trained to argue strong and weak positions equally well.

Be self-aware and tone down your law student-mode around non-students. To a law student, "arguing" is synonymous with "discussing," but to a non-law student, the constant questioning, clarifying, and asserting may feel like a personal attack.

Law students also tend to become overly analytical, which is a great asset in law school and also helpful in making decisions in outside life, but can, like arguing, wear out the people around them. Asked to name his biggest change in personality after one year, a student said:

> I analyze everything legally now. My friend told me he hit a deer the other day. My first question was "Was the deer in the road after you hit it?" "Yes." "Did you leave it there?" "Yes." "You had a duty to move it. You created an unreasonable risk." Last year I would have said, "Oh dang, that sucks. Did it mess up your car very much?"

Other students also recognized this change in their personalities:

- I'm sometimes unable to sufficiently enjoy what a person is saying because I have to analyze the entirety of the situation. Although I think it's good to have an analytical mind, I worry that it's going to affect my ability to truly enjoy and develop my relationships.

- I have noticed I analyze everything about everything now. My fiancé always asks if we can just watch a show or drive down the street without me analyzing every fact about what is going on.

- I often find myself thinking that people's reasoning is faulty and many times I have let them know this. Typically, this situation arises in conversations with my wife and sometimes, if not most times, I come off as a jerk.

Developing analytical skills is an asset, but being *overly* analytical is not always the best path toward leading a full, spontaneous existence. Suppose you've graduated, landed a decent job, and you and your partner are looking to buy your first house. How exciting! You come across a house you both absolutely love. But having been conditioned to overanalyze, you proceed to conduct a thorough cost-benefit analysis that includes weighing the cost against the square footage, floor plan, condition of the back fence, etc.—all worthy considerations, except they ignore what may be the most important factor of all: *You both love the house!*

Law students talk too much about the law and law school.

Law students, especially 1Ls, tend to overwhelm everyone around them by insisting on talking constantly about the law and law school. *Anything* can trigger a law-related response from a law student. If a partner says, "Honey, hold my hand," the student may respond: "Hand! Good old Judge Learned Hand. Now there was a great judge. Have I told you about the famous opinion he wrote in this case where a barge broke free and . . ."[193]

Think I'm exaggerating? Check out the below comment, which made me laugh out loud, from a 1L explaining what she likes to talk about to her boyfriend:

Recently, my boyfriend and I went to a wedding. It was very liturgical and the priest went on forever about promises. So naturally I started thinking enforceable promises—that is, contracts. I perked up in the ceremony and started listening

---

[193]   In *U.S. v. Carroll Towing Co.*, 159 F.2d 169 (2d Cir. 1947), a case you'll study in first-year Torts, Judge Learned Hand set forth a famous algebraic economic cost-benefit formula for determining whether injury-causing conduct was negligent. The formula is $B < P \times L$. B stands for the burden of avoiding a risk of harm, P is the probability that the risk will actually cause harm, and L stands for the severity of the harm if it occurs. If the burden of avoiding the risk is less than the probability of the harm multiplied by the severity of the potential harm, the conduct is unreasonable (i.e., negligent). Conversely, if the burden of avoiding the risk outweighs the probability times the severity of harm, the conduct is reasonable (i.e., non-negligent).

very intently and my boyfriend was sitting there wondering why I was so interested (like most men, he was probably quaking in his boots that I was expecting to catch the bouquet). Seconds after the ceremony was over, I busted out with, "It's a contract! There was offer, acceptance, and the rings are consideration!"

Sometimes I tell him "what I know" but I don't tell him the rule or anything. I guess I do this just to make him realize I really am learning a lot here. Like, for example, we passed a cat that was in the middle of the median on a country highway, fixing to catch a mouse. I told him I could tell him who the cat belongs to, even though it was a stray (law of capture, rules about wild animals on state property). Once I tickled him and he told me to stop, and I kept going and told him, "You know, this is a battery. I'm battering you right now." I also told him about the rules of engagement rings if an affianced pair of our friends happened to call it off before the wedding. I wore his robe and told him I was "trespassing on his chattels," and explained that if I took it home with me, it would be a conversion. Torts actually comes up a lot. But, come to think of it, I really don't tell him anything from Civil Procedure.

Poor bloke. I picture him shaking his head thinking, "Why couldn't she have gone to med school instead?"

While it's great to be excited about learning the law, keep in mind that the non-law students around you aren't going to share that same excitement. Put the shoe on the other foot. Imagine your partner enrolled in a Ph.D. program studying a subject completely foreign to you, say, genetics. Every night after school, your partner waxes rapturously for hours about mitochondrial DNA and hematopoietic stem cells. When you go out with your partner's new classmates, instead of sports, music, or politics, the conversation turns immediately to homologous recombination and dishing about classmates and professors you don't know. How would you feel? Left out? Unimportant?

Moderate your conversations about the law and law school and focus on the good stuff. Generally speaking, subjects like the margin and font requirements for your legal writing memo do not command rapt attention. On the other hand, many loved ones do find unusual cases and legal rules to be interesting. Just be sure to give listeners a context for what you're talking about. As one significant other to a law student explained:

> I find any topic involving law school interesting if it is discussed in a manner courteous to those who are not in law school and who are unfamiliar with law school lingo. Law students love to talk about law school even around those who do not understand words and concepts usually only used in law school. To make law school interesting to non-students, you have to actually consider those not in law school. This is the step most commonly skipped.

Law students can be neglectful.

No one in a relationship wants to feel like they rank anywhere except first in the heart, mind, and soul of their loved one. Unfortunately, a variety of factors can combine to leave the loved ones of law students feeling neglected.

Neglect due to time demands. The time demands of law school can be a major source of discontent and disruption in relationships. One researcher of graduate student marriages observed that "[o]ver time, the graduate student's studies become like a lover to whom the student is totally devoted."[194] That made me laugh because of a comment I received from one of my first-year students at the University of Memphis Cecil C. Humphreys School of Law. "My husband has asked me on numerous occasions if I am having an affair with someone, namely Cecil C. Humphreys." Here's what some other law students said about how the time demands of law school impacted their relationships:

- Lack of time spent together is the biggest problem, especially when I am at home but not really "there" because I'm doing homework. There have been times, such as studying for finals, that my wife hates my computer because I spend more time with it than with her.

- She'd try to draw me away, and though I wanted to, I just had so much to do, the breaks would be short—to eat dinner or talk for a bit. I know this bothered her.

---

[194]   Scheinkman, *supra*, at 359–60.

- Because my wife is the breadwinner and I am the student, I think we both felt going in that I would have more time, both practically and emotionally, to be available to help with our then infant daughter. She has regularly told our friends that she dreads my return to school after vacations, because I "disappear." Ironically, I have always felt like I could have invested so much more in law school and have held back because of my commitments at home.

- I was in a long-distance relationship that did not survive beyond the winter break. We made it through the first semester, but my significant other was often hurt by the lack of time to talk on the phone, which was our only means of interacting. We only saw each other twice during the fall semester. We talked on the phone briefly each day and at night—but there never seemed to be enough time to truly nurture the relationship. The emotional and mental tug I felt from the relationship began to be too much.

Neglect due to preoccupation with law school. A common complaint is that even when law students are physically present, they're mentally absent, preoccupied by law school. An anecdote from a law student recorded by researchers studying the effect of law school on marital relationships offers an amusing snapshot of the problem. The student was describing her thought process on occasions when her husband attempted to be amorous:

> There are times on a Saturday or something, he'll try to be all romantic. He'll come to my office, I'm studying, he'll put his arms around me and he'll be like would you come with me? Let's go to bed. And I have had days where, honestly and this is like kinda sick, . . . I'm just like wondering how fast we can do this because I have reading to do. . . . I'm like, "oh my god ok, we gotta make this quick because I have this and this to do." My husband is trying to be romantic and I'm thinking about torts.[195]

---

[195]   Deanna Boyd McQuillan & Carrie Elizabeth Foote, *Law School and Marriage: Making It Work*, 42 MARRIAGE & FAM. REV. 7, 17 (2008).

Neglect due to exhaustion/lack of energy. Another cause of neglect is that law students simply get worn out physically and mentally from the workload, leaving them with insufficient energy to give to their outside relationships. Two students, one female and one male, respectively, explain:

- Law school was a big adjustment in my marriage. Although my husband is extremely supportive, he would get frustrated with me and school at times. Usually it would happen when I continued to break our "date night" because I wanted to sit at home and watch TV or sleep when I had free time. Law school is very draining because of all of the attention to detail and stress students are under to properly prepare for class. So when I had free time, I did not want to do anything except be alone and not think about anything.

- Oftentimes when I get home I'm tired from a day of waking up early and stretching my brain to the breaking point. After my reading for the night is done, I usually just want to watch a mindless television show or stare at the wall for a few minutes. My wife, on the other hand, loves going outside and doing involved activities. Occasionally she gets frustrated because I'm boring and don't have the drive to do anything fun. I'm not boring! I'm just burned out!

It's essential to carve out time away from law school, not only for your own well-being, but for the sanity of those around you. For couples, a common strategy is to reserve "date nights." But review your schedule carefully in advance to ensure you won't have to back out. Relationship research shows that scheduling and then cancelling date nights is worse than never scheduling them in the first place because it breeds anger and resentment.

I polled significant others of law students as to ways they managed to "get away from law school" with their student. They replied with a long list of great ideas, everything from go-carting to let off steam to "no computer days" to spending a night in a nearby hotel as a type of fantasy vacation. Most of their strategies did not involve or require expensive or excitement-filled vacations or other excursions. Often the simplest pleasures of together-time are the most fulfilling.

Time for loved ones *is* available if you're efficient and organized.

Law school can cause jealousy.

Subsumed within feelings of neglect can be feelings of jealousy arising from the fact that law students spend so much time absorbed in law school and with their new law school friends. This jealousy can assume the form of "priority jealousy," where a partner feels they've been supplanted in the hierarchy of importance in the other's life and/or "exclusivity jealousy," where a partner worries that the other is acting in ways that violate the exclusive compact of a romantic relationship.[196]

Priority jealousy can arise from both the student's fixation on law school itself and the close bonding that occurs among law students. Partners may resent being made to take a backseat to law school and the student's new circle of friends. As one student wrote: "Jealousy is a problem. Spending so much time with students and books, and talking about them to loved ones, may lead the loved one to think that your highest priority is not your relationship but law school and law buddies."

Exclusivity jealousy, also called "romantic jealousy," arises from a concern that the student is engaging in behavior that threatens the exclusivity of an intimate relationship. It doesn't have to involve any kind of physical contact, although that may be part of the underlying fear. It includes any behavior that violates the partner's understanding of his or her exclusive relationship rights, for lack of a better term, such as sharing personal information or going to lunch together.[197]

As an example, a student came to me asking for advice on how to handle a situation where his serious girlfriend was extremely jealous that he had begun studying with a female classmate. The girlfriend insisted he stop studying with her and he didn't know what to do. He insisted the study arrangement

---

[196] Padmal De Silva, *Jealousy in Couple Relationships: Nature, Assessment and Therapy*, 35 BEHAV. RES. & THERAPY 973, 975 (1997) (describing these two types of jealousy).

[197] *Id.*

was innocent and that he loved his girlfriend. Of course, I didn't try to tell him what to do, but I did point out that sometimes we have to do things that are important to our partners even if they seem unreasonable to us.

One point that stood out clearly from the student comments was that jealousy and feelings of neglect are much less of an issue for students who incorporate their partners into their new law school social lives. Several comments paralleled this one: "My partner only expressed jealous feelings toward the beginning of the program when I was hanging out with new friends without him. Once he met my new friends and began attending law school social events with me, most of the jealous feelings seemed to drop off."

From this, we can derive an important piece of advice in maintaining outside relationships: Get your loved ones involved in your law school experience. Introduce them to your new law school friends early on and invite them to law school social events. Invite them to sit in on a class with you, so they can see what it's all about.

Law school stress spills over into relationships.

Researchers have long studied the "spillover effect" of work demands and pressures on non-work relationships. As the name suggests, the spillover theory posits that negative aspects of work, including stress, are often brought home by the worker and can affect the worker's family. No big surprise there. While some are better at compartmentalizing than others, it's difficult to separate major portions of our lives and store them in neatly segregated boxes.

The spillover effect of stress from law school is real, as shown by these student comments:

- Like, right now I'm at about a seven on the stress scale. I overreact to small stimuli, like the other day my boyfriend made a maneuver in a game we played that virtually clinched that I would lose, and I started crying and told him we never played with that rule before, which is unlike me. I'm usually a good sport.

- Fights have stemmed from everything from "Are there any pretty girls in your class?" to "Is your memo more important than this relationship?" I'm, of course, not always innocent either. I remember losing it one night after a long week of classes when I had a light homework load and fell asleep on the couch watching TV. About fifteen minutes later my girlfriend came in and woke me up because she was bored and wanted to go do something. I wasn't happy about being woken up so I started yelling. We fought for about an hour.

- In general, I am on a very short fuse now, so a comment or suggestion that I would otherwise consider with a grain of salt can set me off or piss me off. There have been two instances where my emotional intelligence decreased to that of a shrieking three-year-old and a normal conversation with my boyfriend turned into an outlandish fight. I transformed from a normal person into a scary, scary beast.

In Chapter 20, we discussed strategies for lowering stress, maintaining well-being, and leading a balanced life. To borrow a legal term, your close friends and other loved ones will be third-party beneficiaries of your following those strategies.

Law students may ignore their fair share of household responsibilities.

One of the most dramatic changes in role expectations, and a frequent source of conflict in relationships with law students, concerns the fair division of household responsibilities. In my surveys, this issue was raised almost exclusively by women law students. Their comments included:

- Yes, law school has caused conflict. I feel like I need more help around the house and with general household matters. Prior to school I took care of everything, worked full time, and cooked dinner every night. Now, I still feel pressure to take care of the house, but I don't have the time or energy. I definitely am stressed and I am trying to remember that I chose to do this.

- He mentioned that the house is a big mess and I haven't cooked in months. This made me feel really guilty. Then I got over it and went back to studying. Seriously, my priorities have shifted dramatically. Things that I used to take care of for my family have fallen to my spouse now.

- Stress has primarily come up for us in terms of household expectations. I feel like my husband should just *know* how stressed I am or what a hard day I had. But he *doesn't*. We have had all kinds of spats when I get home from twelve hours of studying and the dogs need a walk or the dishes need to be washed, and I expect him to just take care of it all. Communication is key. It's not fair for him to think that I will have the energy to do household chores at the end of the day, but it's not fair for me to expect that he will just take care of it all himself, despite his full-time job.

In her groundbreaking book, *The Second Shift*, first published in 1989, Arlie Hochschild documented the inequalities in the distribution of household responsibilities between working men and women. The book's title referred to the fact that many women in dual-career couples come home from a long day at work only to begin their second job: taking care of the household and family. With regard to higher education students, studies show that women students traditionally have experienced greater role conflict in this regard than men. Instead of adjusting or shifting their existing roles when they become students, some women attempt to simply add their new role as student on top of their other roles as worker, parent, and spouse, and attempt to perform all of them at the same high level; i.e., the "supermom."[198]

No research exists specific to law students, but whether you are a male or female student, if division of household labor is or becomes an issue in your relationships, the obvious solution is to discuss it and have each party agree to bear his or her fair share of the load. Of course, concurring on the definition of "fair share" can be a sticking point, in part because of what I call the "Who Has It Worse?" syndrome, a situation in which both the law student and the gainfully employed partner each think the other has the easier life.

---

[198] Patricia A.H. Dyk, *Graduate Student Management of Family and Academic Roles*, 36 FAM. REL. 329, 329 (1987) (discussing relevant studies).

Particularly in the first year, students are so wrapped up in the workload and suffocated by the pressures that they can't imagine anything being worse. Meanwhile, non-law students who spend their days "workin' for a living" may have little sympathy for someone whose major life responsibility is simply attending "school." These opposing perceptions may cause both parties to end up stuck in competing thought processes like the following (which I made up):

Non-law student during the day: "Great. She's out sipping a caramel macchiato with her 'study group' while I have to work all day on these stupid reports!"

Law student during the evening: "Nice. He's on the couch with a beer playing video games while I have to work all night on this stupid memo!"

As with most difficult issues in relationships, both sides have valid points. To some extent, law school is a better, easier life than a full-time job, mainly because law students have flexible schedules and more free time during the day than most full-time workers. They also get lengthy breaks between semesters. On the other hand, unlike most employees, a law student's work day doesn't end at 5 or 6 p.m. For many, the hardest parts of the day—reading and briefing cases, outlining, working on their memos—are just starting. For most students, this carries over to weekends and even holidays. And while some jobs are stressful and exhausting, many aren't. They may be boring and unfulfilling, but they aren't necessarily stressful or exhausting. Law students suffer abundant doses of both stress and exhaustion.

If you live with an intimate partner or with your family, the division of household responsibilities is an issue that should be thought about and discussed *prior* to law school, recognizing that everyone will have to be flexible in implementing the plan and making adjustments as events unfold.

Law student debt and lack of revenue can cause financial conflict.

Research shows that money is the most common issue about which couples fight. Particularly relevant to law students and their partners, several studies have found that debt brought into a marriage can be a thorn in the union, and that worries about debt are linked to negative emotional outcomes, such as depression, for young couples.[199] One study of married college students found that couples with minor debt have much higher quality of marriage scores than couples who depend heavily on student loans for income.[200]

As one wife of a law student complained: "Law school is expensive. I really don't want his debt. I get mad because he is in law school and he jokes around saying things like, 'I want to be an importer-exporter.' Well, that is just great because you are in law school wasting away money and causing us financial strain."

This is all the more reason to pay attention to the advice in Chapters 2 and 20: develop a financial plan before arriving at law school and remain dedicated to doing everything possible to minimize your expenditures to keep your loan debt as low as possible.

* * *

When it comes to your outside relationships, here's the bottom line as summed up by a 2L: "Something I wish my family understood is that no matter how much they think they understand about everything I'm doing/going through, *they do not understand!*" Non-law students will never be able to fully understand law students or their lives, but you can educate them and head off problems by reading and discussing this chapter together.

Even better, get them a copy of *The "Companion Text" to Law School: Understanding and Surviving Life with a Law Student* (2012). And you're thinking, "Well, duh, of course you would recommend your own book, McClurg. How convenient." But while dozens of books have been written to prepare students for law school, *The "Companion Text" to Law School* is the only book devoted to preparing students' loved ones.

---

[199] *Id.* (discussing studies).

[200] Bergen & Bergen, *supra*, at 250.

CHAPTER 24

LAW REVIEW, MOOT COURT, AND OTHER EXTRACURRICULAR ACTIVITIES

Your course work will consume most of your time, but a variety of co-curricular and extracurricular activities also take place in law schools. The activities are voluntary, yet some of them require the dedication of hundreds of hours of labor.

Wait! Don't flip ahead yet. While seeing "voluntary" and "hundreds of hours of labor" in the same sentence might seem like an excellent reason to skip this chapter, you'll be amazed by the large percentage of students who actively pursue these extensive extra commitments. Why do they do it? Because, depending on the activity, they allow students to enhance their lawyering skills, enrich their law school experience, find and create a distinct law school identity for themselves, give back to the community, meet and spend time with like-minded students, develop mentoring relationships with faculty, network with lawyers and judges, and, importantly, bolster their resume credentials.

In this chapter, we'll review the most important and common co- and extracurricular activities. Before proceeding, however, remember my warning way back in Chapter 6 about the dangers of overcommitting to extra activities *as a 1L*. Many activities discussed in this chapter are only available to students who have completed their first year, but not all of them.

Law Review

The most reliable career enhancer among extra activities is serving on the law review. Almost every law school publishes a "law review," a student-run, student-edited journal of scholarly legal articles written primarily by law professors, but also by judges, lawyers, and students. The first student-run law review emerged in the late 1800s.

419

Law reviews typically publish four to six issues per year, with each issue containing a few primary articles by outside authors and a few works written by student members of the law review. Some law review articles become influential in the development of the law, while many others are read only by the authors and a few close relatives.

"Making law review" has long been a signature mark of law school academic success, second only to class rank. Often, the two credentials correlate as most top-performing students do indeed participate in law review. Traditionally, this was necessarily the case because the only students invited to participate on law review were those with high class ranks.

Today, most law reviews select members through a summer "write-on competition" at the conclusion of the first year. At some schools, any student can participate in the write-on competition, but many schools impose a minimum GPA requirement to participate. Some law reviews use a dual system combining automatic grade-on qualifiers and write-on participants.

Write-on competition details vary, but they typically include a time-limited writing assignment over a period of days, such as an analysis of a recent case, accompanied by a test on *Bluebook* citation style. One drawback of write-on competitions is their timing. They generally begin shortly after the completion of first-year exams, deterring many qualified, but exhausted students from participating in or completing the competition.

If you have the GPA necessary to qualify, I urge you to participate in the write-on competition, for the reasons discussed below. Many have been the students who have told me they regretted not giving the write-on competition a shot, or who started the competition, but fizzled out before completing it. The odds of making law review are better than students think, particularly, as explained in Chapter 3, in light of shrinking student bodies at most law schools. For example, at my current institution, twenty-six students are invited to join the law review each year out of a pool of write-on competition participants that usually numbers in the low forties. Even if you don't make law review, you'll improve your writing and Bluebooking skills by participating in the competition.

Once students are invited to join law review, they're required to successfully complete one and sometimes two major writing projects that travel under the names "casenote," "note," and "comment." A casenote is an extensive analysis of a significant recent case. Notes and comments (essentially the same thing with different labels) have a broader, topical focus. They usually are thesis-driven works in which the writer identifies a flaw or gap in the law and proposes a solution to fix it. Student law review works require in-depth research and a good deal of writing and rewriting. They average about fifty pages in length with two hundred footnotes. The best of these student works get selected for publication in the law review.

In addition to the writing requirements, staff members are required to do painstaking "cite-checking" of articles that have been accepted by the law review for publication. This involves verifying the accuracy of footnote citations as to both proper *Bluebook* format and substantive content. While anything but fun, these assignments force law review students to become masters of the *Bluebook*, a valuable, but underappreciated skill.

Particularly ambitious and well-qualified students go on to become law review editors (rather than just staff members), which is considered an especially high honor. The editor-in-chief of the law review occupies a law school status equivalent to being the captain of a starship. Each year the current board of editors selects, through an application process, the editors for the next year.

Unlike academic journals in other disciplines, which are often peer-reviewed, law reviews are student-run, much to the chagrin of law professors, who submit the bulk of article manuscripts for publication consideration. In the ultimate role reversal, students accustomed to being lorded over by law professors in every aspect of their student existence suddenly have the upper-hand as professors from around the country—desperate to publish lest they perish—come begging to have their articles published. It's pretty hilarious.

Making matters even more topsy-turvy, once an article is accepted for publication, the students edit it. So now we have law students who only recently exited their first-year legal writing courses telling professors how to write. Classic. On the other hand, a lot of student law review editors prove to be much better researchers and writers than some of the professors and lawyers submitting articles.

Other than the devilish pleasure of telling law professors what do to, what does law review have to offer students other than a lot of hard work? Several things. Students earn credit hours for law review. Many schools give scholarship stipends to editors, at least to the senior editors. Also, pursuant to an ABA-accreditation rule, all upper-level students must complete one substantial writing project as a graduation requirement and law review notes usually satisfy that requirement. Law review also helps members advance their skills as legal researchers and writers. As mentioned, some students get their works published in the law review. Needless to say, graduating law school as a published legal scholar is a heady accomplishment. Additionally, members of the law review, especially the editorial board, enjoy a great deal of comradery.

You may be thinking, "Yeah, I guess that stuff sounds okay, but I still can't see how it justifies voluntarily taking on hundreds of hours of extra work." That's because we haven't addressed the largest practical benefit of law review yet, which is being able to write "Law Review" on your resume.

While it might not be quite the great job-guarantor it once was, law review status still operates as a kind of VIP-admission into the world of legal employment. I used to live and teach in Miami, home of many popular nightclubs in famous South Beach. At the trendy clubs, long lines form behind a rope each night and bouncers at the door pick and choose who gets to come inside. As my students explained it to me, the only ones invited past the rope are the "beautiful people." Being on law review makes you one of the beautiful people in the legal job market.

While not always accurate, many employers use law review membership as a litmus test for evaluating legal talent. Some law firms, especially large ones, won't interview students who were not on law review. The same is true of most federal judges and many state judges when they look to hire judicial law clerks. Being on law review helped me obtain all three of my major legal jobs: judicial law clerk, litigation associate, and law professor.

Didn't qualify for or participate in the law review write-on competition? All is not lost. Far from it. One of the most unusual developments in scholarly legal publishing during the past couple of decades has been the explosion of law school "secondary journals" (so called because they are considered "secondary" to the primary law review), also called "specialty journals." American law schools now publish a staggering 720 specialty law journals,[201] a remarkable increase from the already high 400 counted in the previous edition of *1L of a Ride*. Large, elite schools may have ten or more specialty journals. Small schools may have one or none.

Specialty journals are usually much easier to gain membership to than the law review. Fulfilling the membership requirements is also less daunting. Many specialty journals don't even impose a writing requirement on members, nor do they publish as many issues per year as law reviews. While being a member of a specialty journal is not as prestigious as being on the law review, it still carries resume weight. Moreover, if the specialty journal focuses on an area for which you have a passion, the experience might be more enjoyable and personally fulfilling. Pick a legal subject, any subject, and there's a good chance a law school is publishing a specialized journal devoted to it.

Moot Court

Not as marketable as law review, but still a good resume credential and a lot more fun and exciting, is moot court. "Moot court" is basically "mock court" in an appellate setting, as opposed to a trial setting. Like law reviews, moot court has been around in legal education for a long time, beginning at Harvard Law School in the mid-1840s.

Most law schools have a moot court program. While they vary considerably in their structures and expansiveness, the programs sometimes begin at the ground level with a first-year intramural appellate argument competition. Students who show promise or interest or both can then apply to serve on the school's

---

[201] *See Law Journals: Submissions and Rankings, 2008–2015*, WASH. & LEE U. SCH. L. (last visited Feb. 23, 2017) (listing and ranking all law reviews and secondary journals).

moot court board and moot court "travel teams" as upper-level students.

Moot court competitions, whether intramural or inter-school, operate similarly. Participants receive a package of materials containing an abbreviated appellate record of a fictitious case that is pending on appeal before a high court, often the U.S. Supreme Court. Intramural competitions usually involve teams of two. Each team argues the legal issues raised by the problem against other student teams in front of three-person panels of mock appellate judges, which might include law professors, lawyers, real judges, or law students. The problems usually raise two legal issues, enabling each student to argue one issue during the mock appellate proceeding. After each set of arguments, the panel of judges declares a winning team and that team advances to the next round.

Members of moot court travel teams, which typically include three students, participate in regional and national moot court competitions, of which there are many, against teams from other law schools. The major competitions attract teams from more than 100 schools. Teams are judged both on their written briefs and oral arguments. In big competitions, the judges may include heavyweights from the U.S. Courts of Appeal and, occasionally, even U.S. Supreme Court justices.

Like law review, moot court requires a lot of work. Before even getting to the long rounds of practice arguments leading up to a competition, each competition team must research and write a lengthy appellate brief arguing one side of the issues. In oral argument, however, students must be able to argue both sides. Thus, in round one they may argue "on brief" (i.e., taking the same positions they argued in their written brief), while in round two they may be required to switch positions and argue "off brief." In judging practice rounds, I'm always amazed by the ability of students to accomplish this complete mind-switch in just the few minutes between arguments.

Depending on the school, moot court may carry some of the same benefits as law review, such as credit hours and, for board members, scholarship stipends. Additionally, moot court develops both writing *and* oral advocacy skills. It trains students to think on their feet and work as a part of a team. Moot court accomplishments are more visible than law review. Winning or placing highly in a moot court competition will land the team prominently on the law school website and in other marketing materials.

After reading about law review and moot court, you may be wondering, as many students do, "If I have to choose between law review and moot court, which one should I pick?" It is possible to do both, although I don't recommend it. While a few remarkable students are able to pull off the double-duty without losing a step in either, most students can't do both a high level.

From this reading, the choice may seem obvious: "Hm, let's see. I could choose to spend my time writing and checking hundreds of footnotes or I could argue a case before the Supreme Court. I wonder which would be more fun." You couldn't go wrong with either choice, but if my daughter went to law school and came to me asking which activity to pursue, I wouldn't hesitate before urging her to pursue law review because of the unique emphasis placed on law review by legal employers.

Other Competitions

In addition to moot court, law schools sponsor teams in other types of skills competitions. Trial competitions are the most common type after moot court. Trial competitions generally involve two- or three-member student teams who compete against other student teams, either from the same school or other schools, in mock trial proceedings. Moot court, remember, involves appellate proceedings. Thus, instead of simply making legal arguments to judges, students examine and cross-examine witnesses, admit documentary evidence, and make opening and closing statements to juries.

Depending on your school, opportunities may also exist to participate in mock negotiation, mediation, arbitration, and client counseling competitions. The ABA sponsors national competitions in each of these areas. Negotiation competitions pit law students, acting as lawyers, against other students in attempting to resolve legal problems through negotiation, rather than adversarial legal proceedings. In arbitration and mediation competitions, student teams match up in a mock arbitration or mediation proceeding, increasingly common alternative dispute mechanisms that are less formal than traditional trials. Client counseling competitions involve students interacting with mock clients. The competitions simulate a first consultation with the client at which the student lawyers seek to extract legally relevant information related to the client's problem and analyze and discuss possible courses of action. These competitions offer several of the same rewards as moot court, although they are less prominent in law school landscapes.

The ABA and other organizations also sponsor numerous law student writing competitions in a variety of subject areas.[202] Students submit an essay with the chance to win cash prizes, free trips, and sometimes the opportunity for publication.

Before moving on, stop to take note of one similarity in every co- and extracurricular law school activity discussed thus far: every one involves a competition. And people wonder why law students are competitive. Maybe it's because we don't give them any other choice.

Student Organizations

All law schools permit students to form organizations related to particular student interests. Student organizations enable students to explore and advance legal causes and subjects about which they are passionate, while providing a social outlet and opportunity to network with like-minded people. Joining a student organization is a great way to meet people and enrich your law school experience. Especially if you feel alienated or isolated, as some students do, participating in a student organization can boost your spirits and morale.

Many students also tout the networking benefits of participating in student organizations, which can be important in a tough job climate. As this 1L explained:

> Even for 1Ls, extracurricular activities are important and give access to networking. They have given me a mentor, relationships with upper-level students, Alternative Spring Break experience, and now a clerk position on the executive board of Phi Alpha Delta. These things will hopefully

---

[202]   *See* ABA FOR LAW STUDENTS, WRITING COMPETITIONS AND LAW STUDENT CONTESTS (2015) (listing all individual and team competitions sponsored by the ABA).

distinguish me from my peers who do nothing but study, and will help me to continue to grow my networking base.

(As you know from Chapter 6, she and I differ on the issue of 1L involvement, but I want to give you the benefit of both sides.)

The range of law school student organizations is limited only by a lack of student interest in starting one and keeping it active. It only took a quick web-surfing trip through law school websites for one of my research assistants to compile a list of more than 300 different types of student organizations.[203] Turns out there's a little something for everyone. Student organizations exist for just about every political viewpoint (even anarchy), social cause, legal subject matter area, racial, ethnic, and religious group, and recreational pursuit.

Most law schools also maintain active chapters or inns of the two largest national law school fraternities: Phi Delta Phi and Phi Alpha Delta.[204] Expect to have upper-level students hitting you up to join one or both of them. While both organizations pursue both professional and social goals, Phi Delta Phi is viewed as the more academically oriented of the two, while Phi Alpha Delta is known more for its social activities. Both organizations boast impressive lists of former members, including U.S. Presidents and Supreme Court Justices. Visit their websites for more information.

One other student organization warrants special mention: student government. All law schools have a Student Government Association (SGA), sometimes called the Student Bar Association (SBA). The SGA is made up of elected officers, including a president, vice-president, treasurer, secretary, representatives from each class and, for 1Ls, each section of the first-year class. Depending on the particular officers and law school culture, your SGA may focus primarily on organizing social events or on improving academic life and the reputation of the law school, although most do some of both. When it comes time to vote for SGA officers, don't just vote for your friends, smooth talkers, or candidates who hand out free candy. Vote for

---

[203]   Speaking of surfing, one California law school even has a Surf Club.

[204]   While still usually referred to as a "legal fraternity," Phi Delta Phi converted itself to a "legal honor society" in 2012.

the folks you think will be truly committed to improving the quality of your law school and legal education.

Outside Speakers

Law schools and student organizations often bring in outside speakers, many of them prominent in their fields, to enrich the intellectual life of the school. These can be either individual speakers or groups of speakers brought in for an all-day symposium focused on a particular topic. The Environmental Law Society, for example, may bring in an expert about climate change for a luncheon talk, while the law review may hold a full day symposium on judicial independence or healthcare reform. Most individual presentations are held during lunch and include free food for attendees. If that's the case, take a break from your studies and go to the presentation to grab a bite and some extra knowledge.

CHAPTER 25

RECAPPING LAW SCHOOL'S FIRST YEAR IN THE WORDS OF STUDENTS

I think it's much easier to tell someone else that, to succeed in law school, "You've got to do this, you've got to do that, etc." than it is being the incoming student and having an appreciation for and actually listening to and implementing what someone else is telling you.

> —1L nearing completion of the first year

One of the frustrating aspects about giving advice on how to succeed in law school is the certain knowledge that many students won't follow it. This is true no matter how great the advice. As we near the end of our figurative 1L ride, I thought the best way to reinforce the advice for law school success and well-being that you've been reading would be to hear it retold in the words of those who labored through the real 1L odyssey. Borrowing from humorist Dave Barry, I'm hoping that reading the same advice coming from law students will assure you that "I am not making this up" and help drive home key points.

Shortly before the end of their first year, I posed some combination of the following questions to different entering classes of 1Ls:

- Name one thing you know now (other than the law) that you wish you had known when you started law school.

- As you near the end of your first year, what has surprised you the most about law school compared to your expectations going into it?

- Think back to when you were starting law school, specifically to your fears or concerns. In retrospect, which fear or concern do you think was the most exaggerated as compared to the reality of law school and which fear or concern do you think you most underestimated or overlooked?

- Imagine one of your closest friends or relatives is starting law school. What advice would you give them?

- What is your dominant feeling or sentiment (e.g., relief, nostalgia, frustration, exhaustion) as you near the end of your first year?

Below are representative answers to each question, grouped under subheadings to give them some structure. As you read the student advice, think back and try to connect it to the specific sections of this book where you first heard it. Specifically, think about the C.R.E.D.O. chapter and take note of how many of the tips relate to the habits of being Consistent, Rigorous, Efficient, Diligent, and Organized.

You'll note some overlap in the answers. For example, some students said the importance of not falling behind was the one thing they wished they had known when starting law school, while others listed it as the most important piece of advice they would give to a loved one who was starting law school. Conversely, some students gave opposing comments about the same topic, which is also enlightening. For example, one student listed competitiveness as their most exaggerated fear, while another listed it as their most underestimated fear, showing once again that while many reliable generalizations can be made about law school and law students, no two law school experiences are identical.

QUESTION: Name one thing you know now (other than the law) that you wish you had known when you started law school.

Law School Will Be One of the Most Difficult Challenges of Your Life

- I think the one notion that students have about the law school experience is that it will be difficult. This is universal. I think students underestimate tremendously the type of difficulty that they will encounter. It is not necessarily that the material is always exceptionally difficult to understand, but that the process by which you

learn and the sheer quantity of work required to learn—
let alone master—the subject matter is overwhelming. I
wish that I had some understanding of that before I
started the whole deal.

- I wish I had known how mentally taxing law school was
  going to be. Beyond "learning the law" there is the stress
  of getting good grades, legal writing assignments, moot
  court, etc. Further, trying to balance this stress with the
  normal stress of life (family, relationships, money, etc.) is
  a challenge in and of itself.

- I wish I'd known how easy it is to fail out. I just assumed
  law school would be slightly harder than college—I was
  way off.

But It Can Be Done, So Take Heart

- I wish I'd had the confidence in my abilities at the
  beginning of the year that I have now. I'd stress to readers
  that if they have been accepted to law school, they are
  fully capable of doing well in law school. They didn't get
  there by some mistake in the admissions process. They
  didn't get someone else's letter of acceptance. I think
  there's a tendency to assume that because we've never
  done something, we "can't" do it. We say this sort of thing
  all the time. If a person has never learned to cook, they'll
  say, "I can't cook." In law school, it might be "I can't argue
  a case" because they've never done it. I'd recommend that
  new students do their best to put a stop to that way of
  thinking and say instead, "I haven't learned *yet* to cook"
  or "I haven't learned *yet* to argue a case" or whatever.

It's a Brave New World

- I wish I'd known that the way I'd studied in
  undergraduate school and graduate school would bear no
  resemblance to the way I needed to study in law school if
  I wanted to pass my exams.

- I wish I would have known just how different the whole
  law school experience was going to be from anything else
  I had ever done. I honestly feel that there is nothing in
  undergraduate school that could possibly have prepared

me for law school. The only way to be successful is to try to adapt quickly.

- I wish I had known how to *study*. In undergrad I felt like things came fairly easy and other than writing papers I didn't actually have to sit down and dedicate my time to school material. I had never before *really* reviewed material from class or outlined and these are vital skills you need to apply in law school.

Everyone Has the Same Fears

- That everyone else was just as nervous about some aspect of the whole new experience as I was. Someone very well may have told me that before I started. If they did, I didn't believe them. But it's true. It has taken me two semesters of getting to know others well enough to realize that they are all nervous too. The basis for the nervousness varies drastically, but we all feel it. For some it will be about speaking in class or doing an oral argument. Others are nervous about not being liked, flunking out, or going broke. Amazingly to me, some of the most intelligent students seemed to struggle the most at first. Perhaps because they have always been the shiniest fish in their ponds, they were unaccustomed and uncomfortable with being surrounded by so many true peers. Everyone is struggling with some aspect of the law school experience!

Don't Fall Behind

- You have to stay on top of your obligations and responsibilities EVERY DAY. I don't just mean your reading assignments. You have to make sure to check your email daily and stay on top of other obligations such as signing up for Westlaw training and adding to your outlines on a regular basis. This was a big transition from my undergraduate experience. I would go weeks without checking my email and just cram for a few days before a big test without suffering any dire consequences. If your undergraduate experience was anything like mine, you cannot get away with adhering to the same habits once you start law school.

- I wish that I would have known that everything moves one step ahead in law school. If you are ahead in your readings/preparations, then you are where you need to be.

- If you are merely prepared for each class on a "just-in-time" strategy, you are behind. And if you fall behind, it is impossible to catch up. Although you can get notes from others, double a reading assignment for a class, etc., you simply cannot replace the learning process that comes from actual preparation in advance.

Conscientious Outlining and Periodic Review Are Critical

- How important outlining is and how important it is to keep up with it as you go along. Outlining is a major part of the learning process for me and I did not realize how important it was until I really did it. It doesn't just help you study the material. It allows you to organize the concepts in a logical manner that helps you see the bigger picture.

- Fall semester would have been so much less stressful if I had kept a running outline that was updated biweekly, instead of waiting two weeks before exams to begin making the outline.

- I wish I would have known just how much time it took to study for exams. I wish I would have known that if I put just an hour into studying after class each day it would have made things easier.

Law School Is Competitive

- I think that competition is the white elephant in the room in terms of discussion of the law school experience. Everyone is in a marathon race against the other. Everyone is aware of this—some simply care more than others. However, there is something to be said for being considerate and helpful to your peers. There are people who will go out of their way not to help you lest they give up some tiny thread of comparative advantage. Those students are rarely liked and respected even less. I think it would do our profession and our peers a great deal of good to realize that in the end it does not matter what grades you made or what awards you won. These are important, no doubt. But the relationships that you make now stay with you forever.

- To believe people when they warn how competitive law school is. Looking back, college was like running a 5K for a cause where everyone wanted you to succeed. People are there along the way giving you water and cheering you on. Even the slowest runner is praised for participation. Law school feels more like roller derby. While racing to the finish line, your competition is beating on you, intentionally tripping you up, and pulling your hair out all in an effort to pass you by.

- I wish that I had known exactly how competitive law school is. I think that I kind of knew, but I had no real understanding of the fierceness of the whole system.

Being Organized and Managing Time Efficiently Will Make Your Life Easier

- I think the one thing that I wish I had a better working knowledge of when I started law school is that organization can make the most monumental task attainable.

- Organization makes work easy. It sounds simple, but I never realized I was disorganized. Your desk can be clean and everything can appear perfect, but if you don't know what the fourteen things you have to do at your computer are, then you're wasting time. Simply knowing what needs to be done and when makes it easy to crank out high-quality work quickly. So much time is wasted figuring out what to do and getting the tools to start.

Case Briefs Should Be Brief

- Case briefs should be concise! Really concise. Read the case carefully and underline/highlight important parts but don't waste your time typing every point into a brief. The professor will highlight in class the important points you should get out of the case. Then you can go back and copy anything into your brief that you may not have covered fully.

Don't Be a Transcriber

- Do not transcribe everything the professor says into class notes. The professors' words are important, of course, and if they make a point to slow down and state a specific point of law, transcribe it. But you need to filter their words into notes that you can understand.

Women Experience Law School Differently than Men

- Women tend to underestimate their abilities, while men seem to overestimate theirs. Most girls are just not complimented on their intelligence that often. I'm trying to make a point of doing that more with my daughter and downplaying her appearance, but it's just so second-nature with girls to say "What a pretty dress!" or "Your hair looks so nice today!" and so on. The students who come to mind who I consider lacking in the confidence they fully deserve to have are all female. Many women students have said, "I want to be in a back office" or "I don't want to do litigation" and so on. There's certainly no more competence in being male, but there is definitely more confidence. Even with many law schools having a 50–50 gender balance, the de-emphasis on intelligence that girls experience in relation to the boys they later end up competing against has an effect. This brings us back to what I wished I'd known. Having made it through several scary things in law school (the final exams, the papers, the oral argument) and seeing now that I have the ability to do them, I could have spared myself a lot of needless stress if I'd had a bit of this confidence back in August.

QUESTION: As you near the end of your first year, what has surprised you the most about law school compared to your expectations going into it?

How Much It Changed Me

- What most surprised me about law school is how much it has really changed me. Law school is one of those experiences that can't help but alter a person forever, but in a good way. I think about everything differently now. My perspective on life in general has shifted from what I've learned in law school. Law school has taught me to question and analyze everything, much to the annoyance of my family and friends.

- I am surprised how much law school has changed me. I don't know if that's a good thing or a bad thing.

- It changed how I think about even the most mundane things. I underestimated the impact this would have on the other people in my life. My wife is wonderful and has been very understanding, but law school has been hard on her too. Imagine living with someone who walks around and sees potential lawsuits everywhere he goes. In law school, every case you read is about something that went wrong, so, if you aren't careful, you can become a pessimist very quickly. You begin to approach situations by thinking about what the consequences could be and then taking those consequences to the extreme. I call it "hypothetical hell." My wife tried to tell me this was happening but I didn't believe her until one day when we were discussing how we were going to use our jet-ski the following summer. We had moved farther away from the lake we used to ride on for me to come to law school, so she suggested we rent a slip and keep the jet-ski in the water so that we wouldn't have to tow it every time we wanted to ride. I immediately begin to analyze the liability it could create for us to leave it in the water. "What if a friend wants to borrow it and has an accident?" "What if it gets stolen?" "What if someone hits a boat full of toddlers?" "We need insurance!"

How Much I Love It

- I don't know if I really expected to love law school so much. Before law school, I was excited about beginning a new phase of life, one that I knew would help determine my future professional life. I'm so pleasantly surprised to find that I love coming to school every day. I love reading a case and realizing that I really understand what it's about. Law school is challenging and difficult but there's something so beautiful and reassuring in knowing that I'm right where I'm supposed to be.

- I was surprised most by how much fun I actually had, as opposed to the misery I was expecting. The upper-level students (at orientation and such) do not do a good enough job telling incoming 1Ls to have fun with law school. I think it was due to my classmates' and my ability to enjoy the study of law that made the first year really special. After all, we chose to be here!

The Workload

- Everyone says this, but I really was surprised by the workload, assuming you intend to complete all of your assignments "properly." Before law school I heard everyone talk about how much work it is. I always thought to myself, "I was in the army and I deployed twice to Iraq. I know how to work hard." But I really underestimated the discipline required for law school. Maybe I'm just slower at doing homework than others, but if I did every single homework assignment properly, it would take me at least six hours a day during the week, not including class times. I would also have to put in another ten hours on the weekend to work on outlines and legal writing assignments, two areas I found really difficult to fit in during the week.

- I have been most surprised at how there just are not enough hours in the day to accomplish all the things that need to be done in a day. It is vitally important to streamline your life to remove any distraction that will prevent you from giving every bit of focus to law school. I have learned this the hard way.

How Supportive the Professors and Classmates Are

- I have been pleasantly surprised with how nice my fellow students and professors have been. I had pre-conceived notions coming into law school that the atmosphere would be cutthroat, competitive, and serious all of the time. In one year I have already met great people who I consider more than just regular friends because we had to rely on each other to get through the difficult times.

- I have been pleasantly surprised with how helpful the professors have been. I expected vicious professors who enjoy making first-year students look foolish in front of their peers. I have experienced nothing like that. My professors are all eager to help and meet after class to discuss any issues.

Lack of Feedback

- What surprised me most is the lack of feedback. Because we do not have tests throughout the semester, you don't really get a grasp of your level of understanding of the material. I think this is one of the major reasons that law school is so stressful. There is no feedback, so no matter how much you study you always feel like there is more you should be doing or that you don't understand the material well enough.

How Competitive It Is

- The competitiveness. Grading against the curve changes everything. The college days of sharing notes, helping others, and all working together to get through a tough class are over. The competitive atmosphere of law school is almost hysterical. Point exactly: The last day of my Civil Procedure class the teacher said we were going to do something "fun." We began playing Jeopardy and getting quizzed on the Federal Rules of Civil Procedure (not my idea of fun!). Next thing you know, the entire class was accusing the other side of cheating or crying that the other side's questions were easier. Law school students will not miss any chance to unleash their inner-competiveness and do not mess around when it comes to getting a step ahead in the grades department.

QUESTION: Think back to when you were starting law school, specifically to your fears or concerns. In retrospect, which fear or concern do you think was the most exaggerated as compared to the reality of law school and which fear or concern do you think you most underestimated or overlooked?

Most Exaggerated Fear or Concern

The Socratic method/getting called on.

- The Socratic Method wasn't nearly as bad as I thought it was going to be. I definitely looked really dumb a few times, but it was not anything to go home crying about.

- Most exaggerated fear was definitely the Socratic method. Although it is scary the first time you get called on, the fear quickly diminishes when you realize that you are not expected to get every answer correct. Rather, the professors expect you to have read the material assigned for that class and be able to engage in an open discussion regarding its content. No student knows the correct answer to every question.

- I was extremely concerned with getting called on. There is something about having to respond on command in front of seventy other students and a professor that you do not know very well yet that makes a person lose sleep at night. That was my biggest fear and to be honest it was blown out of proportion. First of all, with a class as big as seventy students, getting called on is not an everyday occurrence even in courses where the professors call on multiple students each day. Second, even when I got called on, most of the time the answers to the questions came to me because I was always prepared for class. Third, I constantly reminded myself that as long as I prepared for class, the professors would not mind if I simply did not know an answer.

Failing/not understanding the material.

- My most exaggerated fear was my fear of failing out law school. I anticipated the material as being so difficult that no amount of work could overcome it. I have found that by reading the material, coming to class, taking good notes, and asking my professors for help when I don't understand something, the material is not insurmountable.

- My most overblown fear was that everyone would be infinitely more intelligent, more articulate, more competent, etc., than me, and that I would be revealed as an impostor and forced to endure the derision of the *real* future lawyers. This would all happen, of course, before I failed out of school. Fortunately, it hasn't played out this way, but the law school atmosphere *is* singularly intense and it intensified my prelaw and first-semester insecurities.

- I expected to not be able to understand the issues we would be discussing in class, especially at the beginning. However, I found that the professors genuinely care that you understand the material. The amount of time you must devote to reading and preparing is enormous, but as long as you are willing to put in that time and work, the information will not be difficult to understand.

Competitiveness.

- The most exaggerated concern was about the competitiveness between students. Before law school a lot of the conversations I had with lawyers and former students went like this: "Oh, it is fiercely competitive. When I was in law school we had a student that [insert ridiculous research sabotage story]." I have found students to be very helpful and amiable toward each other. The only time it feels competitive is when grades come out and some people get a little touchy.

Most Underestimated Fear or Concern

The workload.

- The fear or concern I most underestimated or overlooked was realizing there's not enough time in the day or week to get all the work done. The law school workload requires strict time management and organization. I have always been an organized student and able to handle schoolwork while participating in many other activities. But law school is at a completely different level in terms of the sheer volume of material. To anyone getting ready to start law school or thinking of going to law school, I would tell them to spend time organizing their lives outside of school because once law school starts, there is little time to do much else.

- It was more draining and challenging than I ever thought it would be. I always tell my friends and family that a student cannot be prepared enough for how grueling law school really is. When I was in high school, my teachers would always tell me how difficult college would be one day and that was not true for me personally. However, I am friends with many current attorneys who told me that law school was going to be a whole new ballgame and they could not have been more right. My family threw a party for me on the night before I moved for school and my uncle, a bankruptcy attorney, made a toast to me that ended with "Better you than me." We all laughed at the time, but I did not realize how serious he really was when he made that statement.

- The fear I most underestimated was all the work necessary to prepare for exams my first semester. With all the outlining, reviewing, and collaborating, the time between class and exams quickly disappeared, leaving me more stressed. Time management is essential in law school, especially in that crunch before exams, and I had to learn that one the hard way.

Exams.

- The most underestimated fear was exams. While I knew the whole "one test" thing would be stressful, I did not expect the extreme level of stress I experienced. The two weeks of exams were likely the two most emotionally and physically exhausting weeks I have ever had. Then, to have to wait until the last couple of days before classes restarted to get the grades . . . absolute torture! The excruciating waiting for grades after exams should be deemed a violation of the Eighth Amendment prohibition on cruel and unusual punishment.

Competitiveness.

- One thing I overlooked was the type of students I would be interacting with on a daily basis. You do not get into law school by slacking off or being uninvolved in extracurricular activities. I still am surprised at how so many people are looking for extra ways to set themselves apart. For example, if there is a student government election, job, or scholarship opportunity, there will be intense competition by law students to get it.

- I didn't worry about the competitive atmosphere before coming to law school, and I suppose I should have more. By the competitive atmosphere, I mean the nature of the people who come to law school and how it affects me mentally. Maybe it is just the group of people I hang out with but I wasn't prepared for how much people worry about grades, moot court, summer jobs, etc. Being around highly stressed individuals all of the time is probably the thing I like least about law school. Being somewhat more laidback, I have found it hard to adjust to people constantly "freaking out."

Strain on relationships.

- I underestimated the strain law school would place on my family. Not only is law school an overwhelming responsibility for me, but it places a heavier load on my dear wife to not only work to support us but then spend the majority of her free time caring for our two sons. Luckily, I married a saint and I have been able to strike somewhat of a balance between school and home. I have also found that time away from school with my family helps make me a better student.

Legal writing courses.

- The most underestimated fear was the time allocated toward my two-hour legal research and writing class. In no way was I aware of the time my legal writing class would take away from my core curriculum classes. I was not prepared for the extreme workload it required throughout the entire first year.

- Before school I was more worried about my substantive classes than legal writing. However, once school started I realized Legal Research and Writing was more than I had bargained for. If I knew then what I know now I would have researched legal writing more in my spare time before school started so that I would have been more prepared for the vast difference between writing papers in college and writing papers in law school.

QUESTION: Imagine one of your closest friends or relatives is starting law school. What advice would you give them?

Of all the questions I've used to survey law students, I think this one is my favorite. Casting students in the role of a trusted advisor to a close loved one forced them to think more deeply, advise more bluntly, and get to the heart of some important matters. Some of their answers fall into the realm of "soul searching," while most of their practical advice hammers home fundamental points made throughout this book.

Think Hard About Whether Law School Is Really the Place for You

- Talk to attorneys, consider the financial debt, sit in on a law school class, read a Supreme Court decision, pray/meditate/contemplate about it, understand the pressure involved, do a cost-benefit analysis (even though you may not understand that concept well yet), know that this will be far different from your undergraduate experience, consider the community you are moving to and will be living in for three years.

- I would advise anyone starting law school to make sure that it is truly where you want to be and that you are going *when* you want to be there. I was fortunate enough to take a year after graduating from college to work, relax, and refocus my energy. Several classmates of mine (including one who decided to withdraw after fall semester) regretted not taking time off.

- It is said so often that it sounds cliché, but you have to find in yourself the reason that you want to be here. You have to commit to yourself that you will do this, without fail, no matter what. Kind of like rescuing a baby from a burning building. Once you commit to do it, you follow through with it to the bitter end.

- Oh dear. Well, I don't know. First, I'd ask if they really wanted my advice. I wouldn't try to talk anyone out of it, but I'd advise that they sit in on some classes, talk to a lot of law students, talk to a lot of lawyers, if possible. I'd advise that if they do all those things, they can find out what law school entails and what a legal career entails, and then consider carefully whether it is something they would enjoy. I would say to ask themselves why they're going to law school. If they said something like, "It's all I can do with my degree," I would advise that they think about it some more.

- First I would say, "Are you crazy? You saw what I went through!" Ha ha. And then I would seriously tell them to really give law school a lot of thought. This isn't just something to do just because you can't get a job or you want to stay in school for another three years. If you want to get the most for your money and your time, law school really does become your life. But if law school is your dream, it is worth it. You can't just come to law school to get a quick and easy career, because it's not quick and it's not easy. Law school takes more work than you can imagine, as well as time and patience. There will be days when you want to quit. But if you're there for the right reasons, you will realize that in three years you will have fulfilled your dream and have a degree that will give you a better life. Then all the hard work will seem worth it and you can get right back to the books!

- I would think about giving the typical answer, "Don't go." However, I heard that from both my lawyer parents and all of my friends that I asked prior to law school. It was very discouraging to say the least. The best advice to give someone is if your heart is in law school then you can definitely accomplish it, but make sure to keep true to yourself. Do not let the pressures of law school or the intimidation factor of all the brilliant students surrounding you affect who you are.

Approach Law School Like a Job

- Remember that law school is a full-time job, which is not a bad thing. It requires commitment, and if you are ready for a full-time job that's more interesting than a lot of others, do it. It baffles me that some people complain about the workload when they walk out the door after class ends at 1:00 p.m. Granted, some of those people are doing work at home. But, when 2:30 rolls around and you think that it's time to go home, stop and remember that everyone else your age is either working until 5:00 or they're out looking for a job. Then come right back to your space and work until 5:00. Then enjoy the rest of your night!

- When I started law school, I was told to treat school as a 9 to 5 job and to just stay at school and work for that amount of time whether in class or not. This method didn't really work for me, because I like naps, breaks, etc., but the basic point was helpful. It made me realize that as long as I put in around seven to eight hours of work a day, whether it's preparing for class, being in class, or outlining, I would be fine.

Get Your Life in Order

- Get your life in order because you won't have time for disorganization once you start law school. Have a game plan in advance about when you are going to study, and be prepared to do it religiously.

- I would recommend to someone starting or considering law school to get their personal house in order prior to starting law school. As I observe others struggling with personal matters and difficulties, I feel blessed that my life has not been filled with any of these distractions. I think that learning the law—especially in the first year of law school—is too hard to have to deal with unnecessary distractions. As I observe my peers I think that the two biggest distractions have been either relationships or financial hardships. I would not start law school if I weren't on firm financial footing.

- Make sure you are in a good place psychologically before you commit. The law school atmosphere is very intense and the pressure to excel (or even to just keep up) can be overwhelming at times. The best way to do this is to give yourself some time if you're in a bad place emotionally. Do NOT enroll on the tail end of an emotional crisis. It's important to remove anyone or anything from your life that could potentially distract you from your school work, as being unable to fully focus will greatly intensify any anxiety and stress you already have. Break off toxic romantic relationships and cut ties with unsupportive friends. This may seem brutal but it's absolutely necessary in order to fully face and handle the stress and anxiety of law school.

- I watch as some peers travel to see significant others on the weekends or pine away about someone who is away from them. I think this is a waste of time. I would probably not enter law school and hope that a long distance relationship would work out. I think I would probably just agree to go separate ways. Time is too valuable as a 1L to deal with relationship drama, especially long-distance relationship drama.

Pick a Law School in an Area Where You Will Be Happy Living

- Pick an area that you would like to live in and then choose your law school based on that area. If you are not happy where you are living then you will not be happy in law school. School is going to take up most of your time, but you need to take some time away from the law to relax. It's important that there are things you enjoy doing in the town where you have chosen to go to school. There are good law schools everywhere, so if you like the beach, go to school near the beach; if you like the mountains, go to school near mountains; and if you can't live without seeing your mother every day, go to school near your mother.

Take a Year Off First

- Take a year off. Law School requires a *passionate devotion*. Working for a year will both give you the discipline to approach law school as a job and to know that coming here is the right decision.

Enjoy Your Time Before You Start

- Take a really long vacation before starting school.

Dress for Success

- Always look decent. Impressions are important and people judge you if you wear sweats and flip-flops and don't shower.

Everyone Struggles

- I would tell them that everyone struggles in their own way, be it a bad grade, getting called on when you are unprepared for class, showing up late, or just personal issues. No one's journey through law school is easy, so any struggles you have, remember there are many other students who feel the exact same way as you.

- Remember that EVERYONE is feeling this. . . . I think the Socratic Method (hearing someone give an answer that seems so much more intelligent than whatever you were thinking) and the evaluation method (not having feedback through assignments and midterm tests and what not) can really mess with you. I received an email from a fellow student. She's a student I think people assume "has it all together," and she said, "I feel like I'm hanging on by my fingernails."

- I think the biggest thing to realize and remember is that there are going to be days when you have mental, physical, and emotional breakdowns. Trust me, I probably have two or three a month. And there are going to be days when you really want to hit that person who's ranked in the top ten who keeps talking about his or her grades in front of everyone not ranked in the top ten.

You'll Get Out What You Put into It

- Law school really becomes what you make of it. If you start with a goal of finishing in the top 25 percent of your class, then you'd better accept that studying is going to be a continuous and very large part of your life. If you do, you'll probably meet your goal. If you start law school just as a way to get another degree and procrastinate the career-search process, then just do what you have to do to get by, but don't be disappointed when you aren't in the top of your class. I think every single person has a different perspective on law school and a different way of tackling it. You just have to make it your own!

Be Ready to Work Harder than Ever Before

- Study twice as hard as you think you need to be studying.

- Be ready to spend a lot of time to do a lot of work. Do not go into law school with the attitude that it is anything like undergraduate school. Anyone can do well if they are willing to put in the time and effort.

- Law school is going to be the most serious and difficult task you have ever taken on. You have to go into it wholeheartedly and devote most of your time to it.

- Take a quiet week before you start and try to find that one kernel of motivation that will get you through when you have no energy, desire, or drive left upon which to rely. You will need it.

Getting High Grades Is Not the Only Goal in Life

- Grades are important, but living your life is important also. Professors and deans will stress "grades, grades, grades" and make you feel bad about wanting to have a life. I don't think they do this on purpose, but most professors and deans were in the top ten percent of their class and feel that their sacrifices were worthwhile. The thought of a student actually making a conscious decision to be a *B* or *C* student is ludicrous to the faculty of a law school. Performing as a top 10 percent student can be extremely important depending on which type of job you want when you get out of law school, but it all rests on what YOU want out of life and out of your career. The difference in workload between a *B−* and an *A* is tremendous, and in my opinion, it was not worth the trade-off. I made a conscious decision to lower my goal so that I could participate in other law school activities, spend time hanging out with my husband and my dogs, visit with friends and family, and BBQ poolside. I don't feel bad about it and I don't think anyone else should either.

Relax, Try to Enjoy, and Do the Best You Can

- Relax. Don't worry about using six colors of highlighter to try to absorb every piece of every case. Do the work, try to understand the situation and the rule, and then be willing to put it down and watch a movie. Your ability to produce results is directly proportional to your ability to relax. One of my closest friends is busy burning herself out over law school. Another good friend of mine is doing the same thing at a different law school. They are making their lives hell, ruining their health, and they're frustrated with their understanding. There is a time for work and a time to stop and let your brain recover. Understand the difference.

- Relax. Although law school is a very stressful time, have fun with it. The classes are interesting, you will make amazing friends, and it really can be fun.

- Just do the best you can. Don't try to compare yourself with anyone else or stress too much about the competitive nature of law school because it will only wear you down. The only thing you really have control over is your own performance.

- Approach law school as a learning/training mission rather than as a contest for grades. The second I stopped trying to learn the material enthusiastically and started strategizing as to how to get the best grades, law school became less fun and the stress tripled.

- Have fun! Law school is an amazing journey that teaches one a great deal about themselves and their abilities.

Realize That Non-Law Students Aren't Interested in Hearing About the Law and Law School

- I'd probably tell them that they are about to have their entire lives consumed with the law and conversations about the law. Most of all I would remind them that no matter how interested everyone at the law school is in this stuff, nobody else really cares about it. Try to keep it to yourself because the law does not make for good conversations with friends and family. You'll just come off as boring and weird. I mean outside of lawyers and judges, who could possibly care if a "dog sniff" constitutes a search within the meaning of the Fourth Amendment?

- Be careful about mixing your non-law school friends with your law school friends. Only mix your non-law school friends with law school friends who are capable of conversing about interests other than law school. No non-law school friend wants to be stuck at a table with five law students who only want to talk about law school.

Sort Through Advice Carefully

- Do not listen to anyone else's opinion about professors. Before each semester, I heard that Professor X was pure concentrated evil, or that you can sleep through Professor Y's class, etc. Some information has been helpful, such as what to expect in terms of assignments and exam prep, but most of the rest has been so far off base as to now seem comical.

- It's best to stick to the studying techniques that have worked for you in the past. The first semester I spent an inordinate amount of time perfecting *the* outline of my class notes because that's the studying/organizing technique that law students and professors emphasize the most. Every study advice panel discussion devoted a large portion to outlining success tips: "Have your outline done by this date or you'll probably fail," "By the time you're finished with your outline it should be condensed to x number of pages," "Constantly update and edit your outline so you can be the greatest law student in the world," etc. As a result, in my panic-stricken state of mind, I wasted an absurd amount of time formatting and crafting the perfect outline, and less time actually encoding and understanding the massive amount of information I'd been exposed to over the semester. (Although, I must say, I organized it beautifully.) During the second semester, I still created outlines for my classes but they did not follow the perfectly structured, linear "II, A, i, 1" format I thought was required in the first semester.

Don't Miss Classes

- Do not miss any classes. I have only missed one class since the beginning of the semester and it was for a court date for a traffic ticket. I felt really behind and confused missing just that one lecture. In undergrad it might have been fine to skip every now and then, but I would definitely advise anyone coming to law school not to miss any classes unless they absolutely have to.

Keep Your Emotions in Check

- You're not as smart as you think you are, nor are you as useless as you think you are. You'll go through periods of elation and periods of doubt. Both extremes are false and should be promptly dismissed.

- Don't be afraid of law school. While a little bit of fear is good motivation, too much can be crippling. There is no need to fear your professors, colleagues, or assignments. Most everyone is nice and helpful and most of the assignments and cases are straightforward.

- Do not beat yourself up about things that you cannot control. You will walk into a class and, by design, not know all that you need to know. Recognize that you cannot win every battle. Most of all enjoy the experience.

Make Friends/Develop a Support Network

- Start introducing yourself to other students and try to make friends at orientation. Cliques begin forming then and cliques translate to study groups (which can be a very useful tool, depending on the group). When I say cliques, it's not so much a social thing as a way of finding others who have something in common with you and who, like you, also have no idea what they've gotten themselves into.

- Make as many friends as possible because in order to survive law school the best support system is people who know exactly what you are going through. Plus, friends are helpful for group study sessions and sharing outlines.

- Make friends because you need people who understand what you are going through to keep you sane.

- Get to know your classmates—they are not the enemy. Do not hide books or hoard outlines—share!

- Find one or two people you can really trust and spend large amounts of time studying and outlining with. There will be times when you might miss a class or even when you attend class where you might miss important bits of information from the professor. If you have a few people you can trust, you will be able to cover for each other as well as strengthen each other's notes and outlines, and hold each other accountable. But do not join a study group with too many people because then it becomes counterproductive.

Don't Make Enemies

- Don't make enemies. You know who you like and people you don't really get along with. However, you may very well have to work with these people one day. It is a lesson in humility and maturity that you can work with someone who you don't like.

Don't Fall Behind

- Be organized from day one and never let yourself fall behind. The destructive feelings of being overwhelmed and scared about having fallen behind will finish you off long before you ever have a chance to make a bad grade on an exam.

- I would tell them that when they have extra time, try to get ahead in their work. There is never enough time to get things done in law school, so what you think is free time, really isn't or shouldn't be. Mostly, I would just try to encourage them to stay focused and organized so that they won't get so stressed out.

- DO NOT GET BEHIND ON YOUR WORK. PLAN AHEAD. Six hours over two Saturdays is much better than six hours the weeknight before something is due.

- Keep up! Don't fall behind in your reading. Do your best work at all times. Don't ever cop out and just "phone in" a class hoping that the professor won't call on you.

- Start outlining ASAP. If you wait, you cannot catch back up. Seriously, you cannot catch back up.

Stay Organized

- Take the semester one week at a time and break that week down into days and organize what you need to accomplish that particular day. I am a list maker and that helped me tremendously this year. I placed a giant dry erase board in my room and made lists of assignments that I needed to accomplish that day. As I finished an assignment, I marked it off and moved to the next goal. This kept me organized and gave me satisfaction that I was accomplishing the things that needed to be accomplished.

- Organization is the key. Find a sound plan that works for you. Being able to plan for the seemingly millions of things going on requires attention to detail. Knowing you are well-organized will give you one less thing you have to worry about.

Start Outlines Early/Engage in
Periodic Review

- Start outlining early. If you don't then it's almost impossible to do it at the end of the semester.

- If my little sister was starting law school, I would tell her to review her notes daily or weekly. My problem is that I waited until it was time to outline before I looked back at my notes, and was very unfamiliar with some of the concepts at that point.

- Outline early, at least two weeks before everyone else is starting. If you don't procrastinate, you'll have it all done with a week of class left and you won't be freaking out trying to desperately outline when you should be studying for exams.

Don't Take Short-Cuts

- Do not listen to any of the short-cuts your classmates as well as 2Ls and 3Ls will be all too willing to give. Shortcuts deprive you of the process of truly engaging the material, which is crucial to developing the skills of finding your way into a case and back out with rule in hand. Short-cut websites which provide case briefs do not help you develop the most important skills needed in law school, which are learning to analyze cases, finding the rules and sub-rules, and then applying them to entirely different sets of facts. DO NOT cheat yourself! Follow the C.R.E.D.O.! It worked for me.

Do Your Own Outlines

- "Legendary outlines" by former students do exist, but they won't get you an *A*. Going to class, reading the material, taking your own notes, and studying will do that. There is no cramming in law school. Spacing out in the back playing video games will earn you a fast ticket out.

Sit Up Front

- Sit in the front. This is productive for a couple of reasons. First, I tend to space out a lot and this prevents it. If you're in the first few rows you're visible to the entire class and to your professor. Not only will this ensure you're attentive at least most of the time, but also that you study hard so as not to be embarrassed by being called on. Another benefit is you get to know your professors a bit better and they get to know you. They're a lot less intimidating if you know them as someone other than just a professor. They're usually pretty cool.

Stay in Shape

- Drop the Ho-Ho's and back away from them. They are not your friend. True, they whisper nice, sweet things in your ear, and call out to you in the middle of the night, but when you have to get all gussied up for your oral argument, you're going to look like a fat man in a little suit.

Seek Help from Your Profs

- If something comes up that is beyond your control, go to your professors and ask for help. That's one thing I have always been too proud (or too dumb) to do. I always try to do things on my own. It's okay to sit down with someone and explain that you are overwhelmed.

Back Up Your Work

- Back up your computer work in many places!

Don't Give Up

- Keep your head down and plow through it. At times it will be fun, but at times it will really suck. If you really want to do it, it will be worth it. Just keep pushing through the difficult times.

- Never give up! Repeat after me: "This too shall pass!" And keep smiling.

Take Practice Exams Under Simulated Conditions

- To study for exams, use professors' old exams. Take them like real exams, including timing yourself.

Don't Be a Know-It-All

- Don't become a know-it-all thinking you know everything about the law after a month of law school. Your friends will hate you if you do.

Use Study Aids to Clarify

- There are some teachers who are simply unclear about what they are teaching in class and what you should be learning in the course as a whole. If you find yourself with a teacher like that, don't hesitate to get a study aid or a canned outline to learn the material on your own. Read the assignments, because you need to be familiar with the material, but if the teacher is not getting the job done, make sure you get an understanding from somewhere else.

- My honest opinion: Get the study aids from the get-go and start outlining early! If you don't understand something, consult the professor and extract what you can from the study aids (but only if it falls in line with what the professor is teaching).

Don't Obsess About "Looking Stupid" in Class

- Don't freak out about getting called on in class. Everyone gets called on and everyone feels like they look stupid. However, no one ever remembers but you.

Don't Give Up Your Hobbies/Outside Life

- Law school is difficult and requires a lot of work, but you cannot give up every aspect of your life for law school. It's important to find something you enjoy outside of school with which to fill the limited free time you have. I would not have been able to make it as far as I have, and I realize I still have a long way to go, without being able to do something to relax when I have finished working for the day. I found that playing church-league basketball, playing a round of golf on the weekend, or just hanging out with my friends for a night made opening up my book and diving back into the intricacies of the law the next morning much easier to cope with.

- Make sure you have an outlet outside of school—whether it is tutoring a child, running, playing the guitar, yoga, sewing—just something to do other than study!

- Don't work ALL of the time, only most of it.

- Find time in every day to relax.

- Balance your academic life with your personal life. Don't give up all the things that make you who you are to provide more time for school. There is no way you can be happy if you completely sacrifice the things you do outside of school. If you are unhappy in general your performance in class will suffer.

QUESTION: What is your dominant feeling or sentiment (e.g., relief, nostalgia, frustration, exhaustion) as you near the end of your first year?

Two weeks before the end of the second semester, I posed the above question to a first-year class. Silly me. I naively expected cheerful answers, not taking into account the fact that with five exams still looming, the students weren't thinking—like I was—that they were at "the end" of the first year. Their answers disproportionately centered on anxiety and exhaustion. I'm sure if I asked the same question after exams, the answers would have been a lot more upbeat. Some students, however, were able to look ahead and feel excitement, relief, and a sense of accomplishment for what they'd been through. Overall, the answers reflected the entire spectrum of emotions inherent in being a 1L. Below I included one representative answer for each emotion.

Anxiety/Stress

- I'm full of anxiety. I didn't do well last semester and I have to do much better to remain in school for another year. For the last three weeks or so I have been waking up with nightmares and I have had a difficult time sleeping because I am so nervous about finals.

Despair

- "Dear God! I have two more years of this?" It's kind of like being sent to war and then getting wounded in battle. You start to think you are finally going to get sent home after you heal only to find out you're being sent back to the front line, with even less chance of survival because now you're wounded.

Exhaustion

- EXHAUSTION. I have reached a new level of mental exhaustion I did not know existed.

Frustration

- Frustration. Effort = Results. Plain and simple. I wish I would have spent more time studying and enjoying what I was learning—and less time analyzing what I could do to ensure a decent class rank.

Excitement

- I am energized. I feel excited that I now understand things better. Last semester I was planning a wedding, selling a house, etc. This semester I am focused on school only. That makes ALL the difference in the world. I now enjoy classes more, because I understand things more clearly. I am also at peace now that I have finally accepted the fact that I have no social life outside of classes. I am moving towards the realm of nerd-dom at a steady pace.

Indifference

- I guess I really feel kind of indifferent about it. I am relieved that the first year is coming to a close, but I know there are still two difficult years ahead. I don't really buy into the claim that school gets a lot easier after the first year. I think the students just become accustomed to the demands of the routine.

Numbness

- I am basically numb at this point. I'm looking forward to spending a summer away from law school so I will actually have time to reflect on and re-evaluate my choice to attend.

Pride

- As the year ends, I think I mainly feel proud. Proud of myself for moving across the state, living by myself for the first time, and taking on a world of new responsibilities. Proud for getting through the first year, doing well in my classes, and finding a way to balance school and studying and a social life. Proud to go back home this summer and tell everyone that I just finished my first year of law school . . . and survived!

Relief

- Relief. It is impossible to believe that in just under three weeks I will have survived a WHOLE YEAR of law school. But at the same time there is definitely the end-of-the-year stress as exams approach.

Surprise

- Shock. I cannot believe it went by so fast. It doesn't feel like I'm one-third of the way prepared to be a lawyer.

All of the Above/Mixed Feelings

- Such a mix of emotions . . . relief and exhaustion, but mostly a sense of accomplishment. So amazing to realize that, "Yes, I can do this!"

* * *

I also asked a group of students finishing up their first year whether they would do it all over again knowing what they know now. The vast majority of students said they would. Many said they would do so enthusiastically, answering "Absolutely!," "Definitely!," and "Hell yes!" These answers are consistent with the survey results cited earlier in the book showing that a large majority of law students are satisfied with their law school experience. But not all students feel that way. Some of the students I surveyed said they wouldn't do law school again and others were ambivalent.

One student who said he would *not* do law school again said: "Most of what I know now I had been told at the beginning of the first semester. The problem is I didn't put it to use. Therefore, I believe that I could fall into the same traps."

You now have the information and advice you'll need to avoid falling into those traps and succeeding in law school. It may seem far off, but it won't be long before you'll be finishing your own 1L adventure. Before you know it, you'll be *2L and Back*. Like the rest of life, your time in law school will fly by.

When you reach the end of your 1L ride, I hope you won't find yourself in the position of the student quoted above, bemoaning his unwillingness or inability to heed advice. I'd rather picture you smiling and thinking, "You know, that book I read about the first year gave some really good advice. I'm glad I followed it!"

EPILOGUE: THE END OF A LONG AND GRINDING ROAD

I still remember the day of my last exam of my 1L year. What a feeling! It was like being released from prison. I walked out of the law school into bright sunshine and felt light as air. That night some of my non-law school friends staged a big party at a subterranean den called and painted to resemble Middle Earth, located beneath a block of dorms on the University of Florida campus. (Tolkien was popular on college campuses long before the *Lord of the Rings* and *Hobbit* movies.) We listened to music, watched a weird home movie some of my pals created, drank potent punch, and just hung out.

I was the only law student there. I doubt I mentioned law school the entire night, having learned months earlier that non-law students could care less about it. I did think about it though. I have a distinct memory of sitting in a chair watching the hubbub around me, sipping punch, and feeling blissfully happy, thinking: "I'm done! I can't believe I'm actually done!" Temporarily forgetting, I guess, that I still had two more years to go.

But human nature is funny that way. While I definitely would not want to repeat the first year, like many lawyers, I look back at it with nostalgia and fondness. For better or worse, there has never been another year of my life resembling my 1L experience. I've never learned as much or experienced as much camaraderie in any one year. There was a lot of stress too, but, fortunately, the human psyche seems designed to remember the good over the bad.

Your experience is likely to be similar. For most readers, the first year of law school may still be an abstraction. I hope I succeeded in giving it shape in these pages, but when all is said and done, what I said at the beginning of the book is true. The only way to truly understand and appreciate the 1L experience is to live it. Good luck on your journey. Here's to a smooth ride!

APPENDIX

SAMPLE ESSAY QUESTION

Below is an authentic "issue-spotting/problem-solving" law school exam essay question from my course in Torts. Following the question is the model answer I used to grade the exam. The question addresses a handful of issues in the area of intentional torts, a subject most students will study early on and from which most of the examples in the book were drawn.

Don't worry about the specifics of the law if you're reading this before law school. The question and answer are included primarily to give you an advance feel for what a law school essay question and answer can look like in terms of content and structure. Study the question and answer in conjunction with Chapter 16, which details the most common mistakes students make on law school essay exams. If you're in law school and have covered the intentional torts, the question might make for a nice practice exercise.

INTENTIONAL TORTS ESSAY QUESTION
(115 points/recommended time: 60 minutes)

Sheila and the Shingles (S & S) is a highly successful rock group. Sheila is actually Sheldon Ferndale, lead singer and songwriter for the group. Sheldon decided early on that to be successful in the rock music world, one has to be outrageous and the more outrageous the better. Bizarre and unpredictable stage shows thus became a hallmark of S & S concerts.

At a concert date in Omaha during their 2016 world tour, S & S appeared onstage in military fatigues. Halfway through their hit song, "Take Me Hostage," Sheldon pulled a semiautomatic handgun from his belt, pointed the gun at the crowd and screamed, "Nobody move or I'll shoot."

Most of the audience cheered, thinking this was just another S & S theatrical trick, but some audience members believed it was real and froze in fear. Bernard Boone, sitting in the front row, was not familiar with the reputation of S & S and believed the threat was real. Fearing for his and other audience members' safety, he pulled a handgun from inside his coat and shot at Sheldon. The bullet missed Sheldon, but struck the bass player, Lucky Chord, wounding him in the thigh. None of the band members saw this happen and, in fact, did not realize Lucky had been shot. (The fact that he was writhing on the floor did not tip them off because Lucky frequently played the bass in that position.)

As it turned out, Sheldon was not just engaging in theatrics. Many years of abusing controlled substances had finally caught up with him. He was suffering from an insane delusion in which he believed he was on the front line of a war and that the audience was a wave of terrorists about to attack and kill him. He aimed the gun into the crowd and pulled the trigger.

He shot Matt Madrigal, a 13-year-old boy who was attending the concert with his best friend and his best friend's mother, Wilma. Sheldon then immediately put down the gun and fled the stage, where he was quickly apprehended.

Fortunately, Matt's injury was not serious. He recovered fully. Wilma, however, was traumatized from witnessing Matt's shooting. Wilma went to see a psychologist numerous times in the months following the incident to help her deal with the trauma.

After recovering from his psychotic episode, Sheldon gave a sworn statement to the police that said: "I swear I did not desire to hit anyone when I shot that gun." Assume this statement is credible.

This is an intentional torts question. Do not discuss negligence, even though potential negligence claims exist. Fully discuss and analyze all claims and issues among all potential plaintiffs and defendants arising from this unfortunate series of events, except for potential claims by one band member against another band member. Use subheadings to delineate different party disputes and issues.

* * *

Below is the "model answer" I used to grade the question, including notations of the points range (from zero to the maximum) for each issue. Most students, even those who earn high grades, don't write with the precision and depth of analysis found in professors' model answers, although a few students in every class come very close.

MODEL ANSWER

Several lawsuits are likely to arise out of this unfortunate series of events. They will be discussed separately.

Audience members vs. Sheldon

Members of the concert audience who believed Sheldon's threat have viable claims against him for assault and false imprisonment.

Intent/Sheldon's insanity (point range: 0–15). A preliminary issue applicable to these and other intentional tort claims against Sheldon is his insanity. Sheldon will assert that his insanity prevented him from forming a tortious intent. In his delusional, paranoid state, he was acting in self-defense, thinking the audience was going to attack and kill him. But as we learned in *McGuire v. Almy*, insane people are generally held responsible for their intentional torts. More specifically, insanity does not operate to negate the intent element. As the court in *McGuire* said, for policy reasons such as deterrence and fairness, the law will not inquire into the subjective state of mind of the insane person with a view toward excusing his intentional conduct if it turns out he was acting pursuant to an insane delusion.

Assault (0–10). Audience members *who believed* Sheldon's threat was real should prevail in an assault claim against him. An assault occurs where there is a volitional act intended to cause imminent apprehension of a harmful or offensive bodily contact, and such imminent apprehension results. Sheldon volitionally pointed the gun and expressly threatened to shoot audience members. His intent to create an apprehension could be inferred from his conduct. Any audience member who experienced imminent apprehension of a shooting should prevail. Of course, those audience members who believed it was simply a stage antic would not have sound claims because they were not in imminent apprehension of a harmful contact. Thus, an essential element of assault—the result element—would be missing.

False imprisonment (0–15). Similarly, audience members who believed the threat was genuine may have viable claims for false imprisonment against Sheldon. A false imprisonment requires a volitional act, an intent to confine unlawfully, and a resulting unlawful confinement. When Sheldon wielded the gun, he said, "Nobody move or I'll shoot." The facts state that some audience members "froze in fear." Sheldon acted volitionally, his intent to confine can be inferred from his express statement ordering the audience not to move, and a confinement resulted with regard to any audience member who obeyed the command. A confinement can occur through a threat to use physical force. No actual force is required. The audience members were not required to "test the threat." As with the assault claim, only those audience members who believed the threat was real and did not move because of it would have viable claims.

Lucky Chord v. Bernard Boone

Battery (0–5). Lucky will sue Bernard for battery for shooting him in the leg. Battery requires a volitional act intended to cause a harmful or offensive contact and such a contact results. Here, we had a volitional act and harmful contact, but Bernard may have a defense, one that also calls into question the intent element.

Self-defense and defense of others (0–15). Bernard will assert the privileges of self-defense and defense of others. Self-defense and defense of others apply when one reasonably believes the use of force is necessary to prevent a threatened battery against himself or others and uses a reasonable amount of force under the circumstances. A proportionality rule applies to determine the reasonableness of the amount of force. Thus, one is permitted to use deadly force in self-defense or defense of others only when he reasonably believes deadly force is threatened.

Bernard will argue he was privileged to use deadly force because he reasonably believed Sheldon was about to use deadly force against either him or other audience members. The facts state that he acted "[f]earing for his and other audience members' safety." Given S & S's reputation for bizarre stage shows, one could argue persuasively that an audience member would not have reasonably believed Sheldon's threat was real.

Thus, if Sheldon had been engaged in a stage prank, there's a good chance a court would find the privileges inapplicable. As it turned out, however, the threat was real, which would make it difficult to persuasively assert that Bernard's belief was unreasonable. Thus, the privileges may very well apply, relieving Bernard of liability for shooting Lucky.

No transferred intent (0–12). Lucky may argue that even if Bernard was privileged to use deadly force against Sheldon, he wasn't privileged to shoot Lucky, and that Bernard's intent to shoot Sheldon transferred to Lucky under the doctrine of transferred intent. Transferred intent holds that if one intends to commit an intentional tort, such as a battery, against one person and ends up committing the tort against a different person, the actor's intent is deemed to transfer to the other person (thereby satisfying the intent element).

However, transferred intent would apply only if it was determined that Bernard was *not* privileged to act in self-defense or defense of others. If Bernard's conduct was privileged, there would be no tortious intent to transfer. Thus, Lucky would fail in his battery claim against Bernard if the privileges of self-defense or defense of others are applied.

Matt v. Sheldon

Battery (0–3). Matt will sue Sheldon for battery. The elements of battery have already been stated.

Belief intent (0–15). The only issue would be Sheldon's intent. As already discussed, his insanity would not negate his intent. However, after the incident, Sheldon gave a statement saying "I swear that I did not desire to hit anyone when I shot the gun." The question says to assume this statement is credible, which would mean he lacked desire intent. Two kinds of intent exist, however: desire intent and belief intent. Even if Sheldon lacked desire intent, he could still be liable for battery if he had "belief intent," meaning that when he shot the gun he believed to a substantial certainty that he would hit someone. The facts say Sheldon "aimed the gun into the crowd and pulled the trigger." A fact-finder could infer from his words and conduct that he believed to a substantial certainty that someone in the audience would be hit even if he did not desire to shoot anyone. Sheldon will be liable to Matt for battery.

Wilma v. Sheldon

Intentional infliction of emotional distress (0–15). Wilma will sue Sheldon for intentional infliction of emotional distress (IIED) based on her trauma from witnessing Matt getting shot. IIED allows one to recover against an actor who through extreme and outrageous conduct intentionally or recklessly causes severe emotional distress to another. Although the standard for what qualifies as extreme and outrageous conduct is high, Sheldon's conduct—pulling out a gun and opening fire on a concert audience—probably satisfies it. It is conduct likely to be found to be beyond the bounds of all decency and utterly intolerable in a civilized society. Serious threats of physical violence, as we learned in *Siliznoff,* can constitute extreme and outrageous conduct.

As to the fault element, section 46(1) of the *Restatement (Second) of Torts* adopts a dual intent-recklessness fault standard for IIED. Even if Sheldon didn't intend to cause emotional distress, he was probably at least reckless. Recklessness is conduct that creates a high probability of a harmful consequence as judged by an objective standard. A reasonable person would know that shooting someone at a concert would create a high probability of causing severe emotional distress to a third party.

Whether Wilma's distress qualifies as "severe" would be an issue. She obviously suffered distress, as evidenced by her numerous visits to the psychologist. The fact-finder would have to determine the severity of her distress, probably assisted by expert witnesses. Further fact development would be required.

Bystander limitation (0–10). But Wilma has another problem. As we learned, section 46(2)(b) of the *Restatement (Second) of Torts* imposes an additional limitation in non-family member "bystander" IIED cases such as this one: the requirement that the plaintiff suffer bodily harm flowing from the emotional distress. Matt was unrelated to Wilma and we don't have any facts indicating that Wilma's distress caused her bodily harm. If she didn't suffer bodily harm from her emotional distress, her claim would fail under the *Restatement* test. This issue also would require additional factual development.

INDEX

References are to Pages